JEAN-BAPTISTE POQUELIN was born in Paris in 1622, the son of Jean Poquelin, furniture dealer and upholsterer to the Court. Although it was expected that he would enter his father's business, Molière (Poquelin's assumed name) studied law and received a degree in 1641. His lifelong alliance with the theater began when he met Madeleine Béjart, an actress, playwright and poet. In 1643, under the name of Molière, he signed a contract with eleven other actors, among them Madeleine and and her brother Joseph, incorporating a troupe called The Illustrious Theater. While sharing the leading roles with two other actors, Molière began writing plays. In October, 1658, under the patronage of the King's brother, the company settled in Paris in the Théâtre du Petit-Bourbon. Periodically plagued by financial difficulties, the object of fierce attack because of such stinging masterpieces as *Tartuffe* and *Don Juan*, and also because of his marriage to nineteen-year-old Armande Béjart, Molière nonetheless won the favor of both King and public. In 1665, his company became the King's Troupe, and his pension was raised to six thousand francs. The following year saw the staging of *The Misanthrope*, accompanied by *The Doctor in Spite of Himself*. In 1668, he produced his bitterly comic *The Miser*, and in the four years before his death created such plays as *The Would-Be Gentleman, The Mischievous Machinations of Scapin,* and *The Learned Women*. In 1673, while performing in his last play, *The Imaginary Invalid*, Molière collapsed on stage and died shortly thereafter.

THE MISANTHROPE
and Other Plays
by MOLIÈRE

*Translated,
and with an Introduction,
by Donald M. Frame*

A SIGNET CLASSIC
NEW AMERICAN LIBRARY
TIMES MIRROR
NEW YORK AND SCARBOROUGH, ONTARIO
THE NEW ENGLISH LIBRARY LIMITED, LONDON

SIGNET CLASSIC TRADEMARK REG. U.S. PAT. OFF. AND FOREIGN COUNTRIES
REGISTERED TRADEMARK—MARCA REGISTRADA
HECHO EN CHICAGO, U.S.A.

SIGNET, SIGNET CLASSICS, MENTOR, PLUME, MERIDIAN AND NAL
BOOKS are published in the United States by
The New American Library, Inc.,
1633 Broadway, New York, New York 10019,
in Canada by The New American Library of Canada Limited,
81 Mack Avenue, Scarborough, Ontario M1L 1M8,
in the United Kingdom by The New English Library Limited,
Barnard's Inn, Holborn, London, EC1N 2JR, England.

First Printing, November, 1968

4   5   6   7   8   9   10   11   12

PRINTED IN THE UNITED STATES OF AMERICA

Contents

INTRODUCTION

Molière is probably the greatest and best-loved French author, and comic author, who ever lived. To the reader as well as the spectator, today as well as three centuries ago, the appeal of his plays is immediate and durable; they are both instantly accessible and inexhaustible. His rich resources make it hard to decide, much less to agree, on the secret of his greatness. After generations had seen him mainly as a moralist, many critics today have shifted the stress to the director and actor whose life was the comic stage; but all ages have rejoiced in three somewhat overlapping qualities of his: comic inventiveness, richness of fabric, and insight.

His inventiveness is extraordinary. An actor-manager-director-playwright all in one, he knew and loved the stage as few have done, and wrote with it and his playgoing public always in mind. In a medium in which sustained power is one of the rarest virtues, he drew on the widest imaginable range, from the broadest slapstick to the subtlest irony, to carry out the arduous and underrated task of keeping an audience amused for five whole acts. Working usually under great pressure of time, he took his materials where he found them, yet always made them his own.

The fabric of his plays is rich in many ways: in the intense life he infuses into his characters; in his constant preoccupation with the comic mask, which makes most of his protagonists themselves—consciously or unconsciously—play a part, and leads to rich comedy when their nature forces them to drop the mask; and in the weight of seriousness and even poignancy that he dares to include in his comic vision. Again and again he leads us from the enjoyable but shallow reaction of laughing at a fool to recognizing in that fool others whom we know, and ultimately ourselves; which is surely the truest and deepest comic catharsis.

Molière's insight makes his characters understandable and gives a memorable inevitability to his comic effects. He is seldom completely realistic, of course; his characters, for example, tend to give themselves away more generously and laughably than is customary in life; but it is their true selves they give away. It is an obvious trick, and not very realistic, to have Orgon in *Tartuffe* (Act I, Sc. 4) reply four times to the account of his wife's illness with the question "And Tartuffe?" and reply, again four times, to each report of Tartuffe's gross health and appetite, "Poor fellow!" But it shows us, rapidly and comically, that Orgon's obsession has closed his mind and his ears to anything but what he wants to see and hear. In the following scene, it may be unrealistic to have him in one speech (ll. 276–279) boast of learning from Tartuffe such detachment from worldly things that he could see his whole family die without concern, and in the very next speech (ll. 306–310) praise Tartuffe for the scrupulousness that led him to reproach himself for killing a flea in too much anger. But—again apart from the sheer comedy—it is a telling commentary on the distortion of values that can come from extreme points of view. One of Molière's favorite authors, Montaigne, had written about victims of moral *hubris:* "They want to get out of themselves and escape from the man. That is madness: instead of changing into angels, they change into beasts." Molière is presenting the same idea dramatically, as he does with even more power later (Act IV, scene 3, l. 1293), when Orgon's daughter has implored him not to force her to marry the repulsive Tartuffe, and he summons his will to resist her with these words:

Be firm, my heart! No human weakness now!

These moments of truth, these flashes of unconscious self-revelation that plunge us into the very center of an obsession, abound in Molière, adding to our insight even as they reveal his. And even as he caricatures aspects of himself in the reforming Alceste or in the jealous older lover Arnolphe, so he imparts to his moments of truth not only the individuality of the particular obsession but also the universality of our common share in it.

Molière is one of those widely known public figures whose

private life remains veiled. In his own time gossip was rife, but much of it comes from his enemies and is suspect. Our chief other source is his plays; but while these hint at his major concerns and lines of meditation, we must beware of reading them like avowals or his roles like disguised autobiography.[1]

He was born Jean-Baptiste Poquelin in Paris early in 1622 and baptized on January 15, the first son of a well-to-do bourgeois dealer in tapestry and upholstery. In 1631 his father bought the position of *valet de chambre tapissier ordinaire du roi,* and six years later obtained the right to pass it on at his own death to his oldest son, who took the appropriate "oath of office" at the age of fifteen. Together with many sons of the best families, Jean-Baptiste received an excellent education from the Jesuit Fathers of the Collège de Clermont. He probably continued beyond the basic course in rhetoric to two years of philosophy and then law school, presumably at Orléans.

Suddenly, as it appears to us, just as he was reaching twenty-one, he resigned his survival rights to his father's court position, and with them the whole future that lay ahead of him; drew his share in the estate of his dead mother and a part of his own prospective inheritance; and six months later joined in forming, with and around Madeleine Béjart, a dramatic company, the Illustre-Théâtre. In September 1643 they rented a court-tennis court to perform in; in October they played in Rouen; in January 1644 they opened in Paris; in June young Poquelin was named head of the troupe, and signed himself, for the first time we know of, "de Molière."

Molière's was an extraordinary decision. Apart from the financial hazards, his new profession stood little above pimping or stealing in the public eye and automatically involved minor excommunication from the Church. To write for the theater, especially tragedy, carried no great onus; to be an actor, especially in comedy and farce, was a proof of immorality. Though Richelieu's passion for the stage had improved its prestige somewhat, this meant only that a few voices were raised to maintain its possible innocence against the condemnation of the vast majority.

---

[1] To learn what is established fact we turn to scholars like Michaut and Mornet; for a rich and informed sense of probability, to Fernandez or—with caution—Dussane.

Obviously young Molière was in love with the theater, and had to act. He may also have been already in love with Madeleine Béjart; their contemporaries were probably right in thinking them lovers, though all we actually know is that they were stanch colleagues and business partners. Their loyalty was tested from the first. Although the Béjarts raised all the money they could, after a year and a half in Paris the company failed and had to break up; Molière was twice imprisoned in the Châtelet for debt; he and the Béjarts left Paris to try their luck in the provinces. For twelve years they were on the road, mainly in the south.

For the first five of these they joined the company, headed by Du Fresne, of the Duc d'Épernon in Guyenne. When d'Épernon dropped them, Molière became head of the troupe. From 1653 to 1657 they were in the service of a great prince of the blood, the Prince de Conti, until his conversion. Even with a noble patron, the life was nomadic and precarious, and engagements hard to get. However, the company gradually made a name for itself and prospered. Molière gained a rich firsthand knowledge of life on many levels. In the last few years of their wanderings he tried his hand as a playwright with such plays as *L'Étourdi* and *Le Dépit amoureux*.

At last in 1658 they obtained another chance to play in the capital. On October 24 they appeared before young Louis XIV, his brother, and the court, in the guard room of the old Louvre, in a performance of Corneille's tragedy *Nicomède*, which Molière followed with his own comedy *The Doctor in Love*. Soon they became the Troupe de Monsieur (the King's brother) and were installed by royal order in the Théâtre du Petit-Bourbon. Though they still performed tragedies, they succeeded more and more in comedy, in which Molière was on his way to recognition as the greatest actor of his time.

Within a year he made his mark also as a playwright with *The Ridiculous Précieuses* (November 18, 1659), which, though little more than a sketch, bore the stamp of his originality, keen observation, and rich comic inventiveness.[2] Nearly thirty-eight, Molière was to have thirteen more years to live, and was to live them as though he knew this was all. To his responsibili-

---

[2] Since the fourteen plays (seven in each volume) in the present translation are discussed in the introductory note to each, I shall do little more than mention them here.

ties as director and actor he added a hectic but glorious career
as a very productive playwright, author of thirty-two comedies
that we know, of which a good third are among the comic
masterpieces of world literature. The stress of his many roles,
of deadlines, and of controversy, is well depicted in *The Versailles Impromptu.* Success led to success—and often to more
controversy—but never to respite. He was to be carried off the
stage to his deathbed. No doubt he wanted it that way, or almost that way; for probably no man has ever been more possessed by the theater.

On February 20, 1662, at the age of forty, he married the
twenty-year-old Armande Béjart, a daughter (according to the
mostly spiteful contemporaries) or sister (according to the of-
ficial documents) of Madeleine. Though what we know of their
domestic life is almost nothing, contemporary gossip, a friend's
letter, and Molière's own preoccupation in several plays with
a jealous older man in love with a flighty young charmer,
combine to suggest an uneasy relationship. They had two
sons who died in infancy and a daughter who survived. The
King himself and his sister-in-law (Madame) were god-
father and godmother to the first boy—no doubt to defend
Molière against a charge, or rumor, that he had married his
own daughter.

When the Petit-Bourbon theater was torn down in October
1660 to make way for the new façade of the Louvre, things
looked bad; but the King granted the company the use of
Richelieu's great theater, the Palais-Royal, which remained
Molière's until his death. An early success there was his regular, elaborate verse comedy, *The School for Husbands.* Within
a year of his marriage he wrote his first great play and one
of his most popular, *The School for Wives.* It aroused much
controversy; when Molière published it, he dedicated it to
Madame; the King gave him the support he sought in the
form of a pension of one thousand francs for this "excellent
comic poet." *The Critique of the School for Wives* and *The
Versailles Impromptu* (June and October 1663) completed
Molière's victory in the eyes of the public.

However, his attack on extreme piety and hypocrisy in *Tartuffe* showed him the strength of his enemies. The first three-
act version, performed in May 1664, was promptly banned.
For the next five years much of his time and energy went into

the fight to get it played: petitions, private readings, revisions, private performances. In August 1667 a five-act version entitled *The Impostor* was allowed a second public performance—then also banned. Only in February 1669 was the version that we know put on, with enormous success; and this time it was on the program to stay.

Meanwhile Molière had hit back at his enemies in 1665 in *Don Juan*, which he soon withdrew. In August of that year his company became The King's Troupe, and his pension was raised to six thousand francs. A year later he completed his greatest and most complex play, *The Misanthrope*, which met only a modest success, and the light but brilliant farce that often served as a companion piece, *The Doctor in Spite of Himself*. In 1668 he displayed the bitter comic profundities of *The Miser*; and in the last four years of his life—still to mention only his finest plays—*The Would-Be Gentleman, The Mischievous Machinations of Scapin, The Learned Women,* and *The Imaginary Invalid.*

Molière's last seven years were dogged by pulmonary illness. A bad bout in early 1666 and another in 1667 led him to accept a milk diet and spend much of the next four years apart from his wife in his house in Auteuil. The year before his own death saw those of his old friend Madeleine Béjart and later of his second son. As his health grew worse, he composed—characteristically—his final gay comedy about a healthy hypochondriac. Before its fourth performance, on February 17, 1673, he felt very ill; his wife and one of his actors urged him not to play that evening; he replied that the whole company depended a lot on him and that it was a point of honor to go on. He got through his part, in spite of one violent fit of coughing. A few hours later he was dead. Since he had not been able, while dying, to get a priest to come and receive his formal renunciation of his profession, a regular religious burial was denied at first, and later grudgingly granted—at night, with no notice, ceremony, or service—only after his widow's plea to the King. He died and was buried as he had lived—as an actor.

Translations of Molière abound. Two of the most available, both complete, are by H. Baker and J. Miller (1739) and Henri

Van Laun (1875–76). The former is satisfactory, but its eighteenth-century flavor is not always Molière's; the latter is dull. Better for the modern reader are the versions of selected plays by John Wood (1953 and 1959), George Graveley (1956), and especially three others.

Curtis Hidden Page has translated eight well-chosen plays (Putnam, 1908, 2 vols.) which include three verse comedies done into unrhymed verse. Though it sometimes lacks sparkle, his version is always intelligent and responsible.

Morris Bishop's recent translation of nine plays (one for Crofts Classics, 1950, eight for Modern Library, 1957) is much the best we have for all but two. His excellent selection includes six in prose (*Précieuses, Critique, Impromptu, Physician in Spite of Himself, Would-Be Gentleman, Would-Be Invalid*) and three done into unrhymed verse (*School for Wives, Tartuffe, Misanthrope*). His knowledge of Molière and talent for comic verse make his translation lively and racy, and his occasional liberties are usually well taken.

Richard Wilbur has translated Molière's two greatest verse plays, *The Misanthrope* and *Tartuffe*, into rhymed verse (Harcourt, Brace, & World, Inc., 1955 and 1963). They are the best Molière we have in English. My sense of their excellence is perhaps best stated personally. I have long wanted to try my hand at translating Molière. When the Wilbur *Misanthrope* appeared, I decided not to attempt it unless I thought I would do that play either better or at least quite differently. When I finally tried it, I was surprised to find how different I wanted to make it. Wilbur's end product is superb; but in his *Misanthrope* I sometimes miss the accents of Molière.[3] His *Tartuffe* seems to me clearly better, since it follows the original closely even in detail. Both are beautiful translations. Again and again my quest for sense and for rhymes has led me to the same solution that Wilbur found earlier.

The question whether foreign rhyme should be translated into English rhyme has been often debated and seems to me infinitely debatable. I think a different answer may be appropriate for each poet, and perhaps for each translator. Page explains his rejection of rhyme as something unnatural to good English

---

3 As, for one example, when Alceste's *"Non, elle est générale, et je hais tous les hommes"* (l. 118) becomes "No, I include all men in one dim view . . ."

dramatic verse; but he also recognizes that he often found it harder to avoid rhyme than to use it, and that unrhymed verse is more difficult than rhymed to write well. I think this last point explains my disappointment at some of his and Bishop's lines. Against the point that rhymed dramatic verse is not natural in English, I would argue that it seems to me almost necessary for Molière. Wilbur has made the case brilliantly in his introduction to *The Misanthrope*, pointing to certain specific effects—mock tragedy, "musical" poetic relationships of words, even the redundancy and logic of the argument—which demand rhyme. In my opinion, rhyme affects what Molière says as well as the way he says it enough to make it worthwhile to use it in English, and the loss in precision need not be great.

Fidelity in meter, however, seems clearly to mean putting Molière's alexandrines into English iambic pentameter, and, although allowing some liberties with syllable-count as natural to English, holding rather closely to the precise count that the practice of Molière's day demanded. However, this reduction in length, while translating (which normally lengthens) even from French into English (which normally shortens), often forces the translator to choose between Molière's ever-recurring initial "and's" (and occasional "but's") and some key word in the same line. I have usually chosen to retain the key word; but at times I deliberately have not, for fear of losing too much of Molière's generally easy flow and making him too constipated and sententious.

Molière's characteristic language is plain, correct, functional, often argumentative, not slangy but conversational. Since in French—despite many savory archaisms—he does not generally strike the modern reader as at all archaic, he should not in English. For most of his writing, verse and prose, I have sought an English that is familiar and acceptable today but not obviously anachronistic.

However, there is much truth in Mornet's statement that Molière is one of the few great writers who has no style, but rather all the styles of all his characters. The departures from the norm noted above are as common as the norm itself. The earthy talk of peasants and servants is in constant (and sometimes direct) contrast with the lofty affectation of bluestockings and *précieuses* and the pomposity of pedants; manner as well as matter distinguish a Don Juan from a Sganarelle, Lucile and

Cléonte from Nicole and Covielle; Alceste's explosiveness colors his language and enhances his opposition to Philinte; Charlotte even speaks better French to Don Juan than to her peasant swain Pierrot. To render this infinite variety the translator must call to his aid all the resources of his language—anachronistic or not—that he can command.

A special problem is that of dialect, as in *Don Juan* and *The Doctor in Spite of Himself.* To the dialect of the Ile de France that Molière uses, familiar to his audience, I see no satisfactory equivalent in English. Since part of the dialect humor rests on bad grammar (*"j'avons"* and the like) and rustic oaths, I have tried to suggest this by similar, mainly countrified, lapses and exclamations.

My aim, in short, has been to put Molière as faithfully as I could into modern English, hewing close to his exact meaning and keeping all I could of his form and his verve.

The edition I have mainly relied on for this translation is that of Molière's *Œuvres* by Eugène Despois and Paul Mesnard (Paris: Hachette, 1873–1900, 14 vols.). I have followed the standard stage directions and division of the play into scenes. The stage directions do not normally indicate entrances and exits as such, since in the French tradition these are shown in print by a change of scenes and signalized only in that way.

I should like to acknowledge three debts: to earlier translators, especially Page, Bishop, and Wilbur; to Sanford R. Kadet for his thorough reading of the *Tartuffe* and valuable suggestions; and, as always, to my wife, Katharine M. Frame, for her ready and critical ear and her unfailing encouragement.

DONALD M. FRAME
COLUMBIA UNIVERSITY

The Misanthrope

THE MISANTHROPE

A verse comedy in five acts, first performed June 4, 1666, at the Théâtre du Palais-Royal in Paris by Molière's company, the Troupe du Roi. In his privilege to print the play Molière used the subtitle *Or, The Melancholy Lover (Ou l'Atrabilaire amoureux);* but he later abandoned this. Molière played Alceste; his wife played Célimène; the distribution of the other roles is not known. The play was not a box-office success; after two months it was withdrawn in favor of *The Doctor in Spite of Himself,* and during Molière's lifetime it was performed only a few times a year. However, it won many admirers from the first, and Boileau hailed it as Molière's best.

Within a century Jean-Jacques Rousseau brought out the possibilities of a heroic, if not a tragic, Alceste in what he considers Molière's masterpiece. The author's aim, he argues, is to make virtue ridiculous by pandering to the shallow and vicious tastes of the man of the world; the play would have gained in beauty and consistency if Alceste—with whom he obviously identifies himself—had been meek toward injustice to himself, indignant against public vices; and Philinte the converse. The notion of a tragic Alceste, though not common today, may be dormant, not dead; in any case, it has had a long and vigorous life.

Yet Rousseau was quite right in seeing that Molière had made the play a comedy, and a comedy of virtue. As Ramon Fernandez shows, in the three great plays of the mid 1660's Molière was clearly testing the limits of the comic, struggling to enlarge its domain. In *Don Juan* and *Tartuffe* he had shown that vice is not immune to comic treatment; here he does the same with virtue. Perhaps even more than these two others, this play shows just how serious a Molière comedy

19

can be. Hence the tension of the play, the problems it raises,
the contradictory views it has aroused.

Of Molière's comic intent there is no reasonable doubt; nor
is there much more of his success. Playing the leading comic
role (here, of Alceste), as he always did, from the very first
scene he makes this fully clear. Alceste's constant excessive-
ness is demonstrated from the start: it may be honorable to
protest against the "white lies" of social life, but it is comic
to urge suicide—to one's best friend at that—as the only
atonement for such a crime; the "objective correlative" that
T. S. Eliot speaks of is clearly inadequate. An unconscious
but tyrannical egoist, Alceste is always full of himself; his
speech abounds in what in English would be the vertical pro-
noun, characteristically followed by a statement of how he
wants men to be. In his first two long speeches (ll. 14–28,
41–64) he gives his own motives away as he moves from
the "good reason" of pure principle to the hatred he feels
(l. 43) for social pretense and at last (l. 63 and 53–64
passim) to the clear avowal of what irks him: that stand-
ardized politenes frustrates his thirst to be singled out for
what he alone is.

In the same first scene, after hearing Alceste's theory of
utter frankness, his friend Philinte tests his "theoretical practice" by asking whether he would really say just what he
thinks of them to such grotesques as the tedious Dorilas and
the old coquette Émilie; and Alceste answers a resounding
Yes. The very next scene, however, shows his failure to practice what he preaches. To be sure, he finally makes an enemy
of his sonneteering rival Oronte; but this is only after much more
temporizing and deviousness ("Sir . . ." ll. 267–277; "I don't
say that. But . . ." ll. 352–362), not to mention the obvious
exemplum of what he told another, hypothetical scribbler, than
is at all consistent with the way he says he would, and others
should, behave.

A different kind of inconsistency seems, from the early subtitle
noted above, embedded in Molière's original concept of the play:
Alceste's love for Célimène. To be sure, to most modern readers
at least, this is as endearing and poignant as it is comic. But
here too we find Alceste misled by vanity. From the first he is
sure that she loves him and that his love will prevail and change
her character (ll. 233–237). Later we find—and so does he—

that he is abjectly in love with her (ll. 1371–1390) and ready to accept any explanation that will allow her to "seem faithful," and that her love for him, such as it is, is merely the best she can manage for anyone but herself. The self-assurance of his early statements leads to a comic fall.

The "virtue" that is ridiculed in Alceste is not virtue itself but the unexamined virtue of the theorist—who talks plausibly but does not practice what he preaches—and of the nonconformist, who has eyes for all the vices of society except his own. It is the barnacles on the ship of morality, the excesses and other vices that naturally accompany Alceste's virtues—self-righteousness, inconsistency, and consequently a certain hypocrisy—that Molière holds up to our laughter.

Alceste is by no means merely comic. Characteristically, Molière did not merely play the role, but endowed it with some of his own traits: his love, as an older man, for a younger woman, his eagerness to criticize and correct human foibles.[1] There is obviously something noble about Alceste, for all his comic flaws; and the sincere Éliante, the most trustworthy character in the play, pays homage to it (ll. 1165–1166):

> . . . the sincerity that is his pride
> Has a heroic and a noble side.

Moreover, Molière endows Alceste with a magnetism that is his alone. Not only does Oronte seek to become his friend; he enjoys the devoted friendship of Philinte, and he is the man most loved by the three leading ladies of the play. Moreover, of Célimène's suitors, he is the only one whose love is greater than his vanity.

Even his view of human nature is shared by his main theoretical opponent, Philinte. What separates them is not their opinion of it, but their reactions. Philinte clearly finds it no more shocking (ll. 176–178)

> To see a man unjust, self-seeking, sly,
> Than to see vultures hungry for their prey,
> Monkeys malicious, wolves athirst to slay.

Finally, this view of human nature, expounded so angrily by Alceste and so matter-of-factly by Philinte, seems to be fully

[1] Compare Philinte's remark to Alceste (ll. 157–158)
> The greatest folly of the human mind
> Is undertaking to correct mankind

with, for example, Molière's remark in the preface to *Tartuffe:* "If the function of comedy is to correct men's vices, I don't see why there are to be any privileged ones."

borne out by the action of the play. If it is fair, as I think it is, to regard Alceste, Philinte, and Éliante as in a sense the "we" of the play, and the others as the "they"—the world, or perhaps the court; for all the principal characters are members of high society —then clearly "they" are shown to be vain, unloving, and malicious. The polished world of high society is just a lacquered jungle. And it is at least one of Molière's aims to bring this out even while the principal railer against these vices is made, by his own unwitting flaws, a comic, not a tragic, hero.

THE MISANTHROPE

CHARACTERS

ALCESTE, *in love with Célimène*
PHILINTE, *friend of Alceste*
ORONTE, *in love with Célimène*
CÉLIMÈNE, *beloved of Alceste*
ÉLIANTE, *cousin of Célimène*
ARSINOÉ, *a friend of Célimène*
ACASTE
CLITANDRE } *marquis*
BASQUE, *servant of Célimène*
An OFFICER *of the Tribunal of Marshals of France*
DU BOIS, *servant of Alceste*

    The scene is a salon in Célimène's house in Paris.

ACT I

Scene 1.   ALCESTE, PHILINTE

PHILINTE. Well then? What's wrong?

ALCESTE.   I pray you, let me be.

PHILINTE. Won't you explain this sudden wrath to me?

ALCESTE. Leave me alone, I say; run off and hide.

PHILINTE. Without such anger you should hear my side.

ALCESTE. Not I. I *will* be angry. I *won't* hear.

PHILINTE. The reasons for your fits escape me clear;
And though we're friends, I feel I must insist . . .

ALCESTE. What? I, your friend? Just scratch me off your list.
Till now I have professed to be one, true;
10 But after what I have just seen in you,
I tell you flatly now that here we part;
I want no place in a corrupted heart.

PHILINTE. Then in your eyes, Alceste, I'm much to blame?

ALCESTE. You should go off and die for very shame;
There's no excuse for such an act as yours;
It's one that any decent man abhors.
I see you greet a man like a long-lost friend
And smother him in sweetness without end;
With protestations, offers, solemn vows,
20 You load the frenzy of your scrapes and bows;
When I ask later whom you cherish so,
Even his name, I find, you barely know.
As soon as he departs, your fervor dies,
And you tell *me* he's nothing in your eyes.
Good Lord! You play a base, unworthy role
By stooping to betray your very soul;
And if (which God forbid) I'd done the same,
I'd go right out and hang myself for shame.

PHILINTE. To me the case does not deserve the rope;
30 Pray you, allow me to retain the hope
That I may exercise some leniency
And need not hang myself from the nearest tree.

ALCESTE. With what bad grace this jesting comes from you!

PHILINTE. But seriously, what would you have me do?

ALCESTE. A man should be sincere, and nobly shrink
From saying anything he does not think.

PHILINTE. But when a man embraces you, I find
You simply have to pay him back in kind,
Respond to his effusions as you may,
40 And try to meet offers and vows half-way.

ALCESTE. No, I cannot endure this fawning guile

Employed by nearly all your men of style.
There's nothing I so loathe as the gyrations
Of all these great makers of protestations,
These lavishers of frivolous embraces,
These utterers of empty commonplaces,
Who in civilities won't be outdone,
And treat the good man and the fool as one.
What joy is there in hearing pretty phrases
From one who loud and fulsome sings your praises,   50
Vows friendship, love, esteem for evermore,
Then runs to do the same to any boor?
No, no; a soul that is well constituted
Cares nothing for esteem so prostituted;
Our vanity is satisfied too cheap
With praise that lumps all men in one vast heap;
Esteem, if it be real, means preference,
And when bestowed on all it makes no sense.
Since these new vices seem to you so fine,
Lord! You're not fit to be a friend of mine.   60
I spurn the vast indulgence of a heart
That will not set merit itself apart;
No, singled out is what I want to be;
The friend of man is not the man for me.

PHILINTE. But one who travels in society
Must show some semblance of civility.

ALCESTE. No, I say; an example should be made
Of hypocrites who ply this shameful trade.
A man should be a man, and let his speech
At every turn reveal his heart to each;   70
His own true self should speak; our sentiments
Should never hide beneath vain compliments.

PHILINTE. But utter frankness would, in many a case,
Become ridiculous and out of place.
We sometimes—no offense to your high zeal—
Should rather hide what in our heart we feel.
Would it be either fitting or discreet
To air our views of them to all we meet?
Dealing with someone we dislike or hate,
Must we always be sure to set him straight?   80

ALCESTE. Yes.

PHILINTE.   What? Old Émilie you'd promptly tell
That she has passed the age to be a belle,
And that her makeup is a sorry jest?

ALCESTE. No doubt.

PHILINTE.   Tell Dorilas that he's a pest,
That all his talk has wearied every ear
About his noble blood and brave career?

ALCESTE. Assuredly.

PHILINTE.   You're joking.

ALCESTE.   I am not,
I'll spare no one on this point, not one jot.
It hurts my eyes to see the things I've seen,
90   And court and town alike arouse my spleen.
Dark melancholy seizes me anew
Each time I watch men act the way they do;
Cowardly flattery is all I see,
Injustice, selfishness, fraud, treachery;
I've had my fill; it makes me mad; I plan
To clash head-on with the whole race of man.

PHILINTE. You overdo your philosophic bile;
I see your gloomy fits and have to smile.
We two are like the brothers in *The School*
100   *For Husbands*,[2] who, though reared by the same rule,
Yet . . .

ALCESTE.   Heavens! spare us these inane charades.

PHILINTE. No, really, you should drop your wild tirades.
Your efforts will not change the world, you know,
And inasmuch as frankness charms you so,
I'll tell you, frankly, that this malady
Is treated everywhere as comedy,
And that your wrath against poor humankind
Makes you ridiculous in many a mind.

ALCESTE. By heaven! so much the better! that's first-rate.

2 One of Molière's earlier comedies.

It's a good sign; my joy in it is great.   *110*
All men are so abhorrent in my eyes
That I'd be sorry if they thought me wise.

PHILINTE. Toward human nature you are very spiteful.

ALCESTE. I am; the hate I feel for it is frightful.

PHILINTE. Shall all poor mortals, then, without exception,
Be lumped together in this mass aversion?
Even today you still find now and then . . .

ALCESTE. No, it is general; I hate all men:
For some are wholly bad in thought and deed;
The others, seeing this, pay little heed;   *120*
For they are too indulgent and too nice
To share the hate that virtue has for vice.
Indulgence at its worst we clearly see
Toward the base scoundrel who's at law with me:
Right through his mask men see the traitor's face,
And everywhere give him his proper place;
His wheedling eyes, his soft and cozening tone,
Fool only those to whom he is not known.
That this knave rose, where he deserved to fall,
By shameful methods, is well known to all,   *130*
And that his state, which thanks to these is lush,
Makes merit murmur and makes virtue blush.
Whatever notoriety he's won,
Such honor lacks support from anyone;
Call him a cheat, knave, curséd rogue to boot,
Everyone will agree, no one refute.
Yet everywhere his false smile seems to pay:
Everywhere welcomed, hailed, he worms his way;
And if by pulling strings he stands to gain
Some honor, decent men compete in vain.   *140*
Good Lord! It fairly turns my blood to ice
To see the way men temporize with vice,
And sometimes I've a strong desire to flee
To some deserted spot, from humans free.

PHILINTE. Let's fret less over morals, if we can,
And have some mercy on the state of man;
Let's look at it without too much austerity,

And try to view its faults without severity.
In this world virtue needs more tact than rigor;
150   Wisdom may be excessive in its vigor;
Perfected reason flees extremity,
And says: Be wise, but with sobriety.
The unbending virtue of the olden days
Clashes with modern times and modern ways;
Its stiff demands on mortals go too far;
We have to live with people as they are;
And the greatest folly of the human mind
Is undertaking to correct mankind.
Like you I note a hundred things a day
160   That might go better, done another way,
But notwithstanding all that comes in view,
Men do not find me full of wrath like you;
I take men as they are, with self-control;
To suffer what they do I train my soul,
And I think, whether court or town's the scene,
My calm's as philosophic as your spleen.

ALCESTE. But, sir, this calm, that is so quick to reason,
This calm, is it then never out of season?
If by a friend you find yourself betrayed,
170   If for your property a snare is laid,
If men besmirch your name with slanderous lies,
You'll see that and your temper will not rise?

PHILINTE. Why yes, I see these faults, which make you hot,
As vices portioned to the human lot;
In short, it's no more shock to my mind's eye
To see a man unjust, self-seeking, sly,
Than to see vultures hungry for their prey,
Monkeys malicious, wolves athirst to slay.

ALCESTE. Then I should be robbed, torn to bits, betrayed,
180   Without . . . ? Good Lord! I leave the rest unsaid;
Such reasoning is patently absurd.

PHILINTE. Less talk would help your cause, upon my word:
Outbursts against your foe are out of place;
You should give more attention to your case.

ALCESTE. I'll give it none. That's all there is to say.

PHILINTE. Then who will speak for you and pave the way?

ALCESTE. The justice of my cause will speak for me.

PHILINTE. Is there no judge that you will stoop to see?[8]

ALCESTE. No; don't you think my case is just and clear?

PHILINTE. True, but intrigue is what you have to fear,   *190*
   And . . .

ALCESTE.   No, I'll take no steps, I'll not give in;
   I'm either right or wrong.

PHILINTE.   Don't think you'll win.

ALCESTE. I shall not budge.

PHILINTE.   Your enemy is strong,
   And by collusion he . . .

ALCESTE.   What then? He's wrong.

PHILINTE. You're making a mistake.

ALCESTE.   All right; we'll see.

PHILINTE. But . . .

ALCESTE.   Let me lose my case; that will please me.

PHILINTE. But after all . . .

ALCESTE.   In this chicanery
   I'll see if men have the effrontery,
   And are sufficiently base, vile, perverse,
   To wrong me in the sight of the universe.   *200*

PHILINTE. Oh, what a man!

ALCESTE.   My case—despite the cost,
   For the sheer beauty of it—I'd see lost.

PHILINTE. People would really laugh at you, you know,
   Alceste, if they could hear you talking so.

ALCESTE. Too bad for those who laugh.

---

3 It was normal practice in Molière's France for a litigant to visit his judge while his case was pending.

PHILINTE.   Even this rigor
    Which you require of all with so much vigor,
    This rectitude that you make so much of,
    Do you observe it in the one you love?
    It still amazes me when I see you,
210 Who censor humankind the way you do,
    And see in it so much that you abhor,
    Find in it anyone you can adore;
    And what astonishes me further yet
    Is the strange choice on which your heart is set.
    The candid Éliante finds you attractive,
    Arsinoé the prude would like you active;
    Meanwhile your unconcern with them is plain;
    Instead you are bewitched by Célimène,
    One whose sharp tongue and whose coquettish ways
220 Are just the things in fashion nowadays.
    How is it that in her you tolerate
    Failings which, found in others, rouse your hate?
    Are they no longer faults in one so dear?
    Are they unseen? Are others too severe?

ALCESTE. No, love for this young widow does not blind
    My eyes to all the faults that others find,
    And I, despite my ardor for her, am
    The first to see them and the first to damn.
    But still, for all of that, she has an art;
230 She finds and fills a soft spot in my heart;
    I see her flaws and blame them all I will,
    No matter what I do, I love her still;
    Her grace remains too strong. My love, no doubt,
    Will yet prevail and drive these vices out.

PHILINTE. If you do that, it will be no small coup.
    You think she loves you, then?

ALCESTE.   Indeed I do!
    I'd not love her unless I thought she did.

PHILINTE. But if her fondness for you is not hid,
    Why do your rivals cause you such concern?

240 ALCESTE. A smitten heart wants to possess in turn,
    And all I've come here for is to reveal
    To her all that my passion makes me feel.

PHILINTE. For my part, if mere wishes had a voice,
   Her cousin Éliante would be my choice.
   Her heart esteems you and is stanch and true;
   She'd be a sounder, better match for you.

ALCESTE. You're right, my reason says so every day;
   But over love reason has little sway.

PHILINTE. Your loving hopes I fear that she may flout,
   And . . .

Scene 2.   ORONTE, ALCESTE, PHILINTE

ORONTE.   Éliante, I hear downstairs, is out,   250
   And likewise Célimène, with things to do,
   But since they told me that I might find you,
   I came to tell you frankly, anyway,
   That I esteem you more than tongue can say,
   And that I long have wished and now intend
   To ask you to accept me as a friend.
   Yes, yes, I would see merit have its due;
   In friendship's bond I would be joined with you.
   An ardent friend, as nobly born as I,
   Can surely not be easily passed by.   260
                  (To ALCESTE)
   For you, if you don't mind, my words are meant.

   (At this point ALCESTE is lost in thought and seems not to
          hear that ORONTE is speaking to him.)

ALCESTE. Me, sir?

ORONTE.   You. Are they something to resent?

ALCESTE. No, but your praise of me comes unexpected;
   Such high regard I never had suspected.

ORONTE. My great esteem should come as no surprise,
   And you can claim the like in all men's eyes.

ALCESTE. Sir . . .

ORONTE.   Our whole State possesses nothing higher
  Than all your merit, which men so admire.

ALCESTE. Sir . . .

ORONTE.   Yes, you are far worthier, say I,
270 Than all I see that others rate so high.

ALCESTE. Sir . . .

ORONTE.   If I lie, may heaven strike me dead!
  And, to confirm to you what I've just said,
  Allow me, sir, a heart-to-heart embrace,
  And in your friendship let me find a place.
  Shake on it, if you please. Then it is mine,
  Your friendship?

ALCESTE.   Sir . . .

ORONTE.   What? Then do you decline?

ALCESTE. Sir, most excessively you honor me;
  But friendship asks a bit more mystery,
  And surely we profane its name sublime
280 By using it on all, and all the time.
  Upon enlightened choice this bond depends;
  We need to know each other to be friends,
  And we might prove to be so different
  That both of us might presently repent.

ORONTE. By heaven! That's wisely spoken on that score,
  And I esteem you for it all the more.
  Let us let time prepare friendship's fruition;
  But meanwhile I am at your disposition.
  If you need help at court for anything,
290 You know I have some standing with the King.
  He listens to me, and in every way
  Treats me more decently than I can say.
  In short, consider me as all your own;
  And, since your brilliant mind is widely known,
  I've come to ask your judgment as a friend
  Upon a sonnet that I lately penned,
  And learn whether I ought to publish it.

ALCESTE. For such a judgment, sir, I'm hardly fit.
  So please excuse me.

ORONTE.   Why?

ALCESTE.   For this defect:
  I'm always more sincere than men expect.   300

ORONTE. Exactly what I ask; I could complain
  If, when I urged you to speak clear and plain,
  You then disguised your thought in what you said.

ALCESTE. Since you will have it so, sir, go ahead.

ORONTE. "Sonnet . . ." It is a sonnet. "Hope . . ." You see,
  A lady once aroused some hope in me.
  "Hope . . ." This is nothing grandiose or sublime,
  But just a soft, sweet, tender little rhyme.

  (At each interruption he looks at ALCESTE.*)*

ALCESTE. We shall see.

ORONTE.   "Hope . . ." The style may not appear
  To you sufficiently easy and clear,   310
  And you may think the choice of words is bad.

ALCESTE. We shall see, sir.

ORONTE.   Moreover, let me add,
  A quarter hour was all the time I spent.

ALCESTE. Come, sir; the time is hardly pertinent.

ORONTE. Hope does, 'tis true, some comfort bring,
          And lulls awhile our aching pain;
          But, Phyllis, 'tis an empty thing
          When nothing follows in its train.

PHILINTE. That is a charming bit, and full of verve.

ALCESTE *(aside).* You call that charming? What! You have   320
  the nerve?

ORONTE. My flame you once seemed to invite;
          'Twas pity that you let it live,
          And kept me languishing, poor wight,
          When hope was all you had to give.

PHILINTE. Oh, in what gallant terms these things are put!

ALCESTE *(aside)*. You wretched flatterer! Gallant, my foot!

ORONTE. Should an eternity to wait
      Render my ardor desperate,
      Then my decease shall end my pains.

330
      Your fond concern you well may spare;
      Fair Phyllis, it is still despair
      When hope alone is what remains.

PHILINTE. That dying fall casts a seductive spell.

ALCESTE *(aside, to* PHILINTE*)*. Poisoner, you and your fall
    may go to hell.
  I wish you'd taken one right on your nose.

PHILINTE. I've never heard verses as fine as those.

ALCESTE. Good Lord!

ORONTE.   You flatter me; perhaps you're try-
    ing . . .

PHILINTE. I am not flattering.

ALCESTE *(aside)*.   No, only lying.

ORONTE *(to* ALCESTE*)*. But you, sir, you recall what we
    agreed;
340
  Please be sincere. How do these verses read?

ALCESTE. Questions of talent, sir, are ticklish matters,
  And we all yearn to hear the voice that flatters;
  But when a man—no matter who—one day
  Read me his verses, I made bold to say
  A gentleman must have the will to fight
  Our universal human itch to write,
  That he must overcome his great temptations
  To make a fuss about such recreations,
  And that our eagerness for self-display
350
  Can give us many a sorry role to play.

ORONTE. I think I gather what you're getting at:
  That I am wrong to want . . .

ALCESTE.   I don't say that.
 But frigid writing palls, and can bring down—
 So I told him—a worthy man's renown;
 Though one had every other quality,
 Our weakest points are what men choose to see.

ORONTE. Then with my sonnet, sir, do you find fault?

ALCESTE. I don't say that; but urging him to halt,
 I pointed out to him how, time and again,
 This thirst has spoiled extremely worthy men.   360

ORONTE. Am I like them? Don't I know how to rhyme?

ALCESTE. I don't say that. But, I said, take your time:
 Have you some urgent need to versify
 And see yourself in print? I ask you, why?
 The authors of bad books we may forgive
 Only when the poor wretches write to live.
 Take my advice and overcome temptations,
 Hide from the public all these occupations,
 Against all urgings raise a stout defense,
 And keep your good name as a man of sense;   370
 Don't change it in some greedy printer's stall
 For that of author ridiculed by all.
 —That's what I tried to make this man perceive.

ORONTE. All right. I understand you, I believe.
 About my sonnet, though: may I be told . . . ?

ALCESTE. Frankly, your sonnet should be pigeonholed.
 The models you have used are poor and trite;
 There's nothing natural in what you write.
 What is this "lulls awhile our aching pain"?
            This "nothing follows in its train"?   380
            Or "kept me languishing, poor wight,
             When hope was all you had to give"?
            And "Phyllis, it is still despair
             When hope alone is what remains"?
 This mannered style, so dear to people's hearts,
 From human nature and from truth departs;
 It's purest affectation, verbal play,
 And Nature never speaks in such a way.

Standards today are wretched, I maintain;
390   Our fathers' taste, though crude, was far more sane.
What men now prize gives me far less delight
Than this old song which I will now recite:

　　　If the king had given me
　　　　　Great Paris for my own,
　　　　　And had said the price must be
　　　　　　To leave my love alone,
　　　　I would tell the king Henri:
　　　　　Then take back your great Paris,[4]
　　　　I prefer my love, hey ho,
400   　　　I prefer my love.

The rhyme's not rich, the style is old and rough,
But don't you see this is far better stuff
Then all this trumpery that flouts good sense,
And that here passion speaks without pretence?

　　　　　If the king had given me
　　　　　　Great Paris for my own,
　　　　　And had said the price must be
　　　　　　To leave my love alone,
　　　　I would tell the king Henri:
410   　　　Then take back your great Paris,
　　　　I prefer my love, hey ho,
　　　　　I prefer my love.

That's what a really loving heart might say.
　　　　　(To PHILINTE)
Laugh on. Despite the wits who rule today,
I rate this higher than the flowery show
Of artificial gems, which please men so.

ORONTE. And *I* maintain my verse is very good.

ALCESTE. I'm sure that you have reasons why you should;
But grant my reasons leave to disagree
420   And not let yours impose themselves on me.

ORONTE. Enough for me that others rate it high.

ALCESTE. They have the art of feigning, sir; not I.

ORONTE. Not doubt you think you've quite a share of wit?

4 Pronounce Paree.

ALCESTE. To praise your verse, I should need more of it.

ORONTE. I'll get along without your praise, I trust.

ALCESTE. I hope you're right, sir, for I fear you must.

ORONTE. I'd like to see you try, in your own way,
On this same theme, to show what you could say.

ALCESTE. My verses might be just as bad, I own,
But I'd be careful not to make them known.   *430*

ORONTE. Your talk is high and mighty, and your ways . . .

ALCESTE. Look elsewhere for a man to sing your praise.

ORONTE. My little man, don't take this tone with me.

ALCESTE. Big man, my tone is just what it should be.

PHILINTE *(stepping between them).* Come, gentlemen,
enough! I pray you, no!

ORONTE. My fault, I do admit. And now I'll go.
With all my heart, I am your servant, sir.

ALCESTE. And I, sir, am your humble servitor.

Scene 3.   PHILINTE, ALCESTE

PHILINTE. Well, there you are! You see? By being candid,
Just note in what a nasty mess you've landed;   *440*
Oronte's desire for praise was obvious . . .

ALCESTE. Don't speak to me.

PHILINTE.   But . . .

ALCESTE.   Finis between us.

PHILINTE. You're too . . .

ALCESTE.   Leave me.

PHILINTE.   If . . .

ALCESTE.   Not another
word.

PHILINTE. But what! . . .

ALCESTE.   I'm deaf.

PHILINTE.   But . . .

ALCESTE.   More?

PHILINTE.   This is
absurd.

ALCESTE. Good Lord! I've had enough. Be off with you.

PHILINTE. You don't mean that. Where you go, I go too.

ACT II

Scene 1. ALCESTE, CÉLIMÈNE

ALCESTE. Madame, shall I speak frankly and be brief?
  Your conduct gives me not a little grief;
  It rouses too much bile within my heart,
  And I can see that we shall have to part.   *450*
  I have to tell you this for conscience' sake:
  Sooner or later we must surely break.
  A thousand pledges to the contrary
  I might make, but I could not guarantee.

CÉLIMÈNE. Indeed, your wish to bring me home was kind,
  When scolding me was what you had in mind.

ALCESTE. I do not scold; but what is my dismay,
  Madame, that the first comer makes his way
  Into your heart? By suitors you're beset;
  And I cannot see this without regret.   *460*

CÉLIMÈNE. You blame me for my suitors, this I see.
  Can I prevent people from liking me?
  And when they try to visit me, no doubt
  I ought to take a stick and drive them out?

ALCESTE. A stick, Madame, is not what I suggest,
  Merely a heart less easily impressed.
  I know that everywhere you cast a spell;
  But those your eyes attract you greet too well;
  Your graciousness to all who yield their arms
  Completes the conquering action of your charms.   *470*
  The over-brilliant hopes that you arouse
  Surround you with these suitors and their vows;
  If only your complaisance were less vast,
  This sighing mob would disappear at last.
  But by what spell, Madame, if I may know,

Does your Clitandre contrive to please you so?
In worth and virtue is he so supreme
That you should honor him with your esteem?
His little fingernail is very long:
480   Is that why your regard for him is strong?
Has his blond wig, which has such great effect
Upon society, won your respect?
Do you love him for the ruffles at his knees?
Or do his multitudinous ribbons please?
Is it the charm of his vast German breeches
That, while he plays the slave, your soul bewitches?
Is it his laugh and his falsetto voice
That make of him the suitor of your choice?

CÉLIMÈNE. To take offense at him is most unfair!
490   You know why I must handle him with care,
And that he's pledged his many friends' support
To help me when my lawsuit comes to court.

ALCESTE. Then lose your suit, as bravely as you can,
And do not humor that offensive man.

CÉLIMÈNE. Why, everyone excites your jealousy.

ALCESTE. You welcome everyone so charmingly.

CÉLIMÈNE. But this should reassure your anxious mind:
That all who seek, this same complaisance find;
And you would have more cause for discontent
500   If there were only one recipient.

ALCESTE. But I, Madame, whose jealousy you blame,
In what way is my treatment not the same?

CÉLIMÈNE. Knowing that you are loved sets you apart.

ALCESTE. How can I prove this to my burning heart?

CÉLIMÈNE. To say what I have said exacts a price;
I think such an avowal should suffice.

ALCESTE. But how can I be certain, even then,
You do not say the same to other men?

CÉLIMÈNE. My! That's a charming way to pay your court,
510   And that makes me appear a pretty sort!

Well then, to give you no more cause to sigh,
All I have said I here and now deny.
There's no deceiving to be fearful of
Except your own.

ALCESTE.   Lord! And I'm still in love!
   If I could just get back my heart, I'd bless
   Heaven above for such rare happiness!
   I do my best—and this I don't conceal—
   To break the cruel attachment that I feel;
   But I have toiled in vain, and now I know
   That it is for my sins I love you so.   520

CÉLIMÈNE. It's true, your love for me is matched by none.

ALCESTE. Yes, on that score I'll challenge anyone.
   My love is past belief, Madame; I say
   No one has ever loved in such a way.

CÉLIMÈNE. Indeed, your way is novel, and your aim;
   The only token of your love is blame;
   Your ardor shows itself in angry speech,
   And never was a love so quick to preach.

ALCESTE. It rests with you that this should pass away.
   Let's call a halt to quarreling, I pray,   530
   Speak out with open hearts, then, and begin . . .

Scene 2.   CÉLIMÈNE, ALCESTE, BASQUE

CÉLIMÈNE. What is it?

BASQUE.   It's Acaste.

CÉLIMÈNE.   Well, show him in.

ALCESTE. What? Can one never talk to you alone?
   Must you then always welcome everyone?
   And can you not for just one moment bear
   To have a caller told you are not there?

CÉLIMÈNE. You'd have me quarrel with him too, for sure?

ALCESTE. Some of your courtesies I can't endure.

CÉLIMÈNE. That man would bear a grudge for evermore,
540   If he knew I find the sight of him a bore.

ALCESTE. And why should this make you put on an act?

CÉLIMÈNE. Heavens! Influence is an important fact.
  I don't know why, but people of his sort
  Can talk loud and importantly at court.
  They push their way into each interview;
  They cannot help, but they can damage you;
  And even if your other aid is stout,
  Don't quarrel with these men who love to shout.

ALCESTE. No matter what the reason or the base,
550   You find cause to receive the human race;
  And the precautions that you take, perforce . . .

Scene 3.   BASQUE, ALCESTE, CÉLIMÈNE

BASQUE. Madame, here is Clitandre as well.

ALCESTE (showing that he wants to leave).

                                    Of course.

CÉLIMÈNE. Where are you going?

ALCESTE.   Leaving.

CÉLIMÈNE.   Stay.

ALCESTE.   What for?

CÉLIMÈNE. Stay here.

ALCESTE.   I can't.

CÉLIMÈNE.   I want you to.

ALCESTE.   No more.

These conversations weary me past cure;
This is too much to ask me to endure.

CÉLIMÈNE. You shall remain, you shall.

ALCESTE.   It cannot be.

CÉLIMÈNE. All right, then, go; it's quite all right with me.

Scene 4.   ÉLIANTE, PHILINTE, ACASTE, CLITANDRE,
                ALCESTE, CÉLIMÈNE, BASQUE

ÉLIANTE. Here are the two marquis who've come to call.
   Were they announced?

CÉLIMÈNE.   Indeed. *(To* BASQUE*)* Bring chairs for all.   560
   (To ALCESTE*)* You haven't left?

ALCESTE.   No, Madame. I demand
   That you declare to all just where you stand.

CÉLIMÈNE. Oh, hush.

ALCESTE.   You shall explain yourself today.

CÉLIMÈNE. You're mad.

ALCESTE.   I am not. You shall say your say.

CÉLIMÈNE. Ah!

ALCESTE.   You'll make up your mind.

CÉLIMÈNE.   I think you're joking.

ALCESTE. No, you *shall* choose; this doubt is too provoking.

CLITANDRE. My word! I've just come from the King's levee,
   Where Cléonte played the fool for all to see.
   Has he no friend who could, with kindly tact,
   Teach him the rudiments of how to act?   570

CÉLIMÈNE. Indeed, in social life the man's a dunce;
   His manner startles every eye at once;

And when you see him, later on, once more,
You find him more fantastic than before.

ACASTE. Speaking of characters fantastical,
    I've just endured the greatest bore of all:
    Damon, the talker, kept me, by your leave,
    One hour in the hot sun without reprieve.

CÉLIMÈNE. Yes, his strange mania for reasoning
580   Makes him talk on, and never say a thing;
    His discourse in obscurity abounds,
    And all you listen to is merely sounds.

ÉLIANTE *(To* PHILINTE*)*. Not a bad opening. Soon the
    entire nation
    Will be in danger of annihilation.

CLITANDRE. Timante is quite a character, you know.

CÉLIMÈNE. The man of mystery from top to toe,
    Who gives you a distracted glance, aside,
    Does nothing, yet is always occupied.
    Grimaces lend importance to each word;
590   His high portentousness makes him absurd;
    He interrupts your talk, in confidence,
    To whisper a secret of no consequence;
    At making trifles great he has no peer;
    Even "Good day" he whispers in your ear.

ACASTE. Géralde, Madame?

CÉLIMÈNE.   He tells a tedious tale.
    All but great nobles are beyond the pale;
    He mingles with those of the highest note,
    And none but duke or princess will he quote.
    He is obsessed with rank; his monologues
600   Are all of horses, carriages, and dogs;
    He uses *tu* in speaking to the great,
    And seems to think *Monsieur*[5] is out of date.

CLITANDRE. They say Bélise appreciates his merit.

CÉLIMÈNE. How dry she is in talk, and poor in spirit!

---

5 *Tu*, literally "thou," is the "you" of familiarity or condescension.
Monsieur means both "Mr." and "Sir."

I find it torture to receive her call:
You labor to say anything at all,
And the sterility of her expression
At every moment kills the conversation.
In vain, her stupid silence to annul,
You try each commonplace, however dull: 610
Sunny or rainy weather, heat or frost
Are topics that you rapidly exhaust;
Meanwhile her visit, draining all your strength,
Drags on and on at terrifying length;
You ask the time, you yawn and yawn, but no:
She sits there like a log and will not go. .

ACASTE. What of Adraste?

CÉLIMÈNE.   Oh, what colossal pride!
His love of self has puffed him up inside,
At court he misses due consideration;
So railing at it is his occupation;   620
No post or benefice goes to anyone,
But that he thinks injustice has been done.

CLITANDRE. On young Cléon what will your verdict be?
He entertains the best society.

CÉLIMÈNE. He has a cook who is extremely able;
And what they come to visit is his table.

ÉLIANTE. He serves you nothing but the finest food.

CÉLIMÈNE. He serves himself as well, and that's less good:
His stupid person is a sorry dish
That spoils the taste of fowl and roast and fish.   630

PHILINTE. Some think Damis, his uncle, rather fine.
What do you say?

CÉLIMÈNE.   He is a friend of mine.

PHILINTE. He seems a decent sort, I must admit.

CÉLIMÈNE. Yes, but he tries too hard to be a wit;
He talks so stiltedly you always know
That he's premeditating some *bon mot.*
Since he has set his mind on being clever,
He takes delight in nothing whatsoever;

In all that's written he finds only flaws,
640   And thinks that cleverness forbids applause,
That criticism is a sign of learning,
Enjoyment only for the undiscerning,
And that to frown on any book that's new
Places him high among the happy few;
He looks on common talk with condescension
As much too trivial for his attention;
Folding his arms, from high above the rabble,
He glances down with pity on our babble.

ACASTE. Damme, Madame, that is exactly true.

650   CLITANDRE. There's no one can portray a man like you.

ALCESTE. That's right, my courtly friends, be strong, spare
      none,
Strike hard, and have your sport with everyone;
Yet when one of these victims comes in sight,
Your haste in meeting him is most polite,
And with a kiss and offer of your hand,
You demonstrate that you're at his command.

CLITANDRE. But why blame us? If what is said offends you,
'Tis to Madame that your remonstrance sends you.

ALCESTE. By God, no! 'Tis to you; your fawning laughter
660   Affords her wit just the applause she's after.
Her bent for character assassination
Feeds constantly upon your adulation;
For satire she would have less appetite
Were it not always greeted with delight.
Thus flatterers deserve our main assaults
For leading humans into many faults.

PHILINTE. But why so eager to defend the name
Of those in whom you damn the things we blame?

CÉLIMÈNE. Don't you see, he must be opposed to you?
670   Would you have him accept the common view,
And not display, in every company,
His heaven-sent gift for being contrary?
The ideas of others he will not admit;
Always he must maintain the opposite;

He'd fear he was an ordinary human
If he agreed with any man—or woman.
For him contrariness offers such charms,
Against himself he often turns his arms;
And should another man his views defend,
He will combat them to the bitter end.   680

ALCESTE. The laughers are with you, Madame; you've won.
  Go on and satirize me; have your fun.

PHILINTE. But it is also true you have a way
  Of balking at whatever people say;
  And that your spite, which you yourself avow,
  Neither applause nor censure will allow.

ALCESTE. My God! That's because men are never right;
  It always is the season for our spite;
  I see them on all matters, in all ways,
  Quick with rash censure and untimely praise.   690

CÉLIMÈNE. But . . .

ALCESTE.   No, Madame, you *shall* learn, though
    it kill me,
  With what distaste some of your pleasures fill me,
  And that I find those persons much to blame
  Who foster faults that damage your good name.

CLITANDRE. As for me, I don't know; but I aver
  That up to now I've found no fault in her.

ACASTE. Her charms and grace are evident to me;
  But any faults I fear I cannot see.

ALCESTE. I see them all; she knows the way I feel;
  My disapproval I do not conceal.   700
  Loving and flattering are worlds apart;
  The least forgiving is the truest heart;
  And I would send these soft suitors away,
  Seeing they dote on everything I say,
  And that their praise, complaisant to excess,
  Encourages me in my foolishness.

CÉLIMÈNE. In short, if we're to leave it up to you,
  All tenderness in love we must eschew;

And love can only find its true perfection
710 In railing at the objects of our affection.

ÉLIANTE. Love tends to find such laws somewhat austere,
And lovers always brag about their dear;
Their passion never sees a thing to blame,
And everything is lovely in their flame:
They find perfection in her every flaw,
And speak of her with euphemistic awe.
The pallid one's the whitest jasmine yet;
The frightful dark one is a sweet brunette;
The spindly girl is willowy and free;
720 The fat one bears herself with majesty;
The dowdy one, who's ill-endowed as well,
Becomes a careless and neglectful belle;
The giantess is a divinity;
The dwarf, a heavenly epitome;
With princesses the proud one can compete;
The tricky one has wit; the dull one's sweet;
The tireless talker's charmingly vivacious,
The mute girl modest, womanly, and gracious.
Thus every man who loves beyond compare
730 Loves even the defects of his lady fair.

ALCESTE. And *I*, for my part, claim . . .

CÉLIMÈNE.   Let's end this talk
And step outside for just a little walk.
What? You are leaving, sirs?

CLITANDRE and ACASTE.   No, Madame, no.

ALCESTE. You're certainly afraid that they may go.
Leave when you like, sirs; but I'm warning you,
I shall not leave this place until you do.

ACASTE. Unless Madame should be a little tired,
There's nowhere that my presence is required.

CLITANDRE. I must go later to the King's couchee,
740 But until then I am quite free today.

CÉLIMÈNE. You're joking, surely.

ALCESTE.   No. I need to know
Whether you wish for them, or me, to go.

Scene 5.   BASQUE, ALCESTE, CÉLIMÈNE, ÉLIANTE,
           ACASTE, PHILINTE, CLITANDRE

BASQUE. Sir, there's a man to see you in the hall
   Who says his business will not wait at all.

ALCESTE. Tell him I have no business of such note.

BASQUE. He has a uniform, a great tailcoat
   With pleats and lots of gold.

CÉLIMÈNE.   Please go and see,
   Or let him in.

ALCESTE (*to the* OFFICER).
              What do you want with me?
   Come in, sir.

Scene 6.   OFFICER, ALCESTE, CÉLIMÈNE, ÉLIANTE, ACASTE,
           PHILINTE, CLITANDRE

OFFICER.   Sir, with you I crave a word.

ALCESTE. You may speak up, sir; let your news be heard.   *750*

OFFICER. The Marshals,[6] sir, have ordered me to say
   You must appear before them right away.

ALCESTE. Who, I, sir?

OFFICER.   You yourself.

ALCESTE.   What can they want?

PHILINTE. It's that ridiculous business with Oronte.

[6] The Tribunal of Marshals regulated quarrels among gentlemen.
By this time dueling was on the wane.

CÉLIMÈNE. How's that?

PHILINTE.   They are about to take the sword
Over some verse with which Alceste was bored.
The Marshals want of course to quash the matter.

ALCESTE. They'll never force me to back down and flatter.

PHILINTE. You'll have to follow orders; come, let's go.

760 ALCESTE. What can they reconcile, I'd like to know?
Shall I now, after everything that's passed,
Be sentenced to admire his verse at last?
I don't take back a single thing I said,
I think they're bad.

PHILINTE.   But with a calmer head . . .

ALCESTE. I won't back down; his verse is a disgrace.

PHILINTE. Intransigence like yours is out of place.
Come on.

ALCESTE.   I'll go; but I shall not unsay
One thing I've said.

PHILINTE.   Come, let's be on our way.

ALCESTE. Unless I have the King's express command
770 To like these verses, I have made my stand.
That they are bad, on this I'll never falter,
And that their author well deserves the halter.
        (To CLITANDRE and ACASTE, who laugh)
By God! Messieurs, I never really knew
I was so funny.

CÉLIMÈNE.   Come, be off with you.
Go where you must.

ALCESTE.   I go, Madame, but straight
I shall return to settle our debate.

ACT III

Scene 1. CLITANDRE, ACASTE

CLITANDRE. You glow with satisfaction, dear Marquis:
  You're free from worriment and full of glee.
  But do you think you're seeing things aright
  In taking such occasion for delight?   780

ACASTE. My word! When I regard myself, I find
  No reason for despondency of mind.
  I'm rich, I'm young, I'm of a family
  With some pretention to nobility;
  And through the rank that goes with my condition,
  At court I can aspire to high position.
  For courage, something we must all admire,
  'Tis known I have been tested under fire,
  And an affair of honor recently
  Displayed my vigor and my bravery.   790
  My wit is adequate, my taste discerning,
  To judge and treat all subjects without learning;
  When a new play is shown (which I adore),
  To sit upon the stage, display my lore,
  Determine its success, and stop the show
  When any passage merits my "Bravo!"
  I make a good appearance, rather chic;
  I have fine teeth, an elegant physique.
  And as for dress, all vanity aside,
  My eminence can scarcely be denied.   800
  I could not ask for more regard; I seem
  To have the ladies' love, the King's esteem.
  With all this, dear Marquis, I do believe
  That no man anywhere has cause to grieve.

CLITANDRE. When elsewhere easy conquests meet your eyes,
  Why linger here to utter useless sighs?

ACASTE. I? 'Pon my word, I'm not the sort to bear
A cool reception from a lady fair.
It is for vulgar men, uncouth in dress,
810   To burn for belles who will not acquiesce,
Pine at their feet, endure their cold disdain,
Seek some support from sighs and tears—in vain,
And strive to win by assiduity
What is denied their meager quality.
But men of my class are not made to yearn
For anyone, Marquis, without return.
However fair the girls, however nice,
I think, thank God, we too are worth our price;
If they would claim the heart of one like me,
820   They should in reason pay the proper fee;
And it would be no more than fair that they
Should meet our every overture halfway.

CLITANDRE. Then you are pleased, Marquis, with prospects
here?

ACASTE. They offer me, Marquis, good grounds for cheer.

CLITANDRE. Believe me, leave these fantasies behind;
Dear chap, your self-delusion makes you blind.

ACASTE. Of course, delusion makes me blind; ah, yes.

CLITANDRE. But what assures you of such happiness?

ACASTE. Delusion.

CLITANDRE.   Have you grounds for confidence?

ACASTE. I'm blind.

830   CLITANDRE.   What constitutes your evidence?

ACASTE. I tell you, I'm all wrong.

CLITANDRE.   Well, have you, then,
Received some secret vow from Célimène?

ACASTE. No, I am badly treated.

CLITANDRE.   Tell me, please.

ACASTE. Nothing but snubs.

CLITANDRE.   A truce on pleasantries;
   Tell me what makes you set your hopes so high.

ACASTE. Yours is the luck, and I can only sigh.
   So great is her aversion for my ways
   That I shall hang myself one of these days.

CLITANDRE. Come now, Marquis, to mend our rivalry,
   Let us agree on one thing, you and me: 840
   If either one can show beyond a doubt
   That in her heart he has been singled out,
   The other shall admit defeat and yield,
   Leaving the victor master of the field.

ACASTE. My word! Your notion matches my intent;
   With all my heart and soul I do consent.
   But hush!

Scene 2.   CÉLIMÈNE, ACASTE, CLITANDRE

CÉLIMÈNE. Still here?

CLITANDRE.   Love will not let us go.

CÉLIMÈNE. I heard a carriage in the court below:
   Who is it?

CLITANDRE. I don't know.

Scene 3.   BASQUE, CÉLIMÈNE, ACASTE, CLITANDRE

BASQUE.   Arsinoé
   Is here, Madame.

CÉLIMÈNE.   Why, what can bring her, pray?   850

BASQUE. She's now downstairs talking with Éliante.

CÉLIMÈNE. What can be on her mind? What can she want?

ACASTE. She plays the perfect prude where'er she goes;
   Her ardent zeal . . .

CÉLIMÈNE.   Yes, yes, it's quite a pose:
   Her soul is worldly, and her fondest plan
   Is, by some miracle, to catch a man.
   She can see only with an envious eye
   The suitors someone else is courted by.
   Left all alone, but not the least resigned,
860   She rages at the world that is so blind.
   She tries to hide, by acting like a prude,
   Her obvious and frightful solitude.
   Rather than find her feeble charms to blame,
   She calls the power they lack a cause for shame.
   A suitor, though, is what would please her best,
   Especially if that suitor was Alceste.
   His visits to me make her feel bereft,
   And she pronounces this a kind of theft.
   In jealous spite, which she can hardly bear,
870   She covertly attacks me everywhere.
   In short, a sillier soul I never saw;
   In her absurdity there's not a flaw,
   And . . .

Scene 4.   ARSINOÉ, CÉLIMÈNE.

CÉLIMÈNE. Ah! Madame! Why, what a nice surprise!
   I've missed you so! I can't believe my eyes.

ARSINOÉ. There's something that I think I ought to say.

CÉLIMÈNE. Just seeing you makes this a perfect day.
                      (*Exit* ACASTE *and* CLITANDRE, *laughing.*)

ARSINOÉ. Their leaving now was apropos indeed.

CÉLIMÈNE. Shall we sit down?

ARSINOÉ.   I do not see the need,
   Madame. True friendship should be manifest

In subjects that concern our interest;   880
And since none matter more to you or me
Than those of honor and propriety,
I come to tell you something, as a friend,
On which your reputation may depend.
I spent the other day with virtuous folk,
And, as it happened, 'twas of you they spoke.
And there, Madame, the freedom of your ways
Had the misfortune not to meet with praise.
The many men from whom you seek applause,
The rumors your coquettish manners cause,   890
Found far more censors than they ever ought,
And harsher than I could have wished or thought.
On this, you can imagine where I stood:
I sprang to your defense—as best I could,
Excusing your behavior as well-meant,
And stating I would vouch for your intent.
But there are things, you know as well as I,
We can't excuse, however hard we try;
And so I had to grant the others' claim
That your behavior does not help your name,   900
That it affords you anything but glory,
And makes of you the butt of many a story,
And that your ways, if you amended them,
Might offer less occasion to condemn.
Not that I think you grant more than you ought:
Heaven preserve my mind from such a thought!
But people hanker so for signs of vice,
To live well for oneself does not suffice.
Madame, I think you have too wise a heart
Not to accept this counsel in good part,   910
And to suspect a motive in my breast
Other than fervor for your interest.

CÉLIMÈNE. Madame, do not misjudge my attitude:
Advice like yours is cause for gratitude;
Now let me show my deep appreciation
By counsel that concerns your reputation,
And since I see you show your amity
By telling me what people say of me,
I'll take your kind example as my cue,

920 And let you know the things they say of you.
     I visited some friends the other day—
     People of merit—and it chanced that they
     Sought to define the art of living well.
     On you, Madame, the conversation fell.
     Your prudery, your ready indignation
     Were not, alas! held up for admiration.
     That affectation of a pious face,
     Eternal talk of honor and of grace,
     Your screams and airs of outraged innocence,
930 When a harmless word allows a doubtful sense,
     The self-esteem that gratifies your mind,
     The pitying eye you cast upon mankind,
     Your frequent lessons, and the wrath you vent
     On matters that are pure and innocent:
     All this, to speak without equivocation,
     Madame, gave rise to general condemnation.
     "Why does she wear," they said, "this modest guise,
     This pious mask which all the rest belies?
     Though she would never miss a time to pray,
940 She beats her servants and withholds their pay.
     In church she flaunts her zealous sense of duty,
     Yet paints her face and strives to be a beauty.
     She covers up the nude when it's in paint,
     But of the thing itself makes no complaint."
     Against them all I spoke right up for you,
     Assuring them that none of this was true;
     Still nothing would they do but criticize,
     And they concluded that you would be wise
     To leave the acts of others more alone,
950 And think a little more about your own;
     That we should take an earnest look within
     Before we censure other people's sin;
     That only those whose lives approach perfection
     Are licensed to administer correction;
     And that we leave this better, even then,
     To those whom Heaven has chosen among men.
     Madame, you too have far too wise a heart
     Not to accept this counsel in good part,
     And to suspect a motive in my breast
960 Other than fervor for your interest.

ARSINOÉ. I know we run a risk when we exhort,
　　But I did not expect quite this retort;
　　And since, Madame, it is so very tart,
　　I see my frank advice has stung your heart.

CÉLIMÈNE. Why, not at all, Madame; if we were wise,
　　Such chance for mutual counsel we would prize;
　　And honesty would banish from our mind
　　The blindness toward oneself that plagues mankind.
　　So, if you wish it, we need never end
　　This helpful interchange from friend to friend,　　　970
　　And we can tell each other, *entre nous,*
　　All that you hear of me, and I of you.

ARSINOÉ. Why, nothing can be heard against your name,
　　Madame, and it is I whom people blame.

CÉLIMÈNE. Madame, we either praise or blame, in truth,
　　According to our taste and to our youth.
　　And thus there is one season for romance,
　　Another fitter for a prudish stance.
　　The latter may be suited to the time
　　When our attractiveness has passed its prime:　　　980
　　It helps to cover our pathetic lacks.
　　Some day I may well follow in your tracks:
　　Age brings all things; but who is in the mood,
　　Madame, at twenty, to become a prude?

ARSINOÉ. You flaunt a scant advantage there, in truth,
　　And preen yourself a lot about your youth.
　　If I am just a bit older than you,
　　This is no reason for such great ado;
　　And I confess, Madame, I do not know
　　What passion drives you to attack me so.　　　990

CÉLIMÈNE. And I, Madame, would like to know the reason
　　Why hunting me is never out of season.
　　Why do you blame me for your unsuccess?
　　And can I help it if men seek you less?
　　If I inspire so many men with love,
　　If I am offered daily proofs thereof,
　　Proofs that you wish might be addressed to you,
　　It's not my fault; there's nothing I can do:

The field is free, and I do not prevent
1000   Your charming menfolk to your heart's content.

ARSINOÉ. Come, do you think I envy you that crowd
Of suitors whose attentions make you proud,
And that it is so hard for us to tell
At what a price you hold them in your spell?
Would you have us believe, the way things go,
That it is just your merit charms them so?
That it is with a proper love they burn,
And that they hope for nothing in return?
Vain explanations never do ring true,
1010   No one is fooled; and I know women who,
Though made for every mortal to adore,
Yet do not summon suitors to their door.
From this I think we safely may conclude
That such devotion springs from gratitude,
That no one courts us for our lovely eyes,
And that we pay a price for all their sighs.
So be a little less inclined to gloat
On conquests that deserve such little note;
Correct your disposition to be vain,
1020   And show your fellow humans less disdain.
If we were envious of such as you,
I rather think we could, as others do,
Let ourselves go; and then you soon would find
All can have suitors who are so inclined.

CÉLIMÈNE. Then help yourself, Madame, and we shall see
If you can lure them with this recipe;
And if . . .

ARSINOÉ.   Madame, let's leave things as they are;
More talk would carry both of us too far;
I would have taken leave, as soon I will,
1030   But that my carriage keeps me waiting still.

CÉLIMÈNE. Madame, believe me, you are free to stay
As long as you like; please do not rush away;
But, lest more formal talk from me fatigue you,
Here's someone much more likely to intrigue you;
This gentleman, who comes just when he should,
Will entertain you better than I could.

Alceste, I have a letter I must send,
Or else I shall antagonize a friend.
Please stay here with Madame; I have no doubt
She'll graciously excuse my stepping out.   *1040*

Scene 5.   ALCESTE, ARSINOÉ

ARSINOÉ. She wants the two of us to talk, you see,
   While waiting till my carriage comes for me;
   And she could show me no consideration
   As nice as such a private conversation.
   Truly, people whose merit is supreme
   Attract unanimous love and esteem;
   And by its charm your high distinction earns
   The interest of my heart in your concerns.
   I only wish the court would have the grace
   To set your merit in its proper place: *1050*
   You are ill-treated, and I swear it hurts
   To see you fail to get your true deserts.

ALCESTE. Who, I, Madame? And what should be my claim?
   What service to the state adorns my name?
   What splendid thing have I achieved, in short,
   To justify my preference at court?

ARSINOÉ. The court regards some with a kindly eye
   Which their achievements hardly justify.
   Merit requires a chance to meet some test;
   And yours, which is so plainly manifest,   *1060*
   Should . . .

ALCESTE.   Heavens! forget my merit; be so kind.
   How can the court keep such things on its mind?
   It would be quite a task for it to scan
   The merit that resides in every man.

ARSINOÉ. True merit is most difficult to hide;
   Yours commands high esteem on every side;

And yesterday, in two distinguished places,
I heard important persons sing your praises.

ALCESTE. But undiscerning praise today is cheap,
1070 Madame, and lumps us all in one great heap:
With merit all are equally endowed;
Applause no longer makes us justly proud;
We toss bouquets in one another's face;
And in the news my valet has his place.

ARSINOÉ. I wish your quality was more in view,
And that a post at court appealed to you.
If you would show the slightest inclination,
Machinery would be in operation;
And I have influence to bring to bear
1080 To make your progress smooth beyond compare.

ALCESTE. And there, Madame, what role am I to play?
My character demands I stay away.
And Heaven did not make me of the sort
To get along contentedly at court;
I do not have the virtues that you need
To do your business there and to succeed.
Only in honesty can I compete,
I simply have no talent for deceit;
And anyone who can't equivocate
1090 Should leave the place before it is too late.
Away from court we lack support, no doubt,
And all the titles that are handed out;
But there is consolation for our soul:
We do not have to play a silly role,
Brook the rebuffs that all must undergo,
Admire the verse of Mr. So-and-So,
Burn incense at the shrine of Madam Blank,
And suffer every noble mountebank.

ARSINOÉ. All right; about the court I shall be mute;
1100 But I am much distressed about your suit,
And I could wish, if I may speak my mind,
To see your love more suitably assigned.
You certainly deserve a better fate,
And Célimène is not your proper mate.

ALCESTE. One thing, Madame, I do not comprehend:
  Do you forget this lady is your friend?

ARSINOÉ. Yes; but my conscience has been grieved too long
  At watching you endure so great a wrong;
  Seeing you in this state, I am dismayed,
  And you should know your passion is betrayed.   *1110*

ALCESTE. Your tender sentiments I now discover,
  Madame: what welcome tidings for a lover!

ARSINOÉ. Yes, though she is my friend, I do declare
  That she does not deserve your loving care,
  And that her kindness to you is but show.

ALCESTE. Perhaps, Madame; the heart we cannot know;
  But could you not in charity decline
  To plant such a disloyal thought in mine?

ARSINOÉ. If you would rather look the other way,
  There's no use talking, and I've said my say.   *1120*

ALCESTE. Whatever we are told in this domain,
  Doubt is the thing that gives the greatest pain;
  And I would rather not have information
  Without the chance for clear verification.

ARSINOÉ. Enough said. Very well. To set things right,
  On this score you shall have abundant light.
  Yes, with your own eyes you shall clearly see:
  All you need do is to come home with me;
  Convincing proof I will provide you there
  Of your betrayal by your lady fair;   *1130*
  And if you're cured of your infatuation,
  You might even be offered consolation.

ACT IV

Scene 1. ÉLIANTE, PHILINTE

PHILINTE. I've never seen such stubborn indignation,
　　Or such a difficult accommodation:
　　We could not budge the man, hard as we tried,
　　With all our arguments from every side,
　　Nor has a case of such a curious sort
　　Ever, I think, preoccupied this court.
　　"No, gentlemen," he said, "to this I cling:
1140　I'll concede all, except for this one thing.
　　Why must he bridle and strike out so madly?
　　Is his honor at stake in writing badly?
　　Why must he twist my judgment for the worse?
　　Even a gentleman can write bad verse.
　　These things concern our honor not a whit.
　　That he's a gentleman I do admit,
　　A man of quality, merit, and heart,
　　All that you like—his authorship apart.
　　I'll praise his lavish get-up for its charms,
1150　His skill at dancing, horsemanship, or arms,
　　But praise his verse? That takes a diplomat.
　　And if a man can't write better than that,
　　He should resist rhyming to his last breath—
　　At least, unless it's under pain of death."
　　In short, the best grace and accommodation
　　He found to cover up his irritation
　　Was to seek—thus—to put Oronte at ease:
　　"Sir, I regret that I'm so hard to please,
　　And for your sake I wish with all my heart
1160　I'd thought your sonnet was a work of art."
　　After these words, they had the two embrace,
　　And hastily concluded the whole case.

ÉLIANTE. His actions are peculiar and extreme,
   But, I admit, I hold him in esteem,
   And the sincerity that is his pride
   Has a heroic and a noble side.
   It's an uncommon virtue in this day
   Which I wish others had in the same way.

PHILINTE. The more I see the man, the more I wonder
   At the impassioned spell his heart is under: *1170*
   Considering what Heaven made him of,
   I cannot think how he can fall in love;
   And why he loves your cousin, I confess,
   Is something I can fathom even less.

ÉLIANTE. This clearly shows that love, in human hearts,
   Need not imply community of parts;
   And theories of mutual admiration
   In this case show themselves without foundation.

PHILINTE. But as you see it, is he loved in turn?

ÉLIANTE. That point is far from easy to discern.   *1180*
   Whether she really loves him, who can tell?
   She knows her own emotions none too well:
   Sometimes she's been in love, and never knew it,
   Or thought she was, when there was nothing to it.

PHILINTE. With this cousin of yours, I think he'll find
   More sorrow than has ever crossed his mind;
   And if he had this heart of mine, I swear,
   He promptly would bestow his love elsewhere,
   And, turning in a far better direction,
   Would take advantage of your deep affection.   *1190*

ÉLIANTE. I am not ceremonious, I fear,
   And on these points I like to be sincere:
   His love for her causes me no distress;
   With all my heart I wish her happiness;
   And if the thing were up to me alone,
   I'd let him have her for his very own.
   But if in such a choice, as just might be,
   His love should not be crowned by destiny,
   If she should spurn him for some substitute,

1200   I could be willing to receive his suit;
       And in this case I would not take offense
       To know she had his earlier preference.

PHILINTE. And I do not begrudge him, for my part,
       Madame, the feeling for him in your heart;
       And he himself can tell you even more
       Just how I have advised him on that score.
       But if the bonds of marriage joined those two
       So that he could not pay his court to you,
       My hope would be that I might take his place
1210   And seek to win some measure of your grace,
       Happy if his poor judgment left you free,
       And if that grace, Madame, might fall on me.

ÉLIANTE. Philinte, you're jesting.

PHILINTE.   No indeed, Madame,
       No one could be more earnest than I am,
       And eagerly I wait upon the day
       When I can tell you all I long to say.

                Scene 2.   ALCESTE, ÉLIANTE, PHILINTE

ALCESTE. Ah, Madame! You must help me gain redress
       For an offense that cracks my steadfastness.

ÉLIANTE. What is it? What has made you so upset?

1220   ALCESTE. I've had . . . I cannot understand it yet;
       And the collapse of the whole firmament
       Could never crush me as has this event.
       It's done . . . My love . . . There's nothing I can say.

ÉLIANTE. Try to regain your mind's composure, pray.

ALCESTE. Just Heaven! Must such graces be combined
       With vices worthy of the meanest mind?

ÉLIANTE. But still, what . . . ?

ALCESTE.   Everything is devastated;
  I'm . . . I'm betrayed; why, I'm assassinated!
  Yes, Célimène—can such things be believed?—
  Yes, Célimène's untrue, and I'm deceived.   *1230*

ÉLIANTE. Have you strong reasons for this supposition?

PHILINTE. This might be just an ill-conceived suspicion.
  Your jealous mind, an easy prey to snares . . .

ALCESTE. Good Lord, sir! Won't you mind your own affairs?
  I've proof of her betrayal, all too clear,
  In her own hand, right in my pocket, here.
  Madame, a letter bearing Oronte's name
  Has shown me my disfavor and her shame:
  Oronte, whose suit I thought she viewed askance,
  The one I feared the least of her gallants.   *1240*

PHILINTE. A letter often gives the wrong impression
  And bears a false likeness to a confession.

ALCESTE. Once more, sir, if you please, leave me alone
  And mind your business; let me mind my own.

ÉLIANTE. Alceste, control your temper; all this spite . . .

ALCESTE. Madame, this task belongs to you by right;
  It is with you my heart now seeks relief
  From the torment of overwhelming grief.
  Avenge me on that cousin without shame
  Who basely has betrayed so true a flame;   *1250*
  Avenge me for what I trust your soul abhors.

ÉLIANTE. Avenge you? How?

ALCESTE.   Madame, my heart is yours.
  Take it, replace the faithless Célimène.
  Oh, I'll have my revenge upon her then!
  I want her punished by the deep emotion,
  The heartfelt love, the assiduous devotion,
  The eager duties and the service true
  Which now my heart will sacrifice to you.

ÉLIANTE. Of course I sympathize with what you suffer,
  And I do not disdain the heart you offer;   *1260*
  But it may be the harm is not so great,

And you may drop your vengeance and your hate.
When it's a charming person does us wrong,
Our plans for vengeance do not linger long:
Whatever the offenses we resent,
A guilty loved one is soon innocent;
The harm we wish her has no aftermath;
And nothing passes like a lover's wrath.

ALCESTE. No, Madame, that is not the way I burn;
1270   I'm breaking off with her; there's no return;
Nothing could ever change what I project;
I'd be ashamed to view her with respect.
—Here she is. My blood boils at her approach;
Her turpitude deserves a sharp reproach;
I shall confound her utterly, and then
Bring you a heart quite free of Célimène.

Scene 3. CÉLIMÈNE, ALCESTE

ALCESTE. Great Heavens! Can I control my indignation?

CÉLIMÈNE. Oh dear! What has brought on your agitation?
What do you mean by these portentous sighs
1280   And by the somber passion in your eyes?

ALCESTE. Nothing can match, no, not the ugliest crimes,
The faithlessness you've shown these many times;
The worst that Fate, Hell, wrathful Heaven could do
Never made anything as bad as you.

CÉLIMÈNE. I marvel at these sweet amenities.

ALCESTE. No, no, this is no time for pleasantries.
You should be blushing; you have ample reason,
And I have certain tokens of your treason.
The cause of my distress is all too plain;
1290   My apprehensiveness was not in vain;
My doubts, which you thought odious and unsound,
Have led me to the ill my eyes have found;

My star, though you were skillful to pretend,
Warned me of what I had to apprehend.
But don't presume to make a fool of me
And hope to flout me with impunity.
I know that we cannot control desire,
That love's autonomy must be entire,
That force won't strike a heart's responsive chord,
And that each soul is free to choose its lord.   *1300*
So I would find no subject for complaint
If you had spoken frankly, without feint;
Had you spurned my advances from the first,
I'd have blamed fate and waited for the worst.
But thus to fan my hopes with false acclaim
Is faithless treachery, quite without shame,
Deserving the severest castigation;
And I can freely vent my indignation.
Yes, after such a slight, avoid my path:
I am beside myself with righteous wrath: *1310*
Pierced by the mortal blow with which you slay me,
My reason cannot make my sense obey me;
Ruled by the anger that I feel for you,
I cannot answer for what I may do.

CÉLIMÈNE. Come, please explain this latest of your fits.
Tell me, have you completely lost your wits?

ALCESTE. Yes, yes, I lost them at that fatal hour
When first I fell into your poisonous power,
And when I sought sincerity as well
In the false charms that caught me in their spell.   *1320*

CÉLIMÈNE. Pooh! Of what treachery can you complain?

ALCESTE. Oh, what duplicity! How well you feign!
But I have ready proof at my command.
Just look at this, and recognize your hand.
This note at least should leave you mortified;
Its evidence is not to be denied.

CÉLIMÈNE. Then *this* explains your mood, and all you've
said?

ALCESTE. Can you behold this note, and not turn red?

CÉLIMÈNE. If I should blush, perhaps you'll state the reason?

1330 ALCESTE. What? Are you adding shamelessness to treason?
Do you disown it, as an unsigned note?

CÉLIMÈNE. But why disown a letter that I wrote?

ALCESTE. And you can look at it without dismay
Although its very style gives you away?

CÉLIMÈNE. You really are too patently absurd.

ALCESTE. Against this witness, who could take your word?
And how can you offend me so, and flaunt
Your clear infatuation with Oronte?

CÉLIMÈNE. Oronte! Who says he is the addressee?

1340 ALCESTE. The persons who today gave it to me.
But let's assume it's for some other swain:
Does that give me less reason to complain?
Will that make you less guilty in the end?

CÉLIMÈNE. But if it's written to a lady friend,
Where is the guilt, and what's this all about?

ALCESTE. Oh! that's an artful dodge, a neat way out.
I grant I'd not expected such deceit,
And that just makes my certainty complete.
How can you stoop to such a lame excuse?
1350 And do you really think me that obtuse?
Come, come, let's see in just what way you'll try
To lend support to such an obvious lie,
And by what artifice you will pretend
This ardent note was for a lady friend.
Just tell me how you will explain away
What I shall read . . .

CÉLIMÈNE.   I do not choose to say.
I don't concede to you or anyone
The right to talk to me as you have done.

ALCESTE. Don't take offense; just tell me, if you please,
1360 How you can justify such terms as these.

CÉLIMÈNE. No, I'll do nothing of the kind, I swear.

Think what you like of me; I just don't care.

ALCESTE. Please, show me how this letter could be meant
For any woman, and I'll be content.

CÉLIMÈNE. No, no, it's for Oronte; you must be right;
I welcome his attentions with delight;
In all he says and does, he has a way;
And I'll agree to anything you say.
Make up your mind, let nothing interfere;
But I have heard from you all I will hear.   *1370*

ALCESTE. Heavens! How could such a cruel trick be invented?
And has a heart ever been so tormented?
I come to tax her with her perfidy,
I'm the complainant—and she turns on me!
My pain and my suspicions she provokes.
She won't deny her guilt, but boasts and jokes!
And yet my heart is still too weak and faint
To break the chains that hold it in constraint
And arm itself with generous disdain
Against the object that it loves in vain!   *1380*
Ah, faithless girl, with what consummate skill
You play upon my utter lack of will
And make capital of the vast excess
Of my ill-omened, fatal tenderness!
At least defend yourself for this offense
And drop this claim of guilt, this vain pretense;
Show me the innocence of what you wrote;
My fond heart will forget about the note.
Just try your best to seem faithful, and know
That I will try my best to think you so.   *1390*

CÉLIMÈNE. Your jealous frenzies make you mad, I swear,
And you do not deserve the love I bear.
What makes you think that I would condescend,
On your account, to brazen and pretend?
And why, if my heart leaned another way,
Shouldn't I quite sincerely have my say?
What? Can the way in which I've spoken out
About my feelings leave you any doubt?
Has that such weight against this guarantee?
Can you regard it and not outrage me?   *1400*

And since it's hard for women to confess
Their sentiments of love and tenderness,
Since honor bids us never to reveal
The force of any ardor we may feel,
A man for whom this hurdle is surmounted
Should know our word is not to be discounted.
Shouldn't he be ready to stake his life
On what costs us so much internal strife?
Come, such suspicions earn my indignation;
1410   And you are not worth my consideration.
I am a fool; I'm sorry this is true
And that I still have some regard for you;
I should look elsewhere, that is all too plain,
And give you proper reason to complain.

ALCESTE. Treacherous girl! How can I be so weak?
I cannot trust the sugared words you speak;
Yet fate enjoins—and follow it I must—
That my soul be abandoned to your trust;
Although you may betray me, even so
1420   I must learn to what lengths your heart will go.

CÉLIMÈNE. No, you don't love me in the proper fashion.

ALCESTE. Ah! Nothing can be likened to my passion.
My eagerness to prove it goes so far
That I could wish you worse off than you are.
Yes, I could wish that no one found you charming,
That your predicament was quite alarming,
That Heaven had given you nothing at your birth,
Not rank, nor family, nor any worth,
So that my heart, a gleaming sacrifice,
1430   Might compensate and might alone suffice;
'Twould be my pride and joy, all else above,
To have you owe everything to my love.

CÉLIMÈNE. You surely wish me well in your own way!
I hope to Heaven I never see the day . . .
But here's . . . Monsieur Du Bois. I do declare!

Scene 4.   DU BOIS, CÉLIMÈNE, ALCESTE

ALCESTE. What does this outfit mean, this frightened air?
  What's wrong?

DU BOIS.   Sir . . .

ALCESTE.   Well?

DU BOIS.   I have strange things to tell.

ALCESTE. What are they?

DU BOIS.   Our affairs aren't going well.

ALCESTE. What?

DU BOIS.   Shall I speak?

ALCESTE.   Yes, yes, speak up, and quick.

DU BOIS. Isn't that someone . . . ?

ALCESTE.   Oh! You'll make me sick. *1440*
  Will you speak up?

DU BOIS.   Monsieur, we must give ground.

ALCESTE. How's that?

DU BOIS.   We must decamp without a sound.

ALCESTE. And why?

DU BOIS.   I tell you, sir, we've got to fly.

ALCESTE. What for?

DU BOIS.   We mustn't stop to say good-by.

ALCESTE. But for what reason? What's this all about?

DU BOIS. This reason, sir: we promptly must get out.

ALCESTE. Honestly, I will break your head in two,
  You knave, if that's the best that you can do.

DU BOIS. Sir, a black somber man, in face and dress,
1450   Came to our place—the kitchen door, no less—
And left a paper filled with such a scrawl
You'd have to be a demon to read it all.
It's all about your lawsuit, I've no doubt;
But even Satan couldn't make it out.

ALCESTE. Well then? What of it? Just explain to me:
Why should this paper mean we have to flee?

DU BOIS. A little later, sir, an hour or more,
A man who's been to visit you before
Came in great haste, and finding you not there,
1460   Gave me a message that I was to bear
(Knowing I'm the most dutiful of men),
To tell you . . . Wait, what *is* his name again?

ALCESTE. What did he tell you, wretch? Forget his name.

DU BOIS. Well, he's a friend of yours; it's all the same.
He told me you have got to get away,
And you could be arrested if you stay.

ALCESTE. But why? Nothing specific? Think, man, think.

DU BOIS. No; but he did ask me for pen and ink,
And wrote this note, in which I think you'll see
1470   The explanation of this mystery.

ALCESTE. Well, give it to me.

CÉLIMÈNE.   What's this all about?

ALCESTE. I don't know, but I hope soon to find out.
Come on, you oaf, what are you waiting for?

DU BOIS *(after a long search)*. My goodness, sir! I left it
in your drawer.

ALCESTE. I don't know why I don't . . .

CÉLIMÈNE.   No, that can wait;
You'd better go and set this matter straight.

ALCESTE. It seems that fate, no matter what I do,
Will never let me have a talk with you;
But let me come again ere day is done,
1480   And I shall think for once my love has won.

ACT V

Scene 1. ALCESTE, PHILINTE

ALCESTE. No use. My mind is quite made up, I tell you.

PHILINTE. But must this blow, however hard, compel you . . . ?

ALCESTE. No, you may talk and argue all you can,
Nothing that you can say will change my plan:
On every side such wickedness I find
That I mean to withdraw from humankind.
What? Honor, virtue, probity, the laws
Impugn my enemy and plead my cause;
Everyone knows of my integrity;
I put my trust in right and equity;   *1490*
And yet the outcome leaves me destitute:
Justice is with me, and I lose my suit!
A man whose shame is written on his face
Perjures himself outright, and wins the case!
Good faith gives way before his treachery:
He cuts my throat, and puts the blame on me!
His artificial grimace is so strong
As to taint justice and turn right to wrong!
He gets a court decree to crown his sin,
And not content with having done me in,   *1500*
There's a revolting book in circulation,
A book subject to solemn condemnation,
Deserving to be banned by law—and he
Foully ascribes the authorship to me!
And thereupon Oronte, that evil cheat,
Nods his assent, and seconds the deceit!
Oronte, whose name at court shines bright and clear,
With whom I've always been frank and sincere,
Who comes to me to wheedle and coerce,

73

1510 And make me comment on his wretched verse;
And just because I answer in good sooth,
Refusing to betray him or the truth,
He attests a crime that never did exist
And sets me up as his antagonist!
I'll never have his pardon, count upon it,
For failing to appreciate his sonnet!
Lord! What a sordid and familiar story:
Men led to evil by their itch for glory!
Yes, this is the good faith, the virtuous zeal,
1520 The equity and honor they reveal!
Come, I've endured more than enough from men:
Let's flee this ugly wood, this robbers' den.
And since you men behave the way you do—
Like wolves—I bid my last farewell to you.

PHILINTE. I think your plan's a little premature,
And men are not all that depraved, I'm sure;
Your enemy's charges, it is manifest,
Have not availed to bring on your arrest.
His false report has burst like any bubble,
1530 And might well get him into serious trouble.

ALCESTE. He? He need have no fear at any time:
He has some sort of privilege for crime;
And far from hurting him, this added shame
Will only serve to magnify his name.

PHILINTE. At any rate, I think you will concede
His rumors have been given little heed:
You have no cause at all for worry there;
As for your lawsuit, which was most unfair,
A higher court will surely countermand
This verdict . . .

1540 ALCESTE.   No! I mean to let it stand.
The wrong it does me is so manifest,
I won't appeal it; no, I'll let it rest.
It shows the right downtrodden and maligned,
And I want it exposed to all mankind
As a clear testimony and display
Of all the evil of the present day.
At twenty thousand francs the cost is high;

But for those twenty thousand francs I'll buy
The right to rail against man's wicked state
And look upon it with undying hate.   *1550*

PHILINTE. But still . . .

ALCESTE.   But still, don't press me any more.
What can you tell me further on this score?
Do you mean to justify, right to my face,
The evil conduct of the human race?

PHILINTE. No, no, all that I'll readily concede:
The world is ruled by pure intrigue and greed;
Nothing but trickery prevails today,
And humans should be made some other way.
But should their disaffection for the right
Lead us to try to flee their very sight?   *1560*
These human flaws give us the satisfaction
Of testing our philosophy in action:
In such employment virtue can take pride;
And if goodness were found on every side,
If all men's hearts were docile, frank, and just,
Most of our virtues would but gather rust,
Since they can serve to help us calmly bear
The injustices that face us everywhere.
Just as a heart instinct with virtue can . . .

ALCESTE. Sir, you can talk as well as any man.   *1570*
Your stock of arguments is most profuse,
But now your eloquence is just no use.
Reason bids me retire for my own good:
My tongue will not obey me as it should;
I could not answer for what I might say,
And I'd have a new quarrel every day.
Don't argue, let me wait for Célimène:
I've got to try to talk with her again.
Whether she really loves me, I don't know;
And I must have her answer, yes or no.   *1580*

PHILINTE. Let's wait for her with Éliante upstairs.

ALCESTE. No, I am too oppressed with anxious cares.
Go on and see her; I'll sit here apart
In this dark corner with my gloomy heart.

PHILINTE. That's not good company for any man;
I'll ask Éliante to join us if she can.

Scene. 2.   ORONTE, CÉLIMÈNE, ALCESTE

ORONTE. Yes, Madame, it is for you to decide
Whether a bond between us shall be tied.
I must ask you to answer with precision:
1590   A lover will not stand for indecision.
If you're at all responsive to my flame,
You can reveal that to me without shame;
And as you know, the proof that I request
Is that you end the courtship of Alceste,
Sacrifice him, Madame, and promptly break
All your relations with him for my sake.

CÉLIMÈNE. But why do you attack him with such spirit,
When I've so often heard you praise his merit?

ORONTE. Madame, let's let such explanations be;
1600   The question is just how you feel toward me.
So kindly make your choice between us two,
And my decision will depend on you.

ALCESTE (coming out of his corner). Madame, the gentle-
man's request is just,
And I support it; yes, decide you must.
The same ardor, the same concern are mine;
My love can't do without some clearcut sign;
Matters have gone too far for more delay,
And now's the time for you to have your say.

ORONTE. Sir, I've no wish to be importunate
1610   And bother you, if you're so fortunate.

ALCESTE. Sir, I've no wish to have you share a part—
Even if this be jealous—of her heart.

ORONTE. If your love is more precious in her view . . .

ALCESTE. If she can have the slightest taste for you . . .

ORONTE. I swear I'll leave her to you there and then.

ALCESTE. I swear I'll never see her face again.

ORONTE. Madame, pray tell us what we've come to hear.

ALCESTE. Madame, you can speak freely, without fear.

ORONTE. All you need do is say how you're inclined.

ALCESTE. All you need do is to make up your mind.   *1620*

ORONTE. What? When we ask your choice, you seem put
    out?

ALCESTE. What? Your soul hesitates and seems in doubt?

CÉLIMÈNE. Good Lord! This urgency is out of place,
  And both of you show no more sense than grace.
  My mind's made up about this situation,
  And in my heart there is no hesitation;
  Between you two it is in no suspense,
  And I could well declare its preference.
  But I think it a painful indiscretion
  To utter such a face-to-face confession;   *1630*
  I think these words that are so hard to bear
  Should not be spoken when both men are there;
  I think our hearts betray our inclinations
  Without being forced to such harsh revelations,
  And that there are much gentler ways to use
  When we must tell a lover such bad news.

ORONTE. No, no, the truth! I have no cause to fear it.
  Come, please speak up.

ALCESTE.   And I demand to hear it.
  There's nothing in your openness to scare us;
  Believe me, I've no wish to have you spare us.   *1640*
  You don't need everyone under your sway;
  Enough uncertainty, enough delay:
  Now is the time to answer our demand.
  If you decline, I shall know where I stand;
  Your silence will amount to an admission
  That will corroborate my worst suspicion.

ORONTE. I'm grateful for your indignation, sir;
    And what you say is what I say to her.

CÉLIMÈNE. Oh, how you weary me with this caprice!
1650   Can't you be fair, and let me have some peace?
    Haven't I told you why I will not budge?
    But here comes Éliante: I'll let her judge.

Scene 3. ÉLIANTE, PHILINTE, CÉLIMÈNE, ORONTE,
ALCESTE

CÉLIMÈNE. Cousin, I find myself beset indeed
    By these two men, who seem to have agreed.
    With equal warmth they both insist, my dear,
    That I should make my choice between them clear,
    And, by a sentence uttered face to face,
    That I make one of them give up the chase.
    Has anyone ever behaved this way?

1660 ÉLIANTE. Don't seek my frank opinion on this, pray:
    I'm not the one to ask, as you will find,
    And I'm for people who will speak their mind.

ORONTE. Madame, you may defend yourself in vain.

ALCESTE. No use in being devious, that's plain.

ORONTE. You must speak up, you must, and end this doubt.

ALCESTE. Or if you won't, your silence will speak out.

ORONTE. One word from you, and there'll be no more
    scenes.

ALCESTE. And if you're silent, I'll know what that means.

Scene 4. ACASTE, CLITANDRE, ARSINOÉ, PHILINTE,
ÉLIANTE, ORONTE, CÉLIMÈNE, ALCESTE

ACASTE. Madame, with no offense, we two are here
  To try to get a little matter clear.   *1690*

CLITANDRE. Your presence, sirs, is timely, I declare,
  And you are both involved in this affair.

ARSINOÉ. Madame, my coming must be a surprise,
  But these men would not have it otherwise:
  They both came to me angry and aggrieved
  Over an act too mean to be believed.
  I think there is a goodness in your soul
  That would not let you play so base a role:
  My eyes belied their strongest evidence,
  My friendship overlooked our difference,   *1680*
  And so I came to keep them company
  And see you overthrow this calumny.

ACASTE. Yes, Madame, let's see, with a peaceful mind,
  What sort of explanation you can find.
  You wrote Clitandre this note, now didn't you?

CLITANDRE. It was you wrote Acaste this billet-doux?

ACASTE. To you this handwriting is not obscure,
  Messieurs, and her indulgence, I am sure,
  Has made it known to every person here;
  But this is something for you all to hear.   *1670*
                    (He reads)
  "You're a strange man to condemn my sprightliness and
reproach me with never being so happy as when I'm not
with you. Nothing could be more unjust; and if you don't
come very soon and ask my pardon for this offense, I shall
never forgive you for it as long as I live. Our great lout
of a Viscount . . ."
  He *should* be here.

"Our great lout of a Viscount, whom you complain about first, is a man I never could fancy; and since I watched him for a good three-quarters of an hour spitting into a well to make circles in the water, I have never been able to think well of him. As for the little Marquis . . ."

All vanity aside, gentlemen, that's me.

"As for the little Marquis, who held my hand so long yesterday, I don't know anything as insignificant as his whole person; and the only merit of his kind lies in his cloak and sword. As for the man with the green ribbons . . ."

(To ALCESTE) Your turn, sir.

"As for the man with the green ribbons, he sometimes amuses me with his bluntness and his surly grouchiness; but there are hundreds of times when I find him as tiresome as can be. And as for the man with the jacket . . ."[7]

(To ORONTE) Here's your bundle.

"And as for the man with the jacket, who has gone in for wit and wants to be an author in spite of everyone, I can't give myself the trouble to listen to what he says; and his prose wearies me as much as his poetry. So get it into your head that I don't always have as good a time as you think; that I miss you more than I could wish in all the parties that I'm dragged into; and that a marvelous seasoning for the pleasures we enjoy is the presence of the persons we love."

CLITANDRE. And now here I am.

(He reads)

"Your Clitandre, whom you mention, and who puts on such sweetish airs, is the last man I could be fond of. He is absurd to suppose he is loved; and so are you, to think you are not. To be reasonable, exchange your beliefs for his; and see me as much as you can to help me endure the vexation of being beleaguered by him."

It's a fine character these portraits show,
Madame, and there's a name for it, you know.
Enough: we two shall everywhere impart
This glorious self-portrait of your herat.

---

[7] In all editions from 1682 on, this reads "And as for the man with the sonnet . . ."

ACASTE. I could well speak, I've ample provocation;
  But you're not worthy of my indignation;
  And there are nobler hearts, as you shall see,
  Ready to comfort a *petit marquis*.
                    (Exit ACASTE *and* CLITANDRE*)*

ORONTE. What? You can tear me into shreds this way
  After the things I've seen you write and say!   *1700*
  And your false heart, which seems for love designed,
  Offers itself in turn to all mankind!
  Go to, I've been a dupe too much, too long;
  I *should* be grateful that you've proved me wrong.
  You give me back my heart, a welcome prize,
  And in your loss of it my vengeance lies.
                    (To ALCESTE*)*
  If I was in your way, I no longer am,
  So pray conclude your business with Madame.
                    (Exit ORONTE*)*

ARSINOÉ. Really, that is the blackest action yet.
  I can't keep silent, I am too upset.   *1710*
  How can such treachery be justified?
  I leave the other gentlemen aside;
  But take a man of honor like Alceste,
  Whose heart by your good fortune you possessed,
  Who worshiped you beyond what tongue can say,
  Should he have been . . . ?

ALCESTE.   Madame, allow me, pray,
  To guard my interest here; that's all I ask;
  Don't charge yourself with this superfluous task.
  My heart, though grateful for your vindication,
  Is in no state to pay its obligation;   *1720*
  And if—I have to tell you, for it's true—
  I sought revenge, it would not be with you.

ARSINOÉ. Do you think, sir, that that was in my mind,
  And that I look on you as such a find?
  To tell the truth, I find you very vain
  If that's the kind of thought you entertain.
  To hanker for the leavings of Madame,
  I'd have to be less choosy than I am.
  Come down a peg, open your eyes, give heed:

1730   I'm not the kind of person that you need;
        Keep sighing for her; she is quite a catch;
        I can hardly wait to see so fine a match.

                                    (Exit ARSINOÉ*)*

        ALCESTE. Well! I have held my tongue, for all I see,
            And let everyone speak ahead of me:
            Have my feelings been long enough suppressed?
            And may I now . . . ?

        CÉLIMÈNE.   Yes, tell me all the rest.
            You've every reason to complain your fill
            And reproach me for everything you will.
            I'm wrong, I do confess; my consternation
1740   Leads me to seek no vain extenuation.
            The others' wrath I treated with disdain,
            But I agree, my crime toward you is plain;
            I've earned your bitterness, lost your esteem;
            I know full well how guilty I must seem,
            That everything proclaims I have betrayed you,
            And if you hate me, it's because I've made you.
            Go ahead; I consent.

        ALCESTE.   Ah! traitress, how?
            Can I conquer my passion even now?
            And though I burn to hate you, as you say,
1750   Do you think my heart is ready to obey?
                    (To ÉLIANTE *and* PHILINTE*)*
            See what unworthy tenderness can do;
            Bear witness to my frailty, you two.
            But this is not yet all, I must confess,
            And you shall see me push it to excess,
            Proving that those who call us wise are wrong,
            And that mere human nature is too strong.
                    (To CÉLIMÈNE*)*
            I'm willing to forget the things you've done;
            My soul will find excuse for every one;
            And I'll contrive to view your blackest crimes
1760   As youthful foibles caused by evil times,
            Provided only that your heart agree
            To flee human society with me,
            And that you'll follow me without delay

To the seclusion where I've vowed to stay:
Only thus, in the minds of everyone,
Can you repair the harm your note has done,
And after a scene which noble hearts abhor,
Enable me to love you as before.

CÉLIMÈNE. What! *I* renounce the world before I'm old,
And molder in some solitary hold?   *1770*

ALCESTE. If your love matches mine and is as true,
Why should all other men matter to you?
Why can't I be sufficient to your need?

CÉLIMÈNE. At twenty, solitude is grim indeed.
I fear I lack the loftiness of soul
To undertake so difficult a role.
If marriage can fulfill your aspiration,
I think I could resolve on that relation,
And thus . . .

ALCESTE.   No, never did I hate you so,
And this refusal is the final blow.   *1780*
Since this is something that you cannot do—
Find all in me, as I find all in you—
Go, I refuse you, and at last I sever
My most unworthy ties to you forever.
                    (Exit CÉLIMÈNE. *To* ÉLIANTE*)*
Madame, your beauty is adorned with worth,
You only are sincere in all the earth;
For you my admiration is extreme.
But now please be content with my esteem;
Forgive me if the turmoil in my soul
No longer lets me seek a suitor's role: *1790*
I feel unworthy, and that Heaven's plan
Did not create me for a married man;
That you deserve a hand better than mine,
And not the discard of a heart less fine,
And that . . .

ÉLIANTE.   Follow this notion to the end;
I do not find myself without a friend;
And if I asked Philinte, I understand
He might be happy to accept my hand.

PHILINTE. Madame, if I could have you for my wife,
1800   I'd gladly sacrifice my blood, my life.

ALCESTE. May both of you forever feel like this,
And thus experience true wedded bliss!
While I, betrayed, and overwhelmed with wrong,
Leave an abyss where vices are too strong,
And seek some solitary place on earth
Where one is free to be a man of worth.

(*Exit* ALCESTE)

PHILINTE (*To* ÉLIANTE). Come, Madame, let's do everything we can
To thwart the aims of this unhappy man.

The Doctor in
Spite of Himself

THE DOCTOR IN SPITE OF HIMSELF

A comedy in three acts in prose, first performed on August 6, 1666, at the Théâtre du Palais-Royal in Paris by Molière's Troupe du Roi. Molière played Sganarelle; his wife, Lucinde; the rest of the original distribution of roles is not known. The old story that this play was written to support the unsuccessful *Misanthrope* seems exaggerated; but *The Doctor in Spite of Himself* was an instant hit, was performed together with *The Misanthrope* within a month, and has remained a rival of *Tartuffe* for the title of Molière's most performed play.

Besides some of the details,[1] the outline of the plot is entirely derivative. A medieval fabliau, *Le Vilain mire,* is the original source, though Molière could presumably have known it only through one of many later, printed versions. If, whatever his source, he knew the original ending, his discarding of it would add to our sense of his indifference to logically prepared denouements; for in the original the Sganarelle figure, faced with a pleasanter problem than the threat of hanging, solved it with highly comic logic and ingenuity.[2]

Characteristically, Molière makes the play his own by all kinds of new elements: Sganarelle's inspired quarrel with his

---

[1] Géronte's wish (Act III, sc. 6) to have his daughter become mute again is a clear reminiscence of Rabelais' story (Book III, chapter 34) of the old *Farce of the Mute Wife.*—Sganarelle, one of Molière's stock characters whom we have met already and shall meet again later, is like Mascarille, Scapin, and others in being taken from Italian farce.

[2] His success as an involuntary doctor brought him patients from far and wide; his problem was to get rid of them without killing them by his remedies. He assembled them all, told them that the sickest one of them would have to be killed and burned, and that a potion made of his ashes would cure the rest. None remained to learn who was sickest; so all ended well.

wife Martine, ending inevitably in a beating; her rebuff of
her would-be rescuer; the peasant dialect of Lucas, Jacqueline, and others; Sganarelle's eagerness to feel Jacqueline's
ample breasts, with all the byplay that results; and most of
all Snanarelle's enthusiastic and ingenious adoption of his role
as doctor. (As usual, Molière derives some of his finest comic
effects from having a character play a role within the play.)
Among the delightful results are Sganarelle's feigned reluctance
to take money for his services; his learned paraphrases of
Hippocrates ("In his chapter on hats," Act II, sc. 2) and of
Aristotle, his fluent use of "Latin" once he has ascertained
that no one present knows that language; his lunatic logic
in beating Géronte to make him a doctor, since his own experience has taught him that that is how doctors are made; and
perhaps best of all, when challenged in his statement (Act II,
sc. 4) that the heart is on the right side and the liver on the
left, the eternal comic verity and wide applicability of his remark: "We have changed all that."

In short, the success of *The Doctor in Spite of Himself* is no
accident. Brilliantly inventive and sustained, it is farce at its
richest, truest, and best.

THE DOCTOR IN SPITE OF HIMSELF

CHARACTERS

SGANARELLE, *husband of Martine*
MARTINE, *wife of Sganarelle*
MONSIEUR ROBERT, *neighbor of Sganarelle*
VALÈRE, *servant of Géronte*
LUCAS, *husband of Jacqueline*
GÉRONTE, *father of Lucinde*
JACQUELINE, *wet-nurse at Géronte's and wife of Lucas*
LUCINDE, *daughter of Géronte*
LÉANDRE, *in love with Lucinde*
THIBAUT, *a peasant, father of Perrin*
PERRIN, *a peasant, son of Thibaut*

ACT I

A clearing. The houses of Sganarelle and Monsieur Robert may be seen through the trees.

Scene 1. SGANARELLE, MARTINE *(who enter quarreling)*

SGANARELLE. No, I tell you I won't do anything of the sort, and I'm the one to say and be the master.

MARTINE. And *I* tell *you* that I want you to live to suit me, and I didn't marry you to put up with your carryings-on.

SGANARELLE. Oh, what a weary business it is to have a wife, and how right Aristotle is when he says a wife is worse than a demon!

MARTINE. Just listen to that smart fellow with his half-wit Aristotle!

SGANARELLE. Yes, a smart fellow. Just find me a woodcutter who knows how to reason about things, like me, who served a famous doctor for six years, and who as a youngster knew his elementary Latin book by heart.

MARTINE. A plague on the crazy fool!

SGANARELLE. A plague on the slut!

MARTINE. Cursed be the day when I went and said yes!

SGANARELLE. Cursed be the hornified notary who had me sign my own ruin!

MARTINE. Really, it's a fine thing for you to complain of that affair! Should you let a single moment go by without thanking Heaven for having me for your wife? And did you deserve to marry a person like me?

SGANARELLE. Oh, yes, you did me too much honor, and I had reason to congratulate myself on our wedding night! Oh, my Lord! Don't get me started on that! I'd have a few things to say . . .

MARTINE. What? What would you say?

SGANARELLE. Let it go at that; let's drop that subject. Enough that we know what we know, and that you were very lucky to find me.

MARTINE. What do you mean, lucky to find you? A man who drags me down to the poorhouse, a debauchee, a traitor, who eats up everything I own?

SGANARELLE. That's a lie: I drink part of it.

MARTINE. Who sells, piece by piece, everything in the house.

SGANARELLE. That's living on our means.

MARTINE. Who's taken even my bed from under me.

SGANARELLE. You'll get up all the earlier in the morning.

MARTINE. In short, who doesn't leave a stick of furniture in the whole house.

SGANARELLE. All the easier to move out.

MARTINE. And who does nothing but gamble and drink from morning to night.

SGANARELLE. That's so I won't get bored.

MARTINE. And what do you expect me to do with my family in the meantime?

SGANARELLE. Whatever you like.

MARTINE. I have four poor little children on my hands.

SGANARELLE. Set them on the floor.

MARTINE. Who are constantly asking me for bread.

SGANARELLE. Give them the whip. When I've had plenty to eat and drink, I want everyone in my house to have his fill.

MARTINE. And you, you drunkard, do you expect things to go on forever like this?

SGANARELLE. My good wife, let's go easy, if you please.

MARTINE. And me to endure your insolence and debauchery to all eternity?

SGANARELLE. Let's not get excited, my good wife.

MARTINE. And that I can't find a way to make you do your duty?

SGANARELLE. My good wife, you know that my soul isn't very patient and my arm is pretty good.

MARTINE. You make me laugh with your threats.

SGANARELLE. My good little wife, my love, you're itching for trouble, as usual.

MARTINE. I'll show you I'm not afraid of you.

SGANARELLE. My dear better half, you're asking for something.

MARTINE. Do you think your words frighten me?

SGANARELLE. Sweet object of my eternal vows, I'll box your ears.

MARTINE. Drunkard that you are!

SGANARELLE. I'll beat you.

MARTINE. Wine-sack!

SGANARELLE. I'll wallop you.

MARTINE. Wretch!

SGANARELLE. I'll tan your hide.

MARTINE. Traitor, wiseacre, deceiver, coward, scoundrel, gallowsbird, beggar, good-for-nothing, rascal, villain, thief . . .

SGANARELLE (takes a stick and beats her). Ah! So you want it,
eh?

MARTINE. Oh, oh, oh, oh!

SGANARELLE. That's the right way to pacify you.

Scene 2.   MONSIEUR ROBERT, SGANARELLE, MARTINE

MONSIEUR ROBERT. Hey there, hey there, hey there! Fie! What's
this? What infamy! Confound the rascal for beating his wife
that way!

MARTINE (arms akimbo, forces MONSIEUR ROBERT back as she
talks, and finally gives him a slap). And as for me, I want him
to beat me.

MONSIEUR ROBERT. Oh! Then with all my heart, I consent.

MARTINE. What are you meddling for?

MONSIEUR ROBERT. I'm wrong.

MARTINE. Is it any business of yours?

MONSIEUR ROBERT. You're right.

MARTINE. Just look at this meddler, trying to keep husbands from
beating their wives.

MONSIEUR ROBERT. I take it all back.

MARTINE. What have you got to do with it?

MONSIEUR ROBERT. Nothing.

MARTINE. Have you any right to poke your nose in?

MONSIEUR ROBERT. No.

MARTINE. Mind your own business.

MONSIEUR ROBERT. I won't say another word.

MARTINE. I like to be beaten.

MONSIEUR ROBERT. All right.

MARTINE. It's no skin off your nose.

MONSIEUR ROBERT. That's true.

MARTINE. And you're a fool to come butting in where it's none of your business. (*Slaps* MONSIEUR ROBERT. *He turns toward* SGANARELLE, *who likewise forces him back as he talks, threatening him with the same stick and finally beating and routing him with it.*)

MONSIEUR ROBERT. Neighbor, I beg your pardon with all my heart. Go on, beat your wife and thrash her to your heart's content; I'll help you if you want.

SGANARELLE. Me, I don't want to.

MONSIEUR ROBERT. Oh well, that's another matter.

SGANARELLE. I want to beat her if I want to; and I don't want to beat her if I don't want to.

MONSIEUR ROBERT. Very well.

SGANARELLE. She's my wife, not yours.

MONSIEUR ROBERT. Undoubtedly.

SGANARELLE. I don't take orders from you.

MONSIEUR ROBERT. Agreed.

SGANARELLE. I don't need any help from you.

MONSIEUR ROBERT. That's fine with me.

SGANARELLE. And you're a meddler to interfere in other people's affairs. Learn that Cicero says that you mustn't put the bark between the tree and your finger. *(Beats* MONSIEUR ROBERT *and drives him offstage, then returns to his wife and clasps her hand.)*
Well now, let's us two make peace. Shake on it.

MARTINE. Oh yes! After beating me that way!

SGANARELLE. That's nothing. Shake.

MARTINE. I will not.

SGANARELLE. Eh?

MARTINE. No.

SGANARELLE. My little wife!

MARTINE. No sir.

SGANARELLE. Come on, I say.

MARTINE. I won't do anything of the kind.

SGANARELLE. Come, come, come.

MARTINE. No, I want to be angry.

SGANARELLE. Fie! It's nothing. Come on, come on.

MARTINE. Let me be.

SGANARELLE. Shake, I say.

MARTINE. You've treated me too badly.

SGANARELLE. All right then, I ask your pardon: give me your hand.

MARTINE. I forgive you; *(aside)* but you'll pay for it.

SGANARELLE. You're crazy to pay any attention to that: those little things are necessary from time to time for a good friendship; and five or six cudgel-blows between people in love only whet their affection. There now, I'm off to the woods, and I promise you more than a hundred bundles of kindling wood today.

Scene 3.   MARTINE *(alone)*

MARTINE. All right, whatever face I put on, I'm not forgetting my resentment; and I'm burning inside to find ways to punish you for the beatings you give me. I know very well that a wife always has in hand means of taking revenge on a husband; but that's too delicate a punishment for my gallowsbird. I want a vengeance that he'll feel a bit more; and that would be no satisfaction for the offense I've received.

Scene 4.   VALÈRE, LUCAS, MARTINE

LUCAS. Doggone it! We sure both tooken on one heck of a job; and me, I don't know what I'm gonna come up with.

VALÈRE. Well, what do you expect as the wet-nurse's husband? We have to obey our master; and then we both have an interest in the health of the mistress, his daughter; and no doubt her marriage, put off by her illness, would be worth some kind of present to us. Horace, who is generous, has the best chances of anyone to win her hand; and although she has shown a fondness for a certain Léandre, you know very well that her father has never consented to accept him as a son-in-law.

MARTINE *(musing, aside)*. Can't I think up some scheme to get revenge?

LUCAS. But what kind of wild idea has the master tooken into his head, now that the doctors have used up all their Latin?

VALÈRE. You sometimes find, by looking hard, what you don't find at first; and often in simple places . . .

MARTINE. Yes, I must get revenge, whatever the price; that beating sticks in my crop, I can't swallow it, and . . . *(She says all this still musing, not noticing the two men, so that when she turns around she bumps into them.)* Oh! Gentlemen, I beg your pardon; I didn't see you, and I was trying to think of something that's bothering me.

VALÈRE. Everyone has his problems in this world, and we too are looking for something we would very much like to find.

MARTINE. Would it be anything I might help you with?

VALÈRE. It just might. We're trying to find some able man, some special doctor, who might give some relief to our master's daughter, ill with a disease that has suddenly taken away the use of her tongue. Several doctors have already exhausted all their learning on her; but you sometimes find people with wonderful secrets, with certain special remedies, who can very often do what the others couldn't; and that's what we're looking for.

MARTINE *(aside)*. Oh! What a wonderful scheme Heaven inspires me with to get revenge on my gallowsbird! *(Aloud)* You couldn't have come to a better place to find what you're looking for; and we have a man here, the most marvelous man in the world for hopeless illnesses.

VALÈRE. And, pray, where can we find him?

MARTINE. You'll find him right now in that little clearing over there, spending his time cutting wood.

LUCAS. A doctor cutting wood?

VALÈRE. Spending his time gathering herbs, do you mean?

MARTINE. No, he's an extraordinary man who enjoys that— strange, fantastic, crotchety—you'd never take him for what he is. He goes around dressed in an eccentric way, sometimes affects ignorance, keeps his knowledge hidden, and every day avoids nothing so much as exercising the marvelous talents Heaven has given him for medicine.

VALÈRE. It's an amazing thing that all great men always have some caprice, some little grain of folly mingled with their learning.

MARTINE. This one's mania is beyond all belief, for it sometimes goes to the point of his wanting to be beaten before he'll acknowledge his capacity; and I'm telling you you'll never get the better of him, he'll never admit he's a doctor, if he's in that mood, unless you each take a stick and beat him into confessing in the end what he'll hide from you at first. That's what *we* do when we need him.

VALÈRE. That's a strange mania!

MARTINE. That's true; but afterward, you'll see he does wonders.

VALÈRE. What's his name?

MARTINE. His name is Sganarelle, but he's easy to recognize. He's a man with a big black beard, wearing a ruff and a green and yellow coat.

LUCAS. A green and yaller coat? So he's a parrot doctor?[3]

VALÈRE. But is it really true that he's as skillful as you say?

MARTINE. What? He's a man who works miracles. Six months ago a woman was abandoned by all the other doctors. They thought she'd been dead for a good six hours, and were getting ready to bury her, when they forced the man we're talking about to come. After he'd looked her over, he put a little drop of something or other in her mouth, and that very moment she got up out of bed and right away started walking around her room as if nothing had happened.

LUCAS. Ah!

VALÈRE. It must have been a drop of elixir of gold.

MARTINE. That might well be. Then again, not three weeks ago a youngster twelve years old fell down from the top of the steeple and broke his head, arms, and legs on the pavement. They had no sooner brought our man in than he rubbed the boy's whole body with a certain ointment he knows how to make; and right away the boy got up on his feet and ran off to play marbles.

LUCAS. Ah!

VALÈRE. That man must have a universal cure.

MARTINE. Who doubts it?

LUCAS. By jingo, that's sure the man we need. Let's go get him quick.

[3] In Molière's time, doctors always wore black robes.

VALÈRE. We thank you for the favor you're doing us.

MARTINE. But anyway, be sure to remember what I warned you about.

LUCAS. Tarnation! Leave it to us. If a beating is all it takes, she's our cow.

VALÈRE. That certainly was a lucky encounter for us; and for my part, I'm very hopeful about it.

Scene 5. SGANARELLE, VALÈRE, LUCAS

SGANARELLE *(enters singing, bottle in hand)*. La, la, la!

VALÈRE. I hear someone singing and cutting wood.

SGANARELLE. La, la, la . . . ! My word, that's enough work for a while. Let's take a little breather. *(Drinks)* That wood is salty as the devil. *(Sings)*

> Sweet glug-glug,
> How I love thee!
> Sweet glug-glug
> Of my little jug!
> But everybody would think me too smug
> If you were as full as you can be.
> Just never be empty, that's my plea.
> Come, sweet, let me give you a hug.

(Speaks again) Come on, good Lord, we mustn't breed melancholy.

VALÈRE. There's the man himself.

LUCAS. I think you're right, and we done stumbled right onto him.

VALÈRE. Let's get a closer look.

SGANARELLE *(seeing them, looks at them, turning first toward one then toward the other, and lowers his voice)*. Ah! my little hussy! How I love you, my little jug!

But everybody . . . would think . . . me . . . too smug,
If . . .
What the devil! What do these people want?

VALÈRE. That's the one, no doubt about it.

LUCAS. That's him, his spit an' image, just like they prescribed
him to us.

SGANARELLE *(aside)*. They're looking at me and consulting. What
can they have in mind? *(He puts his bottle on the ground. As
VALÈRE bows to greet him, SGANARELLE thinks he is reaching
down to take his bottle away, and so puts it on the other side
of him. When LUCAS bows in turn, he picks it up again and
clutches it to his belly, with much other byplay.)*

VALÈRE. Sir, isn't your name Sganarelle?

SGANARELLE. How's that?

VALÈRE. I'm asking you if you're not the man named Sganarelle?

SGANARELLE *(turning toward VALÈRE, then toward LUCAS)*. Yes
and no, depending on what you want with him.

VALÈRE. All we want is to pay him all the civilities we can.

SGANARELLE. In that case, my name *is* Sganarelle.

VALÈRE. Sir, we are delighted to see you. We have been addressed to you for something we're looking for; and we come
to implore your aid, which we need.

SGANARELLE. If it's something, sirs, connected with my little
line of business, I am all ready to serve you.

VALÈRE. Sir, you are too kind. But sir, put on your hat, please;
the sun might give you trouble.

LUCAS. Slap it on, sir.

SGANARELLE *(aside)*. These are very ceremonious people.

VALÈRE. Sir, you must not find it strange that we should come
to you. Able men are always sought out, and we are well
informed about your capability.

SGANARELLE. It is true, gentlemen, that I'm the best man in the
world for cutting kindling wood.

VALÈRE. Ah, sir . . . !

SGANARELLE. I spare no pains, and cut it in such a way that it's above criticism.

VALÈRE. Sir, that's not the point.

SGANARELLE. But also I sell it at a hundred and ten sous for a hundred bundles.

VALÈRE. Let's not talk about that, if you please.

SGANARELLE. I promise you I can't let it go for less.

VALÈRE. Sir, we know how things stand.

SGANARELLE. If you know how things stand, you know that that's what I sell them for.

VALÈRE. Sir, you're joking when . . .

SGANARELLE. I'm not joking, I can't take anything off for it.

VALÈRE. Let's talk in other terms, please.

SGANARELLE. You can find it for less elsewhere: there's kindling and kindling; but as for what I cut . . .

VALÈRE. What? Sir, let's drop this subject.

SGANARELLE. I swear you couldn't get it for a penny less.

VALÈRE. Fie now!

SGANARELLE. No, on my conscience, that's what you'll pay. I'm speaking sincerely, and I'm not the man to overcharge.

VALÈRE. Sir, must a person like you waste his time on these crude pretenses and stoop to speaking like this? Must such a learned man, a famous doctor like yourself, try to disguise himself in the eyes of the world and keep his fine talents buried?

SGANARELLE *(aside)*. He's crazy.

VALÈRE. Please, sir, don't dissimulate with us.

SGANARELLE. What?

LUCAS. All this here fiddle-faddle don't do no good; we knows what we knows.

SGANARELLE. What about it? What are you trying to tell me? Whom do you take me for?

VALÈRE. For what you are: for a great doctor.

SGANARELLE. Doctor yourself: I'm not one and I've never been one.

VALÈRE *(aside)*. That's his madness gripping him. *(Aloud)* Sir, please don't deny things any longer; and pray let's not come to regrettable extremes.

SGANARELLE. To what?

VALÈRE. To certain things that we would be sorry for.

SGANARELLE. Good Lord! Come to whatever you like. I'm no doctor, and I don't know what you're trying to tell me.

VALÈRE *(aside)*. I can certainly see we'll have to use the remedy. *(Aloud)* Once more, sir, I beg you to admit what you are.

LUCAS. Dad bust it! No more messin', around; confess frank-like that you're a doctor.

SGANARELLE. I'm getting mad.

VALÈRE. Why deny what everyone knows?

LUCAS. Why all this fuss and feathers? And what good does that done you?

SGANARELLE. Gentlemen, I tell you in one word as well as in two thousand: *I'm not a doctor.*

VALÈRE. You're not a doctor?

SGANARELLE. No.

LUCAS. You ain't no doc?

SGANARELLE. No, I tell you.

VALÈRE. Since you insist, we'll have to go ahead.

(*They each take a stick and beat him.*)

SGANARELLE. Oh, oh, oh! Gentlemen, I'm whatever you like.

VALÈRE. Why, sir, do you force us to this violence?

LUCAS. Why do you give us the botherment of beating you?

VALÈRE. I assure you that I could not regret it more.

LUCAS. By jeepers, I'm sorry about it, honest.

SGANARELLE. What the devil is this, gentlemen? I ask you, is it a joke, or are you both crazy, to insist I'm a doctor?

VALÈRE. What? You still won't give in, and you deny you're a doctor?

SGANARELLE. Devil take me if I am!

LUCAS. It ain't true that you're a doc?

SGANARELLE. No, plague take me! *(They start beating him again.)* Oh, oh! Well, gentlemen, since you insist, I'm a doctor, I'm a doctor; an apothecary too, if you see fit. I'd rather consent to anything than get myself beaten to death.

VALÈRE. Ah! That's fine, sir; I'm delighted to find you in a reasonable mood.

LUCAS. You fair cram my heart with joy when I see you talk thataway.

VALÈRE. I beg your pardon with all my heart.

LUCAS. I begs your excuse for the liberty I done tooken.

SGANARELLE *(aside).* Well now! Suppose I'm the one that's mistaken? Could I have become a doctor without noticing it?

VALÈRE. Sir, you won't regret showing us what you are; and you'll certainly be satisfied with your treatment.

SGANARELLE. But, gentlemen, aren't you making a mistake yourselves? Is it quite certain that I'm a doctor?

LUCAS. Yup, by jiminy!

SGANARELLE. Honestly?

VALÈRE. Beyond a doubt.

SGANARELLE. Devil take me if I knew it!

VALÈRE. What? You're the ablest doctor in the world.

SGANARELLE. Aha!

LUCAS. A doc which has cureded I don't know how many maladies.

SGANARELLE. My Lord!

VALÈRE. A woman had been taken for dead six hours before; she was ready to be buried, when, with a drop of something or other, you brought her back to life and set her walking around the room right away.

SGANARELLE. I'll be darned!

LUCAS. A little boy twelve years old left himself fall from the top of a steeple, from which he got his head, legs, and arms busted; and you, with some kind of ointment or other, you fixed him so he gets right up on his feet and goes off to play marbles.

SGANARELLE. The devil you say!

VALÈRE. In short, sir, you will have every satisfaction with us; and you'll earn whatever you like if you'll let us take you where we mean to.

SGANARELLE. I'll earn whatever I like?

VALÈRE. Yes.

SGANARELLE. Oh! I'm a doctor, there's no denying it. I'd forgotten, but now I remember. What's the problem? Where do we have to go?

VALÈRE. We'll take you. The problem is to go see a girl who's lost her speech.

SGANARELLE. My word! I haven't found it.

VALÈRE. He likes his little joke. Let's go, sir.

SGANARELLE. Without a doctor's gown?

VALÈRE. We'll get one.

SGANARELLE (presenting his bottle to VALÈRE). Hold that, you: that's where I put my potions. (Turning toward LUCAS and spitting on the ground.) You, step on that; doctor's orders.

LUCAS. Land's sakes! That's a doctor I like. I reckon he'll do all right, 'cause he's a real comic.[4]

---

[4] Some have taken this remark as Molière's own disgruntled comment on the mediocre success of The Misanthrope.

ACT II

A room in Géronte's house

Scene 1.   GÉRONTE, VALÈRE, LUCAS, JACQUELINE

VALÈRE. Yes, sir, I think you'll be satisfied; and we've brought you the greatest doctor in the world.

LUCAS. Oh, gee whillikins! You gotta pull up the ladder after that one, and all the rest ain't good enough to take off his shoon.

VALÈRE. He's a man who has performed wonderful cures.

LUCAS. As has cureded some folk as were dead.

VALÈRE. He's a bit capricious, as I've told you; and sometimes he has moments when his mind wanders and he doesn't seem what he really is.

LUCAS. Yup, he likes to clown; and sometimes you'd say, with no offense, that he'd been hit on the head with an axe.

VALÈRE. But underneath it, he's all learning, and very often he says quite lofty things.

LUCAS. When he gets to it, he talks right straight out just like he was reading out of a book.

VALÈRE. His reputation has already spread hereabouts, and everybody is coming to see him.

GÉRONTE. I'm dying to meet him. Bring him to me quick.

VALÈRE. I'll go and get him.

JACQUELINE. Land's sakes, sir, this'un'll do just what the others done. I reckon it'll be just the same old stuff; and the bestest med'cine anyone could slip your daughter, if you're asking me, would be a good handsome husband she had a hankering for.

104

GÉRONTE. Well now! My good wet-nurse, you certainly meddle in lots of things.

LUCAS. Be quiet, Jacqueline, keep to your housework: you ain't the one to stick your nose in there.

JACQUELINE. I told you before and I'll tell you some more that all these here doctors won't do nothing more for her than plain branch water, that your daughter needs something mighty different from rhubarb and senna, and that a husband is the kind of poultice that'll cure all a girl's troubles.

GÉRONTE. Is she in condition now for anyone to want to take her on, with the infirmity she has? And when I was minded to have her married, didn't she oppose my will?

JACQUELINE. I should think she did: you was wanting to pass her a man she don't love. Why didn't you take that Monsieur Léandre that she had a soft spot for? She would've been real obedient; and I'm gonna bet you he'd take her just like she is, if you'd give her to him.

GÉRONTE. That Léandre is not what she needs; he's not well off like the other.

JACQUELINE. He's got such a rich uncle, and he's his hair.

GÉRONTE. All this property to come is just so much nonsense to me. There's nothing like what you've got; and you run a big risk of fooling yourself when you count on what someone else is keeping for you. Death doesn't always keep her ears open to the wishes and prayers of their honors the heirs; and you can grow a long set of teeth when you're waiting for someone's death so as to have a livelihood.

JACQUELINE. Anyway I've always heard that in marriage, as elsewhere, happiness counts more than riches. The pas and mas, they have that goldarned custom of always asking "How much has he got?" and "How much has she got?" and neighbor Peter married off his daughter Simonette to fat Thomas 'cause he had a quarter vineyard more than young Robin, which she'd set her heart on; and now, poor critter, it's turned her yellow as a quince, and she hasn't got her property in all the time since. That's a fine example for *you*, sir. All we got in this world is our pleasure; and I'd rather give my daughter a good husband which she liked than all the revenues in Beauce.

GÉRONTE. Plague take it, Madame Nurse, how you do spit it out! Be quiet, please; you're getting too involved and you're heating up your milk.

LUCAS (*by mistake, tapping* GÉRONTE *on the chest instead of* JACQUELINE). Gosh darn it! Shut up, you're just a meddler. The master don't have no use for your speeches, and he knows what he's got to do. You see to nursing the child you're nurse to, and don't give us none of your big ideas. The master is his daughter's father, and he's good enough and wise enough to see what she needs.

GÉRONTE. Easy! Oh! Easy!

LUCAS. Sir, I want to mortify her a bit, and teach her the respect she owes you.

GÉRONTE. Yes, but those gestures aren't necessary.

Scene 2. VALÈRE, SGANARELLE, GÉRONTE, LUCAS, JACQUELINE

VALÈRE. Sir, prepare yourself. Here comes our doctor.

GÉRONTE. Sir, I'm delighted to have you in my house, and we need you badly.

SGANARELLE (*in a doctor's gown, with a sharply pointed hat*). Hippocrates says . . . that we should both put our hats on.

GÉRONTE. Hippocrates says that?

SGANARELLE. Yes.

GÉRONTE. In what chapter, if you please?

SGANARELLE. In his chapter on hats.

GÉRONTE. Since Hippocrates says it, we must do it.

SGANARELLE. Sir Doctor, since I have heard the wonderful things . . .

GÉRONTE. Whom are you speaking to, pray?

SGANARELLE. You.

GÉRONTE. I'm not a doctor.

SGANARELLE. You're not a doctor?

GÉRONTE. No, really.

SGANARELLE *(takes a stick and beats him just as he himself was beaten)*. You really mean it?

GÉRONTE. I really mean it. Oh, oh, oh!

SGANARELLE. You're a doctor now. I never got any other license.

GÉRONTE. What the devil kind of a man have you brought me?

VALÈRE. I told you he was a joker of a doctor.

GÉRONTE. Yes, but I'd send him packing with his jokes.

LUCAS. Don't pay no attention to that, sir: that's just for a laugh.

GÉRONTE. I don't like that kind of a laugh.

SGANARELLE. Sir, I ask your pardon for the liberty I took.

GÉRONTE. Your servant, sir.

SGANARELLE. I'm sorry . . .

GÉRONTE. That's nothing.

SGANARELLE. For the cudgeling . . .

GÉRONTE. No harm done.

SGANARELLE. That I had the honor of giving you.

GÉRONTE. Let's say no more about it. Sir, I have a daughter who has caught a strange disease.

SGANARELLE. Sir, I'm delighted that your daughter needs me; and I wish with all my heart that you and your whole family needed me too, just to show you how much I want to serve you.

GÉRONTE. I am obliged to you for those sentiments.

SGANARELLE. I assure you that I'm speaking straight from the heart.

GÉRONTE. You do me too much honor.

SGANARELLE. What's your daughter's name?

GÉRONTE. Lucinde.

SGANARELLE. Lucinde! Oh, what a fine name to prescribe for! Lucinde![5]

GÉRONTE. I'll just go and have a look to see what she's doing.

SGANARELLE. Who's that big buxom woman?

GÉRONTE. She's the wet-nurse of a little baby of mine.

SGANARELLE. Plague take it! That's a pretty piece of goods! Ah, nurse, charming nurse, my medicine is the very humble slave of your nurseship, and I'd certainly like to be the lucky little doll who sucked the milk (puts his hand on her breast) of your good graces. All my remedies, all my learning, all my capacity is at your service, and . . .

LUCAS. With your pummission, Mister Doctor, leave my wife be, I beg you.

SGANARELLE. What? Is she your wife?

LUCAS. Yes.

SGANARELLE (makes as if to embrace LUCAS, then, turning toward the nurse, embraces her). Oh! really! I didn't know that, and I'm delighted for the sake of you both.

LUCAS (pulling him away). Easy now, please.

SGANARELLE. I assure you I'm delighted that you're united. I congratulate her (he again makes as if to embrace LUCAS, and, passing under his arms, throws himself on JACQUELINE'S neck) on having a husband like you; and you, I congratulate you on having a wife as beautiful, modest, and well-built as she is.

LUCAS (pulling him away again). Hey! Goldarn it! Not so much compliment, I ask you now.

SGANARELLE. Don't you want me to rejoice with you at such a fine assembly?

5 Here a theatrical tradition has Sganarelle decline the name: Lucindus, Lucinda, Lucindum.

LUCAS. With me, all you like; but with my wife, let's skip these kind of formalities.

SGANARELLE. I take part in the happiness of you both alike; and *(same business as before)* if I embrace you to attest my joy to you, I embrace her as well to attest my joy to her too.

LUCAS *(pulling him away once more)*. Oh! Dad blast it, Mister Doctor, what a lot of fiddle-faddle!

Scene 3. SGANARELLE, GÉRONTE, LUCAS, JACQUELINE

GÉRONTE. Sir, they're going to bring my daughter to you. She'll be here right away.

SGANARELLE. I await her sir, and all medicine with me.

GÉRONTE. Where is it?

SGANARELLE *(tapping his forehead)*. In there.

GÉRONTE. Very good.

SGANARELLE *(trying to touch the nurse's breasts)*. But since I am interested in your whole family, I must take a small sample of your nurse's milk, and inspect her bosom.

LUCAS *(pulling him away and spinning him around)*. Nah, nah, I don't want no truck with that.

SGANARELLE. It's the doctor's job to examine nurses' breasts.

LUCAS. Job nor no job, I'm your servant.

SGANARELLE. Do you really have the audacity to set yourself up against the doctor? Begone!

LUCAS. The heck with that!

SGANARELLE *(looking at him askance)*. I'll give you the fever.

JACQUELINE *(taking LUCAS by the arm and spinning him around)*. That's right, get out of there. Ain't I big enough to defend myself if he does something to me as a person hadn't ought?

LUCAS. Well, me, I don't want him a-feeling you.

SGANARELLE. Fie! The peasant! He's jealous of his wife!

GÉRONTE. Here is my daughter.

Scene 4.   LUCINDE, VALÈRE, GÉRONTE, LUCAS, SGANARELLE,
JACQUELINE

SGANARELLE. Is this the patient?

GÉRONTE. Yes, she's the only daughter I have, and I'd be heart-broken if she were to die.

SGANARELLE. She'd better not! She mustn't die except on doctor's orders.

GÉRONTE. Come, come, a chair![6]

SGANARELLE. That's not such a bad-looking patient, and I maintain that a really healthy man would make out all right with her.

GÉRONTE. You've made her laugh, sir.

SGANARELLE. That's fine. When the doctor makes the patient laugh, that's the best possible sign. Well! What's the problem? What's wrong with you? Where does it hurt?

LUCINDE (answers in sign language, putting her hand to her mouth, her head, and under her chin). Hah, heeh, hoh, hah.

SGANARELLE. Eh? What's that you say?

LUCINDE (same gestures as before). Hah, heeh, hoh, hah, hah, heeh, hoh.

SGANARELLE. What?

LUCINDE. Hah, heeh, hoh.

[6] Chairs were relatively rare luxuries in Molière's France. By ordering a regular chair, not a folding stool, Géronte shows his respect for the learned doctor.

SGANARELLE *(imitating her)*. Hah, heeh, hoh, hah, hah: I don't understand you. What the devil kind of language is that?

GÉRONTE. Sir, that's her illness. She's been struck dumb, and up to now no one has been able to learn the reason why; and it's an accident that has put off her marriage.

SGANARELLE. And why so?

GÉRONTE. The man she is to marry wants to wait until she's cured to make things final.

SGANARELLE. And who is the fool that doesn't want his wife to be dumb? Would God mine had that disease! I'd be the last one to want to cure her.

GÉRONTE. Anyway, sir, we beg you to make every effort to relieve her of her trouble.

SGANARELLE. Oh! Don't worry. Tell me now, does this trouble bother her a lot?

GÉRONTE. Yes, sir.

SGANARELLE. Very good. Does she feel great pains?

GÉRONTE. Very great.

SGANARELLE. That's just fine. Does she go—you know where?

GÉRONTE. Yes.

SGANARELLE. Copiously?

GÉRONTE. I don't know anything about that.

SGANARELLE. Does she achieve laudable results?

GÉRONTE. I'm no expert in those matters.

SGANARELLE *(turning to the patient)*. Give me your arm. That pulse shows your daughter is dumb.

GÉRONTE. Why yes, sir, that's her trouble! You found it the very first thing.

SGANARELLE. Aha!

JACQUELINE. Just lookit how he guessed her illness!

SGANARELLE. We great doctors, we know things right away. An

ignorant one would have been embarrassed and would have gone and told you "It's this" or "It's that"; but *I* hit the mark on the first shot, and I inform you that your daughter is dumb.

GÉRONTE. Yes; but I wish you could tell me what it comes from.

SGANARELLE. Nothing easier: it comes from the fact that she has lost her speech.

GÉRONTE. Very good; but the reason, please, why she has lost her speech?

SGANARELLE. All our best authors will tell you that it's the stoppage of the action of her tongue.

GÉRONTE. But still, what are your views about this stoppage of the action of her tongue?

SGANARELLE. Aristotle, on that subject, says . . . some very fine things.

GÉRONTE. I believe it.

SGANARELLE. Oh! He was a great man!

GÉRONTE. No doubt.

SGANARELLE *(raising his forearm)*. An utterly great man: a man who was greater than I by all of that! So, to get back to our reasoning, I hold that this stoppage of the action of her tongue is caused by certain humors, which among us scholars we call peccant humors: peccant, that is to say . . . peccant humors; because the vapors formed by the exhalations of the influences arising in the region where the maladies lie, when they come . . . so to speak . . . to . . . Do you understand Latin?

GÉRONTE. Not in the least.

SGANARELLE *(getting up in astonishment)*. You don't understand Latin?

GÉRONTE. No.

SGANARELLE *(assuming various comical poses)*. *Cabricias arci thuram, catalamus, singulariter, nominativo haec Musa,* "the Muse," *bonus, bona, bonum, Deus sanctus, estne oratio latinas?*

Etiam, "yes." *Quare,* "why?" *Quia substantivo et adjectivum concordat in generi, numerum, et casus.*[7]

GÉRONTE. Oh! Why did I never study?

JACQUELINE. Land! That's an able man!

LUCAS. Yup, that's so purty I can't make out a word of it.

SGANARELLE. Now when these vapors I'm speaking of come to pass from the left side, where the liver is, to the right side, where the heart is, it happens that the lungs, which in Latin we call *armyan,* having communication with the brain, which in Greek we call *nasmus,* by means of the vena cava, which in Hebrew we call *cubile,*[8] on its way encounters the said vapors, which fill the ventricles of the omoplate; and because the said vapors—follow this reasoning closely, I beg you— and because the said vapors have a certain malignity . . . Listen to this carefully, I conjure you.

GÉRONTE. Yes.

SGANARELLE. Have a certain malignity, which is caused . . . Be attentive, please.

GÉRONTE. I am.

SGANARELLE. Which is caused by the acridity of the humors engendered in the concavity of the diaphragm, it happens that these vapors . . . *Ossabandus, nequeys, nequer, potarinum, quipsa milus.* That's exactly what is making your daughter dumb.

JACQUELINE. Oh! That man of ourn! Ain't that well said?

LUCAS. Why ain't *my* tongue that slick?

GÉRONTE. No one could reason any better, no doubt about it. There's just one thing that surprised me: the location of the liver and the heart. It seems to me that you place them otherwise than they are; that the heart is on the left side and the liver on the right side.

---

[7] Traditionally, as Sganarelle winds up this hodge-podge of gibberish and elementary Latin phrases with the word *casus* ("case," or "fall"), he throws himself back in his chair too hard, and falls over in it on his back. He remains in this position during the next two remarks.

[8] These are all invented names, except that *cubile* is Latin for *bed.*

SGANARELLE. Yes, it used to be that way; but we have changed all that, and now we practice medicine in a completely new way.

GÉRONTE. That's something I didn't know, and I beg your pardon for my ignorance.

SGANARELLE. No harm done, and you're not obliged to be as able as we are.

GÉRONTE. To be sure. But, sir, what do you think needs to be done for this illness?

SGANARELLE. What I think needs to be done?

GÉRONTE. Yes.

SGANARELLE. My advice is to put her back in bed and have her take, as a remedy, a lot of bread steeped in wine.

GÉRONTE. And why that, sir?

SGANARELLE. Because in bread and wine mixed together there is a sympathetic virtue that makes people speak. Haven't you noticed that they don't give anything else to parrots, and that they learn to speak by eating that?

GÉRONTE. That's true. Oh, what a great man! Quick, lots of bread and wine!

SGANARELLE. I'll come back toward evening and see how she is. (To the nurse) Hold on, you. Sir, here is a nurse to whom I must administer a few little remedies.

JACQUELINE. Who? Me? I couldn't be in better health.

SGANARELLE. Too bad, nurse, too bad. Such good health is alarming, and it won't be a bad thing to give you a friendly little bloodletting, a little dulcifying enema.

GÉRONTE. But, sir, that's a fashion I don't understand. Why should we go and be bled when we haven't any illness?

SGANARELLE. No matter, it's a salutary fashion; and just as we drink on account of the thirst to come, so we must have ourselves bled on account of the illness to come.

JACQUELINE (starting to go off). My Lord! The heck with that, and I don't want to make my body into a drugstore.

SGANARELLE. You are resistant to remedies, but we'll manage to bring you to reason.   (*Exit* JACQUELINE)
  (*To* GÉRONTE) I bid you good day.

GÉRONTE. Wait a bit, please.

SGANARELLE. What do you want to do?

GÉRONTE. Give you some money, sir.

SGANARELLE (*holding out his hand behind, beneath his gown, while* GÉRONTE *opens his purse*). I won't take any, sir.

GÉRONTE. Sir . . .

SGANARELLE. Not at all.

GÉRONTE. Just a moment.

SGANARELLE. By no means.

GÉRONTE. Please!

SGANARELLE. You're joking.

GÉRONTE. That's that.

SGANARELLE. I'll do nothing of the sort.

GÉRONTE. Eh?

SGANARELLE. Money is no motive to me.

GÉRONTE. I believe it.

SGANARELLE (*after taking the money*). Is this good weight?

GÉRONTE. Yes, sir.

SGANARELLE. I'm not a mercenary doctor.

GÉRONTE. I'm well aware of it.

SGANARELLE. I'm not ruled by self-interest.

GÉRONTE. I have no such idea.

Scene 5. SGANARELLE, LÉANDRE

SGANARELLE *(looking at his money)*. My word! That's not too bad; and if only . . .

LÉANDRE. Sir, I've been waiting for you a long time, and I come to implore your assistance.

SGANARELLE *(taking his wrist)*. That's a very bad pulse.

LÉANDRE. I'm not sick, sir, and that's not why I've come to see you.

SGANARELLE. If you're not sick, why the devil don't you say so?

LÉANDRE. No. To put the whole thing in a word, my name is Léandre, and I'm in love with Lucinde, whom you've just examined; and since, because of her father's bad disposition, I'm denied all access to her, I'm venturing to beg you to serve my love, and give me a chance to carry out a scheme I've thought up to say a word or two to her on which my happiness and my life depend absolutely.

SGANARELLE *(feigning anger)*. Whom do you take me for? How can you dare come up and ask me to serve you in your love, and try to degrade the dignity of a doctor to this type of employment?

LÉANDRE. Sir, don't make so much noise.

SGANARELLE. *I* want to make noise. You're an impertinent young man.

LÉANDRE. Ah! Gently, sir.

SGANARELLE. A dunderhead.

LÉANDRE. Please!

SGANARELLE. I'll teach you that I'm not the kind of man for that, and that it's the height of insolence . . .

LÉANDRE *(pulling out a purse and giving it to him)*. Sir . . .

SGANARELLE. To want to use me . . . I'm not speaking about you, for you're a gentleman, and I would be delighted to do you a service; but there are some impertinent people in the world who come and take people for what they're not; and I admit that makes me angry.

LÉANDRE. I ask your pardon, sir, for the liberty that . . .

SGANARELLE. Don't be silly. What's the problem?

LÉANDRE. You shall know, then, sir, that this llness that you want to cure is make-believe. The doctors have reasoned in due form about it, and have not failed to say that it came, some say from the brain, some from the intestines, some from the spleen, some from the liver; but it is certain that love is the real cause of it, and that Lucinde hit upon this illness only to deliever herself from a threatened marriage. But, for fear we may be seen together, let's get out of hre, and as we walk I'll tell you what I would like from you.

SGANARELLE. Let's go, sir: you've given me an inconceivable fondness for your love; and unless I'm no doctor, either the patient will die or else she'll be yours.

ACT III

Géronte's garden

Scene 1. SGANARELLE, LÉANDRE

LÉANDRE. It seems to me I don't look bad this way as an apothecary; and since the father has scarcely ever seen me, this change of costume and wig may well succeed, I think, in disguising me to his eyes.

SGANARELLE. No doubt about it.

LÉANDRE. All I could wish would be to know five or six big medical terms to adorn my speech and make me seem like a learned man.

SGANARELLE. Come, come, all that is unnecessary: the costume is enough, and I know no more about it than you.

LÉANDRE. What?

SGANARELLE. Devil take me if I know anything about medicine! You're a good sort, and I'm willing to confide in you, just as you are confiding in me.

LÉANDRE. What? You're not really . . . ?

SGANARELLE. No, I tell you: they made me a doctor in spite of me. I had never bothered my head about being that learned; and all my studies went only up to seventh grade. I don't know what put this idea into their heads; but when I saw that they absolutely insisted on my being a doctor, I decided to be one, at the expense of whom it may concern. However, you'd never believe how the mistaken idea has gotten around, and how everybody is hell-bent on thinking me a learned man. They come looking for me from all directions; and if things keep on this way, I believe I'll stick to medicine

all my life. I think it's the best trade of all; for whether
you do well or badly, you're always paid just the same.
Bad work never comes back onto our backs, and we cut
the material we work on as we please. A cobbler making
shoes could never botch a piece of leather without paying
for the broken crockery; but in this work we can botch a
man without its costing us anything. The blunders are never
ours, and it's always the fault of the person who dies. In
short, the best part of this profession is that there's a decency, an unparalleled discretion, among the dead; and you
never see one of them complaining of the doctor who killed
him.

LÉANDRE. It's true that dead men are very decent folk on that
score.

SGANARELLE *(seeing some men coming toward him)*. There
are some people who look as though they were coming to
consult me. Go ahead and wait for me near your sweetheart's house.

Scene 2.   THIBAUT, PERRIN, SGANARELLE

THIBAUT. Sir, we done come to see you, my son Perrin and me.

SGANARELLE. What's the matter?

THIBAUT. His poor mother, her name is Perrette, is sick in bed
these six months now.

SGANARELLE *(holding out his hand to receive money)*. And what
do you expect me to do about it?

THIBAUT. We'd like, sir, for you to slip us some kind of funny
business for to cure her.

SGANARELLE. I'll have to see what she's sick of.

THIBAUT. She's sick of a proxy, sir.

SGANARELLE. Of a proxy?

THIBAUT. Yes, that is to say she's all swelled up all over; and they say it's a whole lot of seriosities she's got inside her, and that her liver, her belly, or her spleen, whatever you want to call it, 'stead of making blood don't make nothing but water. Every other day she has a quotigian fever, with pains and lassitules in the muskles of her legs. You can hear in her throat phleg-ums like to choke her; and sometimes she gets tooken with syncopations and compulsions till I think she done passed away. In our village we got a 'pothecary, all respect to him, who's given her I don't know how many kinds of stuff; and it costs me more'n a dozen good crowns in enemas, no offense, and beverages he had her take, in jacinth confusions and cordial portions. But all that stuff, like the feller said, was just a kind of salve that didn't make her no better nor no worse. He wanted to slip her one certain drug that they call hermetic wine; but me, frankly, I got scared that would send her to join her ancestors; and they do say those big doctors are killing off I don't know how many people with that there invention.[9]

SGANARELLE (still holding out his hand and signaling with it for money). Let's get to the point, my friend, let's get to the point.

THIBAUT. The fact is, sir, that we done come to ask you to tell us what we should do.

SGANARELLE. I don't understand you at all.

PERRIN. Sir, my mother is sick; and here be two crowns that we've brung you so you'll give us some cure.

SGANARELLE. Oh! Now *you*, I understand you. Here's a lad who speaks clearly and explains himself properly. You say that your mother is ill with dropsy, that her whole body is swollen, that she has a fever and pains in her legs, and that she is sometimes seized with syncopes and convulsions, that is to say, fainting spells?

PERRIN. Oh, yes, sir, that's exactly it.

SGANARELLE. I understood you right away. You have a father

---

[9] A big medical controversy of the time concerned the value of emetic wine, which contained antimony.

who doesn't know what he's talking about. Now you're asking me for a remedy?

PERRIN. Yes, sir.

SGANARELLE. A remedy to cure her?

PERRIN. That's what we got in mind.

SGANARELLE. Look, here's a piece of cheese that you must have her take.

PERRIN. Cheese, sir?

SGANARELLE. Yes, it's a specially prepared cheese containing gold, coral, pearls, and lots of other precious things.

PERRIN. Sir, we be much obliged to you; and we'll have her take this right away.

SGANARELLE. Go ahead. If she dies, don't fail to give her the best burial you can.

Scene 3.   JACQUELINE, SGANARELLE; LUCAS *(backstage)*

SGANARELLE. Here's that beautiful nurse. Ah, nurse of my heart, I'm delighted that we meet again, and the sight of you is the rhubarb, cassia, and senna that purge my soul of all its melancholy!

JACQUELINE. Well I swan, Mister Doctor, you say that too purty for me, and I don't understand none of your Latin.

SGANARELLE. Fall ill, nurse, I beg you; fall ill for my sake: it would give me all the pleasure in the world to cure you.

JACQUELINE. I'm your servant, sir: I'd much rather not have no one cure me.

SGANARELLE. How sorry I am for you, fair nurse, for having a jealous, troublesome husband like the one you have!

JACQUELINE. What would you have me do, sir? It's a penance

for my sins. Where the goat is tied, that's where she's got to graze.

SGANARELLE. What? A clod like that! A man who's always watching you, and won't let anyone talk to you!

JACQUELINE. Mercy me, you ain't seen nothin' yet, and that's only a little sample of his bad humor.

SGANARELLE. Is it possible? And can a man have a soul so base as to mistreat a person like you? Ah, lovely nurse, I know people, and not far from here either, who would think themselves happy just to kiss the little tips of your footsies! Why must so lovely a person have fallen into such hands, and must a mere animal, a brute, a lout, a fool . . . ? Pardon me, nurse, if I speak in this way of your husband.

JACQUELINE. Oh, sir, I know good and well he deserves all them names.

SGANARELLE. Yes, nurse, he certainly does deserve them; and he would also deserve to have you plant a certain decoration on his head, to punish him for his suspicions.

JACQUELINE. It's quite true that if I was only thinking about him, he might drive me to some strange carryings-on.

SGANARELLE. My word! It wouldn't be a bad idea for you to take vengeance on him with someone else. He's a man, I tell you, who really deserves that; and if I were fortunate enough, beautiful nurse, to be chosen to . . .

(At this point they both notice LUCAS, *who was in back of them all the time listening to their talk. They go off in opposite directions, the doctor with comical byplay.)*

Scene 4.   GÉRONTE, LUCAS

GÉRONTE. Hey there, Lucas! Haven't you seen our doctor around?

LUCAS. Yup, tarnation take it! I seen him, and my wife too.

GÉRONTE. Then where can he be?

LUCAS. I dunno, but I wish he'd go to the devil in hell.

GÉRONTE. Go take a look and see what my daughter is doing.

Scene 5. SGANARELLE, LÉANDRE, GÉRONTE

GÉRONTE. Ah, sir! I was just asking where you were.

SGANARELLE. I was busy in your courtyard—expelling the superfluity of my potations. How is the patient?

GÉRONTE. A little worse since taking your prescription.

SGANARELLE. Very good: that's a sign that it's working.

GÉRONTE. Yes; but as it works, I'm afraid it will choke her.

SGANARELLE. Don't worry; I have remedies that make light of everything, and I'll wait for her in her death agony.

GÉRONTE. Who's this man you're bringing with you?

SGANARELLE (gesturing like an apothecary giving an enema). He's . . .

GÉRONTE. What?

SGANARELLE. The one . . .

GÉRONTE. Eh?

SGANARELLE. Who . . .

GÉRONTE. I understand.

SGANARELLE. Your daughter will need him.

Scene 6.   JACQUELINE, LUCINDE, GÉRONTE, LÉANDRE,
                            SGANARELLE

JACQUELINE. Sir, here's your daughter as wants to take a little walk.

SGANARELLE. That will do her good. Mister Apothecary, go along and take her pulse a bit so that I can discuss her illness with you presently.

(At this point he draws GÉRONTE *to one side of the stage, and, passing one arm over his shoulders, puts his hand under his chin and turns him back toward himself whenever* GÉRONTE *tries to watch what his daughter and the apothecary are doing together.)* Sir, it's a great and subtle question among the learned whether women are easier to cure than men. I beg you to listen to this, if you please. Some say no, others say yes; and *I* say yes and no: inasmuch as the incongruity of the opaque humors that are found in the natural temperament of women, is the reason why the brutish part always tries to gain power over the sensitive part, we see that the inequality of their opinions depends on the oblique movement of the moon's circle; and since the sun, which darts its rays over the concavity of the earth, finds . . .

LUCINDE. No, I'm utterly incapable of changing my feelings.

GÉRONTE. That's my daughter speaking! Oh, what wonderful virtue in that remedy! Oh, what an admirable doctor! How obliged I am to you for this marvelous cure! And what can I do for you after such a service?

SGANARELLE *(walking around the stage and wiping his brow).* That's an illness that gave me a lot of trouble!

LUCINDE. Yes, father, I've recovered my speech; but I've recovered it to tell you that I shall never have any other husband than Léandre, and that there's no use your trying to give me Horace.

GÉRONTE. But . . .

LUCINDE. Nothing can shake my resolution.

GÉRONTE. What . . . ?

LUCINDE. All your fine objections will be in vain.

GÉRONTE. If . . .

LUCINDE. All your arguments will be no use.

GÉRONTE. I . . .

LUCINDE. It's a thing I'm determined on.

GÉRONTE. But . . .

LUCINDE. There is no paternal authority that can force me to marry in spite of myself.

GÉRONTE. I've . . .

LUCINDE. All your efforts will not avail.

GÉRONTE. He . . .

LUCINDE. My heart could never submit to this tyranny.

GÉRONTE. There . . .

LUCINDE. And I'll cast myself into a convent rather than marry a man I don't love.

GÉRONTE. But . . .

LUCINDE *(in a deafening voice)*. No. By no means. Nothing doing. You're wasting your time. I won't do anything of the sort. That's settled.

GÉRONTE. Oh! What a rush of words! There's no way to resist it. Sir, I beg you to make her dumb again.

SGANARELLE. That's impossible for me. All I can do for your service is to make you deaf, if you want.

GÉRONTE. Many thanks! *(To* LUCINDE*)* Then do you think . . . ?

LUCINDE. No. All your reasons will make no impression on my soul.

GÉRONTE. You shall marry Horace this very evening.

LUCINDE. I'll sooner marry death.

SGANARELLE. Good Lord! Stop, let me medicate this affair. Her illness still grips her, and I know the remedy we must apply.

GÉRONTE. Is it possible, sir, that you can also cure this illness of the mind?

SGANARELLE. Yes. Leave it to me, I have remedies for everything, and our apothecary will serve us for this cure. *(Calls the apothecary.)* One word. You see that the ardor she has for this Léandre is completely contrary to her father's will, that there is no time to lose, that the humors are very inflamed, and that it is necessary to find a remedy promptly for this ailment, which could get worse with delay. For my part, I see only one, which is a dose of purgative flight, which you will combine properly with two drams of matrimonium in pill form. She may make some difficulty about taking this remedy; but since you are an able man at your trade, it's up to you to persuade her and make her swallow the dose as best you can. Go along and get her to take a little turn around the garden, so as to prepare the humors, while I talk to her father here; but above all don't waste time. The remedy, quickly, the one specific remedy!

Scene 7.   GÉRONTE, SGANARELLE

GÉRONTE. What are those drugs, sir, that you just mentioned? It seems to me I've never heard of them.

SGANARELLE. They are drugs used in great emergencies.

GÉRONTE. Did you ever see such insolence as hers?

SGANARELLE. Daughters are sometimes a little headstrong.

GÉRONTE. You wouldn't believe how crazy she is about this Léandre.

SGANARELLE. The heat of the blood does this to young minds.

GÉRONTE. For my part, ever since I discovered the violence of this love, I've managed to keep my daughter always locked up.

SGANARELLE. You've done wisely.

GÉRONTE. And I've kept them from having any communication together.

SGANARELLE. Very good.

GÉRONTE. Some folly would have resulted if I'd allowed them to see each other.

SGANARELLE. No doubt.

GÉRONTE. And I think she'd have been just the girl to run off with him.

SGANARELLE. That's prudent reasoning.

GÉRONTE. I've been warned that he's making every effort to speak to her.

SGANARELLE. What a clown!

GÉRONTE. But he'll be wasting his time.

SGANARELLE. Ha, ha!

GÉRONTE. And I'll keep him from seeing her, all right.

SGANARELLE. He's not dealing with a dolt, and you know tricks of the game that he doesn't. Smarter than you is no fool.

Scene 8. LUCAS, GÉRONTE, SGANARELLE

LUCAS. Dad blast it, sir, here's a lot of ruckus: your daughter's done run off with her Léandre. The 'pothecary, that was him; and Mister Doctor here's the one as pufformed that fine operation.

GÉRONTE. What? Assassinate me in that way! Here, get a policeman! Don't let him get out. Ah, traitor! I'll have the law on you.

LUCAS. Hah! By jingo, Mister Doctor, you'll be hung: just don't move outa there.

Scene 9. MARTINE, SGANARELLE, LUCAS

MARTINE. Oh, Good Lord! What a time I've had finding this house! Tell me, what's the news of the doctor I provided for you?

LUCAS. Here he be. Gonna be hung.

MARTINE. What? My husband hanged? Alas! What's he done?

LUCAS. He fixed it for our master's daughter to get run away with.

MARTINE. Alas! My dear husband, is it really true they're going to hang you?

SGANARELLE. As you see. Oh!

MARTINE. Must you let yourself die in the presence of all these people?

SGANARELLE. What do you expect me to do about it?

MARTINE. At least if you'd finished cutting our wood, I'd have some consolation.

SGANARELLE. Get out of here, you're breaking my heart.

MARTINE. No, I mean to stay to give you courage in the face of death, and I won't leave you until I see you hanged.

SGANARELLE. Oh!

Scene 10. GÉRONTE, SGANARELLE, MARTINE, LUCAS

GÉRONTE. The constable will be here soon, and they'll put you
in a place where they'll be answerable for you to me.

SGANARELLE *(hat in hand)*. Alas! Can't this be changed to a
modest cudgeling?

GÉRONTE. No, no, justice will take its course . . . But what's
this I see?

Scene 11. LÉANDRE, LUCINDE, JACQUELINE, LUCAS,
GÉRONTE, SGANARELLE, MARTINE

LÉANDRE. Sir, I come to reveal Léandre to you and restore
Lucinde to your power. We both intended to run away
and get married; but this plan has given way to a more
honorable procedure. I do not aim to steal your daughter
from you, and it is only from your hands that I wish to
receive her. I will tell you this, sir: I have just received
letters informing me that my uncle has died and that I
am heir to all his property.

GÉRONTE. Sir, I have the highest consideration for your virtues,
and I give you my daughter with the greatest pleasure in
the world.

SGANARELLE. That was a close shave for medicine!

MARTINE. Since you're not going to be hanged, you can thank
me for being a doctor; for I'm the one who procured you
that honor.

SGANARELLE. Yes, you're the one who procured me quite a
beating.

LÉANDRE. The result is too fine for you to harbor resentment.

SGANARELLE. All right: I forgive you for the beatings in consideration of the dignity you've raised me to; but prepare henceforth to live in the greatest respect with a man of my consequence, and bear in mind that the wrath of a doctor is more to be feared than anyone can ever believe.

The Miser

THE MISER

A prose comedy in five acts, first performed on September 9, 1668, at the Théâtre du Palais-Royal in Paris by Molière's Troupe du Roi. All we know of the distribution of roles is that Molière played Harpagon, and Béjart, La Flèche. The play was a success almost from the first.

Molière's borrowings are at their most conspicuous here: from Ariosto, the *commedia dell' arte,* Boisrobert, Larivey, and beyond all these to his—and their—main source, the *Aulularia* of Plautus. Yet the play has a life and vigor of its own, independent of its models.

The basic situation is grim and ugly. Harpagon's avarice dominates the entire action, reducing everyone he touches to either inanition or revolt, and making him not only the father of Cléante, but also his rival in love and his money-lender. Yet Molière's ingenuity keeps the play comic with such inventions as the incredible list of secondhand objects—even to that "pleasing curio" the stuffed lizard—that Harpagon would force Cléante to take as part of his loan; the vanity that mingles with Harpagon's stinginess and dictates his ingenious plans for the supper he is to give; the description of his starving horses; the unforgettable hats—still a universal symbol of multiple jobs —worn by Maître Jacques; Frosine's panegyrics on the charms of elderly lovers; Harpagon's manic soliloquy on the loss of his money-box; and the sustained *quid pro quo* (inspired, to be sure, by Plautus) of the long scene between Harpagon and Valère where each, unbeknownst to the other, is speaking about the object of his own love and obsession—Valère about Élise, Harpagon about his money-box.

The play is full of the language of money applied to love and (by Harpagon) the language of love applied to money; so that even its vocabulary reminds us constantly of the

irreducible conflict of values between Harpagon and everyone
else. A typical comic hero of Molière in this, Harpagon never
changes; and his power and obduracy are such that, much as
in *Tartuffe*, no happy ending is logically possible. Evil begets
evil, and Molière has given it a large place in his comedy. Its
natural result would be an ugly impasse. The happy ending
that Molière provides instead, romanesque and unprepared, reveals this clearly even as it keeps the play within the domain
of the comic muse. And the ending is happy even for Harpagon,
as well as comic, as he worms his way out of giving a dowry,
paying the wedding expenses and the officer's fee, gets a promise
of a new suit for the wedding—and goes off to see the
newly-restored money-box that is his one true love.

THE MISER

CHARACTERS

HARPAGON, *father of Cléante and Élise, and suitor to Mariane*
CLÉANTE, *son of Harpagon, in love with Mariane*
ÉLISE, *daughter of Harpagon, in love with Valère*
VALÈRE, *son of Anselme, in love with Élise*
MARIANE, *in love with Cléante, and courted by Harpagon*
ANSELME, *father of Valère and Mariane*
FROSINE, *a woman who lives by her wits*
MAÎTRE SIMON, *a broker*
MAÎTRE JACQUES, *Harpagon's cook and coachman*
LA FLÈCHE, *Cléante's valet*
DAME CLAUDE, *servant of Harpagon*
BRINDAVOINE, LA MERLUCHE, *lackeys of Harpagon*
The OFFICER *and his* CLERK

*The scene is in Paris: Harpagon's living room,
with a garden to the rear.*

ACT I

Scene 1. VALÈRE, ÉLISE

VALÈRE. What, charming Élise, you are growing melancholy, after the obliging assurances you were good enough to give me of your faith? I see you sigh, alas! in the midst of my joy! Tell me, is it in regret at having made me happy, and do you repent of the signed engagement which my ardor wrung from you?

ÉLISE. No, Valère, I cannot repent of anything I do for you. I feel myself drawn to it by too sweet a power, and I haven't even the strength to wish that these things were not so. But to tell you the truth, the outcome gives me some uneasiness; and I am very much afraid that I may love you a little more than I ought.

VALÈRE. Oh! What can you fear, Élise, in the kindness you bear me?

ÉLISE. Alas! A hundred things at once: a father's anger, a family's reproaches, the censures of society; but more than anything, Valère, a change in your heart, and that criminal coolness with which those of your sex most often repay any too ardent proof of an innocent love.

VALÈRE. Ah! Do not do me the wrong of judging me by others. Suspect me of anything, Élise, rather than of failing in what I owe you; I love you too much for that, and my love for you will last as long as my life.

ÉLISE. Ah, Valère, everyone says the same thing. Men are all alike in their words; and it is only their actions that show them to be different.

VALÈRE. Since actions alone reveal what we are, then at least wait and judge my heart by these, and don't look for crimes of mine in the unjust fears of dire forebodings. Do not murder me, I beg you, with the painful blows of an outrageous suspicion; and give me time to convince you, by a thousand upon a thousand proofs, of the sincerity of my flame.

ÉLISE. Alas! How easily we let ourselves be persuaded by the persons we love! Yes, Valère, I regard your heart as incapable of deceiving me. I believe that you love me with a genuine love, and that you will be faithful to me; I do not in the least want to doubt it, and I confine my concern to my fear of the blame that I may receive.

VALÈRE. But why this anxiety?

ÉLISE. I would have nothing to fear if everyone saw you with the same eyes as I do, and I find enough in your person to justify the things I do for you. For its defense, my heart has all your merit, supported by the aid of a gratitude by which Heaven binds me to you. At every moment I recall the astounding peril that first brought us to each other's sight; that surprising generosity that made you risk your life to steal mine from the fury of the waves; those most tender cares that you showed me after having drawn me out of the water, and the assiduous homage of that ardent love which neither time nor difficulties have discouraged, and which, making you neglect both kindred and country, detains you here, keeps your fortune disguised for my sake, and has reduced you, in order to see me, to take on the functions of a servant of my father's. All this of course has a marvelous effect on me, and is enough in my eyes to justify to me the engagement I was able to consent to; but perhaps it is not enough to justify it to others, and I am not sure that they will share my feelings.

VALÈRE. Of all that you have mentioned, it is only by my love alone that I claim to deserve anything from you; and as for the scruples you have, your father himself takes only too good care to justify you to everyone; and the excess of his avarice and the austere way he lives with his children could authorize even stranger things. Pardon me, charming Élise, if I speak of him thus before you. You know that on that score one can say no good of him. But anyway, if I can find my parents again, as I hope to, we shall not have much trouble in winning him over. I am waiting impatiently for news of them, and if I don't hear any soon I'll go myself and look for it.

ÉLISE. Ah! Valère, don't budge from here, I beg you; and just think about getting into my father's good graces.

VALÈRE. You see how I am going about it, and the adroit complaisance I have had to employ to make my way into his service; what a mask of sympathy and conformity of feelings I disguise myself under to please him, and what a part I play with him every day so as to win his affection. I am making admirable progress in this; and I find that to win men, there is no better way than to adorn oneself before their eyes with their inclinations, fall in with their maxims, praise their defects, and applaud whatever they do. One need have no fear of overdoing the complaisance; and even though the way you trick them is visible, even the shrewdest are great dupes when it comes to flattery; and there is nothing so absurd or so ridiculous that you can't make them swallow it if you season it with praise. Sincerity suffers a bit in the trade I am plying; but when you need men, you simply have to adjust to them; and since that's the only way to win them over, it's not the fault of those who flatter, but of those who want to be flattered.

ÉLISE. But why don't you also try to win my brother's support, in case the maidservant should take it into her head to reveal our secret?

VALÈRE. You can't humor them both; and the father's spirit and the son's are things so opposed that it's hard to be in the confidence of both at the same time. But you, for your part, work on your brother, and use the affection there is between you to bring him over to our interests. Here he comes. I'll withdraw. Take this time to speak to him; and don't tell him anything about our affairs except what you see fit.

ÉLISE. I don't know whether I'll have the strength to confide this to him.

Scene 2.   CLÉANTE, ÉLISE

CLÉANTE. I'm very glad to find you alone, sister; and I was burning to talk to you, to let you in on a secret.

ÉLISE. Here I am ready to listen, brother. What have you to tell me?

CLÉANTE. Many things, sister, all wrapped up in a word: I'm in love.

ÉLISE. You're in love?

CLÉANTE. Yes, I'm in love. But before I go any further, I know that I'm dependent on a father, and that the name of son subjects me to his will; that we should not plight our troth without the consent of those who brought us into the world; that Heaven has made them masters of our affections, and that we are enjoined not to dispose of these without their guidance; that not being prepossessed by any mad ardor, they are in much better shape not to make a mistake than we, and to see much better what is right for us; that we must rather trust the lights of their prudence than the blindness of our passion; and that the impetuosity of youth most often drags us over terrible precipices. I tell you all this, sister, so that you won't take the trouble to tell it to me; for the fact is my love won't listen to anything, and I beg you not to make any remonstrances.

ÉLISE. Brother, have you pledged yourself to the one you love?

CLÉANTE. No, but I am resolved to; and I conjure you, once again, not to bring up any reasons to dissuade me.

ÉLISE. Am I so strange a person, brother?

CLÉANTE. No, sister, but you're not in love; you do not know the sweet violence that tender love exerts over our hearts; and I am apprehensive of your wisdom.

ÉLISE. Alas, brother! Let's not speak of my wisdom! There is no one who does not lack it, at least once in his life; and if I open my heart to you, I may appear to your eyes much less wise than yourself.

CLÉANTE. Ah! Would to Heaven that your heart, like mine . . .

ÉLISE. Let's finish with your affair first, and tell me who is the one you love.

CLÉANTE. A young person who has lived in this neighborhood only a short time, and who seems to be made to inspire love in all who see her. Sister, nature has formed nothing lovelier; and I felt myself transported from the moment I saw her. Her name is Mariane, and she lives under the guidance of an old mother who is nearly always sick, and for whom this lovable girl has such affection as cannot be imagined. She serves her, sympathizes with her, and consoles her, with a tenderness that would touch your soul. She goes about the things she does in the most charming manner in the world, and a thousand graces shine in all her actions: a most attractive sweetness, an engaging kindness, an adorable modesty, a . . . Ah, sister! I wish you had seen her.

ÉLISE. I see much of her, brother, in the things you tell me; and to understand what she is, it is enough for me that you love her.

CLÉANTE. I have secretly learned that they are not very well off, and that even with their discreet way of living they are hard put to it to make ends meet with what little they have. Just imagine, sister, what a joy it can be to restore the fortunes of a person we love; to give some little help, adroitly, to the modest needs of a virtuous family; and think how frustrating it is for me to see that because of a father's avarice I am powerless to taste this joy and to display to this beauty any token of my love.

ÉLISE. Yes, brother, I can see well enough what your vexation must be.

CLÉANTE. Ah! Sister, it's worse than you could believe. For after all, can anything be more cruel than this rigorous economy that is inflicted on us, this extraordinary parsimony in which we are made to languish? And what good will it do us to have money if it comes to us only when we are no longer at a good age to enjoy it, and if, even to maintain myself, I now have to go into debt on all sides, if like you I am reduced to seeking help every day from tradesmen to have enough to wear decent clothes? At all events I wanted to talk to you and ask you to help me to sound out my father about my feelings; and if I find him opposed, I am resolved to go away with this lovely girl and enjoy whatever fortune Heaven may will to offer us. To this end I am hunting everywhere for money to borrow; and if your affairs, sister, are like mine, and if our father must oppose our desires, we shall both leave him and free ourselves from this tyranny in which his insupportable avarice has held us for so long.

ÉLISE. It is quite true that every day he gives us more and more reason to regret our mother's death, and that . . .

CLÉANTE. I hear his voice. Let's go somewhere nearby to finish our talk in private; and afterward we'll join forces to attack his obduracy.

Scene 3.   HARPAGON, LA FLÈCHE

HARPAGON. Out of here right now, and no back-talk. Come on, get out of my house, you past master of thievery, you gallows-bird!

LA FLÈCHE *(aside).* I've never seen anything as mean as this cursed old man, and, subject to correction, I think he has the devil in him.

HARPAGON. You're muttering between your teeth.

LA FLÈCHE. Why are you kicking me out?

HARPAGON. You're a fine one, you scoundrel, to ask me for my reasons. Get out quick, before I beat your brains out.

LA FLÈCHE. What have I done to you?

HARPAGON. You've done enough to make me want you to get out.

LA FLÈCHE. Your son, my master, gave me orders to wait for him.

HARPAGON. Go wait for him in the street, and don't stay in my house planted bolt upright like a sentry watching what goes on and making your profit from everything. I don't want to have eternally before me a spy on my affairs, a traitor, whose cursed eyes besiege all my actions, devour what I possess, and ferret around everywhere to see if there isn't anything to rob.

LA FLÈCHE. How the devil do you expect anyone to go about robbing you? Are you a robbable man, when you lock up everything and stand guard day and night?

HARPAGON. I'll lock up what I see fit and stand guard as I like. Isn't that just like one of those spies, who keep watch on whatever you do? *(Aside)* I tremble for fear he may have suspected something about my money. *(Aloud)* Wouldn't you be just the man to start the rumor that I have money hidden in my house?

LA FLÈCHE. You have money hidden?

HARPAGON. No, you rogue, I didn't say that. *(Aside)* He drives me mad. *(Aloud)* I'm wondering whether maliciously you wouldn't go start a rumor that I have.

LA FLÈCHE. Heigho! What does it matter to me whether you have or you don't have, if it comes to the same thing for us?

HARPAGON. A reasoner, are you? I'll give you a piece of that reasoning about your ears. *(He raises his hand to give him a slap.)* Once more, get out of here.

LA FLÈCHE. All right! I'm going.

HARPAGON. Wait. Aren't you taking something of mine with you?

LA FLÈCHE. What would I be taking of yours?

HARPAGON. Come here, let me see. Show me your hands.

LA FLÈCHE. Here they are.

HARPAGON. The others.[1]

LA FLÈCHE. The others?

HARPAGON. Yes.

LA FLÈCHE. Here they are.

HARPAGON *(pointing to* LA FLÈCHE's *breeches).* Haven't you put something in there?

LA FLÈCHE. See for yourself.

HARPAGON *(feeling at the bottom of* LA FLÈCHE's *breeches).* These big breeches are cut out to become receivers for stolen goods; and I wish somebody had been hanged for making them.

LA FLÈCHE *(aside).* Ah! How well a man like this would deserve what he fears! And what joy I would have in robbing him!

HARPAGON. Eh?

LA FLÈCHE. What?

HARPAGON. What are you saying about robbing?

[1] This comic bit about the "other" hands is borrowed from Plautus, *Aulularia,* Act IV, scene 4.

LA FLÈCHE. I say for you to search me everywhere to see if I've been robbing you.

HARPAGON. That's what I mean to do. *(Searches in* LA FLÈCHE's *pockets.)*

LA FLÈCHE. A plague on miserliness and misers!

HARPAGON. How's that? What's that you say?

LA FLÈCHE. What did I say?

HARPAGON. Yes, what did you say about miserliness and misers?

LA FLÈCHE. I said a plague on miserliness and misers.

HARPAGON. Whom are you referring to?

LA FLÈCHE. Misers.

HARPAGON. And who are these misers?

LA FLÈCHE. Niggards and skinflints.

HARPAGON. But whom do you mean by that?

LA FLÈCHE. What are you worrying about?

HARPAGON. I'm worrying about what I must.

LA FLÈCHE. Do you think I mean you?

HARPAGON. I think what I think; but I want you to tell me whom you're talking to when you say that.

LA FLÈCHE. I'm talking . . . I'm talking to my hat.

HARPAGON. And I might just be talking to your thick head.

LA FLÈCHE. Will you stop me from cursing misers?

HARPAGON. No, but I'll stop you from chattering and being insolent. Shut up.

LA FLÈCHE. I'm not mentioning any names.

HARPAGON. I'll thrash you if you speak.

LA FLÈCHE. If the cap fits, wear it.

HARPAGON. Will you shut up?

LA FLÈCHE. Yes—against my will.

HARPAGON. Aha!

LA FLÈCHE *(turning out one of the pockets in his jerkin)*. There, here's another pocket; are you satisfied?

HARPAGON. Come on, give it back to me without a search.

LA FLÈCHE. What?

HARPAGON. What you took from me.

LA FLÈCHE. I didn't take anything at all from you.

HARPAGON. Honestly?

LA FLÈCHE. Honestly.

HARPAGON. Farewell, and go to all the devils in hell.

LA FLÈCHE. That's a nice kind of dismissal.

HARPAGON. Anyway, I charge it against your conscience. *(Alone)* That's a gallowsbird of a valet, who bothers me a lot, and I don't like to see that limping cur around.[2]

Scene 4.   ÉLISE, CLÉANTE, HARPAGON

HARPAGON *(alone)*. It's certainly no small trouble to keep a large sum of money in the house; and happy is the man who has all his pile well invested, and keeps around only what he needs for his expenses. It's quite a job to think up a safe hiding-place anywhere in the whole house; for to me, strong-boxes are suspect, and I don't ever want to trust them; I regard them as just the right bait for thieves, and they're always the first thing they go for. However, I don't know whether I did well to bury in my garden the ten thousand crowns I was paid back yesterday. Ten thousand crowns in gold in your house is a rather . . . *(CLÉANTE and ÉLISE appear, talking in low voices.)* O Heavens! I must have betrayed myself! My excitement carried me away, and I think I spoke out loud while talking this over with myself. *(To CLÉANTE and ÉLISE)* What is it?

[2] Louis Béjart, who played La Flèche, had a limp.

CLÉANTE. Nothing, father.

HARPAGON. Have you been there long?

ÉLISE. We've only just arrived.

HARPAGON. You heard . . .

CLÉANTE. What, father?

HARPAGON. Just now . . .

ÉLISE. What?

HARPAGON. What I just said.

CLÉANTE. No.

HARPAGON. Oh, yes you did, yes you did.

ÉLISE. I *beg* your pardon.

HARPAGON. I see perfectly well that you heard a few words of it. The fact is I was talking to myself about how hard it is to find any money nowadays, and I was saying that any man is fortunate who can have ten thousand crowns in his house.

CLÉANTE. We were hesitating to speak to you for fear of interrupting you.

HARPAGON. I'm very glad to tell you this so you won't get things wrong and imagine I'm saying that I'm the one who has ten thousand crowns.

CLÉANTE. We don't enter into your affairs.

HARPAGON. Would God I had ten thousand crowns!

CLÉANTE. I don't think . . .

HARPAGON. It would be a fine thing for me.

ÉLISE. Those are things . . .

HARPAGON. I could certainly use them.

CLÉANTE. I think . . .

HARPAGON. That would be quite all right with me.

ÉLISE. You're . . .

HARPAGON. And I wouldn't complain as I do that times are hard.

CLÉANTE. Good Lord, father! You've no cause to complain, and everyone knows you're well enough off.

HARPAGON. What? I'm well enough off! Those who say so are liars. Nothing could be more false, and it's a bunch of scoundrels who spread all those rumors.

ÉLISE. Don't get angry.

HARPAGON. It's a strange thing that my own children betray me and become my enemies!

CLÉANTE. Is it being your enemy to say that you have money?

HARPAGON. Yes. That kind of talk, and the expenses you incur, will be the reason why one of these days they'll come and cut my throat in my own house in the belief that I'm made of gold pieces.

CLÉANTE. What great expense do I incur?

HARPAGON. What expense? Is there anything more scandalous than that sumptuous costume that you flaunt around the town? I was scolding your sister yesterday, but this is even worse. That's what cries to Heaven for vengeance; and to take you from head to foot, there'd be enough there to provide a handsome annuity. I've told you twenty times, son, all your ways displease me very much; you're putting on the marquis act like mad; and to go around dressed as you are, you must be robbing me.

CLÉANTE. What? How could I rob you?

HARPAGON. How do I know? Then how do you get the wherewithal to support the way you live?

CLÉANTE. I, father? I gamble; and since I'm very lucky, I put all my winnings on my back.

HARPAGON. That's a very bad way to do. If you're lucky at gambling, you should profit by it, and invest the money you win at decent interest so as to get it back some day. But I'd really like to know, not to speak of the rest, what's the use of all those ribbons you're decked out with from head to foot, and whether half a dozen laces are not enough to fasten a pair of breeches? It's necessary indeed to use money on wigs when you can wear home-grown hair, which costs nothing.

I'll bet that in wigs and ribbons you have at least twenty pistoles' worth; and twenty pistoles in a year bring in eighteen francs six sous and eight deniers, even at only one denier interest on twelve.

CLÉANTE. You're right.

HARPAGON. Let's leave that and talk about something else. (CLÉANTE *and* ÉLISE *exchange glances.*) Huh? (*Aside*) I think they're making signs to each other to steal my purse. (*Aloud*) What do those gestures mean?

ÉLISE. My brother and I are arguing over who shall speak first; and we both have something to tell you.

HARPAGON. And I too have something to tell you both.

CLÉANTE. It's about marriage, father, that we want to speak to you.

HARPAGON. And it's marriage too that I want to talk to you about.

ÉLISE. Oh, father!

HARPAGON. Why that exclamation? Is it the word or the thing, daughter, that frightens you?

CLÉANTE. Marriage may frighten us both, in the way you may understand it; and we fear that our feelings may not be in accord with your choice.

HARPAGON. Have a little patience. Don't be alarmed. I know what you both need; and neither of you will have any reason to complain about anything I intend to do. And to begin at one end of the story: (*To* CLÉANTE) tell me, have you seen a young person named Mariane, who lives not far from here?

CLÉANTE. Yes, father.

HARPAGON. (*To* ÉLISE) And you?

ÉLISE. I've heard of her.

HARPAGON. What do you think of the girl, son?

CLÉANTE. A very charming person.

HARPAGON. Her face?

CLÉANTE. Extremely modest and full of intelligence.

HARPAGON. Her air and manner?

CLÉANTE. Admirable, beyond a doubt.

HARPAGON. Don't you think a girl like that is well worth thinking about?

CLÉANTE. Yes, father.

HARPAGON. And would be a desirable match?

CLÉANTE. Very desirable.

HARPAGON. And gives every promise of making a good wife?

CLÉANTE. Without a doubt.

HARPAGON. And a husband would have satisfaction with her?

CLÉANTE. Assuredly.

HARPAGON. There is one little difficulty: I'm afraid she won't bring with her as much money as one might expect.

CLÉANTE. Ah, father! The money doesn't matter when it's a question of marrying a good woman.

HARPAGON. I beg your pardon, I beg your pardon. But there is this to be said, that if she doesn't bring as much money as one would like, one can try to make it up in other ways.

CLÉANTE. To be sure.

HARPAGON. Well, I'm very glad to see that you share my sentiments; for her modest bearing and her gentleness have won my heart, and I'm determined to marry her, provided she has *some* dowry.

CLÉANTE. Huh?

HARPAGON. What's that?

CLÉANTE. You are determined, you say . . . ?

HARPAGON. To marry Mariane.

CLÉANTE. Who, you? You?

HARPAGON. Yes, me, me, me. What does this mean?

CLÉANTE. I feel a sudden dizziness, and I'm leaving.

HARPAGON. It won't amount to anything. Go into the kitchen quick and have a good drink—of fresh water. *(Exit CLÉANTE)* There's one of your dainty young men for you, with no more vigor than a chicken. Well, daughter, that's what I've decided for myself. As for your brother, I've picked out for him a certain widow that a man came to talk to me about this morning; and as for you, I'm giving you to Seigneur Anselme.

ÉLISE. To Seigneur Anselme?

HARPAGON. Yes, a mature man, prudent and wise, who's not over fifty and who's said to be very wealthy.

ÉLISE *(with a curtsey)*. I don't want to get married, father, if you please.

HARPAGON *(mimicking the curtsey)*. And I, my little daughter, my pet, I want you to get married, if you please.

ÉLISE *(with another curtsey)*. I beg your pardon, father.

HARPAGON *(mimicking the curtsey)*. I beg your pardon, daughter.

ÉLISE *(with another curtsey)*. I am Seigneur Anselme's very humble servant; but with your permission, I won't marry him.

HARPAGON *(mimicking the curtsey)*. I am your very humble valet; but with your permission, you will marry him this evening.

ÉLISE. This evening?

HARPAGON. This evening.

ÉLISE *(with another curtsey)*. That shall not be, father.

HARPAGON *(mimicking the curtsey)*. That shall be, daughter.

ÉLISE. No.

HARPAGON. Yes.

ÉLISE. No, I tell you.

HARPAGON. Yes, I tell you.

ÉLISE. That's something you shall not force me to.

HARPAGON. That's something I shall force you to.

ÉLISE. I'll kill myself rather than marry such a husband.

HARPAGON. You shall not kill yourself, and you shall marry him. But just look at that impertinence! Who ever saw a daughter talk to her father that way?

ÉLISE. Who ever saw a father marry off his daughter that way?

HARPAGON. It's a match to which no one could object; and I bet that everyone will approve of my choice.

ÉLISE. And I bet that no reasonable person could approve of it.

HARPAGON. Here's Valère. Do you want to have him judge between us in this matter?

ÉLISE. I consent.

HARPAGON. Will you be governed by his judgment?

ÉLISE. Yes, I'll abide by what he says.

HARPAGON. That's settled.

Scene 5.   VALÈRE, HARPAGON, ÉLISE

HARPAGON. Here, Valère! We've elected you to tell us which of us is right, my daughter or I.

VALÈRE. It's you, sir, beyond dispute.

HARPAGON. Do you know what we're talking about?

VALÈRE. No, but you couldn't be wrong, and you are reason itself.

HARPAGON. I want to give her this evening as her husband a man as rich as he is wise; and the wench tells me to my face that she wouldn't dream of taking him. What do you say to that?

VALÈRE. What do I say to that?

HARPAGON. Yes.

VALÈRE. Well, ah . . .

HARPAGON. What?

VALÈRE. I say that fundamentally I agree with you, and you can't fail to be right. But at the same time she's not entirely in the wrong, and . . .

HARPAGON. What? Seigneur Anselme is an important match, a gentleman who is a nobleman,[3] mild, sedate, wise, and well off, and who has no children left him from his first marriage. Could she find better?

VALÈRE. That's true. But she might say to you that this is hurrying things a bit, and that there ought to be at least some time to see if her inclination can be reconciled with . . .

HARPAGON. It's an opportunity we must quickly seize by the forelock. I find an advantage here that I wouldn't find elsewhere; he undertakes to take her without dowry.

VALÈRE. Without dowry?

HARPAGON. Yes.

VALÈRE. Ah! I say no more. Do you see? That's a completely convincing reason; you have to give in to that.

HARPAGON. It's a considerable saving for me.

VALÈRE. Assuredly, there's no denying that. It is true that your daughter may point out to you that marriage is a more important affair than some may think; that the happiness or unhappiness of her whole lifetime is at stake; and that a commitment that must last until death should never be made except with great precautions.

HARPAGON. Without dowry.

VALÈRE. You're right. That decides the whole thing, of course. There are people who might tell you that on such occasions a daughter's inclinations are something that should no doubt be considered, and that this great disparity of age, temperament, and feelings makes a marriage subject to very unpleasant accidents.

HARPAGON. Without dowry.

VALÈRE. Ah! There's no answer to that, as anyone knows; who

---

[3] In Molière's day, *gentilhomme* (gentleman) meant a nobleman by birth, while a nobleman might be only recently ennobled.

the devil can go against that? It's not that there aren't a lot of
fathers who would rather look out for their daughters' satisfaction than for the money they might give away; who would
not want to sacrifice them to self-interest, and would seek
more than anything else to infuse into a marriage that sweet
conformity which maintains in it at all times honor, tranquillity, and joy, and which . . .

HARPAGON. Without dowry.

VALÈRE. That's true; that stops every mouth: *without dowry*.
How can anyone resist a reason like that one?

HARPAGON (*aside, looking toward the garden*). What's that? It
seems to me I hear a dog barking. Could somebody be after
my money? (*To* VALÈRE) Don't move, I'll be right back.
                                                        (*Exit*)

ÉLISE. Are you joking, Valère, to talk to him the way you do?

VALÈRE. It's so as not to exasperate him and to get around him
the better. To oppose his feelings head on is the way to spoil
everything; and there are some people whom you have to take
only from an angle, temperaments hostile to any resistance,
restive natures, who shy from the truth, who always balk at
the straight road of reason, and whom you can lead only by
gradually turning them in the direction you want them to go.
Pretend to give your consent to what he wants, you'll get your
way better, and . . .

ÉLISE. But this marriage, Valère?

VALÈRE. We'll find some roundabout way to break it off.

ÉLISE. But what can we come up with, if it's to take place
this evening?

VALÈRE. You must ask for a delay, and pretend to have some
illness.

ÉLISE. But they'll discover the pretense if they call the doctors.

VALÈRE. Are you joking? What do they know about it? Come,
come, with them you can have whatever illness you please,
they'll find reasons to tell you where it comes from.

HARPAGON (*returning; to himself*). It's nothing, thank God.

VALÈRE. Finally, our last resort is that flight can make us safe from everything; and if your love, fair Elise, is capable of a strength . . . *(Seeing* HARPAGON*)* Yes, a daughter must obey her father. She must not consider how a husband looks, and when the great argument of *without dowry* is involved, she must be ready to take whatever is given her.

HARPAGON. Good. That's the way to talk.

VALÈRE. Sir, I ask your pardon if I get carried away a bit and make bold to talk to her as I am doing.

HARPAGON. What? I'm delighted, and I want you to assume absolute power over her. *(To* ÉLISE*)* Yes, it's no use trying to run away. I give him the authority that Heaven gives me over you, and I mean to have you do whatever he tells you.

VALÈRE. *(To* ÉLISE*)* Now will you resist my remonstrances! *(To* HARPAGON*)* Sir, I'm going to follow her and continue the lessons I was teaching her.

HARPAGON. Yes, I'll be much obliged. Assuredly . . .

VALÈRE. It's good to keep a tight rein on her.

HARPAGON. That's true. We must . . .

VALÈRE. Don't you worry. I think I can bring her around.

HARPAGON. Do, do. I'm off to take a little turn in town, and I'll be right back.

VALÈRE. Yes, money is more precious than anything in the world, and you should thank Heaven for giving you such a fine man for a father. He knows what life is about. When someone offers to take a girl without dowry, one shouldn't look any further. Everything is wrapped up in that, and *without dowry* takes the place of beauty, youth, birth, honor, wisdom, and probity.

HARPAGON. Ah! Good boy! Spoken like an oracle. Happy the man who can have a servant like him!

ACT II

Scene 1. CLÉANTE, LA FLÈCHE

CLÉANTE. Ah! You scoundrel, where in the world have you been hiding? Didn't I give you orders . . . ?

LA FLÈCHE. Yes, sir, and I came here to wait for you and not stir; but your honorable father, that most ungracious of men, drove me out against my will, and I ran the risk of a beating.

CLÉANTE. How is our affair going? Things are more urgent than ever; and since I last saw you I have found out that my father is my rival.

LA FLÈCHE. Your father in love?

CLÉANTE. Yes, and I had all kinds of trouble not to let him see how much this news upset me.

LA FLÈCHE. Him, meddling in love! What the devil does he think he's doing? Is he trying to play some kind of a joke on everybody? And was love made for people built like him?

CLÉANTE. For my sins, this passion had to come into his head.

LA FLÈCHE. But why keep your love a mystery to him?

CLÉANTE. To give him less reason for suspicion, and to keep the easiest ways open to myself, in case of need, to prevent this marriage. What answer did they give you?

LA FLÈCHE. My word, sir, people who borrow are very unfortunate; and a person has to put up with some pretty strange things when, like you, he has to pass through the hands of the money-lenders.

CLÉANTE. The deal won't come off?

LA FLÈCHE. Pardon me. Our Maître Simon, the broker they gave us, an active man and full of zeal, says he has done wonders for you; and he insists that your face alone won his heart.

CLÉANTE. I'll get the fifteen thousand francs I'm asking for?

LA FLÈCHE. Yes, but on a few little conditions that you will have to accept if you want these things to be done.

CLÉANTE. Did he have you talk to the person who is to lend the money?

LA FLÈCHE. Oh, really, now, it doesn't work that way. He takes even more care to remain unknown than you, and these are much greater mysteries than you think. They won't tell his name at all, and today they are to bring the two of you together in a house borrowed for the purpose, to learn from your own mouth about your means and your family; and I have no doubt at all that your father's name alone will make things easy.

CLÉANTE. And especially since our mother is dead, and they can't keep me from coming into her estate.

LA FLÈCHE. Here are a few articles that he dictated himself to our go-between, to be shown you before doing anything:
Provided that the lender see all his securities, and that the borrower be of age and of a family whose estate is ample, solid, secure, clear and free of all encumbrance, a good precise statement of obligation shall be executed before a notary, the most honest man possible, who to this purpose shall be chosen by the lender, to whom it is most important that the act be drawn up in due form.

CLÉANTE. There's nothing to object to in that.

LA FLÈCHE. *The lender, to have no scruples on his conscience, undertakes to lend the money at only one denier for eighteen.*

CLÉANTE. One denier for eighteen! Gad! That's honorable. There's no reason to complain.

LA FLÈCHE. That's true.
But since the said lender does not have at hand the sum in question, and, to please the borrower, is himself constrained to borrow it from another at the rate of one denier

for five, it will be proper that the said first borrower shall pay this interest, without prejudice to the rest, considering that it is only to oblige him that the said lender undertakes to borrow this.

CLÉANTE. What the devil! What a bloodsucker! What a robber! That's more than one denier for four.

LA FLÈCHE. That's true; that's just what I said. That's something for you to see about.

CLÉANTE. What do you expect me to see? I need money, and I'll simply have to consent to everything.

LA FLÈCHE. That's the answer I gave.

CLÉANTE. Is there anything else?

LA FLÈCHE. Just one little article more.

Of the fifteen thousand francs that are asked, the lender will be able to pay out in cash only twelve thousand, and for the remaining thousand crowns[4] the borrower will have to take the used clothing, effects, and jewelry listed in the following memorandum, and which the said lender has set, in good faith, at the most moderate price that was possible for him.

CLÉANTE. What does this mean?

LA FLÈCHE. Listen to the memorandum.

First, one four-poster bed with hangings of Hungarian lace[5] very handsomely applied to an olive-colored cloth, with six chairs and a counterpane of the same; the whole lot in very good condition and lined with light shot taffeta in red and blue.

Plus one tester of good Aumale serge, in old rose, with silk fringes.

CLÉANTE. What does he expect me to do with that?

LA FLÈCHE. Wait.

Plus one tapestry hanging representing the loves of Gombaut and Macée.[6]

Plus one big walnut table with twelve columns or turned

---

4 The crown equaled three francs.
5 A very common material.
6 From a bucolic novel in vogue long before, under Henry IV.

*legs, which can be pulled out at either end, and provided
with its six stools to go under it.*

CLÉANTE. Gad, what have I to do . . . ?

LA FLÈCHE. Have patience.
   *Plus three large muskets all inlaid with mother-of-pearl,
with the three forked rests for them.*
   *Plus one brick furnace with two retorts and three flasks,
very useful for those with an interest in distilling.*

CLÉANTE. I'm going mad.

LA FLÈCHE. Take it easy.
   *Plus one Bologna lute furnished with all its strings, or
nearly all.*
   Plus one game of "trou-madame"[7] *and one checkerboard,
with one game of "goose"*[8] *renewed from the Greeks, very
suitable for passing the time when one has nothing to do.*
   *Plus one lizard skin, three and a half feet long, stuffed
with hay, a very pleasing curio to hang from the ceiling of
a room.*
   *The whole lot aforementioned, honestly worth more than
four thousand five hundred francs, and reduced to a thousand crowns through the discretion of the lender.*

CLÉANTE. The plague choke him with his discretion, the traitor,
the cutthroat! Did you ever hear of such usury? And isn't
he content with the insane interest he demands without
also forcing me to take, for three thousand francs, the old
relics he picks up? I won't get two hundred crowns for all
that; and yet I've simply got to make up my mind to consent to what he wants, for he's in a position to make me
accept anything, and the scoundrel has got me with a dagger at my throat.

LA FLÈCHE. No offense, sir, but I see you precisely on the
highroad to ruin that Panurge[9] took, taking money in advance, buying dear, selling cheap, and eating your wheat in
the blade.

7 A form of bagatelle played with a cue and balls on a board with arches
and holes.
8 A game played with counters on a board.
9 In Rabelais, *Gargantua and Pantagruel*, Book III, chapter 2. The
quotation, which begins with "taking money," is word for word.

CLÉANTE. What do you want me to do? That's what young men are reduced to by the cursed avarice of fathers; and after that people wonder why sons wish their fathers would die.

LA FLÈCHE. I must admit that yours would make the most sedate man in the world angry at his niggardliness. Heaven be praised, I have no great inclination to be hanged; and among my colleagues whom I see dabbling in a lot of little deals, I know how to steer clear, and keep prudently out of all those gallantries that smell the least bit of the gallows; but to tell you the truth, by the way he acts, he would really tempt me to rob him; and in robbing him I would think I was performing a meritorious action.

CLÉANTE. Give me that memorandum a second for another look.

Scene 2. MAÎTRE SIMON, HARPAGON, CLÉANTE, LA FLÈCHE

MAÎTRE SIMON. Yes, sir, it's a young man who needs money. His affairs make it urgent for him to get some, and he'll put up with everything you prescribe.

HARPAGON. But do you think, Maître Simon, that there's no risk? And do you know the name, the means, and the family of the man you are speaking for?

MAÎTRE SIMON. No, I can't give you full information on all that, and it was only by chance that I was put in touch with him; but you will be informed about everything by himself, and his man has assured me that you will be satisfied when you know him. All I can tell you is that his family is very rich, he has already lost his mother, and he will guarantee, if you want, that his father will die in the next eight months.

HARPAGON. Well, that's something. Charity, Maître Simon, obliges us to do favors to people when we can.

MAÎTRE SIMON. Of course.

LA FLÈCHE *(softly, to* CLÉANTE*)*. What does this mean? Our Maître Simon talking to your father?

CLÉANTE *(softly, to* LA FLÈCHE*)*. Could someone have told him who I am? And would you be the man to betray us?

MAÎTRE SIMON. Aha! You are certainly in a hurry! Who told you it was here? *(To* HARPAGON*)* At least it wasn't I, sir, who revealed to them your name and address; but in my opinion there's no great harm in that. These are people of discretion, and you can work things out together here.

HARPAGON. What's this?

MAÎTRE SIMON. This gentleman is the person who wants to borrow from you the fifteen thousand francs I spoke to you about.

HARPAGON. What, you scoundrel? It's you who abandon yourself to these guilty extremities?

CLÉANTE. What, father? It's you who lend yourself to these shameful actions?

(Exit MAÎTRE SIMON and LA FLÈCHE)

HARPAGON. It's you who are trying to ruin yourself by such disgraceful borrowings?

CLÉANTE. It's you who are trying to enrich yourself by such criminal usury?

HARPAGON. Do you really dare appear before me after this?

CLÉANTE. Do you really dare show your face to the world after this?

HARPAGON. Tell me, aren't you ashamed to descend to such debauch? to plunge headlong into frightful expenses? and to squander shamefully the money that your parents amassed for you by the sweat of their brow?

CLÉANTE. Don't you blush to dishonor your position by the deals you make? to sacrifice glory and reputation to the insatiable desire to pile up one crown-piece on another, and to outdo, in the matter of interest, the most infamous dodges that the most notorious usurers ever invented?

HARPAGON. Get out of my sight, you rogue! Get out of my sight!

CLÉANTE. Which one is more criminal, in your opinion, the man who buys a sum of money he needs, or the man who steals a sum of money that he has no use for?

HARPAGON. Out of here, I tell you, and don't torment my ears.   *(Exit* CLÉANTE*)*
I'm not sorry about this adventure; and it's a warning to me to keep an eye more than ever on all his actions.

Scene 3.   FROSINE, HARPAGON

FROSINE. Sir . . .

HARPAGON. Wait a moment; I'll come back and talk to you. *(Aside)* It's about time I went and took a little look at my money.

Scene 4.   LA FLÈCHE, FROSINE

LA FLÈCHE *(not seeing* FROSINE*)*. It's an utterly comic adventure. Somewhere he must have a whole big warehouse of used furniture, for we didn't recognize anything in the memorandum we have.

FROSINE. Oh, it's you, my poor La Flèche? Fancy meeting you!

LA FLÈCHE. Aha! It's you, Frosine. What are you doing here?

FROSINE. What I do everywhere else: serving as a go-between, making myself useful to people, and profiting as best I can from the little talents I may have. You know that in this world you have to live by your wits, and that Heaven has given people like me no other revenue than intrigue and ingenuity.

LA FLÈCHE. Do you have some business with the master of the house?

FROSINE. Yes, I'm handling a little matter for him for which I hope to be compensated.

LA FLÈCHE. By him? Oh, my word! You'll be very clever if you get anything out of him; and I warn you that in here money is very expensive.

FROSINE. There are certain services that are wondrously effective.

LA FLÈCHE. I am your humble servant, and you don't yet know *Seigneur* Harpagon. Seigneur Harpagon is of all humans the least human human; the mortal of all mortals who is hardest and most close-fisted. There is no service that drives his gratitude to the point of making him open his hands. Praise, esteem, and good will in words, friendliness—all you like; but money—nothing doing. There is nothing more dry and arid than his good graces and his compliments; and *give* is a word for which he has such an aversion that he never says *I give you*, but *I lend you good day.*

FROSINE. Good Lord! I know the art of milking men, I have the secret of winning their tenderness, tickling their hearts, and finding their soft spots.

LA FLÈCHE. Useless trifles here. I defy you to soften up the man in question in the matter of money. On that score he's cruel, so cruel as to drive anyone to despair; a person could die and he wouldn't budge. In a word, he loves money, more than reputation, honor, and virtue; and the sight of anyone asking for it throws him into convulsions. That's striking him in his vulnerable spot, that's piercing his heart, that's tearing out his entrails; and if . . . But he's coming back; I'm off.

Scene 5. HARPAGON, FROSINE

HARPAGON. *(Aside)* Everything is as it should be. *(To* FROSINE*)* Well, what is it, Frosine?

FROSINE. Oh my Heavens, how well you look! And what a picture of health you are!

HARPAGON. Who, me?

FROSINE. I've never seen you looking so fresh and sprightly.

HARPAGON. Really?

FROSINE. What? You've never in your life been as young as you are now; and I see people of twenty-five who are older than you.

HARPAGON. And yet, Frosine, I'm a good sixty years old.

FROSINE. Well, sixty, what's that? A lot indeed! That's the flower of life, and you're just coming into your prime.

HARPAGON. That's true; but nevertheless, as I see it, twenty years less would do me no harm.

FROSINE. Are you joking? You don't need that, and you're built to live to a hundred.

HARPAGON. You think so?

FROSINE. Indeed I do. You show all the indications of it. Hold still a moment. Oh, look, right there between your eyes, there's a sign of long life!

HARPAGON. You're an expert in those things?

FROSINE. Certainly. Show me your hand. Oh, my goodness, what a life line!

HARPAGON. How's that?

FROSINE. Don't you see where that line goes to?

HARPAGON. Well, what does that mean?

FROSINE. My word! I said a hundred; but you'll pass six score.

HARPAGON. Is it possible?

FROSINE. They'll have to kill you, I tell you; and you'll bury your children and your children's children.

HARPAGON. Splendid. How is our business going?

FROSINE. Need you ask? And do I ever take a hand in anything without making it come out? Above all I have a marvelous talent for matchmaking; there aren't two people in the world that I couldn't find a way to pair off in a

short time; and I think that if I took it into my head I could marry the Grand Turk to the Republic of Venice. Of course there were no such great difficulties in this affair. Since I have dealings with the ladies, I've talked to them both about you at length, and I've told the mother about the designs you had formed on Mariane, from seeing her pass in the street and take the air at her window.

HARPAGON. She answered . . .

FROSINE. She received the proposal with joy; and when I gave her to understand that you were very anxious to have her daughter present this evening at the signing of your own daughter's marriage contract, she consented without difficulty and entrusted her to me for that purpose.

HARPAGON. You see, Frosine, I am obliged to give a supper for Seigneur Anselme, and I'd like very much for her to share in the treat.

FROSINE. You're right. After dinner she's to pay a visit to your daughter, and from there she plans to go and make a trip to the fair, and then come to the supper.

HARPAGON. Well! They'll go together in my carriage, which I'll lend them.

FROSINE. That's just the thing for her.

HARPAGON. But Frosine, have you talked with the mother about the dowry she can give her daughter? Did you tell her that she had to bestir herself, make some effort, and bleed herself, for an occasion like this one? For after all, one does not marry a girl unless she brings something.

FROSINE. What? She's a girl that will bring you twelve thousand francs a year.

HARPAGON. Twelve thousand francs a year!

FROSINE. Yes. In the first place, she's trained and brought up to eat very sparingly; she's a girl accustomed to live on salad, milk, cheese, and apples, and consequently she will have no need of a well-served table, nor exquisite consommés, nor eternal broths of peeled barley, nor the other delicacies that another woman would require; and that is no such small matter but that it will amount every year to three

thousand francs at the least. Besides that she has no taste
for anything but very simple dress, and does not like fancy
clothes or rich jewelry or sumptuous furnishings, which
others of her sex go in for so heartily; and this item is
worth more than four thousand francs a year. Moreover,
she has a horrible aversion to gambling, which is not a
common trait in today's women; and I know one in our
neighborhood who lost twenty thousand francs at "trente-et-
quarante" this year. But let's take only a quarter of that.
Five thousand francs a year for gambling, and four thousand
francs on clothes and jewelry, that makes nine thousand
francs; and a thousand crowns that we put down for food:
doesn't that give you your twelve thousand francs of hard
money per year?

HARPAGON. Yes, that's not bad; but there's nothing real in that
accounting.

FROSINE. Pardon me! Isn't it something real to bring you in
marriage a great sobriety, the inheritance of a great love of
simplicity in adornment, and the acquisition of a great fund
of hatred for gambling?

HARPAGON. It's just a joke to try to make up a dowry for
me out of all the expenses that she won't incur. I won't
give any quittance for what I don't receive; and I've got
to get some money out of this.

FROSINE. Good Lord! You'll get plenty; and they spoke to
me of certain money they have abroad that you will become master of.

HARPAGON. We'll have to look into that. But Frosine, there's
another thing that worries me. The girl is young, as you
see; and young folk ordinarily like only those like themselves and seek only their company. I'm afraid that a man
of my age may not be to her taste; and that that may come
to produce in my house certain little disorders that would
not suit me.

FROSINE. Ah, how little you know her! That's another pe-
culiarity I was going to mention to you. She has a frightful
aversion for young men, and loves only old ones.

HARPAGON. She?

FROSINE. Yes, she. I wish you had heard her talk on the subject. She can't abide the sight of a young man at all; but she is never more delighted, she says, than when she can see a handsome old man with a majestic beard. The eldest are the most charming for her, and I warn you not to go making yourself look younger than you are. She wants a man at the very least to be in his sixties; and not four months ago, all ready to be married, she flatly broke off the marriage on the grounds that her sweetheart revealed that he was only fifty-six and didn't put on spectacles to sign the contract.

HARPAGON. Just on those grounds?

FROSINE. Yes. She says that fifty-six is no satisfaction to her; and most of all, she favors noses that wear spectacles.

HARPAGON. What you're telling me is a very novel thing.

FROSINE. It goes further than I could tell you. In her bedroom you see a few pictures and prints; but what do you think they are? Adonises, Cephaluses,[10] Parises, and Apollos? No; fine portraits of Saturn, of King Priam, of old Nestor, and of good father Anchises on the shoulders of his son.[11]

HARPAGON. That's admirable! I never would have thought it; and I am delighted to learn that her taste runs that way. Indeed, if I'd been a woman, I wouldn't have liked young men.

FROSINE. I should think not. Young men are a fine lot, for anyone to love! They're pretty boys with running noses, fine show-offs, to make anyone crave their skin; and I'd certainly like to know what relish there is to them.

HARPAGON. As for me, I don't find any; and I don't know how it is that there are women who love them so.

FROSINE. You'd have to be raving mad. To find youth attractive! Does that make sense? Those blond youngsters, are they men? And can anybody take to those creatures?

10 Cephalus was loved by Eos for his beauty.
11 Aeneas carried his father Anchises out of Troy on his shoulders when the city was destroyed by the Greeks.

HARPAGON. That's what I keep saying every day: with their voices like milk-fed hens, and their three little wisps of beard turned up like a cat's whiskers, their wigs of tow, their flowing breeches, and all unbuttoned over the stomach!

FROSINE. Oh, they're mighty well got up indeed compared with a man like you! Now you, you're a man. There's something here to satisfy the sight; and this is the way you have to be built and dressed to inspire love.

HARPAGON. You like my looks?

FROSINE. Do I? You're irresistible, and your face is fit for a painting. Turn around a little, please. Couldn't be better. Let me see you walk. There's a fine figure of a man—trim, free and easy as it should be, and with no sign of imperfection.

HARPAGON. I've nothing serious, thank God. There's just my catarrh that gets me from time to time.

FROSINE. That's nothing. Your catarrh is not unbecoming to you, and you cough with grace.

HARPAGON. Just tell me now: hasn't Mariane seen me yet? Hasn't she noticed me passing by?

FROSINE. No, but we've talked a lot about you. I've described your person to her, and I did not fail to praise your merit, and the advantage it would be for her to have a husband like you.

HARPAGON. You've done well, and I thank you for it.

FROSINE. I *would* like to make one small request of you, sir. (HARPAGON *looks severe.*) I have a lawsuit that I'm on the point of losing for lack of a little money; and you could easily enable me to win the case, if you were to show me a little kindness.—You could never believe how delighted she will be to see you. (HARPAGON *looks cheerful again.*) Ah, how pleased with you she will be! And what a wonderful effect that old-fashioned ruff of yours will have on her fancy! But above all she'll be charmed with your breeches, attached as they are to your doublet with laces; it's enough to make her crazy about you; and a lover with laced-up breeches will be a wonderful treat for her.

HARPAGON. Really, I'm enchanted to have you tell me this.

FROSINE. Truly, sir, this lawsuit is a matter of very great consequence to me. *(HARPAGON looks severe again.)* I'm ruined if I lose it; and some small assistance would put my affairs back in order.—I wish you'd seen how delighted she was to hear me talk about you. *(HARPAGON looks cheerful again.)* Joy shone in her eyes at the account of your qualities; and in short, I made her extremely impatient to see this marriage all settled.

HARPAGON. You've given me great pleasure, Frosine; and I confess I'm extremely obliged to you.

FROSINE. I beseech you, sir, to give me the little assistance I'm asking of you. *(HARPAGON looks severe again.)* It will put me on my feet again, and I'll be eternally grateful to you.

HARPAGON. Good-by. I'm going to finish my letters.

FROSINE. I assure you, sir, that you could never give me relief in greater need.

HARPAGON. I'll give orders to have my carriage all ready to take you two to the fair.

FROSINE. I wouldn't trouble you if I weren't forced to by necessity.

HARPAGON. And I'll see to it that we have supper early, so as not to make you ill waiting.

FROSINE. Don't refuse me the favor I'm begging you for.—You couldn't believe, sir, the pleasure that . . .

HARPAGON. I'm off. Someone's calling me. See you anon. *(Exit)*

FROSINE. I hope a fever gets you, you stingy dog, and takes you straight to the devil! The skinflint held out against all my attacks! But I mustn't give up the business for all that; and in any case I've got the other side, from which I am certain to get a good reward.

ACT III

Scene 1. HARPAGON, CLÉANTE, ÉLISE, VALÈRE, DAME CLAUDE,
MAÎTRE JACQUES, BRINDAVOINE, LA MERLUCHE

HARPAGON. All right, come here all of you while I give you my
orders for this evening and assign everyone his job. Come
here, Dame Claude. Let's start with you. *(She is holding
a broom.)* Good, I see you're armed. I entrust you with the
task of cleaning up everywhere; and above all, take care
not to rub the furniture too hard, for fear of wearing it out.
Besides that, I assign to you the government of the bottles
during the supper; and if there's one missing or anything
broken, I'll hold you responsible and deduct it from your
wages.

MAÎTRE JACQUES *(aside).* A politic punishment.

HARPAGON. Off you go. *(Exit* DAME CLAUDE*)* You, Brindavoine,
and you, La Merluche, I establish you in charge of rinsing
the glasses and serving the drink; but only when people are
thirsty, and not in the manner of some impertinent lackeys
who egg people on and put them in mind of drinking when
they're not thinking about it. Wait until they ask you more
than once, and remember always to take around plenty of
water.

MAÎTRE JACQUES. Yes, pure wine goes to your head.

LA MERLUCHE. Shall we be taking off our aprons, sir?

HARPAGON. Yes, when you see the people coming; and take
care not to spoil your clothes.

BRINDAVOINE. You know very well, sir, that one of the fore-
flaps of my doublet is covered with a big spot of oil from the
lamp.

168

LA MERLUCHE. And me, sir, I got a big hole in the seat of my breeches, and with all respect, people can see . . .

HARPAGON. Peace. Arrange that adroitly against the wall, and always face the company. (HARPAGON *puts his hat in front of his doublet to show* BRINDAVOINE *what he must do to hide the oil spot.*) And you, always hold your hat thus when you serve. (*To* ÉLISE) As for you, daughter, you'll keep an eye on what is cleared away, and take care that nothing is wasted. That's quite fitting for a daughter. But meanwhile prepare to receive my fiancée well. She's coming to visit you and take you to the fair with her. Do you hear what I'm telling you?

ÉLISE. Yes, father.

HARPAGON. And you, my fine fop of a son, whom I am kind enough to forgive for that matter just now, don't go and take it into your head to show her a sour face either.

CLÉANTE. I, father, a sour face? And for what reason?

HARPAGON. Oh Lord! We know the way children carry on whose fathers remarry, and how they usually look at what we call a stepmother. But if you want me to lose all remembrance of your latest escapade, I recommend to you above all to greet this person with a friendly face, and in short to give her the best welcome you possibly can.

CLÉANTE. To tell you the truth, father, I can't promise you to be very glad that she is to become my stepmother; I'd be lying if I told you so; but as for receiving her well and showing her a friendly face, I promise to obey you to the letter on that score.

HARPAGON. All right, be sure you do.

CLÉANTE. You'll see that you have no reason to complain.

HARPAGON. You will do wisely. Valère, help me in this. Here now, Maître Jacques, come here, I've kept you for the last.

MAÎTRE JACQUES. Is it your coachman, sir, or your cook that you want to speak to? For I'm both.

HARPAGON. Both.

MAÎTRE JACQUES. But which one first?

HARPAGON. The cook.

MAÎTRE JACQUES. Then wait, please. (*He takes off his coachman's overcoat and hat and appears dressed as a cook.*)

HARPAGON. What the devil kind of a ceremony is that?

MAÎTRE JACQUES. I await your orders.

HARPAGON. I have committed myself, Maître Jacques, to giving a supper this evening.

MAÎTRE JACQUES (*aside*). Will wonders never cease?

HARPAGON. Now tell me, will you give us a good meal?

MAÎTRE JACQUES. Yes, if you give me plenty of money.

HARPAGON. What the devil, always money! They seem to have nothing else to say but "Money, money, money." Oh, that's the only word in their mouths: "Money." Always talking about money! That's the sword by their bedside, money.

VALÈRE. I've never heard a more pointless answer than that. That's a great wonder, to make a good meal with lots of money! It's one of the easiest things in the world, and any poor fool can do as much; but to show some ability you've got to talk about making a good meal with little money.

MAÎTRE JACQUES. A good meal with little money!

VALÈRE. Yes.

MAÎTRE JACQUES. Upon my word, Mr. Steward, you'll do us a favor by showing us that secret, and taking over my job as cook, since you're meddling with being a factotum here.

HARPAGON. Be quiet. What will we need?

MAÎTRE JACQUES. There's Mr. Steward of yours, who'll give you a good meal for little money.

HARPAGON. Hey! I want you to answer me.

MAÎTRE JACQUES. How many of you will there be at table?

HARPAGON. There'll be eight or ten of us; but figure on only eight; when there's enough to eat for eight, there's certainly enough for ten.

VALÈRE. Obviously.

MAÎTRE JACQUES. Well! You'll need four big soups, and five courses.[12] Soups . . . entrées . . .

HARPAGON. What the devil! That's enough to treat a whole town.

MAÎTRE JACQUES. A roast . . .

HARPAGON (*putting his hand over* MAÎTRE JACQUES' *mouth*). Ah, traitor! You're eating up everything I own.

MAÎTRE JACQUES. Side dishes . . .

HARPAGON. Still at it?

VALÈRE. Do you want to make everybody burst? And did the master invite people in order to kill them with too much food? Go read up a bit on the precepts for health, and ask the doctors if there's anything more prejudicial to man than eating to excess.

HARPAGON. He's right.

VALÈRE. Learn, Maître Jacques, you and the likes of you, that a table overloaded with food is a deathtrap; that to be a true friend to those you invite, frugality must reign in the meals you give; and that, as one of the ancients put it, *we must eat to live, and not live to eat.*[13]

HARPAGON. Ah! That's well put! Come here, let me embrace you for that saying. That's the finest precept I've ever heard in my life. *We must live to eat, and not eat to li* . . . No, that's not it. How does it go?

VALÈRE. *That we must eat to live, and not live to eat.*

HARPAGON. Yes. (*To* MAÎTRE JACQUES) Do you hear? (*To* VALÈRE) Who was the great man who said that?

VALÈRE. I don't remember his name now.

HARPAGON. Remember to write down those words for me; I want to have them engraved in letters of gold on the mantelpiece in my dining room.

12 Here the 1682 edition gives a long enumeration of choice dishes.
13 A famous ancient saying attributed by Plutarch to Socrates.

VALÈRE. I won't fail to. And for your supper, you need only leave it to me: I'll arrange it all as it should be.

HARPAGON. Then do.

MAÎTRE JACQUES. All the better; I'll have that much less trouble.

HARPAGON. We'll have to have some of those things that people don't eat much of and that fill you up right away: a good fat lamb stew, and a potted pie well stuffed with chestnuts.

VALÈRE. Rely on me.

HARPAGON. Now, Maître Jacques, my carriage needs to be cleaned.

MAÎTRE JACQUES. Wait. This is for the coachman. *(He puts his coat on again.)* You were saying . . . ?

HARPAGON. That my carriage needs to be cleaned and my horses got ready to drive to the fair . . .

MAÎTRE JACQUES. Your horses, sir? My word, they're in no condition at all to walk. I won't tell you that they're down on their litter, the poor beasts don't have any, and it would be no way to talk; but you make them observe such austere fasts that they are nothing any more but ideas or phantoms or shadows of horses.

HARPAGON. They're sick indeed! They don't do anything.

MAÎTRE JACQUES. And because they don't do anything, sir, don't they need to eat anything? It would be much better for them, poor creatures, to work a lot and eat likewise. It breaks my heart to see them so emaciated; for the fact is I have such a tender feeling for my horses that when I see them suffer, it seems to be happening to me. Every day I take things out of my own mouth for them; and, sir, it's a sign of too harsh a nature if a man has no pity on his neighbor.

HARPAGON. It won't be any great effort to go as far as the fair.

MAÎTRE JACQUES. No, sir, I haven't the heart to drive them, and it would go against my conscience to give them the whip in the state they're in. How do you expect them to drag a carriage when they can't even drag themselves along?

VALÈRE. Sir, I'll get our neighbor Le Picard to take on the job of driving them; and we'll need him here too to get the supper ready.

MAÎTRE JACQUES. So be it. I'd still rather they died under someone else's hand than mine.

VALÈRE. Maître Jacques is acting very reasonable.

MAÎTRE JACQUES. Mr. Steward is acting very indispensable.

HARPAGON. Peace!

MAÎTRE JACQUES. Sir, I can't stand flatterers; and I see that whatever he does, his perpetual checks on the bread and the wine, the wood, the salt, and the candles, are nothing but scratching your back and getting on your good side. That makes me mad, and I'm angered every day to hear what people say about you; for after all I have a soft spot in my heart for you in spite of myself; and after my horses, you are the person I like best.

HARPAGON. Might I learn from you, Maître Jacques, what people say about me?

MAÎTRE JACQUES. Yes, sir, if I could be sure it wouldn't make you angry.

HARPAGON. No, not in the least.

MAÎTRE JACQUES. Pardon me. I know very well that I'd put you in a rage.

HARPAGON. Not at all. On the contrary, it will give me pleasure, and I'm very glad to learn how people talk about me.

MAÎTRE JACQUES. Since you want it, sir, I'll tell you frankly that people everywhere make fun of you; that from every side they toss a hundred jokes at us on your account; and that they couldn't be more delighted than in catching you with your pants down and telling stories constantly about your stinginess. One man says that you have special almanacs printed in which you double the number of fast days and vigils, so as to profit by the fasts that you force upon your household. Another says that you always have a quarrel ready to pick with your valets when it's time for presents or for them to leave you, so you can find a reason for not giving them anything. This man tells how you took the cat of one of your neighbors to court for having eaten up the remains of a leg of lamb of yours. That man tells how you were caught one night going, yourself, to steal your horses' oats; and that your coachman, who was the one before me, in the dark, gave you I don't know how many blows with a stick, which you never wanted to say anything about. In short, do you want me to tell you how it is? A man can't go anywhere where he won't hear you hauled over the coals; you are a by-word and a laughingstock to everybody; and nobody ever speaks about you except as a miser, a skinflint, a penny-pincher and a usurer.

HARPAGON *(beating him)*. You are a numbskull, a rogue, and an impudent scoundrel.

MAÎTRE JACQUES. Well! Didn't I guess right? You wouldn't believe me. I told you I'd make you angry if I told you the truth.

HARPAGON. That'll teach you how to talk.

Scene 2.   MAÎTRE JACQUES, VALÈRE

VALÈRE *(laughing)*. From what I can see, Maître Jacques, your frankness is ill repaid.

MAÎTRE JACQUES. By gad, Mr. Upstart, you who like to play important, it's none of your business. Laugh at your own beatings when you get them, and don't come laughing at mine.

VALÈRE. Ah! Sir Maître Jacques, don't be angry, I beg you.

MAÎTRE JACQUES. *(Aside)* Oh! sweet talk! I'll play tough, and if he's fool enough to be afraid of me, I'll give him a bit of a drubbing. *(Aloud)* Do you realize, Mr. Laugher, that me, I'm not laughing, and that if you make me mad I'll make you laugh out of the other side of your mouth? (MAÎTRE JACQUES *pushes* VALÈRE *to the end of the stage, threatening him.*)

VALÈRE. Eh! gently.

MAÎTRE JACQUES. What do you mean, gently? That doesn't suit me.

VALÈRE. I pray you.

MAÎTRE JACQUES. You're an impertinent fellow.

VALÈRE. Sir Maître Jacques.

MAÎTRE JACQUES. I won't give you two cents for your "Sir Maître Jacques." If I take a stick to you, I'll give you a sound thrashing.

VALÈRE (makes him retreat as much as he had done). What, a stick?

MAÎTRE JACQUES. Oh, I don't mean that.

VALÈRE. Do you realize, Mr. Big Shot, that I'm just the man to thrash you?

MAÎTRE JACQUES. I don't doubt it.

VALÈRE. That take you all in all you're nothing but a scum of a cook?

MAÎTRE JACQUES. I know that very well.

VALÈRE. And that you don't know me yet?

MAÎTRE JACQUES. I beg your pardon.

VALÈRE. You'll thrash me, you say?

MAÎTRE JACQUES. I said it as a joke.

VALÈRE. And I have no taste for your jokes. (Beats him.) Better learn that you're a bad joker.   (Exit)

MAÎTRE JACQUES. A plague on sincerity! It's a bad trade. Henceforth I give it up, and I'll never speak the truth again. All right for my master; he has a certain right to beat me; but as for this Mr. Steward, I'll be revenged on him if I can.

Scene 3.   FROSINE, MARIANE, MAÎTRE JACQUES

FROSINE. Maître Jacques, do you know if your master is at home?

MAÎTRE JACQUES. Yes indeed he is, I know it only too well.

FROSINE. Please tell him that we're here.

Scene 4.   MARIANE, FROSINE

MARIANE. Ah, Frosine, what a strange state I'm in! And if I must say what I feel, how I dread the sight of him!

FROSINE. But why? And what are you worried about?

MARIANE. Alas! How can you ask? And can't you imagine the alarm of a person just about to see the torture that's in store for her?

FROSINE. I see well enough that to die pleasantly, Harpagon isn't the torture that you'd like to embrace; and I can tell by your face that that blond youngster you spoke to me about is a bit on your mind.

MARIANE. Yes, Frosine, it's something against which I don't even want to defend myself; and the respectful visits he has paid us have, I admit, had some effect on my soul.

FROSINE. But have you found out who he is?

MARIANE. No, I don't know who he is; but I know that he's made in such a way as to be loved; that if things could be left to my choice, I'd take him rather than another man; and that he contributes no little to make me find a frightful torment in the husband they want to give me.

FROSINE. My Lord! All these young fops are attractive, and

have a good line; but most of them are poor as church mice; and it's better for you to take an old husband who'll give you plenty of money. I admit that the senses are not so well taken care of on the side I'm talking about, and that there are some distasteful things to put up with with such a husband; but that's not made to last, and his death, believe me, will soon put you in a position to take a more attractive one, who will make up for everything.

MARIANE. Good Lord, Frosine! It's a strange business when, to be happy, we must wish for someone else's decease; and death does not always fall in with all the plans we make.

FROSINE. Don't be silly. You're marrying him only on condition that he leave you a widow soon; and that must be one of the articles in the contract. He would be very impertinent not to die inside of three months.—Here he is in person.

MARIANE. Ah! Frosine, what a face!

Scene 5.   HARPAGON, FROSINE, MARIANE

HARPAGON. Don't be offended, my beauty, if I come to you with spectacles on. I know that your charms strike the eye enough, are visible enough, by themselves, and that there's no need of glasses to perceive them; but after all, it is through glasses that we observe the stars; and I maintain and guarantee that you are a star, but a star that is the loveliest star in the land of stars. Frosine, she doesn't answer a word, and, it seems to me, shows no joy in seeing me.

FROSINE. That's because she's still all overcome; and then, girls are always ashamed to show at first what they feel in their souls.

HARPAGON. You're right. There now, my pretty, here's my daughter coming to greet you.

Scene 6.   ÉLISE, HARPAGON, MARIANE, FROSINE

MARIANE. I've owed you a visit, Madame, and I'm late in paying it.

ÉLISE. You've done what I should have done, Madame, and *I* should have come to see *you* first.

HARPAGON. You see she's a big girl; but bad weeds always grow.

MARIANE *(aside, to* FROSINE*)*. Oh, what an unpleasant man!

HARPAGON. What is the pretty thing saying?

FROSINE. That she thinks you're admirable.

HARPAGON. You do me too much honor, adorable pet.

MARIANE *(aside)*. What a beast!

HARPAGON. I'm only too obliged to you for these sentiments.

MARIANE *(aside)*. I can't stand it any longer.

HARPAGON. Here's my son too, coming to pay his respects to you.

MARIANE *(aside, to* FROSINE*)*. Ah! Frosine, what an encounter! This is just the one I was telling you about.

FROSINE *(to* MARIANE*)*. It's an amazing coincidence.

HARPAGON. I see that you're astonished to see that I have such grown-up children; but I'll soon be rid of them both.

Scene 7.   CLÉANTE, HARPAGON, ÉLISE, MARIANE, FROSINE

CLÉANTE *(to* MARIANE*)*. Madame, to tell you the truth, this is a coincidence I certainly wasn't expecting; and my father surprised me no little when he told me just now of the plan he had made.

MARIANE *(to* CLÉANTE*)*. I may say the same thing. This is an unforeseen encounter that surprised me as much as it did you; and I was not prepared for such an adventure.

CLÉANTE. It is true that my father, Madame, can make no finer choice, and that the honor of seeing you is a real joy to me; but for all that, I will not assure you that I am delighted with the plan you might have to become my stepmother. I confess to you, that compliment is too difficult for me; and by your leave, that is a title I do not wish you. This speech will appear brutal in the eyes of some people; but I am sure that you will be the person to take it aright; that this is a marriage, Madame, for which you may well imagine I must have some repugnance; that you are not unaware, knowing what I am, how it clashes with my interests; and that, in short, you are willing to have me tell you, with my father's permission, that if things depended on me, this marriage would not take place.

HARPAGON. That's a very impertinent compliment. What a fine confession to make to her!

MARIANE. And I, to answer you, must tell you that things are very much the same with me; and that if you would feel repugnance to see me as your stepmother, I would doubtless feel no less to see you as my stepson. Please don't believe that it is I who am trying to give you this distress. I would be very sorry to cause you any displeasure; and if I do not find myself forced to it by some absolute power, I give you my word that I shall not consent to this marriage that makes you unhappy.

HARPAGON. She's right: a stupid compliment demands a like answer. I beg your pardon, my beauty, for my son's impertinence. He's a young fool, who doesn't yet know the consequence of the words he says.

MARIANE. I promise you that what he said to me did not offend me at all; on the contrary, he gave me pleasure by thus explaining his true feelings to me. I like an avowal of that kind from him; and if he had spoken in any other way, I would esteem him the less for it.

HARPAGON. It's very kind of you to want to excuse his faults thus. Time will make him wiser, and you'll see that he'll change his feelings.

CLÉANTE. No, father, I am not capable of changing them, and I earnestly implore Madame to believe this.

HARPAGON. Just see how wild he is! He goes on stronger than ever.

CLÉANTE. Do you want me to betray my heart?

HARPAGON. Still at it? How would you like to change your tune?

CLÉANTE. Well, since you want me to speak in another vein, allow me, Madame, to put myself in my father's place and admit to you that I have seen nothing in the world as charming as you; that I can conceive nothing equal to the happiness of pleasing you; and that to be called your husband is a glory, a felicity that I would prefer to the destinies of the greatest princes on earth. Yes, Madame, the happiness of possessing you is in my eyes the fairest of all fortunes; I set my whole ambition on that; there is nothing I am incapable of doing to make so precious a conquest; and the most powerful obstacles . . .

HARPAGON. Gently, son, if you please.

CLÉANTE. It's a compliment I'm paying for you to Madame.

HARPAGON. My Lord! I've a tongue to explain myself with, and I don't need an advocate like you. (To the SERVANTS) Come on, bring some chairs.

FROSINE. No, it's better that we go to the fair right now, so as to get back sooner and then have plenty of time to talk to you.

HARPAGON. Then have them put the horses to the carriage. I pray you to excuse me, my beauty, if I didn't think to give you a little refreshment before leaving.

CLÉANTE. I've arranged for that, father, and I've had brought here a few basinsful of China oranges, sweet lemons, and preserves,[14] which I have sent for on your behalf.

HARPAGON (aside, to VALÈRE). Valère!

VALÈRE (to HARPAGON). He's out of his mind.

CLÉANTE. Do you think it's not enough, father? Madame will please be kind enough to excuse it.

14 These were all great luxuries in Molière's day.

MARIANE. That was not necessary.

CLÉANTE. Madame, have you ever seen a brighter diamond than the one you see my father has on his finger?

MARIANE. It's true that it's very sparkling.

CLÉANTE (*takes it from his father's finger and gives it to* MARIANE). You must see it from close up.

MARIANE. Certainly it's very beautiful and casts great luster.

CLÉANTE (*stands in front of* MARIANE, *who tries to return it*). No, Madame, the hands it is in are too beautiful. It's a present that my father has given you.

HARPAGON. I?

CLÉANTE. Isn't it true, father, that you want Madame to keep it for your sake?

HARPAGON (*aside, to his son*). What?

CLÉANTE (*To* HARPAGON). A fine question! (*To* MARIANE) He's signaling me to make you accept it.

MARIANE. I don't want . . .

CLÉANTE. Are you joking? He wouldn't think of taking it back.

HARPAGON (*aside*). I'm getting mad!

MARIANE. It would be . . .

CLÉANTE (*still keeping* MARIANE *from returning the ring*). No, I tell you, you would offend him.

MARIANE. Please . . .

CLÉANTE. Not at all.

HARPAGON (*aside*). Plague take . . .

CLÉANTE. Now he's shocked at your refusal.

HARPAGON (*aside, to his son*). Ah, traitor!

CLÉANTE. You see he's getting desperate.

HARPAGON (*aside, to his son, threatening him*). You cutthroat!

CLÉANTE. Father, it's not my fault. I'm doing what I can to make her keep it; but she's obstinate.

HARPAGON (aside, to his son, in a fury). You scoundrel!

CLÉANTE. You are the reason, Madame, why my father is scolding me.

HARPAGON (aside, to his son, with the same grimaces). The villain!

CLÉANTE. You will make him ill. Please, Madame, don't resist any longer.

FROSINE. My Lord! What a to-do! Keep the ring, since the gentleman wants you to.

MARIANE. So as not to make you angry, I'll keep it for now; and I'll find another time to return it to you.

Scene 8.   HARPAGON, MARIANE, FROSINE, CLÉANTE,
BRINDAVOINE, ÉLISE

BRINDAVOINE. Sir, there's a man here that wants to speak to you.

HARPAGON. Tell him I'm busy, and to come back another time.

BRINDAVOINE. He says he's bringing you some money.

HARPAGON. I beg your pardon. I'll be right back.

Scene 9.   HARPAGON, MARIANE, CLÉANTE, ÉLISE, FROSINE,
LA MERLUCHE

LA MERLUCHE (comes running in, and knocks HARPAGON down). Sir . . .

HARPAGON. Oh! I'm dead.

CLÉANTE. What is it, father? Did you hurt yourself?

HARPAGON. The traitor certainly got money from my debtors to make me break my neck.

VALÈRE. It won't be anything.

LA MERLUCHE. Sir, I beg your pardon, I thought I was doing the right thing to come running.

HARPAGON. What did you come for, you murderer?

LA MERLUCHE. To tell you that both your horses have lost their shoes.

HARPAGON. Have them taken promptly to the smith's.

CLÉANTE. While we're waiting for them to be shod, father, I'll do the honors of the house for you, and take Madame into the garden, where I'll have the refreshments served.

HARPAGON. Valère, keep an eye on all this, and please take care to save me as much of it all as you can, to send back to the storekeeper.

VALÈRE. Enough said.

HARPAGON. O you rascal of a son, do you want to ruin me?

ACT IV

Scene 1. CLÉANTE, MARIANE, ÉLISE, FROSINE

CLÉANTE. Let's come back in here, this place is much better. There are no suspicious people around any more, and we can talk freely.

ÉLISE. Yes, Madame, my brother has confided to me the passion he feels for you. I know the chagrins and vexations that such crossings can cause; and, I assure you, it is with extreme tenderness that I take an interest in your adventure.

MARIANE. It's a sweet consolation to see a person like you espousing one's interests; and I conjure you, Madame, always to keep this generous friendship for me, so capable of softening the cruelties of fortune.

FROSINE. My word! You are both unfortunate that you didn't inform me about your affair before all this. I would certainly have averted this trouble, and I wouldn't have brought things to the point where they are.

CLÉANTE. What's the use? It's my evil destiny that willed it so. But, lovely Mariane, what have you decided?

MARIANE. Alas! Am I in a position to decide anything? And in my dependent situation, can I do anything but wish?

CLÉANTE. No other support for me in your heart than mere wishes? No well-intentioned pity? No helpful kindness? No active affection?

MARIANE. What can I say to you? Put yourself in my place, and see what there is I can do. Advise me yourself, order me; I put myself in your hands, and I think you are too reasonable to

184

try to require of me anything but what honor and propriety permit.

CLÉANTE. Alas! To what straits you reduce me, by confining me to what is allowed by the frustrating feelings of rigorous honor and scrupulous propriety!

MARIANE. But what would you have me do? Even if I could override a quantity of considerations to which our sex is obliged, I have some consideration for my mother. She has always brought me up with extreme tenderness, and I could not bring myself to cause her any displeasure. Do your best to work on her; use every means to win her over. You can do and say anything you want, I give you my permission; and if all that's needed is for me to declare myself in your favor, I am willing to consent to make her an avowal myself of all that I feel for you.

CLÉANTE. Frosine, my poor dear Frosine, would you help us out?

FROSINE. My word! Need you ask? I would like to with all my heart. You know I'm naturally quite humane; Heaven did not make my heart of bronze, and I'm only too tender in doing little favors when I see people wholeheartedly and honorably in love. What can we do in this matter?

CLÉANTE. Please give it a little thought.

MARIANE. Give us some ideas.

ÉLISE. Find some scheme to break up what you've done.

FROSINE. That's pretty hard. (To MARIANE) As for your mother, she's not altogether unreasonable, and it might be possible to win her over and persuade her to transfer to the son the gift she wants to make to the father. (To CLÉANTE) But the problem I find is that your father is your father.

CLÉANTE. That's just it.

FROSINE. I mean that he'll hold a grievance if he finds himself turned down, and he'll be in no mood then to give his consent to your marriage. To do this right, we'd have to have the refusal come from him, and try to find some means to give him a distaste for your person.

CLÉANTE. You're right.

FROSINE. Yes, I know I'm right. That's what we need; but the devil of it is finding the means. Wait! Suppose we had some woman fairly well along, who had my kind of talent, and could act well enough to counterfeit a lady of quality, with the help of a retinue gotten up in haste, and with some strange title of marquise or viscountess, let's suppose from lower Brittany; I would be skillful enough to make your father believe she was a wealthy woman with a hundred thousand crowns in ready cash besides her houses; that she was madly in love with him and so eager to be his wife that she would give him everything she had in the marriage contract; and I have no doubt that he would lend an ear to the proposition. For after all he loves you very much, I know, but he loves money a little bit more. And if, dazzled by this bait, he had once consented to what concerns you, it would make little difference later that he was disillusioned when he came to try to see more clearly into the possessions of our marquise.[15]

CLÉANTE. All that is very well thought out.

FROSINE. Leave it to me. I've just remembered a friend of mine who will be just the person we want.

CLÉANTE. Be assured of my gratitude, Frosine, if you can bring this off. But, charming Mariane, let us begin, I pray you, by winning over your mother; it would be a lot accomplished, at any rate, to break off this marriage. For your part, I conjure you, make every possible effort to this end; use all the power you have over her through the fondness she has for you; employ, and don't hold back, the eloquent graces, the all-powerful charms that Heaven has placed in your eyes and mouth; and please don't forget any of those tender words, those sweet prayers, and those touching caresses to which, I am persuaded, nothing can be refused.

MARIANE. I'll do everything I can, and I won't forget a single thing.

15 This plan of Frosine's has no sequel.

Scene 2. HARPAGON, CLÉANTE, MARIANE, ÉLISE, FROSINE

HARPAGON *(aside and still unseen).* Well now! My son is kissing the hand of his prospective stepmother, and his prospective stepmother is not defending herself very hard. Can there be some mystery beneath all this?

ÉLISE. Here is my father.

HARPAGON. The carriage is all ready. You can leave when you please.

CLÉANTE. Since you're not going, father, I'll take them.

HARPAGON. No, stay. They'll go all alone perfectly well; and I need you.

(The ladies exit.)

Scene 3. HARPAGON, CLÉANTE

HARPAGON. Now tell me, apart from her being your stepmother, what do you think of this person?

CLÉANTE. What do I think of her?

HARPAGON. Yes, her manner, her figure, her beauty, her mind?

CLÉANTE. Ho, hum.

HARPAGON. But then what?

CLÉANTE. To speak frankly, I didn't find her up to what I'd thought. Her manner is that of an out-and-out coquette; her figure is rather clumsy, her beauty very mediocre, and her mind quite ordinary. Don't think, father, that this is to make you lose your taste for her; for as stepmothers go, I like this one as well as another.

HARPAGON. And yet you were saying to her just now . . .

CLÉANTE. I said a few sweet nothings to her in your name, but that was to please you.

HARPAGON. So that you would not have any inclination for her?

CLÉANTE. I? Not at all.

HARPAGON. I'm sorry; for that ruins an idea that had come into my mind. Seeing her here, I got to thinking about my age; and it struck me that people may find fault with me to see me marrying so young a girl. That consideration was about to make me give up the plan; and since I've asked for her hand, and have pledged my word to her, I would have given her to you, but for the aversion you show.

CLÉANTE. To me?

HARPAGON. To you.

CLÉANTE. In marriage?

HARPAGON. In marriage.

CLÉANTE. Listen: it's true she's not much to my taste; but to please you, father, I'll make up my mind to marry her, if you want.

HARPAGON. I? I'm more reasonable than you think; I don't want to force your inclination.

CLÉANTE. Pardon me; I'll force myself for your sake.

HARPAGON. No, no; a marriage can't be happy without inclination.

CLÉANTE. That's something, father, that may come later; and they say that love is often a fruit of marriage.

HARPAGON. No; on the man's side this is not a risk to take; and there are unhappy consequences to which I have no wish to commit myself. If you had felt some inclination for her, well and good: I would have had you marry her instead of me; but that not being the case, I'll stick to my original plan and marry her myself.

CLÉANTE. Well, father, since that's the way things are, I must open my heart to you, I must reveal our secret to you. The truth is that I have loved her ever since the day when I first saw her, out for a walk; that my plan just now was to ask you to let me have her for my wife; and that all that held me back was your declaration of your feelings, and my fear of displeasing you.

HARPAGON. Have you paid her any visits?

CLÉANTE. Yes, father.

HARPAGON. Many times?

CLÉANTE. A good many, considering the time there has been.

HARPAGON. Were you well received?

CLÉANTE. Very well, but without their knowing who I was; and that's what caused Mariane's surprise just now.

HARPAGON. Have you declared your passion to her, and the intention you had to marry her?

CLÉANTE. Of course; and I've even made some overtures to her mother about it.

HARPAGON. Did she listen to your proposal on her daughter's behalf?

CLÉANTE. Yes, very civilly.

HARPAGON. And does the daughter fully return your love?

CLÉANTE. Judging by appearances, father, I am persuaded that she has some affection for me.

HARPAGON (aside). I'm very glad to have learned such a secret, and that's just what I wanted to know. (To CLÉANTE) Now then, son, do you know what's ahead? You will have to make up your mind, if you please, to get rid of your love; to stop all your pursuit of a person whom I intend for myself; and shortly to marry the woman who is destined for you.

CLÉANTE. So, father, that was the game you were playing with me! Well! Since this is what things have come to, I declare to you that I will never give up my passion for Mariane, that I will go to any extreme to dispute your conquest of her, and that if you have a mother's consent on your side, I may perhaps have other resources fighting for me.

HARPAGON. What, you gallowsbird? You have the audacity to poach on my preserves?

CLÉANTE. You're the one who's poaching on mine; and I was the first one there.

HARPAGON. Am I not your father? And don't you owe me respect?

CLÉANTE. These are not matters in which children are obliged to defer to fathers; and love is no respecter of persons.

HARPAGON. I'll make you respect me all right—with a good stick!

CLÉANTE. All your threats will have no effect.

HARPAGON. You shall give up Mariane.

CLÉANTE. Absolutely not.

HARPAGON. Give me a stick immediately.

Scene. 4.   MAÎTRE JACQUES, HARPAGON, CLÉANTE

MAÎTRE JACQUES. Now, now, now, gentlemen, what is all this? What are you thinking of?

CLÉANTE. I don't care a bit.

MAÎTRE JACQUES. Oh, sir, gently!

HARPAGON. To talk to me with such impudence!

MAÎTRE JACQUES. Oh, sir, please!

CLÉANTE. I won't give an inch.

MAÎTRE JACQUES. What? To your father?

HARPAGON. Let me at him.

MAÎTRE JACQUES. What? Your son? For me it would be another matter.

HARPAGON. Maître Jacques, I'll make you yourself the judge of this matter, to show how right I am.

MAÎTRE JACQUES. I agree. *(To* CLÉANTE*)* Move off a bit.

HARPAGON. I'm in love with a girl whom I mean to marry; and this gallowsbird has the insolence to love her too, and to aspire to her hand in spite of my orders.

MAÎTRE JACQUES. Oh! He's wrong.

HARPAGON. Isn't it a frightful thing for a son to want to go into rivalry with his father? And shouldn't he, out of respect, abstain from meddling with my inclinations?

MAÎTRE JACQUES. You're right. Let me speak to him, and you stay there. *(Crosses the stage to* CLÉANTE.*)*

CLÉANTE. Well, yes, since he wants to choose you as judge, I won't back down; I don't care who it is; and I too am willing to leave it to you, Maître Jacques, to judge our difference.

MAÎTRE JACQUES. You do me too much honor.

CLÉANTE. I'm in love with a young lady who returns my affection and tenderly accepts the offer of my love; and my father takes it into his head to come and disturb our love by asking for her hand.

MAÎTRE JACQUES. He is certainly wrong.

CLÉANTE. Isn't he ashamed, at his age, to think of marrying? Is it becoming to him to be still in love? And shouldn't he leave that occupation to young men?

MAÎTRE JACQUES. You're right, he can't be serious. Let me have a word with him. *(Goes back to* HARPAGON.*)* Well! Your son isn't as strange as you say, and he's listening to reason. He says that he knows the respect he owes you, that he was carried away only in the first heat of anger, and that he will not refuse to submit to whatever you like, provided you are willing to treat him better than you do, and give him some person in marriage that he'll have reason to be pleased with.

HARPAGON. Ah! Tell him, Maître Jacques, that on those conditions he can hope for anything from me; and that except for Mariane, I give him the freedom to choose anyone he wants.

MAÎTRE JACQUES. Let me handle it. *(Crosses to* CLÉANTE.*)* Well, your father isn't as unreasonable as you make him out to be; and he told me that it was your outbursts that made him angry; that all he objects to is your way of acting; and that he will be quite disposed to grant you what you wish, provided you are willing to go about matters nicely, and show him the deference, respect, and submission that a son owes to his father.

CLÉANTE. Ah! Maître Jacques, you can assure him that if he grants me Mariane, he will always find me the most submissive of men, and that I will never do anything except by his wishes.

MAÎTRE JACQUES (to HARPAGON). That's done. He agrees to everything you say.

HARPAGON. That's just wonderful.

MAÎTRE JACQUES (to CLÉANTE). Everything is settled. He's satisfied with your promises.

CLÉANTE. Heaven be praised!

MAÎTRE JACQUES. Gentlemen, all you have to do is talk it over. Now you are agreed; and you were going to have a quarrel because you didn't understand each other.

CLÉANTE. Dear Maître Jacques, I shall be obliged to you all my life.

MAÎTRE JACQUES. Don't mention it, sir.

HARPAGON. You've given me great pleasure, Maître Jacques, and that deserves a reward. (Feels in his pocket, while MAÎTRE JACQUES holds out his hand; then pulls out his handkerchief.) Go along with you; I'll remember this, I assure you.

MAÎTRE JACQUES. I kiss your hands.

Scene 5.   CLÉANTE, HARPAGON

CLÉANTE. I beg your pardon, father, for having lost my temper.

HARPAGON. That's nothing.

CLÉANTE. I assure you, I'm as sorry as I can be.

HARPAGON. And I'm as happy as I can be to find you reasonable.

CLÉANTE. How good of you to forget my fault so quickly!

HARPAGON. It's easy to forget children's faults when they remember their duty.

CLÉANTE. What? Do you bear me no resentment for all my outrageous conduct?

HARPAGON. You oblige me not to, by the submission and respect you show me.

CLÉANTE. I promise you, father, that to the grave I shall carry in my heart the memory of your goodness.

HARPAGON. And *I* promise *you* that there is nothing you may not obtain from me.

CLÉANTE. Ah! father, I ask nothing more of you; and you've given me enough by giving me Mariane.

HARPAGON. How's that?

CLÉANTE. I say, father, that I'm only too delighted with you, and that I find all I want in your kindness in granting me Mariane.

HARPAGON. Who says anything about granting you Mariane?

CLÉANTE. You, father.

HARPAGON. I?

CLÉANTE. Of course.

HARPAGON. What? You're the one who promised to give her up.

CLÉANTE. I, give her up?

HARPAGON. Yes.

CLÉANTE. Not at all.

HARPAGON. You haven't given up your hopes for her?

CLÉANTE. On the contrary, I'm more determined than ever.

HARPAGON. What, you blackguard? At it again?

CLÉANTE. Nothing can change me.

HARPAGON. Let me at you, you traitor.

CLÉANTE. Do what you like.

HARPAGON. I forbid you to come into my sight again.

CLÉANTE. That's fine with me.

HARPAGON. I abandon you.

CLÉANTE. Abandon all you like.

HARPAGON. I disown you as my son.

CLÉANTE. So be it.

HARPAGON. I disinherit you.

CLÉANTE. Whatever you like.

HARPAGON. And I give you my curse.

CLÉANTE. I have no use for your gifts.

Scene 6. LA FLÈCHE, CLÉANTE

LA FLÈCHE *(coming from the garden with a money-box).* Ah, sir! I was just looking for you! Quick, follow me.

CLÉANTE. What's going on?

LA FLÈCHE. Follow me, I tell you; we're in luck.

CLÉANTE. How's that?

LA FLÈCHE. Here is what we need.

CLÉANTE. What?

LA FLÈCHE. I've had my eye on this all day.

CLÉANTE. What is it?

LA FLÈCHE. Your father's treasure, which I've nabbed.

CLÉANTE. How did you manage?

LA FLÈCHE. I'll tell you everything. Let's run, I hear him shouting.

Scene 7.   HARPAGON

45

HARPAGON *(shouting* "Stop, thief!" *from the garden, and coming in without his hat).* Stop, thief! Stop, thief! Assassin! Murderer! Justice, just Heaven! I'm ruined, I'm assassinated, they've cut my throat, they've stolen my money. Who can it be? What has become of him? Where is he? Where is he hiding? What shall I do to find him? Which way shall I run? Which way shall I not run? Isn't he there? Isn't he here? Who is it? Stop! *(Catches his own arm.)* Give me back my money, you scoundrel . . . Oh, it's me. My mind is troubled, and I don't know where I am, who I am, or what I'm doing. Alas! My poor money, my poor money, my dear friend! They've deprived me of you; and since you are taken from me, I've lost my support, my consolation, my joy; all is finished for me, and there's nothing more for me to do in the world; without you, it's impossible for me to live. It's all over, I can't go on; I'm dying, I'm dead, I'm buried. Isn't there anyone who will bring me back to life by giving me back my dear money, or by telling me who took it? Eh? What do you say? . . . It's no one. Whoever it was that did it, he must have watched his opportunity with great care; and he chose just the time when I was talking to my traitor of a son. Let's go out; I'm going to fetch the law, and have everyone in my house put to the torture: maidservants, valets, son, daughter, and myself too. *(Looking at the audience)* What a lot of people assembled! There's no one my eyes light on but gives me suspicions, and everyone looks like my thief. Eh? What are they talking about over there? About the man who robbed me? What's that noise they're making up there? Is my thief there? For Heaven's sake, if anyone has any news of my thief, I implore him to tell me. Isn't he hiding there among you? . . . They're all looking at me and laughing. You'll see, beyond a doubt they're all involved in my robbery. Let's go, quick, officers, policemen, provosts, judges, racks, gallows, and executioners. I'll have everybody hanged; and if I don't find my money, I'll hang myself afterward.

ACT V

Scene 1. HARPAGON, *the* OFFICER, *his* CLERK

OFFICER. Leave it to me: I know my job, thank God. Today's not the first time I've been involved in solving a theft; and I wish I had as many thousand-franc bags as I've had people hanged.

HARPAGON. It's in the interest of every magistrate to take this affair in hand; and if they don't get me my money back, I'll demand justice of justice itself.

OFFICER. We must take all the necessary steps. You say there was in this money-box . . . ?

HARPAGON. Ten thousand crowns in cash.

OFFICER. Ten thousand crowns!

HARPAGON. Ten thousand crowns.

OFFICER. That's a considerable theft.

HARPAGON. There is no punishment great enough for the enormity of this crime; and if it remains unpunished, the most sacred things are no longer safe.

OFFICER. In what denominations was this sum?

HARPAGON. In good louis d'or and pistoles of full weight.

OFFICER. Whom do you suspect of this theft?

HARPAGON. Everyone; and I want you to arrest the whole town and the suburbs.

OFFICER. If you'll take my advice, we must try not to frighten anyone, and seek quietly to collect some evidence, so as then to proceed with full rigor to recover the money that has been taken from you.

Scene 2.   MAÎTRE JACQUES, HARPAGON, OFFICER, CLERK

47

MAÎTRE JACQUES (*speaking to someone offstage as he enters*). I'll be back. I want his throat cut right away; I want his feet grilled, I want him put in boiling water, and then hung from the rafters.

HARPAGON. Who? The man who robbed me?

MAÎTRE JACQUES. I'm talking about a sucking pig that your steward has just sent me, and I want to fix him for you according to my fancy.

HARPAGON. We're not talking about that; and here is this gentleman, to whom there are other things to talk about.

OFFICER. Don't be frightened. I'm not the man to cause a scandal, and things will be done quietly.

MAÎTRE JACQUES. Is the gentleman one of your supper party?

OFFICER. In this matter, my good friend, you must hide nothing from your master.

MAÎTRE JACQUES. My word, sir! I'll show you all I know how to do, and I'll treat you as best I can.

HARPAGON. That's not the point.

MAÎTRE JACQUES. If I don't give you as good a meal as I'd like, that's the fault of that Mr. Steward of ours, who has clipped my wings with the scissors of his economy.

HARPAGON. Traitor, we're talking about something besides supper; and I want you to tell me some news about the money that was stolen from me.

MAÎTRE JACQUES. Somebody stole some money from you?

HARPAGON. Yes, you scoundrel; and I'm going to hang you if you don't give it back to me.

OFFICER. *(To* HARPAGON*)* Good Lord! Don't mistreat him. I can see from his face that he's an honest man, and that without having to be thrown into prison, he'll tell you what you want to know. *(To* MAÎTRE JACQUES*)* Yes, my friend, if you confess it all to us, you won't come to any harm, and you'll be suitably rewarded by your master. Somebody took his money today, and you can't help knowing something about this business.

MAÎTRE JACQUES *(aside)*. Here is just what I need to get revenge on our steward. Ever since he came here he's been the favorite; they listen only to his advice; and I also have that beating of a while ago on my mind.

HARPAGON. What are you ruminating about?

OFFICER. Let him be. He's preparing to give you satisfaction; and I told you he was an honest man.

MAÎTRE JACQUES. Sir, if you want me to tell you how things are, I think it was your dear Mr. Steward who did the job.

HARPAGON. Valère?

MAÎTRE JACQUES. Yes.

HARPAGON. He, who seems so faithful to me?

MAÎTRE JACQUES. Himself. I think he's the one who robbed you.

HARPAGON. And on what grounds do you think so?

MAÎTRE JACQUES. On what grounds?

HARPAGON. Yes.

MAÎTRE JACQUES. I think so . . . on the grounds that I think so.

OFFICER. But you have to say what evidence you have.

HARPAGON. Did you see him hanging around the place where I'd put my money?

MAÎTRE JACQUES. Yes indeed. Where was your money?

HARPAGON. In the garden.

MAÎTRE JACQUES. Exactly! I saw him hanging around the garden. And what was the money in?

HARPAGON. In a money-box.

MAÎTRE JACQUES. The very thing. I saw him with a money-box.

HARPAGON. And that money-box, what is it like? I can easily tell if it's mine.

MAÎTRE JACQUES. What is it like?

HARPAGON. Yes.

MAÎTRE JACQUES. It's like . . . it's like a money-box.

OFFICER. That's understood. But describe it a bit so we can tell.

MAÎTRE JACQUES. It's a big money-box.

HARPAGON. The one stolen from me is small.

MAÎTRE JACQUES. Oh, yes, it's small, if you look at it that way; but I call it big for what it contains.

OFFICER. And what color is it?

MAÎTRE JACQUES. What color?

OFFICER. Yes.

MAÎTRE JACQUES. Its color is . . . well, a certain color . . . Can't you help me find the word?

HARPAGON. Huh?

MAÎTRE JACQUES. Isn't it red?

HARPAGON. No, gray.

MAÎTRE JACQUES. Why yes, grayish red: that's what I meant.

HARPAGON. There's no doubt whatever: that's certainly the one. Write it down, sir, write down his deposition. Heavens! Whom can I trust from now on? I mustn't swear to anything any more; and I think after this I'd be capable of robbing myself.

MAÎTRE JACQUES. Sir, here he comes back. For goodness' sake, don't go and tell him that I'm the one who told you this.

Scene 3.   VALÈRE, HARPAGON, OFFICER, CLERK,
MAÎTRE JACQUES

HARPAGON. Come here! Come and confess the foulest action, the most horrible crime ever committed.

VALÈRE. What do you want, sir?

HARPAGON. What, traitor, don't you blush for your crime?

VALÈRE. Why, what crime are you talking about?

HARPAGON. What crime am I talking about, you wretch? As if you didn't know what I mean! There's no use your trying to disguise it; the business is uncovered, and I've just learned everything. How could you take advantage of my kindness so, and make your way into my house on purpose to betray me and play a trick like this on me?

VALÈRE. Sir, since the whole thing is revealed to you, I won't attempt to get around it and deny it.

MAÎTRE JACQUES *(aside).* Oho! Could I have guessed right without realizing it?

VALÈRE. It was my intention to speak to you about it, and for that I wanted to wait for a favorable occasion; but since things are as they are, I conjure you not to be angry, and to be willing to hear my reasons.

HARPAGON. And what fine reasons can you give me, you infamous robber?

VALÈRE. Ah, sir! I have not deserved those names. It is true that I have committed an offense against you; but after all, my fault is pardonable.

HARPAGON. What, pardonable? An ambush, a murder like that one?

VALÈRE. Please don't get angry. When you've heard me, you'll see that the harm is not as great as you make it out.

HARPAGON. The harm is not as great as I make it out! What, you gallowsbird? My blood, my entrails?

VALÈRE. Your blood, sir, hasn't fallen into bad hands. I am of a rank that will do it no harm, and there is nothing in all this that I cannot well repair.

HARPAGON. That's my intention all right, and to have you restore what you've stolen from me.

VALÈRE. Your honor, sir, shall be fully satisfied.

HARPAGON. There's no question of honor in this. But tell me, what led you to this act?

VALÈRE. Alas! Can you ask?

HARPAGON. Yes indeed I do ask.

VALÈRE. A god who bears his own excuses for everything he makes people do: the god of Love.

HARPAGON. Love?

VALÈRE. Yes.

HARPAGON. A fine kind of love, a fine kind of love! My word! Love for my louis d'or!

VALÈRE. No, sir, it was not your riches that tempted me; that's not what dazzled me; and I protest that I have no aspirations to all your wealth, provided you leave me the one treasure I have.

HARPAGON. That I won't, by all the devils in hell! I won't leave it to you. Will you look at that insolence, to want to keep what he's stolen from me!

VALÈRE. Do you call that stealing?

HARPAGON. Do I call it stealing? A treasure like that?

VALÈRE. It's a treasure, that's true, and beyond a doubt the most precious that you have; but you won't be losing it by leaving it to me. On my knees I ask you for it, this most charming treasure; and to do right, you must grant it to me.

HARPAGON. I'll do nothing of the sort. What is all this?

VALÈRE. We have promised a mutual faith to each other, and have taken a vow never to abandon one another.

HARPAGON. That's a wonderful vow and a delightful promise!

VALÈRE. Yes, we've pledged ourselves to belong to one another forever.

HARPAGON. I'll put a stop to that, I assure you.

VALÈRE. Nothing but death can separate us.

HARPAGON. That's being devilishly enamored of my money.

VALÈRE. I've already told you, sir, that it was not self-interest that drove me to do what I did. My heart did not act for the reasons you think, and a nobler motive inspired that resolution in me.

HARPAGON. Next we'll find that it's out of Christian charity that he wants my money. But I'll take care of that; and the law, you barefaced rogue, will give me satisfaction for all this.

VALÈRE. You will do as you wish about that, and here I am ready to suffer all the violence you please; but I beg you to believe at least that if wrong has been done, I am the only one to accuse, and in all this your daughter is not at all to blame.

HARPAGON. Indeed, I can believe that; it would be mighty strange if my daughter had had a hand in this crime. But I want to have my own back, and for you to confess what spot you've used for a hiding-place.

VALÈRE. I? There is no hiding-place, and your treasure is still in your house.

HARPAGON (aside). O my dear money-box! (To VALÈRE) Hasn't left my house?

VALÈRE. No, sir.

HARPAGON. Now, just tell me: you haven't touched . . . ?

VALÈRE. I, touched? Oh! You wrong us both; and the ardor with which I burn is wholly pure and respectful.

HARPAGON *(aside).* Burn for my money-box!

VALÈRE. I'd rather die than show any offensive notion to one who is too decent and honorable for that!

HARPAGON *(aside).* My money-box too honorable!

VALÈRE. I have limited my desires to feasting my eyes; and nothing criminal has profaned the passion that her lovely eyes have inspired in me.

HARPAGON *(aside).* The lovely eyes of my money-box! He talks about it like a lover about a mistress!

VALÈRE. Dame Claude, sir, knows the truth of the matter, and she can testify to you that . . .

HARPAGON. What? My serving-woman is an accomplice in the affair?

VALÈRE. Yes, sir, she was a witness to our engagement; and it was after recognizing that my love was honorable that she helped me persuade your daughter to plight me her troth and receive mine.

HARPAGON *(aside).* Eh? Is fear of the law making his mind wander? *(To* VALÈRE*)* What's all this gibberish about my daughter?

VALÈRE. I say, sir, that I had all the difficulty in the world in prevailing on her modesty to consent to what my love desired.

HARPAGON. Whose modesty?

VALÈRE. Your daughter's; and it was not until yesterday that she could make up her mind that we should sign a mutual promise of marriage.

HARPAGON. My daughter has signed you a promise of marriage?

VALÈRE. Yes, sir, even as I too have signed one for her.

HARPAGON. O Heavens! Another disgrace!

MAÎTRE JACQUES *(to the* OFFICER*).* Write it down, sir, write it down.

HARPAGON. Trouble piled on trouble! Despair on despair! Come,

sir, do the duty of your office, and draw me up the indict-
ment against him as a thief and a suborner.

VALÈRE. Those names are not due me; and when it is known
who I am . . .

Scene 4. ÉLISE, MARIANE, FROSINE, HARPAGON, VALÈRE, MAÎTRE JACQUES, OFFICER, CLERK

HARPAGON. Ah, you wicked daughter! daughter unworthy of a
father like me! So this is how you practice the lessons I've
given you? You let yourself fall in love with an infamous
thief, and you pledge him your troth without my consent?
But you'll be surprised, both of you. *(To* ÉLISE) Four solid
walls shall answer for your conduct; *(to* VALÈRE) and a
good gallows will give me satisfaction for your audacity.

VALÈRE. It will not be your passion that will judge the affair;
and I shall at least be heard before being condemned.

HARPAGON. I was wrong to say the gallows, and you shall be
broken alive on the wheel.

ÉLISE *(on her knees before her father).* Ah! father, be a little
more humane in your feelings, I implore you, and don't
push matters to the utmost violence of paternal power.
Don't surrender to the first impulses of your passion; give
yourself time to consider what you mean to do. Take the
trouble to have a better look at the man you are offended
with: he is very different than he appears to your eyes; and
you will find it less strange that I have given myself to him
when you know that but for him you would long since have
had me no longer. Yes, father, he's the one who saved me from
that great peril I was in in the water, and to whom you
owe the life of that very daughter whom . . .

HARPAGON. All that is nothing; and it would have been much
better for me if he had let you drown than do what he's
done.

ÉLISE. Father, I conjure you, by your paternal love, to . . .

HARPAGON. No, no, I won't hear a thing, and justice must take its course.

MAÎTRE JACQUES *(aside)*. You'll pay me for my beating.

FROSINE *(aside)*. Here's a fine kettle of fish.

50

Scene 5.   ANSELME, HARPAGON, ÉLISE, MARIANE, FROSINE,
VALÈRE, MAÎTRE JACQUES, OFFICER, CLERK

51

ANSELME. What is it, Seigneur Harpagon? I find you all upset.

HARPAGON. Ah! Seigneur Anselme, you see in me the most unfortunate of men; and here's a lot of confusion and disorder over the contract that you have come to sign. I'm being assassinated in my property, I'm being assassinated in my honor; and here is a traitor, a scoundrel, who has violated all the most sacred rights, who has wormed his way into my house under the title of a domestic to steal my money and suborn my daughter.

VALÈRE. Who's thinking of your money, that you're making such a strange fuss about?

HARPAGON. Yes, they've given each other a promise of marriage. This affront concerns you, Seigneur Anselme, and it is you who should become his prosecutor and bring a lawsuit against him to take revenge on his insolence.

ANSELME. It's not my plan to get myself married by force, and to lay any claim to a heart that has already given itself; but as regards your interests, I am ready to espouse them just like my own.

HARPAGON. This gentleman here is an honest officer who, from what he has told me, won't forget any part of the duty of his office. *(To the* OFFICER) Charge him properly, sir, and make things good and criminal.

VALÈRE. I don't see what crime they can make of my passion for your daughter; and as for the punishment you think

I may be condemned to for our engagement, when they know who I am . . .

HARPAGON. I don't care a rap for all these stories; and today the world is full of these people who steal their nobility, these impostors who take advantage of their obscurity to dress themselves insolently in the first illustrious name that comes into their head.

VALÈRE. Then know that I have too sound a heart to adorn myself with anything that isn't mine, and that all Naples can bear witness to my birth.

ANSELME. Easy now! Be careful of what you're going to say. You're taking a bigger risk than you think; and you're speaking in the presence of a man to whom all Naples is known, and who can easily see through any story you tell.

VALÈRE (*proudly putting on his hat*). I am not the man to fear anything, and if Naples is known to you, you know who was Don Thomas d'Alburcy.

ANSELME. Indeed I do know; and few men have known him better than I.

HARPAGON. I don't care a rap about Don Thomas or Don Martin. (*He sees two candles burning, and blows one out.*)

ANSELME. Pray let him speak, we'll see what he wants to say about him.

VALÈRE. I want to say that he is the man who gave me life.

ANSELME. He?

VALÈRE. Yes.

ANSELME. Come, you're jesting. Try some other story that may succeed better, and don't hope to save yourself with this imposture.

VALÈRE. Be careful what you say. This is no imposture, and I'm asserting nothing that is not easy for me to justify.

ANSELME. What? You dare to call yourself the son of Don Thomas d'Alburcy?

VALÈRE. Yes, I dare; and I'm ready to maintain this truth against anyone at all.

ANSELME. This is amazing audacity. Then learn, to your confusion, that at least sixteen years ago the man you're telling us about perished at sea with his wife and children while trying to save their lives from the cruel persecutions that accompanied the disorders in Naples,[16] and that caused many noble families to be exiled.

VALÈRE. Yes; but learn, to *your* confusion, that his son, seven years old, was saved from that shipwreck with one servant by a Spanish vessel, and that this son who was saved is the man speaking to you now; learn that the captain of that vessel, touched by my lot, took me into his friendship. He had me brought up as his own son, and arms were my profession as soon as I was old enough; I learned not long ago that my father was not dead, as I had always thought; passing through this town on my way to look for him, an accident arranged by Heaven made me see the charming Élise; the sight of her made me a slave to her beauty; and the violence of my love and the severities of her father made me resolve to enter his household and send someone else in quest of my parents.

ANSELME. But what other proofs, besides your words, can assure us that this is not some fable that you've built upon a truth?

VALÈRE. The Spanish captain; a ruby signet-ring that belonged to my father; an agate bracelet that my mother had put on my arm; old Pedro, the servant who escaped from the shipwreck with me.

MARIANE. Alas! from your words I myself can attest here and now that this is no imposition; and everything you say makes me know clearly that you are my brother.

VALÈRE. You, my sister?

MARIANE. Yes. My heart was stirred from the moment you opened your mouth; and our mother, who will be delighted to see you, has told me a thousand times about our family's misfortunes. Heaven did not make us perish either in that sad shipwreck; but it saved our lives only at the cost of our freedom; and it was pirates who picked us up, my

16 Probably an allusion to the revolt by Masaniello in 1647.

mother and me, from a bit of the wreckage of our ship.
After ten years of slavery, a happy chance restored our
liberty to us, and we returned to Naples, where we found
all our property sold, without being able to find any news
of my father. We took passage to Genoa, where my mother
went to collect some wretched remains of an inheritance
that had been torn to bits; and from there, fleeing the
barbaric injustice of her relatives, she came to these parts,
where she has lived little better than a languishing life.

ANSELME. O Heaven! How great are the works of your power!
And how well you show that it is for you alone to work
miracles! Embrace me, my children, and both mingle your
transports with those of your father.

VALÈRE. You are our father?

MARIANE. It's you my mother mourned so?

ANSELME. Yes, my daughter, yes, my son, I am Don Thomas
d'Alburcy, whom Heaven saved from the waves with all
the money he had on him, and who, having thought you all
dead for more than sixteen years, was preparing, after much
voyaging, to seek, in marriage with a sweet and decent
woman, the consolation of a new family. The little safety
I could see for my life if I returned to Naples made me
renounce that place forever; and having managed to sell
what I owned, I have settled down here, where, under the
name of Anselme, I have tried to put aside the sorrows
of that other name that has caused me so many misfortunes.

HARPAGON. That's your son?

ANSELME. Yes.

HARPAGON. I hold you responsible for paying me ten thousand
crowns that he stole from me.

ANSELME. *He* stole from you?

HARPAGON. Himself.

VALÈRE. Who told you that?

HARPAGON. Maître Jacques.

VALÈRE (*to* MAÎTRE JACQUES). You're the one who says that?

MAÎTRE JACQUES. You see I'm not saying a thing.

HARPAGON. Oh, yes you did; here's the officer who took the deposition.

VALÈRE. Can you think me capable of such a cowardly act?

HARPAGON. Capable or not capable, I want my money back.

Scene 6. CLÉANTE, VALÈRE, MARIANE, ÉLISE, FROSINE,
HARPAGON, ANSELME, MAÎTRE JACQUES, LA FLÈCHE,
OFFICER, CLERK

52

CLÉANTE. Don't worry, father, and don't accuse anyone. I have learned news of your affair, and I come here to tell you that if you will make up your mind to let me marry Mariane, your money will be returned to you.

HARPAGON. Where is it?

CLÉANTE. Don't be concerned about it; it's in a place where I can answer for it, and everything depends on me alone. It's up to you to tell me what you decide; and you can choose either to give me Mariane or to lose your money-box.

HARPAGON. Hasn't anything been taken out of it?

CLÉANTE. Nothing at all. See whether it's your intention to agree to this marriage and join your consent to that of her mother, who gives her her freedom to make a choice between the two of us.

MARIANE. But you don't know that that consent is not enough, and that Heaven has just restored to me, together with a brother, whom you see, a father, from whom you must obtain me.

ANSELME. Heaven does not give me back to you, my children, to oppose your wishes. Seigneur Harpagon, you know very well that a young person's choice will fall on the son rather than on the father. Come, don't make anyone tell you what it is not necessary to hear, and consent, as I do, to this double marriage.

HARPAGON. To take counsel, I must see my money-box.

CLÉANTE. You shall see it safe and sound.

HARPAGON. I have no money to give my children in marriage.

ANSELME. Well, I have enough for them; don't let that worry you.

HARPAGON. Will you undertake to meet all the expenses of these two marriages?

ANSELME. Yes, I undertake that. Are you satisfied?

HARPAGON. Yes, provided you have a suit made for me for the weddings.

ANSELME. Agreed. Come, let's enjoy the bliss that this happy day offers us.

OFFICER. Hold on, gentlemen! Hold on! Easy, if you please. Who is going to pay me for my depositions?

HARPAGON. We want no part of your depositions.

OFFICER. Yes, but *I* don't intend to have taken them for nothing.

HARPAGON *(pointing to* MAÎTRE JACQUES*)*. For your payment, here is a man I give you to hang.

MAÎTRE JACQUES. Alas! What is a man to do? They give me a beating for telling the truth, and they want to hang me for lying.

ANSELME. Seigneur Harpagon, you must forgive him for this imposture.

HARPAGON. Then you'll pay the officer?

ANSELME. So be it. Let's go quickly and share our joy with your mother.

HARPAGON. And I, to see my dear money-box.

The Would-Be Gentleman

THE WOULD-BE GENTLEMAN

A comedy-ballet in five acts, in prose, performed by Molière's Troupe du Roi, first for the King at Chambord on October 14, 1670, then for the public at the Théâtre du Palais-Royal in Paris on November 23, 1670. Molière played Monsieur Jourdain; his wife, Lucile; Du Croisy, the Philosophy Master; Mlle. Beauval, Nicole; Lulli, the Mufti; and Hubert may have created the role of Madame Jourdain, which he is known to have played fifteen years later. The play was a considerable success from the first.

Though Molière, as usual, borrowed from various predecessors (Strepsiades, the character who learns from Socrates in Aristophanes' *The Clouds,* is an ancestor of that late bloomer Monsieur Jourdain), his main sources and resources are his own. However, the initial idea came from elsewhere. About a year before the first performance, a Turkish envoy named Soliman had made something of a sensation in France, notably by his pride and disdain for French pomp. Amid general curiosity and pique, Louis XIV asked his favorite entertainers, Molière and the ambitious—and ingenious—Italian composer Lulli, to collaborate on some sort of Turkish ceremony, with music and dancing and buffoonish interludes. The resulting music and dance is Lulli's, the play Molière's.

Thus Molière's initial aim was apparently to create a little drama—a "little funny business," as his hero would say—that would prepare a suitable butt for the Turkish foolishness to follow. The project must have grown on him; for, starting with almost nothing, he created one of his most delightful comic figures. Moreover, the play is almost half over (about Act III, sc. 3) before he gets really to the plot at all. Until then it is all a presentation of Monsieur Jourdain, the middle-aged innocent agog for learning and for imitating persons of quality, as he shows off his new clothes and new skills to those who surround him: the smug and quarrelsome private tutors, the

213

flattering tailors, and occasionally the tart and level-headed Madame Jourdain and Nicole.

Unambitious but workmanlike, the plot effectively does its job: to put Monsieur Jourdain's would-be-nobiliary vanity into conflict with a sound marriage for his daughter, and to end that conflict by the farcical disguise of Cléonte as the son of the Grand Turk and of his valet Covielle as his Turkish servant and interpreter.

Many admirers of Molière seem unnecessarily apologetic about *The Would-Be Gentleman* because it is neither a pure farce fantasy stage-managed by a consummate actor, like *The Mischievous Machinations of Scapin,* nor a profound exploration of the limits of comedy like *Tartuffe, Don Juan,* or *The Misanthrope.* Even if it does not lend itself to subtle analysis, this play needs no apology. It has earned its success by being funny as hell, for five acts; which is no mean trick.

Though it is often classified as farce and is rarely satiric or serious, I would classify it rather as pure comedy, full of the eternal verities of the comic. Among these—to draw only on the first three acts—I would place the lofty speech and ludicrous quarrel of the Philosophy Master; the many versions of the billet-doux for Dorimène; the fencing lesson that Monsieur Jourdain tries to give Nicole; the bow to Dorimène. Perhaps even more rewarding are the many sublime finds that are the heart of comedy: "Give me my gown so I'll hear better"; "There's lamb in it"; the bow Monsieur Jourdain wants to learn for "a marquise named Dorimène"; the three operations of the mind: the first, the second, and the third; and of course the bit that has become a byword by filling a comic need, Monsieur Jourdain's discovery that without knowing it he has been speaking prose all his life.

To such humor as this, which informs the play, the proper reaction is not analysis (not even self-analysis) but simple gratitude. *The Would-Be Gentleman* may not teach us much; but to many of us the world is a better place because Molière wrote it.

THE WOULD-BE GENTLEMAN

CHARACTERS

MONSIEUR JOURDAIN, *a bourgeois*[1]
MADAME JOURDAIN, *his wife*
LUCILE, *their daughter*
NICOLE, *a maidservant*
CLÉONTE, *in love with Lucile*
COVIELLE, *Cléonte's valet*
DORANTE, *a count, in love with Dorimène*
DORIMÈNE, *a marquise*
MUSIC MASTER
MUSIC MASTER'S PUPIL
DANCING MASTER
FENCING MASTER
PHILOSOPHY MASTER
MASTER TAILOR
JOURNEYMAN TAILOR
Two LACKEYS
Several SINGERS, INSTRUMENTALISTS, DANCERS, COOKS, TAILOR'S
 APPRENTICES, *and other characters in the ballets*

The scene is Paris, in Monsieur Jourdain's home.

---

[1] Monsieur Jourdain's lavish costume is mainly described in Act I,
scene 2.

215

ACT I

The overture is played by a large group of instruments. The MUSIC MASTER'S PUPIL *is seen at center stage, at a table, composing a tune that* MONSIEUR JOURDAIN *has commissioned for a serenade.*

Scene 1.   MUSIC MASTER, DANCING MASTER, *three* SINGERS, *two* VIOLINISTS, *four* DANCERS

MUSIC MASTER *(to his musicians).* Come on, come into this room and rest here until he comes.

DANCING MASTER *(to his dancers).* And you, too, on this side.

MUSIC MASTER *(to the* PUPIL*).* Is it done?

PUPIL. Yes.

MUSIC MASTER. Let's see . . . That's fine.

DANCING MASTER. Is it something new?

MUSIC MASTER. Yes, it's an air for a serenade that I had him compose here while we're waiting for our man to wake up.

DANCING MASTER. May I see what it is?

MUSIC MASTER. You'll hear it, with the words, when he comes. He won't be long.

DANCING MASTER. Ours are no small jobs now.

MUSIC MASTER. That's true. We've found here just the man we both need. This Monsieur Jourdain is a nice income for us, with the visions of nobility and gallantry that he's taken into his head; and your dance and my music might well wish that everyone was like him.

DANCING MASTER. Not entirely; and I wish he had more understanding than he does of the things we offer him.

MUSIC MASTER. It's true that he understands them badly, but he pays for them well; and that's what our arts need nowadays more than anything else.

DANCING MASTER. As for me, I confess, I get some enjoyment out of appreciation; I care about applause; and I maintain that in all the fine arts it's a pretty painful torture to display ourselves to fools, to endure the barbarous reaction of a stupid man to our compositions. There is pleasure—don't tell me there isn't—in working for people who are capable of sensing the fine points of an art, who can offer a sweet reception to the beauties of a work, and, by gratifying approval, repay you for your labor. Yes, the most delightful reward you can receive for the things you do is to see them understood, to see them fêted by an applause that honors you. There is nothing, in my opinion, that pays us better than that for all our fatigues; and enlightened praises are exquisite delights.

MUSIC MASTER. I agree, and I relish them as you do. There is certainly nothing as gratifying as the applause you speak of. But that adulation does not keep you alive; praise by itself does not make a man well off; you have to mix in something solid; and the best way to praise is to praise with the open hand. Indeed, this is a man of scant understanding, who talks nonsense about everything and applauds only the wrong things; but his money corrects the judgments of his mind; there is discernment in his purse; he praises in cash; and this ignorant bourgeois is worth more to us, as you see, than the enlightened noble lord who brought us in here.

DANCING MASTER. There is something in what you say; but I think you put too much emphasis on money; and self-interest is such a base thing that an honorable man should never show any attachment for it.

MUSIC MASTER. All the same, you are perfectly willing to receive the money our man gives you.

DANCING MASTER. Certainly; but I don't set all my happiness in it, and I wish that with all his money he also had a little taste.

MUSIC MASTER. I wish he did too, and that's what we're both working for as best we can. But in any case, he's giving us a chance to make ourselves known in society; and on behalf of the others he will pay for what the others will praise for him.

DANCING MASTER. Here he comes.

Scene 2.   MONSIEUR JOURDAIN, *two* LACKEYS, MUSIC MASTER, DANCING MASTER, VIOLINISTS, SINGERS, *and* DANCERS

MONSIEUR JOURDAIN. Well, gentlemen, what is it to be? Will you show me your little funny business?

DANCING MASTER. What? What little funny business?

MONSIEUR JOURDAIN. Why, the . . . what you may call it, your prologue or dialogue of song and dance.

DANCING MASTER. Aha!

MUSIC MASTER. You find us all ready.

MONSIEUR JOURDAIN. I've kept you waiting a little, but that's because today I'm having myself dressed like people of quality; and my tailor has sent me some silk stockings that I thought I'd never get on.

MUSIC MASTER. We are here only to await your leisure.

MONSIEUR JOURDAIN. I ask you both not to go away until they've brought me my coat, so you can see me in it.

DANCING MASTER. Whatever you please.

MONSIEUR JOURDAIN. You'll see me decked out right from head to foot.

MUSIC MASTER. We've no doubt of it.

MONSIEUR JOURDAIN (*showing his dressing-gown*). I've had this India print made up for me.

DANCING MASTER. It's very handsome.

MONSIEUR JOURDAIN. My tailor told me that people of quality went around like this in the morning.

MUSIC MASTER. It's most becoming to you.

MONSIEUR JOURDAIN. Lackeys! Hey, my two lackeys!

FIRST LACKEY. What do you wish, sir?

MONSIEUR JOURDAIN. Nothing. It was just to see if you hear me all right. *(To the two* MASTERS*)* What do you think of my liveries?

DANCING MASTER. They're magnificent.

MONSIEUR JOURDAIN *(opening his dressing-gown and displaying his tight red velvet breeches and green velvet jacket).* And here's a little casual outfit to do my exercises in in the morning.

MUSIC MASTER. Very gallant.

MONSIEUR JOURDAIN. Lackeys!

FIRST LACKEY. Sir?

MONSIEUR JOURDAIN. The other lackey!

SECOND LACKEY. Sir?

MONSIEUR JOURDAIN. Hold my gown. *(To the* MASTERS*)* How do I look this way?

DANCING MASTER. Very good; couldn't be better.

MONSIEUR JOURDAIN. Let's have a look at this thing of yours.

MUSIC MASTER. First I'd like you to hear an air he has just composed for the serenade you asked me for. He's one of my pupils who has a remarkable talent for this kind of thing.

MONSIEUR JOURDAIN. Yes; but you shouldn't have had it done by a pupil, and you're not too good to have done the job yourself.

MUSIC MASTER. You mustn't let the word *pupil* mislead you, sir. Pupils of this kind know as much about it as the greatest masters, and this air is as beautiful as can be. Just listen.

MONSIEUR JOURDAIN. Give me my gown so I'll hear better

. . . Wait, I think I'll be better without a gown . . . No, give it back to me, that'll be better.

SINGER.

> *I languish night and day; great is my woe*
> *Since my enslavement to your cruelties;*
> *If thus you treat someone who loves you so,*
> *How, Iris, must you treat your enemies?*

MONSIEUR JOURDAIN. That song seems a bit lugubrious to me, it puts a man to sleep, and I wish you could liven it up a bit here and there.

MUSIC MASTER. Sir, the music must be suited to the words.

MONSIEUR JOURDAIN. I learned a really pretty one some time ago. Wait . . . la, la . . . how does it go?

DANCING MASTER. My word, I don't know!

MONSIEUR JOURDAIN. There's lamb in it.

DANCING MASTER. Lamb?

MONSIEUR JOURDAIN. Yes. Ah! *(Sings)*

> *I thought my little Pam*
> *Was sweet as she was fair,*
> *I thought my little Pam*
> *Was sweet as any lamb.*
> *Alas! There's nothing like her,*
> *None crueler anywhere;*
> *She's worse than any tiger!*

Isn't that pretty?

MUSIC MASTER. Couldn't be prettier.

DANCING MASTER. And you sing it well.

MONSIEUR JOURDAIN. That's without having learned music.

MUSIC MASTER. You should learn it, sir, just as you are learning the dance. These are two closely related arts.

DANCING MASTER. And they open a man's mind to beautiful things.

MONSIEUR JOURDAIN. Do people of quality learn music too?

MUSIC MASTER. Yes, sir.

MONSIEUR JOURDAIN. Then I'll learn it. But I don't know where I'll find the time; for besides the fencing master who's teaching me, I've also taken on a philosophy master, who's due to begin this morning.

MUSIC MASTER. Philosophy is something; but music, sir, music . . .

DANCING MASTER. Music and the dance . . . Music and the dance, that's all you need.

MUSIC MASTER. There's nothing so useful in a state as music.

DANCING MASTER. There's nothing so necessary to men as the dance.

MUSIC MASTER. Without music a state cannot subsist.

DANCING MASTER. Without the dance a man couldn't do anything.

MUSIC MASTER. All the disorders, all the wars we see in the world come only from not learning music.

DANCING MASTER. All the misfortunes of men, all the deadly disasters that history is full of, the blunders of politicians, the mistakes of great captains—all these have come just from not knowing how to dance.

MONSIEUR JOURDAIN. How's that?

MUSIC MASTER. Doesn't war come from a lack of union among men?

MONSIEUR JOURDAIN. That's true.

MUSIC MASTER. And if all men learned music, wouldn't that be the way to achieve concord, and to see universal peace in the world?

MONSIEUR JOURDAIN. You're right.

DANCING MASTER. When a man has committed a lapse in conduct, whether in his family affairs, or in the government of a state, or in the command of an army, don't people always say: "So-and-so has made a misstep in such-and-such a matter?"

MONSIEUR JOURDAIN. Yes, people say that.

DANCING MASTER. And making a misstep, can that come from anything but not knowing how to dance?

MONSIEUR JOURDAIN. That's true, you're both right.

DANCING MASTER. That's to show you the excellence and utility of dancing and music.

MONSIEUR JOURDAIN. I understand that now.

MUSIC MASTER. Do you want to see our two things?

MONSIEUR JOURDAIN. Yes.

MUSIC MASTER. I've told you already, this is a little essay I once composed on the various passions that music can express.

MONSIEUR JOURDAIN. Very good.

MUSIC MASTER *(to the* SINGERS*).* Come on, step forward. *(To* MONSIEUR JOURDAIN*)* You must imagine that they're dressed as shepherds.

MONSIEUR JOURDAIN. Why always shepherds? That's all you see everywhere.

DANCING MASTER. When you have people speak to music, for verisimilitude you have to go in for the pastoral. Singing has always been assigned to shepherds; and it's hardly natural in dialogue for princes or bourgeois to sing their passions.

MONSIEUR JOURDAIN. All right, all right. Let's see.

DIALOGUE IN MUSIC
between a WOMAN SINGER *and two* MEN SINGERS

WOMAN.

> *A heart that love holds in its sway*
> *To countless cares must always be a prey;*
> *They talk as though we sigh and languish pleasantly,*
> *And yet, for all they say,*
> *Nothing is quite so sweet as to be free.*

FIRST MAN.

> *Nothing is quite so sweet as the tender passion*
> *That lovingly can fashion*
> *One single heart of two.*

. *Without loving desires there is no happiness:*
Take love from life and you'll confess
You take away its pleasures too.

SECOND MAN.
    It would be sweet to enter love's domain
If, seeking faith in love, we did not seek in vain;
    But alas! Cruel heartlessness!
One cannot find a faithful shepherdess,
And that inconstant sex, unworthy to be born,
Should make men give up love in utter scorn.

FIRST MAN.
    Longing so sweet,

WOMAN.
    Freedom and bliss,

SECOND MAN.
    Sex full of deceit,

FIRST MAN.
    What's dearer than this?

WOMAN.
    How you exalt me!

SECOND MAN.
    How you revolt me!

FIRST MAN.
    Ah! for the sake of love give up this hatefulness.

WOMAN.
    You can be made to see
    A faithful shepherdess.

SECOND MAN.
    Alas! Where can she be?

WOMAN.
    Since our sex is so maligned,
    Here: I give my heart to you.

SECOND MAN.
    Shepherdess, but shall I find
    That it will be always true?

WOMAN.

> *Well, let's try it out and see*
> *Which of us is the truer lover.*

SECOND MAN.

> *Whichever fails in constancy,*
> *Over that one may the gods' wrath hover!*

ALL THREE SINGERS.

> *So fair is love's dart,*
> *Let's yield to its heat;*
> *Ah! loving is sweet*
> *For the faithful in heart!*

MONSIEUR JOURDAIN. Is that all?

MUSIC MASTER. Yes.

MONSIEUR JOURDAIN. I think it's well worked out, and there are some rather pretty little remarks in it.

DANCING MASTER. Here, for my piece, is a little attempt to show the most beautiful movements and attitudes with which a dance can be varied.

MONSIEUR JOURDAIN. Is it still shepherds?

DANCING MASTER. They're whatever you like. *(To the* DANCERS*)* Let's go.

Four DANCERS *execute all the different movements and all the kinds of steps that the* DANCING MASTER *directs them to. This dance makes up the* FIRST INTERLUDE.

ACT II

Scene 1. MONSIEUR JOURDAIN, MUSIC MASTER, DANCING MASTER, LACKEYS

MONSIEUR JOURDAIN. Now that's not bad at all, and those fellows really jig around well.

MUSIC MASTER. When the dance is combined with music, that will be even more effective, and you'll see something gallant in the little ballet we've arranged for you.

MONSIEUR JOURDAIN. That's for later, anyway; and the person for whom I've had all this done is to do me the honor of coming to dinner here.

DANCING MASTER. Everything's ready.

MUSIC MASTER. Furthermore, sir, this is not enough. A person like you, who do things in a big way and who have an inclination for beautiful things, should give a concert at home every Wednesday or Thursday.

MONSIEUR JOURDAIN. Do people of quality have them?

MUSIC MASTER. Yes, sir.

MONSIEUR JOURDAIN. Then I'll have some. Will it be good?

MUSIC MASTER. Beyond a doubt. You'll need three voices: a soprano, an alto, and a bass, which will be accompanied by a bass viol, a theorbo, and a harpsichord for the sustained bass, with two violins to play the refrains.

MONSIEUR JOURDAIN. We'll have to put in a trumpet marine[2] too. The trumpet marine is an instrument I like, and it's harmonious.

[2] Despite its name, the trumpet marine is a single-stringed instrument with a long neck and a loud rumbling note. It was especially popular with street musicians.

MUSIC MASTER. Let us decide things.

MONSIEUR JOURDAIN. Anyway, don't forget to send me some musicians soon to sing at table.

MUSIC MASTER. You'll have everything you need.

MONSIEUR JOURDAIN. But above all, see that the ballet is nice.

MUSIC MASTER. You'll be pleased with it, and, among other things, with certain minuets you'll see in it.

MONSIEUR JOURDAIN. Ah! The minuet is my dance, and I want you to see me dance it. (*To the* DANCING MASTER) Come on, Master.

DANCING MASTER. A hat, sir, if you please. (MONSIEUR JOUR-DAIN *takes a* LACKEY's *hat and puts it on over his nightcap, removing it for the deep bows involved in the dance. The* DANCING MASTER *takes his hand, sings the music, and gives directions.*) La, la, la; La, la, la, la, la, la; La, la, la, once again; La, la, la; La, la. Keep time, if you please. La, la, la, la. Your leg straight. La, la, la. Don't move your shoulders so much. La, la, la, la, la; La, la, la, la, la. Your arms look crippled. La, la, la, la, la. Lift your head. Turn your toes out. La, la, la. Body straight.

MONSIEUR JOURDAIN. Euh?

MUSIC MASTER. That couldn't be better.

MONSIEUR JOURDAIN. By the way. Teach me how I should make a bow to greet a marquise; I'll soon need it.

DANCING MASTER. A bow to greet a marquise?

MONSIEUR JOURDAIN. Yes, a marquise named Dorimène.

DANCING MASTER. Give me your hand.

MONSIEUR JOURDAIN. No. All you have to do is do it; I'll remember.

DANCING MASTER. If you want to greet her with great respect, you must first make a bow stepping backward, then walk toward her with three forward bows, and on the last one bow to the level of her knees.

MONSIEUR JOURDAIN. Just do it for me. Good.

FIRST LACKEY. Sir, here's your fencing master.

MONSIEUR JOURDAIN. Tell him to come in here and give me my lesson. *(To the* DANCING MASTER *and the* MUSIC MASTER*)* I want you to watch me perform.

Scene 2.   FENCING MASTER, MUSIC MASTER, DANCING MASTER,
MONSIEUR JOURDAIN, *two* LACKEYS

FENCING MASTER *(after putting a foil in* MONSIEUR JOURDAIN's *hand)*. Come, sir, the salute. Body straight. Weight a bit more on the left thigh. Legs not so far apart. Your feet on the same line. Your wrist in line with your hip. The point of your sword level with your shoulder. Arm not extended quite so far. Left hand at eye level. Left shoulder more in quart. Head up. Confident look. Forward. Body firm. Engage my foil in quart, and follow through. One, two. Recover. Thrust again, feet firm. A jump back. When you make your thrust, sir, the sword must start first, and the body must be out of the way. One, two. Come on, engage my foil in tierce, and follow through. Forward. Body firm. Forward. Lunge from there. One, two. Recover. Thrust again. A jump back. On guard, sir, on guard. *(As he calls "On guard," the* FENCING MASTER *scores two or three touches on* MONSIEUR JOURDAIN.*)*

MONSIEUR JOURDAIN. Euh?

MUSIC MASTER. You're doing wonders.

FENCING MASTER. I've told you already, the whole secret of swordplay consists in just two things: in giving, and in not receiving; and as I showed you the other day by demonstrative reasoning, it is impossible for you to receive if you know how to turn your opponent's sword away from the line of your body; which depends simply on a tiny movement of your wrist either to the inside or to the outside.

MONSIEUR JOURDAIN. Then in that way a man, without being brave, is sure of killing his man and not being killed?

FENCING MASTER. Absolutely. Didn't you see the demonstration?

MONSIEUR JOURDAIN. Yes.

FENCING MASTER. And it's in that way that you see how much consideration we should enjoy in a state, and how far superior the science of arms is to all the useless sciences like dancing, music, and . . .

DANCING MASTER. Gently, Mr. Sword-Waver; don't speak of the dance except with respect.

MUSIC MASTER. I pray you, learn to speak better of the excellence of music.

FENCING MASTER. You are funny people, to try to compare your sciences with mine.

MUSIC MASTER. Just look at this very important person!

DANCING MASTER. That's a funny-looking beast, with his chest-protector!

FENCING MASTER. My little dancing master, I could teach you how to dance! And you, my little musician, I could really make you sing!

DANCING MASTER. Mr. Swashbuckler, I'll teach you your trade!

MONSIEUR JOURDAIN (to the DANCING MASTER). Are you mad, to pick a fight with him, when he understands tierce and quart, and knows how to kill a man by demonstrative reasoning?

DANCING MASTER. I don't care a rap for his demonstrative reasoning or his tierce and his quart.

MONSIEUR JOURDAIN. Gently, I tell you.

FENCING MASTER. What? You impertinent little . . . !

MONSIEUR JOURDAIN. There now, Fencing Master!

DANCING MASTER. What? You big cart horse!

MONSIEUR JOURDAIN. There now, Dancing Master!

FENCING MASTER. If I jump on you . . .

MONSIEUR JOURDAIN. Gently!

DANCING MASTER. If I lay a hand on you . . .

MONSIEUR JOURDAIN. Easy!

FENCING MASTER. I'll tan your hide so . . .

MONSIEUR JOURDAIN. Please!

DANCING MASTER. I'll give you such a drubbing . . .

MONSIEUR JOURDAIN. I beg you!

MUSIC MASTER. Just let us be and we'll teach him how to talk!

MONSIEUR JOURDAIN. Good Lord! Stop it!

Scene 3.   PHILOSOPHY MASTER, MUSIC MASTER, DANCING MASTER, FENCING MASTER, MONSIEUR JOURDAIN, LACKEYS

MONSIEUR JOURDAIN. Hello, Mr. Philosopher, you've come in the nick of time with your philosophy. Come here a minute and make peace between these people.

PHILOSOPHY MASTER. Why, what is it? What's wrong, gentlemen?

MONSIEUR JOURDAIN. They've gotten angry over the preference of their professions, to the point of exchanging insults and wanting to come to blows.

PHILOSOPHY MASTER. How now, gentlemen! Should a man become so angry? And haven't you read the learned treatise that Seneca composed on anger? Is there anything more base and shameful than this passion, which turns a man into a wild beast? And shouldn't reason be the mistress of all our impulses?

DANCING MASTER. Why, sir, he comes and insults us both, sneering at the dance, which I practice, and at music, which is *his* profession!

PHILOSOPHY MASTER. A wise man is above all the insults that

may be paid him; and the great response we should make to affronts is moderation and patience.

FENCING MASTER. They both have the audacity to want to compare their professions with mine.

PHILOSOPHY MASTER. Should that move you? It is not over vainglory and rank that men should dispute among themselves; what distinguishes us perfectly from one another is wisdom and virtue.

DANCING MASTER. I maintain against him that the dance is a science to which one cannot pay too much honor.

MUSIC MASTER. And I, that music is one that all ages have revered.

FENCING MASTER. And I maintain against them that the science of arms is the most beautiful and necessary of all sciences.

PHILOSOPHY MASTER. And what is philosophy to be then? I find all three of you mighty impertinent to speak with such arrogance in my presence and impudently to give the name of science to things that should not even be honored with the name of art, and that can only be comprised under the name of miserable trades of gladiator, singer, and mountebank!

FENCING MASTER. Go on, you dog of a philosopher!

MUSIC MASTER. Go on, you good-for-nothing pedant!

DANCING MASTER. Go on, you egregious pedagogue!

PHILOSOPHY MASTER. What? Why, you rascals . . . (He throws himself upon them, and all three beat him, continuing until their exit.)

MONSIEUR JOURDAIN. Mr. Philosopher!

PHILOSOPHY MASTER. Wretches! Insolent scoundrels!

MONSIEUR JOURDAIN. Mr. Philosopher!

FENCING MASTER. Confound the brute!

MONSIEUR JOURDAIN. Gentlemen!

PHILOSOPHY MASTER. Impudent clowns!

MONSIEUR JOURDAIN. Mr. Philosopher!

DANCING MASTER. Devil take the stupid ass!

MONSIEUR JOURDAIN. Gentlemen!

PHILOSOPHY MASTER. Blackguards!

MONSIEUR JOURDAIN. Mr. Philosopher!

MUSIC MASTER. The devil with him and his impertinence!

MONSIEUR JOURDAIN. Gentlemen!

PHILOSOPHY MASTER. Rogues! Beggars! Traitors! Impostors!

MONSIEUR JOURDAIN. Mr. Philosopher, Gentlemen, Mr. Philosopher, Gentlemen, Mr. Philosopher!
                    (Exit the four MASTERS, still fighting.)
Oh, fight all you please! There's nothing I can do about it, and I'm not going to ruin my gown trying to separate you. I'd be mighty crazy to butt in there among them and get a smack that would hurt me.

Scene 4.   PHILOSOPHY MASTER, MONSIEUR JOURDAIN

PHILOSOPHY MASTER *(straightening his neckband as he returns).* Let's get to our lesson.

MONSIEUR JOURDAIN. Ah, sir, I'm sorry about the blows they gave you.

PHILOSOPHY MASTER. That's nothing. A philosopher knows how to take things as they come, and I'm going to compose a satire against them in the style of Juvenal, which will really tear them to shreds. Enough of that. What do you want to learn?

MONSIEUR JOURDAIN. Everything I can, for I'm just dying to be learned; and I'm furious that my father and mother didn't make me study every kind of learning when I was young.

PHILOSOPHY MASTER. That's a reasonable sentiment: *Nam sine doctrina vita est quasi mortis imago.* You understand that, and you know Latin, no doubt.

MONSIEUR JOURDAIN. Yes, but act as though I didn't know it: explain to me what that means.

PHILOSOPHY MASTER. That means that without knowledge, life is little but an image of death.

MONSIEUR JOURDAIN. That Latin is right.

PHILOSOPHY MASTER. Haven't you some first principles, some rudiments of the sciences?

MONSIEUR JOURDAIN. Oh, yes! I know how to read and write.

PHILOSOPHY MASTER. Where do you want to begin? Do you want me to teach you logic?

MONSIEUR JOURDAIN. What is this logic?

PHILOSOPHY MASTER. That's what teaches us the three operations of the mind.

MONSIEUR JOURDAIN. What are these three operations of the mind?

PHILOSOPHY MASTER. The first, the second, and the third. The first is sound conception by means of universals. The second, sound judgment by means of categories; and the third, sound drawing of consequences by means of the figures *Barbara, Celarent, Darii, Ferio, Baralipton,* and so forth.

MONSIEUR JOURDAIN. Those words are too crabbed. I don't like that logic. Let's learn something else that's prettier.

PHILOSOPHY MASTER. Do you want to learn moral philosophy?

MONSIEUR JOURDAIN. Moral philosophy?

PHILOSOPHY MASTER. Yes.

MONSIEUR JOURDAIN. What does this moral philosophy say?

PHILOSOPHY MASTER. It treats of happiness, teaches men to moderate their passions, and . . .

MONSIEUR JOURDAIN. No, let's leave that alone. I'm as bilious as all the devils in hell; and I don't care what moral philosophy says, I want to get as angry as I like when I feel like it.

PHILOSOPHY MASTER. Is it physics that you want to learn?

MONSIEUR JOURDAIN. What kind of business is this physics about?

PHILOSOPHY MASTER. Physics is the science which explains the principles of natural things and the properties of bodies; which discourses on the nature of the elements, of metals, minerals, stones, plants, and animals, and teaches us the causes of all the meteors, rainbows, will-o'-the-wisps, comets, lightning, thunder, thunderbolts, rain, snow, hail, winds, and whirlwinds.

MONSIEUR JOURDAIN. There's too much racket in that, too much hullabaloo.

PHILOSOPHY MASTER. Then what do you want me to teach you?

MONSIEUR JOURDAIN. Teach me spelling.

PHILOSOPHY MASTER. Most gladly.

MONSIEUR JOURDAIN. After that, you'll teach me the almanac, so I'll know when there's a moon and when there isn't.

PHILOSOPHY MASTER. Very well. To follow your idea properly and treat this matter as a philosopher should, we must begin according to the order of these things, by an exact knowledge of the nature of the letters and the different ways in which they are all pronounced. And on that point I have this to tell you, that the letters are divided into vowels, so called because they express the voiced sounds, and into consonants, so called because they sound with the vowels and merely mark the various articulations of the voiced sounds. There are five vowels or voiced sounds: A, E, I, O, U.

MONSIEUR JOURDAIN. I understand all that.

PHILOSOPHY MASTER. The vowel A, pronounced *Ah*, is formed by opening the mouth wide: A.

MONSIEUR JOURDAIN. A, A. Yes.

PHILOSOPHY MASTER. The vowel E, pronounced *Euh*, is formed by bringing the lower jaw close to the upper one: A, E.

MONSIEUR JOURDAIN. A, E, A, E. My word, yes! Ah, how beautiful that is!

PHILOSOPHY MASTER. And the vowel I, pronounced *Ee*, by bringing the jaws even closer together and stretching the corners of the mouth toward the ears: A, E, I.

MONSIEUR JOURDAIN. A, E, I, I, I, I. That's true! Long live learning!

PHILOSOPHY MASTER. The vowel O is formed by opening the jaws again and bringing the lips closer together both at the corners and above and below: O.

MONSIEUR JOURDAIN. O, O. Nothing could be more true. A, E, I, O, I, O. That's admirable! I, O, I, O.[3]

PHILOSOPHY MASTER. The opening of the mouth makes precisely a sort of little circle that represents an O.

MONSIEUR JOURDAIN. O, O, O. You're right. O. Ah, what a beautiful thing it is to know something!

PHILOSOPHY MASTER. The vowel U, pronounced Ü,[4] is formed by bringing the teeth close together but not quite touching, and sticking out both lips, bringing them also close to each other but not quite touching: U.

MONSIEUR JOURDAIN. U, U. There's nothing truer than that. U.

PHILOSOPHY MASTER. Your two lips stick out as if you were making a pout; whence it comes about that if you want to make that kind of a face at someone and deride him, all you can say to him is: U.

MONSIEUR JOURDAIN. U, U. That's true. Ah! Why didn't I study earlier, to know all that?

PHILOSOPHY MASTER. Tomorrow we'll have a look at the other letters, which are the consonants.

MONSIEUR JOURDAIN. Are there as curious things about them as about these?

PHILOSOPHY MASTER. Beyond a doubt. The consonant D, for example, is pronounced by applying the tip of the tongue above the upper teeth: DA.

MONSIEUR JOURDAIN. DA, DA. Yes. Ah! Beautiful! Simply beautiful!

---

3 Here the actor imitates a donkey's bray.
4 The French *u*, which is like the German *ue* or *ü*.

PHILOSOPHY MASTER. The F, by pressing the upper teeth on the lower lip: FA.

MONSIEUR JOURDAIN. FA, FA. It's the truth! Ah, Father and Mother, how I blame you!

PHILOSOPHY MASTER. And the R, by raising the tip of the tongue up against the upper palate, so that, being brushed by the air as it comes out with force, it yields to it, and always returns to the same place, making a kind of vibration: RRA.

MONSIEUR JOURDAIN. R, R, RA; R, R, R, R, RA. That's true! Oh, what an able man you are! And how much time I've wasted! R, R, R, RA.

PHILOSOPHY MASTER. I'll explain all these curious facts to you thoroughly.

MONSIEUR JOURDAIN. Please do. By the way, I must confide in you. I'm in love with a person of high quality, and I'd like you to help me write her something in a little note I want to drop at her feet.

PHILOSOPHY MASTER. Very well.

MONSIEUR JOURDAIN. It will be gallant, yes?

PHILOSOPHY MASTER. Beyond a doubt. Is it verse that you want to write her?

MONSIEUR JOURDAIN. No, no, no verse.

PHILOSOPHY MASTER. You want only prose?

MONSIEUR JOURDAIN. No, I don't want either prose or verse.

PHILOSOPHY MASTER. It has to be one or the other.

MONSIEUR JOURDAIN. Why?

PHILOSOPHY MASTER. For the reason, sir, that there is nothing to express ourselves in but prose or verse.

MONSIEUR JOURDAIN. There's nothing but prose or verse?

PHILOSOPHY MASTER. That's right, sir: whatever isn't prose is verse, and whatever isn't verse is prose.

MONSIEUR JOURDAIN. And the way we talk, what's that then?

PHILOSOPHY MASTER. Prose.

MONSIEUR JOURDAIN. What? When I say: "Nicole, bring me my slippers and give me my nightcap," that's prose?

PHILOSOPHY MASTER. Yes, sir.

MONSIEUR JOURDAIN. Bless my soul! I've been talking prose for over forty years without knowing it, and I'm ever so grateful to you for teaching me that. So: I'd like to put in a note to her: "Lovely marquise, your beautiful eyes make me die of love"; but I'd like to have that put in a gallant style, and nicely turned.

PHILOSOPHY MASTER. Say that the flames from her eyes reduce your heart to ashes; that you suffer for her night and day the torment of a . . .

MONSIEUR JOURDAIN. No, no, no, I don't want all that; I just want what I told you: "Lovely marquise, your beautiful eyes make me die of love."

PHILOSOPHY MASTER. You really should extend the thing a bit.

MONSIEUR JOURDAIN. No, I tell you, all I want in the note is just those words; but fashionably turned, nicely arranged in the proper style. Please just tell me, to give me an idea, the various ways that can be put.

PHILOSOPHY MASTER. First of all, you can put them just as you've said: "Lovely marquise, your beautiful eyes make me die of love." Or else: "Of love make me die, lovely marquise, your beautiful eyes." Or else: "Your eyes beautiful of love make me, lovely marquise, die." Or else: "Die your beautiful eyes, lovely marquise, of love make me." Or else: "Make me your beautiful eyes die, lovely marquise, of love."

MONSIEUR JOURDAIN. But of all those ways, which is the best?

PHILOSOPHY MASTER. The one you said: "Lovely marquise, your beautiful eyes make me die of love."

MONSIEUR JOURDAIN. And yet I've never studied, and I did that at the very first try. I thank you with all my heart, and please come early tomorrow.

PHILOSOPHY MASTER. I shall not fail to.   *(Exit)*

MONSIEUR JOURDAIN *(to his* LACKEYS*)* What? Hasn't my coat arrived yet?

SECOND LACKEY. No, sir.

MONSIEUR JOURDAIN. That confounded tailor is certainly keeping me waiting, for a day when I have so much to do. That makes me mad. A quartan fever seize that blackguard of a tailor! Devil take the tailor! A plague on the tailor! If I had him here now, that detestable tailor, that dog of a tailor, that traitor of a tailor, I'd . . .

Scene 5.   MASTER TAILOR, JOURNEYMAN TAILOR *(carrying* MONSIEUR JOURDAIN*'s coat),* MONSIEUR JOURDAIN, LACKEYS

MONSIEUR JOURDAIN. Ah, there you are! I was just about to get angry with you.

MASTER TAILOR. I couldn't come any sooner, and I've had twenty of my men at work on your coat.

MONSIEUR JOURDAIN. The silk stockings you sent me were so tight that I had all the trouble in the world getting them on, and there are already two stitches broken.

MASTER TAILOR. They'll stretch all you need, and more.

MONSIEUR JOURDAIN. Yes, if I keep breaking stitches. Also, the shoes you made me hurt terribly.

MASTER TAILOR. Not at all, sir.

MONSIEUR JOURDAIN. What do you mean, not at all?

MASTER TAILOR. No, they don't hurt you.

MONSIEUR JOURDAIN. And *I* tell *you* they hurt me.

MASTER TAILOR. You're imagining it.

MONSIEUR JOURDAIN. I imagine it because I feel it. That's a fine kind of talk!

MASTER TAILOR. Look, here is the handsomest coat in all the court, and the best harmonized. It's a masterpiece to have invented a dignified coat that isn't black, and I defy the most creative tailors to match it in half a dozen tries.

MONSIEUR JOURDAIN. What in the world is this? You've put the flowers upside down.

MASTER TAILOR. You didn't tell me you wanted them right side up.

MONSIEUR JOURDAIN. Is that something you have to specify?

MASTER TAILOR. Yes, really. All persons of quality wear them this way.

MONSIEUR JOURDAIN. Persons of quality wear the flowers upside down?

MASTER TAILOR. Yes, sir.

MONSIEUR JOURDAIN. Oh, then that's fine.

MASTER TAILOR. If you wish, I'll put them right side up.

MONSIEUR JOURDAIN. No, no.

MASTER TAILOR. You have only to say so.

MONSIEUR JOURDAIN. No, I tell you; you did right. Do you think the coat will look well on me?

MASTER TAILOR. A fine question! I defy a painter with his brush to make you anything more becoming. I have one man who for putting together petticoat-breeches is the greatest genius in the world, and another who for assembling a doublet is the hero of our age.

MONSIEUR JOURDAIN. Are the wig and the plumes as they should be?

MASTER TAILOR. Everything is fine.

MONSIEUR JOURDAIN (*looking at the* MASTER TAILOR's *coat*). Aha, Mr. Tailor! There's some of my material from the last coat you made me. I recognize it all right.

MASTER TAILOR. The fact is that the material seemed to me so beautiful that I decided to cut a coat from it for me.

MONSIEUR JOURDAIN. Yes, but you shouldn't have cut it from my material.

MASTER TAILOR. Do you want to try on your coat?

MONSIEUR JOURDAIN. Yes, give it to me.

MASTER TAILOR. Wait. It doesn't go on that way. I've brought some men to dress you to music, and this kind of coat is to be put on with ceremony. Hello there! Come in, all of you. Put this coat on the gentleman in the way you do for persons of quality.

(Four TAILOR'S APPRENTICES *enter, of whom two take off the breeches worn for* MONSIEUR JOURDAIN's *exercises, and two others the jacket; then they put his new coat on him; and he promenades among them and shows off his coat to them to see if it looks good—all this to the music of the whole orchestra.)*

JOURNEYMAN TAILOR. Will the gentleman[5] please give the apprentices something to drink his health with?

MONSIEUR JOURDAIN. What did you call me?

JOURNEYMAN TAILOR. The gentleman.

MONSIEUR JOURDAIN. "The gentleman!" That's what it means to be gotten up as a person of quality! Just go on always dressing as a bourgeois, and nobody will call you "the gentleman." Here, that's for "the gentleman."

JOURNEYMAN TAILOR. My Lord, we're much obliged to you.

MONSIEUR JOURDAIN. "My Lord," oh, oh, "My Lord!" Wait, my friend: "My Lord" deserves something, and that's no small term, "My Lord." Here, this is what My Lord gives you.

JOURNEYMAN TAILOR. My Lord, we're all going to drink to the health of Your Eminence.

MONSIEUR JOURDAIN. "Your Eminence!" Oh, oh, oh! Wait, don't go away. "Your Eminence" to me! My word, if he goes on as far as "Your Highness," he'll get the whole purse. Here, this is for My Eminence.

---

[5] The title "gentleman" was restricted to a man of noble birth, whereas that of "nobleman" was often used of a man whose nobility had been acquired during his lifetime.

JOURNEYMAN TAILOR. My Lord, we thank you very humbly for your liberality.

MONSIEUR JOURDAIN. A good thing he stopped; I was going to give him the whole thing.

The four TAILOR'S APPRENTICES *express their joy in a dance that constitutes the* SECOND INTERLUDE.

ACT III

Scene 1. MONSIEUR JOURDAIN, LACKEYS

MONSIEUR JOURDAIN. Follow me while I go and show off my coat a bit around town; and above all be careful both of you to walk immediately in my footsteps so that people can clearly see that you belong to me.

LACKEYS. Yes, sir.

MONSIEUR JOURDAIN. Call Nicole for me, so I can give her a few orders. . . . Don't move, here she is.

Scene 2. NICOLE, MONSIEUR JOURDAIN, LACKEYS

MONSIEUR JOURDAIN. Nicole!

NICOLE. What is it?

MONSIEUR JOURDAIN. Listen.

NICOLE. Hee, hee, hee, hee, hee!

MONSIEUR JOURDAIN. What are you laughing at?

NICOLE. Hee, hee, hee, hee, hee, hee!

MONSIEUR JOURDAIN. What does that hussy mean?

NICOLE. Hee, hee, hee! The way you're dressed! Hee, hee, hee!

MONSIEUR JOURDAIN. How's that?

NICOLE. Oh, oh, Lord have mercy! Hee, hee, hee, hee, hee!

MONSIEUR JOURDAIN. What kind of a rascal is this? Are you making fun of me?

NICOLE. No, sir, I'd hate to do that. Hee, hee, hee, hee, hee, hee!

MONSIEUR JOURDAIN. I'll give you one on the nose if you laugh any more.

NICOLE. Sir, I can't help it. Hee, hee, hee, hee, hee, hee!

MONSIEUR JOURDAIN. Aren't you going to stop?

NICOLE. Sir, I ask your pardon; but you look so funny that I can't keep from laughing. Hee, hee, hee!

MONSIEUR JOURDAIN. Will you look at that insolence!

NICOLE. You're really a sketch like that. Hee, hee!

MONSIEUR JOURDAIN. I'll . . .

NICOLE. I beg you to excuse me. Hee, hee, hee, hee!

MONSIEUR JOURDAIN. Look here, if you laugh the least bit more, I swear I'll give you the biggest slap that ever was given.

NICOLE. Well, sir, it's all over, I won't laugh any more.

MONSIEUR JOURDAIN. Take good care that you don't. Now, to get ready, you must clean . . .

NICOLE. Hee, hee!

MONSIEUR JOURDAIN. Clean up properly . . .

NICOLE. Hee, hee!

MONSIEUR JOURDAIN. You must, I say, clean up the parlor, and . . .

NICOLE. Hee, hee!

MONSIEUR JOURDAIN. Again!

NICOLE. Look here, sir, just beat me and let me laugh to my heart's content. That'll do me more good. Hee, hee, hee, hee, hee!

MONSIEUR JOURDAIN. I'm getting mad.

NICOLE. Please, sir, I beg you to let me laugh. Hee, hee, hee!

MONSIEUR JOURDAIN. If I catch you . . .

NICOLE. Sir-ir, I'll blow-ow up if I don't laugh. Hee, hee, hee!

MONSIEUR JOURDAIN. Why, did anyone ever see such a hussy as that? She comes and laughs insolently in my face, instead of taking orders from me!

NICOLE. What do you want me to do, sir?

MONSIEUR JOURDAIN. To think, you wench, about getting my house ready for the company that's due to come soon.

NICOLE. Ah, faith! I've no more wish to laugh; and all your company makes such a mess in here that that word is enough to put me in a bad humor.

MONSIEUR JOURDAIN. I suppose that for your sake I should close my door to everybody?

NICOLE. You should at least close it to certain people.

Scene 3.   MADAME JOURDAIN, MONSIEUR JOURDAIN, NICOLE, LACKEYS

MADAME JOURDAIN. Aha! Here's a new one! What in the world, my dear husband, is that get-up? Is this some kind of joke, to have got yourself decked out like that, and do you want to have people everywhere make fun of you?

MONSIEUR JOURDAIN. My dear wife, there's none but the fools, male and female, who'll make fun of me.

MADAME JOURDAIN. Well, really, they haven't waited until now to do it, and it's been a long time now that your carryings-on have been making everybody laugh.

MONSIEUR JOURDAIN. And just who is this *everybody,* if you please?

MADAME JOURDAIN. This everybody is people who are right, and who have more sense than you. For my part, I'm scandalized at the life you're leading. I don't know what our house is any more; you'd think it was Mardi Gras every day; and from morning on, for fear we might miss it, we hear a great uproar of fiddlers and singers that disturbs the whole neighborhood.

NICOLE. Madame is quite right. I can't keep my house clean any more, with that train of people that you invite home. They have feet that go hunting for mud in every quarter of town to bring it here; and poor Françoise is almost worn out scrubbing the floors that your fine masters come and muddy up regularly every day.

MONSIEUR JOURDAIN. Well now, Nicole, our servant, you've got a mighty sharp line of chatter for a peasant girl.

MADAME JOURDAIN. Nicole is right, and she has better sense than you. I'd like to know what you think you can do with a dancing master at your age.

NICOLE. And with a great big master sword player, who comes stamping around and shakes the whole house and loosens all the tiles in the parlor floor?

MONSIEUR JOURDAIN. Be quiet, my maidservant and my wife.

MADAME JOURDAIN. Do you want to learn dancing for the time when your legs are gone?

NICOLE. Or do you have a hankering to kill somebody?

MONSIEUR JOURDAIN. Be quiet, I tell you: you are both ignoramuses, and you don't know the prerogatives of all that.

MADAME JOURDAIN. You should much rather be thinking of marrying off your daughter, who's of an age to be provided with a husband.

MONSIEUR JOURDAIN. I'll think about marrying off my daughter when a good match for her comes along; but I also want to think about learning the finer things of life.

NICOLE. I've also heard, Madame, that to top it off, today he took on a philosophy master.

MONSIEUR JOURDAIN. Indeed I did. I want to have wit and be able to reason about things among people of culture.

MADAME JOURDAIN. Won't you be going to school one of these days and having yourself whipped, at your age?

MONSIEUR JOURDAIN. Why not? Would God I could get whipped right now in front of everybody, and know the things they learn in school!

NICOLE. Faith, yes! That would do you a lot of good!

MONSIEUR JOURDAIN. Undoubtedly.

MADAME JOURDAIN. All that is mighty necessary for running your house!

MONSIEUR JOURDAIN. Of course it is. You're both talking like fools, and I'm ashamed of your ignorance. (To MADAME JOURDAIN) For example, you, do you know what it is you're saying right now?

MADAME JOURDAIN. Yes, I know that what I'm saying is very well said, and that you should do some thinking about living in a different way.

MONSIEUR JOURDAIN. I'm not talking about that. I'm asking you, what are the words that you're saying now?

MADAME JOURDAIN. They're very sensible words, and your conduct is scarcely that.

MONSIEUR JOURDAIN. I'm not talking about that, I tell you. I ask you: what I speak with you, what I'm saying to you right now, what is it?

MADAME JOURDAIN. Stuff and nonsense.

MONSIEUR JOURDAIN. Oh, no, it's not that! What we're both saying, the language we're speaking right now?

MADAME JOURDAIN. Well?

MONSIEUR JOURDAIN. What is that called?

MADAME JOURDAIN. That's called whatever you want to call it.

MONSIEUR JOURDAIN. It's prose, ignoramus.

MADAME JOURDAIN. Prose?

MONSIEUR JOURDAIN. Yes, prose. Everything that's prose is not verse; and everything that's not verse is not prose. Well, that's what it means to study. (To NICOLE) And you, do you know what you have to do to say U?

NICOLE. How's that?

MONSIEUR JOURDAIN. Yes. What do you do when you say U?

NICOLE. What?

MONSIEUR JOURDAIN. Just say U, to see.

NICOLE. Well then, U.

MONSIEUR JOURDAIN. Well, what is it you do?

NICOLE. I say U.

MONSIEUR JOURDAIN. Yes; but when you say U, what do you do?

NICOLE. I do what you tell me.

MONSIEUR JOURDAIN. Oh, what a strange business it is to have to deal with idiots! You thrust your lips out and bring the upper jaw close to the lower one: U. Do you see? U. I make a pout: U.

NICOLE. Yep, that's real purty.

MADAME JOURDAIN. That *is* admirable.

MONSIEUR JOURDAIN. It's something else again if you'd seen O, and DA, DA, and FA, FA.

MADAME JOURDAIN. What *is* all this rigmarole?

NICOLE. What does all this cure you of?

MONSIEUR JOURDAIN. It makes me mad to see ignorant women.

MADAME JOURDAIN. Go on, you ought to send all those people on their way, with their tomfoolery.

NICOLE. And especially that great lout of a fencing master, who fills my whole house with dust.

MONSIEUR JOURDAIN. Well, you've certainly got that fencing master on the brain. I want to show you how impertinent you are right now. (He has the foils brought and gives one to NICOLE.) Here you are. Demonstrative reasoning, the line of the body. When you thrust in quart, all you have to do is this; and when you thrust in tierce, all you have to do is this. That's the way never to get killed; and isn't that fine, to be certain of how you'll come out when you fight with somebody? There, try a thrust at me, to see.

NICOLE *(making several thrusts at* MONSIEUR JOURDAIN, *and as many touches)*. Well, what about it?

MONSIEUR JOURDAIN. Easy now! Hold on! Oh, gently! Devil take the hussy!

NICOLE. You told me to thrust.

MONSIEUR JOURDAIN. Yes, but you're thrusting in tierce before thrusting in quart, and you won't wait for me to parry.

MADAME JOURDAIN. You're crazy, my dear husband, with all your fancies; and this has all happened to you since you've been taking it into your head to hang around the nobility.

MONSIEUR JOURDAIN. When I hang around the nobility, I show my judgment, and that's better than hanging around your bourgeoisie.

MADAME JOURDAIN. Oh yes indeedy! There's a lot to be gained by going around with your noblemen, and you've done good business with that fine Monsieur le Comte that you're so stuck on.

MONSIEUR JOURDAIN. Peace. Think what you're saying. Do you know, my dear wife, that you don't know whom you're talking about when you talk about him? He's a person of more importance than you think, a lord who's well considered at court, and who talks to the King just as I'm talking to you. Isn't that a very honorable thing for me, for people to see a person of such quality coming to my house so often, calling me his dear friend, and treating me as if I were his equal? You'd never guess how good he is to me; and in front of everybody he shows me regards that leave me embarrassed myself.

MADAME JOURDAIN. Yes, he's good to you and shows you regards; but he borrows your money.

MONSIEUR JOURDAIN. Well! Isn't it an honor for me to lend money to a man of that rank? And can I do less for a lord who calls me his dear friend?

MADAME JOURDAIN. And this lord, what does he do for you?

MONSIEUR JOURDAIN. Things that would astonish people, if they knew them.

MADAME JOURDAIN. And what are they?

MONSIEUR JOURDAIN. Enough. I can't explain it all. Sufficient that if I've lent him money, he'll give it back to me all right, and before long.

MADAME JOURDAIN. Yes, just count on that.

MONSIEUR JOURDAIN. Of course; hasn't he told me so?

MADAME JOURDAIN. Yes, yes; he won't fail—not to do so.

MONSIEUR JOURDAIN. He's given me his word as a gentleman.

MADAME JOURDAIN. Fiddlesticks!

MONSIEUR JOURDAIN. Well now, you are mighty obstinate, my good wife. I tell you he'll keep his word, I'm sure.

MADAME JOURDAIN. And *I'm* sure he won't, and that all the attentions he shows you are only to cajole you.

MONSIEUR JOURDAIN. Be quiet; here he is.

MADAME JOURDAIN. That's all we need. Perhaps he's coming to get another loan from you; and I lose my appetite when I see him.

MONSIEUR JOURDAIN. Be quiet, I tell you.

Scene 4.   DORANTE, MONSIEUR JOURDAIN,
MADAME JOURDAIN, NICOLE

DORANTE. My dear friend Monsieur Jourdain,[6] how are you?

MONSIEUR JOURDAIN. Very well, sir, at your service.

6 As a form of address, *Monsieur* (or *Madame*) alone was polite in Molière's day; the form *Monsieur* (or *Madame*) *Jourdain* was pointedly impolite. Of course Monsieur Jourdain, in addressing Dorante, uses the polite form *Monsieur* (Sir) alone.

DORANTE. And Madame Jourdain here, how is she?

MADAME JOURDAIN. Madame Jourdain is doing as well as she can.

DORANTE. Well, Monsieur Jourdain, how elegant you are!

MONSIEUR JOURDAIN. As you see.

DORANTE. You look very smart in that coat, and we have no young men at court who are better turned out than you are.

MONSIEUR JOURDAIN. Heh, heh!

MADAME JOURDAIN (aside). He scratches him where he itches.

DORANTE. Turn around. That's utterly gallant.

MADAME JOURDAIN (aside). Yes, just as stupid from the rear as from the front.

DORANTE. Upon my word, Monsieur Jourdain, I was extraordinarily impatient to see you. You are the man I esteem the most in all the world, and I was talking about you just this morning in the King's bedchamber.

MONSIEUR JOURDAIN. You do me great honor, sir. (To MADAME JOURDAIN) In the King's bedchamber!

DORANTE. Come now, put on your hat.

MONSIEUR JOURDAIN. Sir, I know the respect that I owe you.

DORANTE. Good Lord, put it on! No ceremony between us, pray.

MONSIEUR JOURDAIN. Sir . . .

DORANTE. Put it on, I tell you, Monsieur Jourdain; you are my friend.

MONSIEUR JOURDAIN. Sir, I am your humble servant.

DORANTE. I won't put mine on unless you do.

MONSIEUR JOURDAIN (putting his hat on). I'd rather be uncivil than a nuisance.

DORANTE. I'm your debtor, as you know.

MADAME JOURDAIN (aside). Yes, we know it only too well.

DORANTE. You have generously lent me money on several occasions, and you have certainly obliged me with the best grace in the world.

MONSIEUR JOURDAIN. Sir, you're joking.

DORANTE. But I know how to repay what is lent me, and to recognize favors done me.

MONSIEUR JOURDAIN. I don't doubt it, sir.

DORANTE. I want to settle things up with you, and I've come here to clear up our accounts together.

MONSIEUR JOURDAIN (to MADAME JOURDAIN). Well! You see how silly you were, my good wife.

DORANTE. I'm a man who likes to pay up his debts as soon as he can.

MONSIEUR JOURDAIN (to MADAME JOURDAIN). I told you so!

DORANTE. Let's see now, what do I owe you?

MONSIEUR JOURDAIN (to MADAME JOURDAIN). There you are with your ridiculous suspicions!

DORANTE. Do you have a good recollection of all the money you've lent me?

MONSIEUR JOURDAIN. I think so. I've kept a little memorandum. Here it is. Given to you once, two hundred louis.

DORANTE. That's true.

MONSIEUR JOURDAIN. Another time, six score.

DORANTE. Yes.

MONSIEUR JOURDAIN. And another time, a hundred and forty.

DORANTE. You're right.

MONSIEUR JOURDAIN. These three items make four hundred and sixty louis, which come to five thousand and sixty francs.

DORANTE. The accounting is very good indeed. Five thousand and sixty francs.

MONSIEUR JOURDAIN. One thousand eight hundred and thirty-two francs to your plume-seller.

DORANTE. Precisely.

MONSIEUR JOURDAIN. Two thousand seven hundred and eighty francs to your tailor.

DORANTE. That's true.

MONSIEUR JOURDAIN. Four thousand three hundred and seventy-nine francs twelve sous eight deniers to your clothier.

DORANTE. Very good. Twelve sous eight deniers: the account is exact.

MONSIEUR JOURDAIN. And one thousand seven hundred and forty-eight francs seven sous four deniers to your saddler.

DORANTE. That's all exactly right. What does it come to?

MONSIEUR JOURDAIN. Sum total, fifteen thousand eight hundred francs.

DORANTE. Sum total is correct: fifteen thousand eight hundred francs. Now, add another two hundred pistoles that you're going to give me, that will make precisely eighteen thousand francs, which I'll pay you the first chance I get.

MADAME JOURDAIN (*to* MONSIEUR JOURDAIN). Well! Didn't I guess it all right?

MONSIEUR JOURDAIN (*to* MADAME JOURDAIN). Peace!

DORANTE. Will that inconvenience you, to give me what I've mentioned?

MONSIEUR JOURDAIN. Oh, no!

MADAME JOURDAIN (*to* MONSIEUR JOURDAIN). This man milks you like a cow.

MONSIEUR JOURDAIN. Be quiet.

DORANTE. If it's inconvenient for you, I'll look elsewhere.

MONSIEUR JOURDAIN. No, sir.

MADAME JOURDAIN (*to* MONSIEUR JOURDAIN). He won't be content until he's ruined you.

MONSIEUR JOURDAIN (*to* MADAME JOURDAIN). Shut up, I tell you.

DORANTE. You have only to tell me if it embarrasses you.

MONSIEUR JOURDAIN. Not at all, sir.

MADAME JOURDAIN (*to* MONSIEUR JOURDAIN). He's a real wheedler.

MONSIEUR JOURDAIN (*to* MADAME JOURDAIN). Shut up, you.

MADAME JOURDAIN (*to* MONSIEUR JOURDAIN). He'll suck you dry to your last sou.

MONSIEUR JOURDAIN (*to* MADAME JOURDAIN). Will you shut up?

DORANTE. I have plenty of people who would be overjoyed to lend me money; but since you are my best friend, I thought I would wrong you if I asked anyone else.

MONSIEUR JOURDAIN. You do me too much honor, sir. I'll go get what you want.

MADAME JOURDAIN (*to* MONSIEUR JOURDAIN). What? Are you going to give him that too?

MONSIEUR JOURDAIN (*to* MADAME JOURDAIN, *as he makes his exit*). What am I to do? Do you want me to refuse a man of that rank, who talked about me this morning in the King's bedchamber?

MADAME JOURDAIN. Go on, you're a real dupe.

Scene 5. DORANTE, MADAME JOURDAIN, NICOLE

DORANTE. You seem quite melancholy. What's the matter, Madame Jourdain?

MADAME JOURDAIN. My head's bigger than my fist, and it's not swollen at that.

DORANTE. And your charming daughter, where is she? I don't see her.

MADAME JOURDAIN. My charming daughter is fine where she is.

DORANTE. How is she getting along?

MADAME JOURDAIN. She's getting along on her own two legs.

DORANTE. Don't you want to come with her one of these days to see the ballet and comedy that are being performed before the King?

MADAME JOURDAIN. Yes indeed, we really want to laugh, really want to laugh we do.

DORANTE. I think, Madame Jourdain,,you had plenty of suitors in your younger days, pretty and good-humored as you were.

MADAME JOURDAIN. Land's sakes, sir! Is Madame Jourdain decrepit and doddering already?

DORANTE. Ah! Faith, Madame Jourdain, I beg your pardon. I wasn't thinking that you're still young, and I'm very absent-minded. I beg you to excuse my impertinence.

Scene 6. MONSIEUR JOURDAIN, MADAME JOURDAIN, DORANTE, NICOLE

MONSIEUR JOURDAIN. Here are two hundred louis exactly.

DORANTE. I assure you, Monsieur Jourdain, that I'm at your service, and I'm burning to do you a favor at court.

MONSIEUR JOURDAIN. I'm only too obliged to you.

DORANTE. If Madame Jourdain wants to see the entertainment before the King, I'll see that she gets the best seats in the house.

MADAME JOURDAIN. Madame Jourdain kisses your hands.

DORANTE (aside to MONSIEUR JOURDAIN). Our fair marquise, as I told you in my note, will come here soon for the ballet and the meal, and I finally got her to consent to the party you want to give her.

MONSIEUR JOURDAIN (aside to DORANTE). Let's go a little farther away, for good reason.

DORANTE. It's a week since I've seen you, and I haven't told you the latest about the diamond you placed in my hands to present to her on your behalf; but the fact is I've had all the trouble in the world in overcoming her scruples, and it's only today that she's made up her mind to accept it.

MONSIEUR JOURDAIN. How did she like it?

DORANTE. She thought it was wonderful; and unless I'm much mistaken, the beauty of that diamond will set you high in her regard.

MONSIEUR JOURDAIN. Would God!

MADAME JOURDAIN (*to* NICOLE). Once he's with him, he can't leave him.

DORANTE. I made the most to her of the richness of this present and the greatness of your love.

MONSIEUR JOURDAIN. These are kindnesses, sir, that overwhelm me; and I am most greatly embarrassed to see a person of your rank lower himself for my sake to do what you're doing.

DORANTE. Are you joking? Between friends, does one stop at this sort of scruple? And wouldn't you do the same thing for me if the occasion should arise?

MONSIEUR JOURDAIN. Oh, certainly, and with all my heart!

MADAME JOURDAIN (*to* NICOLE). How his presence weighs on me!

DORANTE. For my part, I don't worry about anything when a friend needs a service; and when you confided to me the passion you had formed for this charming marquise whom I knew, you saw that right away I freely offered myself to serve your love.

MONSIEUR JOURDAIN. That's true, these are kindnesses that embarrass me.

MADAME JOURDAIN (*to* NICOLE). Won't he ever go away?

NICOLE (*to* MADAME JOURDAIN). They like to be together.

DORANTE. You took the right approach to touch her heart. Above all else women like the expenditures people make for them; and your frequent serenades and continual bouquets, that

superb display of fireworks on the water, the diamond she has
received on your behalf, and the party you are preparing for
her—all this speaks to her far better in favor of your love than
any words you might have said to her yourself.

MONSIEUR JOURDAIN. There are no expenditures I would not
make if thereby I could find the way to her heart. A woman
of quality has ravishing charms for me, and it's an honor
I would buy at any price.

MADAME JOURDAIN (*to* NICOLE). What can they be talking about
for so long? Go up quietly and lend an ear a bit.

DORANTE. You will soon enjoy at your ease the pleasure of seeing her, and your eyes will have all the time you want to be
satisfied.

MONSIEUR JOURDAIN. To be completely free, I've arranged for
my wife to go and dine at my sister's and stay on the whole
time after dinner.

DORANTE. You have acted prudently, and your wife might have
embarrassed us. I've given the necessary orders for you to
the cook, and for all the things that are needed for the ballet.
It's a composition of my own; and provided the execution
comes up to my idea, I'm sure it will be found . . .

MONSIEUR JOURDAIN (*noticing that* NICOLE *is listening, and
giving her a slap*). Well, you're mighty impertinent! (*To*
DORANTE) Let's get out of here, if you please.

Scene 7. MADAME JOURDAIN, NICOLE

NICOLE. Faith, Madame! Curiosity cost me something; but I
think I smell a rat, and they're talking about some affair
where they don't want you to be.

MADAME JOURDAIN. Today's not the first time, Nicole, that I've
had suspicions about my husband. Unless I'm utterly mistaken,
he's trying to promote some amour, and I'm trying to find
out what it may be. But let's think about my daughter. You

know about Cléonte's love for her. He's a man I like, and I
want to help his suit and give him Lucile if I can.

NICOLE. To tell the truth, Madame, I'm most delighted to see
that this is your feeling; for if you like the master, I like the
valet no less, and I could wish that our marriage might take
place in the shadow of theirs.

MADAME JOURDAIN. Go and speak to him for me, and tell him
to come and see me as soon as he can, so that together we
can ask my husband for my daughter's hand.

NICOLE. I'll run and do it with joy, Madame, and I couldn't be
given a pleasanter errand.   (*Exit* MADAME JOURDAIN.)
I think I'm going to make the men very happy.

Scene 8.   CLÉONTE, COVIELLE, NICOLE

NICOLE. Ah, there you are, just at the right time. I am a bearer
of joyful news, and I come . . .

CLÉONTE. Go away, perfidious girl, and don't come and beguile
me with your traitorous words.

NICOLE. Is that the way you receive . . . ?

CLÉONTE. Go away, I tell you. Go to your faithless mistress
right away and tell her that she will never again in her life
delude the too simple Cléonte.

NICOLE. What sort of caprice is that? My poor dear Covielle,
give me some idea of what this means.

COVIELLE. My poor dear Covielle! You little minx! Come on,
quick, get out of my sight, wretched girl, and leave me in
peace!

NICOLE. What? You too . . . !

COVIELLE. Get out of my sight, I tell you, and never speak to me
again in your life!

NICOLE. Well! What's bitten the two of them? Let's go and
inform my mistress of this fine how-do-you-do.

Scene 9.   CLÉONTE, COVIELLE

CLÉONTE. What? Treat a sweetheart in that way, and a sweetheart who is the most faithful and passionate of all sweethearts!

COVIELLE. It's a frightful thing, what they're doing to the two of us.

CLÉONTE. I reveal for a certain person all the ardor and all the tenderness imaginable; I love nothing in the world but her, and have her alone in my mind; she constitutes all my cares, all my desires, all my joy; I speak of her alone, think of her alone, dream of her alone, breathe through her alone, my heart lives in her alone: and this is the fitting reward for so much affection! I go two days without seeing her, which for me are two frightful centuries; I meet her by chance; my heart, at the sight of her, is all transported, my joy bursts out on my face, I fly toward her in ecstasy; and the faithless creature turns her eyes away from me and passes brusquely by, as if she had never seen me in her life!

COVIELLE. I say the same things as you do.

CLÉONTE. Is it possible, Covielle, for anything to match this perfidy of the ingrate Lucile?

COVIELLE. Or that, sir, of that hussy Nicole?

CLÉONTE. After so many ardent sacrifices, sighs, and vows that I've offered to her charms!

COVIELLE. After so many assiduous homages, so many attentions and services I've done for her in the kitchen!

CLÉONTE. So many tears that I've shed at her knees!

COVIELLE. So many buckets of water that I've drawn from the well for her!

CLÉONTE. So much ardor I've shown in cherishing her more than myself!

COVIELLE. So much heat I've endured turning the spit in place of her!

CLÉONTE. She flees me with disdain!

COVIELLE. She turns her back on me with effrontery!

CLÉONTE. It's perfidy worthy of the greatest punishments.

COVIELLE. It's a betrayal that deserves a thousand slaps in the face.

CLÉONTE. Don't ever take it into your head, I pray you, to speak to me on her behalf.

COVIELLE. I, sir! God forbid!

CLÉONTE. Don't come to me with excuses for this faithless girl's action.

COVIELLE. Have no fear.

CLÉONTE. No, you see, all you may say to defend her will be no use.

COVIELLE. Who has that in mind?

CLÉONTE. I want to preserve my resentment against her, and break off all relations with her.

COVIELLE. I consent to that.

CLÉONTE. Perhaps that Monsieur le Comte who goes to her house has caught her eye; and her mind, I can see, is letting itself be dazzled by rank. But, for my own honor, I must forestall the revelation of her inconstancy. I mean to keep step with her in this change toward which I see her hurrying, and not let her have all the glory of leaving me.

COVIELLE. That's very well said, and I, on my own account, share all your feelings.

CLÉONTE. Lend a hand to my spite, and support my resolve against any remains of love that might speak to me on her behalf. Tell me, I beseech you, all the bad things you can about her; paint me a portrait of her person that will make her contemptible to me; and point out to me clearly, to destroy my taste for her, all the defects you can see in her.

COVIELLE. She, sir! She's a girl who puts on a lot of airs, an affected bit of goods, a fine one for you to be so much in love with! I see nothing in her that isn't very ordinary, and you can find a hundred girls that will be more worthy of you. In the first place, her eyes are small.[7]

CLÉONTE. That's true, her eyes are small; but they're full of fire; they're the most brilliant, the most piercing in the world, the most touching to be seen anywhere.

COVIELLE. Her mouth is large.

CLÉONTE. Yes; but there are graces to be seen in it that you don't see in other mouths; and that mouth, when you see it, inspires desires, is the most attractive, the most loving in the world.

COVIELLE. As for her figure, it's not tall.

CLÉONTE. No, but it's graceful and well built.

COVIELLE. She affects nonchalance in her speech and in her actions.

CLÉONTE. That's true; but she does so with grace, and her manners are engaging; they have an indefinable charm that insinuates itself into the heart.

COVIELLE. As for wit . . .

CLÉONTE. Ah, that she has, Covielle, of the most subtle and delicate kind.

COVIELLE. Her conversation . . .

CLÉONTE. Her conversation is charming.

COVIELLE. She's always serious.

CLÉONTE. Do you want broad playfulness, everlasting expansive gaiety? And do you find anything sillier than women who laugh at everything?

COVIELLE. But finally, she's as capricious as anybody in the world.

CLÉONTE. Yes, she is capricious, I agree; but in beautiful women everything looks good, we put up with anything from beautiful women.

7 There is a tradition that what follows is a portrait of Molière's wife Armande, who played Lucile.

COVIELLE. Since that's the way it goes, I see perfectly well that you want to love her forever.

CLÉONTE. I? I'd rather die; and I'm going to hate her as much as I've loved her.

COVIELLE. And how, if you find her so perfect?

CLÉONTE. That's how my revenge will be the more brilliant, and how I mean to show my strength of heart all the better, by hating her, by leaving her, beautiful, attractive, and lovable as I find her to be . . . Here she is.

Scene 10.   CLÉONTE, LUCILE, COVIELLE, NICOLE

NICOLE. For my part, I was utterly scandalized.

LUCILE. It can only be what I'm telling you, Nicole. But here he is.

CLÉONTE (to COVIELLE). I won't even speak to her.

COVIELLE. I'll follow your example.

LUCILE. Why, what is it, Cléonte? What's the matter?

NICOLE. What's wrong with you, Covielle?

LUCILE. What makes you so distressed?

NICOLE. What's put you in such a bad humor?

LUCILE. Are you struck dumb, Cléonte?

NICOLE. Have you lost your tongue, Covielle?

CLÉONTE. What a crime!

COVIELLE. What a couple of Judases!

LUCILE. I see perfectly well that our recent encounter has troubled your mind.

CLÉONTE. Aha! They see what they've done.

NICOLE. Our greeting this morning got your goat.

COVIELLE. They've guessed where the shoe pinches.

LUCILE. Isn't it true, Cléonte, that that's the cause of your vexation?

CLÉONTE. Yes, perfidious woman, it is, since speak I must. And let me tell you that you shall not triumph in your faithlessness as you expect, that I mean to be the first to break with you, and that you shall not have the advantage of sending me away. No doubt I'll have trouble in conquering the love I have for you, it will cause me distress, I shall suffer for a time; but I'll get over it, and I'll sooner pierce my own heart than be so weak as to return to you.

COVIELLE. Same here.

LUCILE. That's a lot of fuss over nothing. I want to tell you, Cléonte, what it was made me avoid your greeting this morning.

CLÉONTE. No, I won't listen to a thing.

NICOLE. I want to let you know the reason we went by so quickly.

COVIELLE. I won't hear a thing.

LUCILE. Know that this morning . . .

CLÉONTE. No, I tell you.

NICOLE. Learn that . . .

COVIELLE. No, traitress.

LUCILE. Listen!

CLÉONTE. No such thing.

NICOLE. Let me speak.

COVIELLE. I'm deaf.

LUCILE. Cléonte!

CLÉONTE. No.

NICOLE. Covielle!

COVIELLE. Not a bit.

LUCILE. Stop!

CLÉONTE. Nonsense!

NICOLE. Hear me!

COVIELLE. Fiddlesticks!

LUCILE. One moment.

CLÉONTE. Not at all.

NICOLE. A little patience.

COVIELLE. Bunk.

LUCILE. Two words!

CLÉONTE. No, it's all over.

NICOLE. One word!

COVIELLE. We're all through.

LUCILE. Well! Since you won't listen to me, keep on thinking what you're thinking, and do as you please.

NICOLE. Since that's how you're acting, take it any way you like.

(Up to this point the girls have been following the young men around the stage; from now on the young men follow the girls.)

CLÉONTE. All right, let's know the reason for such a fine greeting.

LUCILE. I don't feel like telling it any more.

COVIELLE. All right, just tell us this story.

NICOLE. Me, I don't want to tell it to you any more.

CLÉONTE. Say what . . .

LUCILE. No, I won't say a thing.

COVIELLE. Tell me . . .

NICOLE. No, I'm not telling a thing.

CLÉONTE. Please.

LUCILE. No, I tell you.

COVIELLE. Out of charity . . .

NICOLE. Nothing doing.

CLÉONTE. I beg you.

LUCILE. Let me be.

COVIELLE. I conjure you.

NICOLE. Get out of here.

CLÉONTE. Lucile!

LUCILE. No.

COVIELLE. Nicole!

NICOLE. Not a bit.

CLÉONTE. In the name of the gods!

LUCILE. I won't.

COVIELLE. Speak to me.

NICOLE. Not at all.

CLÉONTE. Clear up my doubts.

LUCILE. No, I'll do nothing of the sort.

COVIELLE. Cure my mind.

NICOLE. No, I don't feel like it.

CLÉONTE. Well! Since you care so little about ending my pain and justifying yourself for your unworthy treatment of my flame, you see me, ingrate, for the last time, and I'm going far away from you to die of grief and love.

COVIELLE. And I'm going to follow in his footsteps.

LUCILE. Cléonte!

NICOLE. Covielle!

CLÉONTE. Eh?

COVIELLE. What is it?

LUCILE. Where are you going?

CLÉONTE. Where I told you.

COVIELLE. We're going to die.

LUCILE. You're going to die, Cléonte?

CLÉONTE. Yes, cruel girl, since you want it.

LUCILE. *I* want you to die?

CLÉONTE. Yes, you want it.

LUCILE. Who says so?

CLÉONTE. Isn't it wanting it not to want to clear up my suspicions?

LUCILE. Is that my fault? If you'd been willing to listen to me, wouldn't I have told you that the incident this morning that you're complaining about was caused by the presence of an old aunt of mine who absolutely insists that the mere approach of a man dishonors a girl, who preaches us sermons perpetually on this subject, and who pictures all men to us as devils whom we must flee.

NICOLE. That's the secret of the matter.

CLÉONTE. You're not deceiving me, Lucile?

COVIELLE. You're not handing me a line?

LUCILE. Nothing could be more true.

NICOLE. That's the thing as it is.

COVIELLE *(to* CLÉONTE*)*. Do we give in to this?

CLÉONTE. Ah, Lucile! With one word from your lips, how many things you can appease in my heart! And how easily we let ourselves be persuaded by the persons we love!

COVIELLE. How easily we get softened up by these confounded creatures!

Scene 11.   MADAME JOURDAIN, CLÉONTE, LUCILE, COVIELLE, NICOLE

MADAME JOURDAIN. I'm very glad to see you, Cléonte, and you're here at the right time. My husband's coming; take your chance quickly to ask him for Lucile's hand in marriage.

CLÉONTE. Ah, Madame, how sweet these words are to me, and how they flatter my desires! Could I receive a more charming order, a more precious favor?

Scene 12. MONSIEUR JOURDAIN, MADAME JOURDAIN, CLÉONTE, LUCILE, COVIELLE, NICOLE

CLÉONTE. Sir, I didn't want to get anyone else to make a request of you that I have long been meditating. It concerns me closely enough for me to take it on myself; and so, without beating around the bush further, I will tell you that the honor of being your son-in-law is a glorious favor that I beg you to grant me.

MONSIEUR JOURDAIN. Before giving you an answer, sir, I ask you to tell me if you are a gentleman.

CLÉONTE. Sir, most people don't hesitate much on this question. The word is easy to throw around. People have no scruples about assuming this title, and usage today seems to authorize the theft of it. For my part, I admit, I have slightly more delicate feelings about this matter. I think that any imposture is unworthy of an honorable man, and that there is cowardice in disguising what Heaven had us born to be, in adorning ourselves in the eyes of the world with a stolen title, in trying to pass ourselves off for what we are not. To be sure, I was born of ancestors who have held honorable positions. I have acquired the honor of six years of service under arms, and I have enough means to hold a pretty passable position in society. But with all that, I don't want to give myself a title that others in my place would feel entitled to assume, and I will tell you frankly that I am not a gentleman.

MONSIEUR JOURDAIN. Shake on it, sir; my daughter is not for you.

CLÉONTE. How's that?

MONSIEUR JOURDAIN. You're not a gentleman, you shall not have my daughter.

MADAME JOURDAIN. What are you talking about with your gentleman business? Are *we* sprung from Saint Louis's rib?

MONSIEUR JOURDAIN. Be quiet, wife; I can see you coming.

MADAME JOURDAIN. Are we both descended from anything but good bourgeois?

MONSIEUR JOURDAIN. There goes your tongue!

MADAME JOURDAIN. And wasn't your father a tradesman just like mine?

MONSIEUR JOURDAIN. Plague take the woman! She's never failed. If your father was a tradesman, too bad for him; but as for mine, it's only the ill-informed who say so. As for me, all I have to say to you is that I want to have a gentleman for my son-in-law.

MADAME JOURDAIN. Your daughter needs a husband who is suited to her, and she'd be much better off with an honorable man who is rich and attractive than with a beggarly and unattractive gentleman.

NICOLE. That's true. In our village we have the gentleman's son who's the biggest oaf and the stupidest lout I've ever seen.

MONSIEUR JOURDAIN. Shut up, you, with your impertinence. You're always butting into the conversation. I have enough money for my daughter, all I need is honor, and I want to make her a marquise.

MADAME JOURDAIN. A marquise?

MONSIEUR JOURDAIN. Yes, a marquise.

MADAME JOURDAIN. Alas! God forbid!

MONSIEUR JOURDAIN. It's something I've decided on.

MADAME JOURDAIN. It's something *I'll* never consent to. Marriages above your station are always subject to unpleasant drawbacks. I don't want a son-in-law to be able to reproach my daughter for her parents, and for her to have children who are ashamed to call me their grandma. If she had to come and visit me decked out like a grand lady, and by mistake failed to greet someone in the neighborhood, right away people wouldn't fail to say a hundred stupid things. "Do you see that Madame la Marquise," they'd say, "with her high and mighty airs? That's Monsieur Jourdain's daughter, who was only too happy, when she was little, to play at being a fine lady with us. She wasn't always as lofty as she is now, and both her grandfathers used to sell cloth by the Porte Saint-Innocent. They piled up some wealth for their children, which they may be paying mighty dear for now in the other world, and you just don't get that rich by being honest folk." I don't want all that gossip; and in a word, I want a man who will feel obliged to me for my daughter, and to whom I can say: "Sit down there, my son-in-law, and have dinner with me."

MONSIEUR JOURDAIN. Those are certainly the sentiments of a petty mind, to want to remain always in lowliness. Don't answer me further; my daughter shall be a marquise in spite of everybody; and if you get me angry, I'll make her a duchess.   *(Exit)*

MADAME JOURDAIN. Cléonte, don't lose heart yet. Follow me, my daughter, and come and tell your father resolutely that if you don't get him, you won't marry anyone.

Scene 13.   CLÉONTE, COVIELLE

COVIELLE. You made a fine success of it with your fine sentiments.

CLÉONTE. Well, what would you have me do? On that score I have scruples that example cannot overcome.

COVIELLE. Are you joking, to take the matter seriously with a man like that? Don't you see he's crazy? And was it costing you anything to accommodate yourself to his fancies?

CLÉONTE. You're right; but I didn't think you had to give your proofs of nobility to be the son-in-law of Monsieur Jourdain.

COVIELLE. Ha, ha, ha!

CLÉONTE. What are you laughing about?

COVIELLE. An idea that comes to my mind to play a trick on our man and have you get what you want.

CLÉONTE. How's that?

COVIELLE. It's a really funny notion.

CLÉONTE. What is it then?

COVIELLE. There has been a certain masquerade performed for a little while that would do perfectly here, and that I'd like to work into a hoax I want to perpetrate on this ridiculous man of ours. The whole thing smacks a bit of low comedy; but with him you can risk anything, you don't have to be too careful; and he's the man to play his own part in it to perfection, to lend himself easily to all the nonsense we take it into our heads to tell him. I have the actors, I have the costumes all ready; just leave it to me.

CLÉONTE. But tell me . . .

COVIELLE. I'll tell you all about it. Let's leave, he's coming back.

Scene 14.   MONSIEUR JOURDAIN, LACKEY

MONSIEUR JOURDAIN. What the devil is all this? They have nothing to reproach me for but the noble lords; and I don't think anything is as fine as to associate with noble lords. With them there is nothing but honor and civility; and I wish it had cost me two fingers off my hand, and I'd been born a count or a marquis.

LACKEY. Sir, here is Monsieur le Comte, and a lady on his arm.

MONSIEUR JOURDAIN. Oh my Lord! I have some orders to give. Tell them I'll be here right away.

Scene 15.   DORIMÈNE, DORANTE, LACKEY

LACKEY. The master says like he'll be here right away.

DORANTE. Very good.

DORIMÈNE. I don't know, Dorante; this is another strange thing
I'm doing here, letting you take me into a house where I don't
know anybody.

DORANTE. Then what place, Madame, would you have my love
choose to entertain you, since, to avoid publicity, you want
neither your house nor mine?

DORIMÈNE. But you don't mention that I'm becoming involved
imperceptibly every day by accepting excessive tokens of your
passion. I try to defend myself against these things, but you
wear down my resistance; and you have a polite obstinacy
which makes me come around gradually to whatever you like.
It began with the frequent visits; the declarations came next,
which brought after them the serenades and entertainments,
which were followed by the presents. I opposed all that; but
you don't give up, and step by step you overcome my resolutions. For me, I can no longer answer for anything, and I
think that in the end you'll persuade me to marriage, which
I have put so far from my mind.

DORANTE. Faith, Madame! You should be married already. You're
a widow, and dependent only on yourself. I am my own
master, and I love you more than my life. What is to keep you
from making my happiness complete this very day?

DORIMÈNE. Good Lord, Dorante! Many qualities on both sides
are needed to live happily together; and the two most reasonable people in the world often have trouble in forming a union
to their satisfaction.

DORANTE. You can't be serious, Madame, in picturing so many
difficulties in this; and the experience you have had proves
nothing about all the others.

DORIMÈNE. Anyway, I still come back to this: the expenditures
I see you make for me worry me for two reasons: one, they
commit me more than I would like; and two, I am sure
—no offense—that you do not make them without financial
embarrassment; and I don't want that.

DORANTE. Ah, Madame, those are trifles; and it's not by those . . .

DORIMÈNE. I know what I'm saying; and among other things,
the diamond you forced me to accept is so valuable . . .

DORANTE. Oh, Madame! Please don't make so much of something that my love finds unworthy of you; and permit . . . Here's the master of the house.

Scene 16.   MONSIEUR JOURDAIN, DORIMÈNE, DORANTE, LACKEY

MONSIEUR JOURDAIN *(after making two bows as he steps forward, and finding himself too close to* DORIMÈNE). A little farther back, Madame.

DORIMÈNE. How's that?

MONSIEUR JOURDAIN. One step back, if you please.

DORIMÈNE. What?

MONSIEUR JOURDAIN. Step back a bit, for the third.

DORANTE. Madame, Monsieur Jourdain knows his etiquette.

MONSIEUR JOURDAIN. Madame, it's a very great glory for me to find myself so fortunate as to be so happy as to have the happiness that you have had the goodness to grant me the grace of doing me the honor of honoring me with the favor of your presence; and if I also had the merit of meriting a merit like yours, and if Heaven . . . envious of my good fortune . . . had granted me . . . the advantage of finding myself worthy . . . of the . . .

DORANTE. Monsieur Jourdain, that's enough of that. Madame does not like great compliments, and she knows that you are a man of wit. *(Aside, to* DORIMÈNE) He's a good bourgeois, rather ridiculous, as you see, in all his manners.

DORIMÈNE *(aside, to* DORANTE). It's not hard to see that.

DORANTE. Madame, this is the best of my friends.

MONSIEUR JOURDAIN. You do me too much honor.

DORANTE. A complete man of the world.

DORIMÈNE. I have much esteem for him.

MONSIEUR JOURDAIN. I've done nothing yet, Madame, to deserve that favor.

DORANTE *(aside, to* MONSIEUR JOURDAIN). Be very careful, at any rate, that you don't speak to her about the diamond you gave her.

MONSIEUR JOURDAIN *(aside, to* DORANTE). Couldn't I just ask her how she likes it?

DORANTE *(aside, to* MONSIEUR JOURDAIN). What? See that you don't. That would be vulgar of you; and to act as a man of the world, you have to behave as though it wasn't you who gave her that present. *(Aloud)* Madame, Monsieur Jourdain says he is delighted to see you in his house.

DORIMÈNE. He honors me greatly.

MONSIEUR JOURDAIN *(aside, to* DORANTE). How obliged I am to you, sir, for speaking to her thus for me!

DORANTE *(aside, to* MONSIEUR JOURDAIN). I had frightful difficulty in getting her to come.

MONSIEUR JOURDAIN *(aside, to* DORANTE). I don't know how to thank you for it.

DORANTE. He says, Madame, that he thinks you're the most beautiful person in the world.

DORIMÈNE. That's very gracious of him.

MONSIEUR JOURDAIN. Madame, the graciousness is all on your side; and . . .

DORANTE. Let's think about eating.

LACKEY. Everything is ready, sir.

DORANTE. Then let's sit down, and send in the musicians.

Six COOKS, *who have prepared the feast, perform a dance together, which makes up the* THIRD INTERLUDE. *After that, they bring in a table covered with various dishes.*

ACT IV

Scene 1. DORANTE, DORIMÈNE, MONSIEUR JOURDAIN, *two* MEN
SINGERS, *a* WOMAN SINGER, LACKEYS

DORIMÈNE. Why, Dorante! This is a really magnificent meal!

MONSIEUR JOURDAIN. You're joking, Madame, and I wish it
was more worthy of being offered to you.
(They all take their seats at the table.)

DORANTE. Monsieur Jourdain is right, Madame, to speak in this
way, and he obliges me by doing you the honors of his house
so well. I agree with him that the meal is not worthy of you.
Since it was I who ordered it, and since I do not have the
sophistication of our friends in this matter, you don't have a
very learned meal here, and you will find in it some gastro-
nomic incongruities and some barbarisms in the matter of
good taste. If Damis had had a hand in it, everything would
be according to the rules; there would be elegance and erudition everywhere; and he would not fail, himself, to overpraise
to you all the parts of the meal that he would serve, and to
make you agree to his high capacity in the science of tidbits:
to talk to you of his rolls cooked on the edge of the oven,
golden brown, crusted all over, crunching delicately under
the teeth; of a wine with a velvety savor, armed with a youthful vigor that is not too dominating; a breast of lamb gar-
nished with parsley; a loin of Normandy veal, just so long,
white, delicate, and like real almond paste under your teeth;
partridges seasoned with a surprising bouquet; and for his
masterpiece, a plump young turkey flanked by squabs, in a
pearly bouillon, crowned with white onions wedded to
chicory. But as for me, I confess my ignorance; and as Monsieur Jourdain has very well said, I wish the meal were more
worthy of being offered you.

DORIMÈNE. My only reply to this compliment is to eat as I am doing.

MONSIEUR JOURDAIN. Ah, what beautiful hands!

DORIMÈNE. The hands are very ordinary, Monsieur Jourdain; but no doubt you mean to speak of the diamond, which is very beautiful.

MONSIEUR JOURDAIN. I, Madame! God forbid that I should mean to speak of it; that would not be acting like a man of the world, and the diamond is a very small thing.

DORIMÈNE. You're very hard to please.

MONSIEUR JOURDAIN. You are too kind . . .

DORANTE. Come, serve some wine to Monsieur Jourdain and to these gentlemen, who will do us the kindness of singing us a drinking air.

DORIMÈNE. It's a marvelous seasoning for good cheer, to combine it with music, and I find myself being admirably entertained here.

MONSIEUR JOURDAIN. Madame, it's not . . .

DORANTE. Monsieur Jourdain, let's be quiet for these gentlemen; what they will tell us will be better than anything we could say.
(*The* MUSICIANS *take glasses and sing two drinking songs, accompanied by the whole orchestra.*)

First Drinking Song

Just a wee drop of wine, Phyllis, to start the round.
Ah! Ah! How in your hands a glass is full of charms!
*   You and the wine, you lend each other arms,*
And for you both my love is doubled at a bound.
*   So you and I let's swear, between us three,*
*   Love that shall always be.*

Wetting your mouth, it is embellished with love's shafts,
And as you see, by it your mouth is set on fire;
*   Each of the other fills me with desire;*
Of you and it I drink intoxicating drafts.

So you and I let's swear, between us three,
Love that shall always be.

Second Drinking Song

Friends, let's drink, let's pass the glass.
Time invites us, and it's fleeting.
Let's enjoy life and this meeting
All we can, alas!
When we've passed the gloomy brink,
Our links with wine and love we sever,
So let's hurry up and drink;
We can't drink forever.

Leave discussion to the asses
On man's true felicity.
For our own philosophy
Finds it in the glasses.
Riches, learning, and renown
Don't remove care and distress;
Only when we drink it down
Can we taste happiness.

Chorus

Come on, then, wine all round, come on, then, pour, boys, pour,
Keep pouring, keep pouring, till no one asks for more.

DORIMÈNE. I don't think it's possible to sing better, and that's quite lovely.

MONSIEUR JOURDAIN. I still see something lovelier here, Madame.

DORIMÈNE. Well! Monsieur Jourdain is more gallant than I thought.

DORANTE. Why, Madame, what do you take Monsieur Jourdain for?

MONSIEUR JOURDAIN. I certainly wish she'd take me for what I could mention.

DORIMÈNE. Still at it?

DORANTE. You don't know him.

MONSIEUR JOURDAIN. She'll know me whenever she likes.

DORIMÈNE. Oh! I give it up.

DORANTE. He's a man who always has an answer ready. But Madame, you aren't noticing that Monsieur Jourdain eats all the morsels you touch.

DORIMÈNE. Monsieur Jourdain is a man who delights me.

MONSIEUR JOURDAIN. If I could delight your heart, I would be . . .

Scene 2.   MADAME JOURDAIN, MONSIEUR JOURDAIN, DORIMÈNE, DORANTE, MUSICIANS, LACKEYS

MADAME JOURDAIN. Aha! I find nice company here, and I can easily see that I wasn't expected. So it's on account of this fine affair, my worthy husband, that you were so eager to send me to dinner at my sister's? I've just seen a sort of theater downstairs, and here I see a banquet fit for a wedding. This is how you spend your money, and this is the way you entertain ladies in my absence, and offer them music and a play, while you send me packing?

DORANTE. What do you mean, Madame Jourdain? And what kind of fancies do you have, to take it into your head that your husband is spending his money, and that he's the one who's giving this party for Madame? Pray learn that I'm the one; that all he's doing is just lending me his house, and that you should be a little more careful about the things you say.

MONSIEUR JOURDAIN. Yes, you impertinent woman, it's Monsieur le Comte who is offering all this to Madame, who is a lady of quality. He is doing me the honor of taking my house and wanting me to be with him.

MADAME JOURDAIN. That's a lot of nonsense; I know what I know.

DORANTE. Madame Jourdain, put on a better pair of spectacles.

MADAME JOURDAIN. I have no use for spectacles, sir, and I see clear enough. I've sensed things for a long time, and I'm not a fool. For a great lord, it's very mean of you to lend a hand as you do to my husband's follies. And you, Madame, for a great lady, it's neither nice nor decent of you to sow dissension in a family and allow my husband to be in love with you.

DORIMÈNE. Why, what is the meaning of all this? Come, Dorante, this is a poor joke to expose me to the silly delusions of this madwoman. *(Exit)*

DORANTE. Madame, stay! Madame, where are you running off to?

MONSIEUR JOURDAIN. Madame! Monsieur le Comte, make my excuses to her, and try to bring her back . . . *(Exit DORANTE.)* *(To MADAME JOURDAIN)* Ah! You impertinent woman, that was a fine performance! You come and affront me in front of everyone, and you drive people of quality out of my house!

MADAME JOURDAIN. I don't care a rap about their quality.

MONSIEUR JOURDAIN. Confound you, I don't know what keeps me from cracking your skull with the leftovers of the meal you came and broke up.
(The LACKEYS remove the table.)

MADAME JOURDAIN. I don't care a rap about that. It's my rights I'm defending, and all the women will be on my side. *(Exit)*

MONSIEUR JOURDAIN. You do well to avoid my anger. *(Alone)* She certainly arrived at a bad time. I was in the mood to say some pretty things, and I never had felt so full of wit. . . . What's all this?

Scene 3. COVIELLE *(in Oriental costume, with a long beard)*, MONSIEUR JOURDAIN, LACKEYS

COVIELLE. Sir, I don't know whether I have the honor of being known to you.

MONSIEUR JOURDAIN. No, sir.

COVIELLE. I knew you when you were no bigger than that *(holding his hand not far above the floor)*.

MONSIEUR JOURDAIN. Me?

COVIELLE. Yes, you were the handsomest child in the world, and all the ladies would take you in their arms to kiss you.

MONSIEUR JOURDAIN. To kiss me!

COVIELLE. Yes. I was a great friend of your honorable late father.

MONSIEUR JOURDAIN. Of my honorable late father!

COVIELLE. Yes. He was a very fine gentleman.

MONSIEUR JOURDAIN. What's that you say?

COVIELLE. I say he was a very fine gentleman.

MONSIEUR JOURDAIN. My father!

COVIELLE. Yes.

MONSIEUR JOURDAIN. You knew him well?

COVIELLE. Certainly.

MONSIEUR JOURDAIN. And you knew him to be a gentleman?

COVIELLE. Beyond a doubt.

MONSIEUR JOURDAIN. Then I don't know what the world is coming to.

COVIELLE. How's that?

MONSIEUR JOURDAIN. There are some stupid people who try to tell me that he was a merchant.

COVIELLE. He, a merchant? That's sheer calumny; he never was. All he did was that he was very obliging, very helpful; and since he was a real connoisseur of cloth, he went around and picked it out everywhere, had it brought to his house, and gave it to his friends for money.

MONSIEUR JOURDAIN. I'm delighted to know you, so that you can give that testimony, that my father was a gentleman.

COVIELLE. I'll maintain it in front of everybody.

MONSIEUR JOURDAIN. I'll be much obliged to you. What brings you here?

COVIELLE. Since the time when I knew your honorable late father—a fine gentleman, as I've told you—I've traveled all over the world.

MONSIEUR JOURDAIN. All over the world!

COVIELLE. Yes.

MONSIEUR JOURDAIN. It must be a long way to those parts.

COVIELLE. Yes indeed. I've been back only four days from all my long journeys; and because of the interest I take in all that concerns you, I come to announce to you the best news in the world.

MONSIEUR JOURDAIN. What's that?

COVIELLE. You know that the son of the Grand Turk is here?

MONSIEUR JOURDAIN. I? No.

COVIELLE. What? He has an utterly magnificent retinue; everybody's going to see him; and he has been received in this country as a lord of great importance.

MONSIEUR JOURDAIN. Upon my word! I didn't know that.

COVIELLE. What's advantageous about it for you is that he is in love with your daughter.

MONSIEUR JOURDAIN. The son of the Grand Turk?

COVIELLE. Yes; and he wants to be your son-in-law.

MONSIEUR JOURDAIN. My son-in-law, the son of the Grand Turk?

COVIELLE. The son of the Grand Turk, your son-in-law. Since I went to see him and understand his language perfectly, he had a talk with me; and after some other conversation he said to me: *"Acciam croc soler ouch alla moustaph gidelum amanahem varahini oussere carbulath,"*[8] that is to say: "Have you by any chance seen a beautiful young person who is the daughter of Monsieur Jourdain, a Parisian gentleman?"

8 The "Turkish" throughout is mostly gibberish.

MONSIEUR JOURDAIN. The son of the Grand Turk said that about me?

COVIELLE. Yes. When I answered that I knew you personally and had seen your daughter, he said to me: "Ah! *Marababa sahem*," that is to say: "Ah! How I love her!"

MONSIEUR JOURDAIN. *Marababa sahem* means "Ah! How I love her!"

COVIELLE. Yes.

MONSIEUR JOURDAIN. Faith! You do well to tell me so, for personally I would never have thought that *marababa sahem* meant "Ah! How I love her!" What a wonderful language this Turkish is!

COVIELLE. More wonderful than you'd believe. Do you know what *cacaracamouchen* means?

MONSIEUR JOURDAIN. *Cacaracamouchen?* No.

COVIELLE. It means "My dear heart."

MONSIEUR JOURDAIN. *Cacaracamouchen* means "My dear heart"?

COVIELLE. Yes.

MONSIEUR JOURDAIN. That is marvelous! *Cacaracamouchen,* "My dear heart." Who'd have thought it? That amazes me.

COVIELLE. Finally, to complete my embassy, he is coming to ask for your daughter in marriage; and to have a father-in-law who is worthy of him, he wants to make you a *Mamamouchi,* which is a certain great dignity of his country.

MONSIEUR JOURDAIN. A *Mamamouchi?*

COVIELLE. Yes, a *Mamamouchi;* that is to say, in our language, a paladin. Paladins are some of those ancient . . . In short, a paladin. There's nothing nobler than that in the world, and you'll move on a par with the greatest lords on earth.

MONSIEUR JOURDAIN. The son of the Grand Turk does me great honor, and I beg you to take me to meet him and give him my thanks.

COVIELLE. What? He's right on his way here.

MONSIEUR JOURDAIN. He's on his way here?

COVIELLE. Yes; and he's bringing everything for the ceremony of your ennoblement.

MONSIEUR JOURDAIN. That's very prompt.

COVIELLE. His love can bear no delay.

MONSIEUR JOURDAIN. All that embarrasses me in all this is that my daughter is a stubborn girl who's gone and set her mind on a certain Cléonte, and she swears she won't marry anyone but him.

COVIELLE. She'll change her feelings when she sees the son of the Grand Turk; and then there's a wonderful coincidence here, that the son of the Grand Turk bears a very close resemblance to this Cléonte. I've just seen Cléonte, he was pointed out to me; and her love for the one may easily pass to the other, and . . . I hear him coming; here he is.

Scene 4. CLÉONTE *(in Turkish costume, with three*
PAGES *carrying his train),* MONSIEUR JOURDAIN,
COVIELLE *(disguised)*

CLÉONTE. *Ambousahim oqui boraf, Iordina, salamalequi.*

COVIELLE. That is to say, "Monsieur Jourdain, may your heart all year round be like a rosebush in bloom!" These are obliging modes of expression in those countries.

MONSIEUR JOURDAIN. I am the very humble servant of his Turkish Highness.

COVIELLE. *Carigar camboto oustin moraf.*

CLÉONTE. *Oustin yoc catamalequi basum base alla moran.*

COVIELLE. He says: "May Heaven give you the strength of lions and the prudence of serpents!"

MONSIEUR JOURDAIN. His Turkish Highness does me too much honor, and I wish him all sorts of prosperity.

COVIELLE. *Ossa binamen sadoc babally oracaf ouram.*

CLÉONTE. *Bel-men.*

COVIELLE. He says that you should go with him quickly and prepare for the ceremony, so he may then see your daughter and conclude the marriage.

MONSIEUR JOURDAIN. All those things in two words?

COVIELLE. Yes, the Turkish language is like that, it says a lot in a few words. Go quickly where he wants you to.

Scene 5.   DORANTE, COVIELLE

COVIELLE. Ha, ha, ha! Faith! That's really funny! What a dupe! If he'd learned his part by heart he couldn't play it better. Ha, ha! I beg you, sir, to help us here in something that's going on.

DORANTE. Ha, ha! Covielle, who would have recognized you? What a get-up that is!

COVIELLE. You see. Ha, ha!

DORANTE. What are you laughing at?

COVIELLE. At something, sir, that well deserves it.

DORANTE. What's that?

COVIELLE. I'd give you lots of tries, sir, to guess the stratagem we're using with Monsieur Jourdain to bring him around to give his daughter to my master.

DORANTE. I can't guess the stratagem, but I can guess that it won't fail to work, since you're undertaking it.

COVIELLE. I know, sir, that the beast is known to you.

DORANTE. Tell me what it's all about.

COVIELLE. Be good enough to move a little farther away, to make room for what I see coming. You'll be able to see part of the story, and I'll tell you the rest.

The Turkish ceremony ennobling MONSIEUR JOURDAIN *is performed as a dance to music, and composes the* FOURTH INTERLUDE.[9]

Six dancing TURKS *enter gravely, two by two, to a Turkish march. As they dance, they wave three long carpets, and finally raise them high; the Turkish Singers and Instrumentalists pass under them. Four* DERVISHES *accompany the* MUFTI *to close the procession.*

The TURKS *put their carpets on the ground and kneel on them. The* MUFTI *remains standing in the middle, raises his eyes to Heaven in a burlesque invocation, grimaces, and moves his hands beside his head like wings. The* TURKS *bow and touch their foreheads to the floor, singing "Alli," return to a kneeling position, singing "Alla," and continue this alternation until the invocation is over; then all rise to their feet and join in the words "Alla ekber."*

Then the DERVISHES *bring on* MONSIEUR JOURDAIN *dressed as a Turk, clean-shaven, without turban or saber. The* MUFTI *sings.*

MUFTI.

> Se ti sabir,
> Ti respondir;
> Se non sabir,
> Tazir, tazir.
> Mi star Mufti.
> Ti, qui star ti?
> Non intendir:
> Tazir, tazir.[10]

(Two DERVISHES *take* MONSIEUR JOURDAIN *out. The* MUFTI *questions the* TURKS *about* MONSIEUR JOURDAIN's *religion.)*

MUFTI. Dice, Turque, qui star quista.
      Anabaptista, anabaptista?

TURKS. Ioc.[11]

---

[9] The version of the Turkish Ceremony offered here is the fullest one known. It first appeared in the 1682 edition of the play.

[10] If you know,/ You answer;/ If you no know,/ Be quiet, be quiet./ Me be Mufti./ You, who be you?/ You don't understand:/ Be quiet, be quiet.

[11] Tell me, Turk, who be this?/ An Anabaptist, Anabaptist?/ No.—*Ioc* (no) is a real Turkish word.

MUFTI. Zwinglista?

TURKS. Ioc.

MUFTI. Coffita?

TURKS. Ioc.

MUFTI. Hussita? Morista? Fronista?[12]

TURKS. Ioc. Ioc. Ioc.

MUFTI. Ioc. Ioc. Ioc.
    Star pagana?

TURKS. Ioc.

MUFTI. Luterana?

TURKS. Ioc.

MUFTI. Puritana?

TURKS. Ioc.

MUFTI. Bramina? Moffina? Zurina?[13]

TURKS. Ioc. Ioc. Ioc.

MUFTI. Ioc. Ioc. Ioc.
    Mahometana? Mahometana?

TURKS. Hey valla! Hey valla!

MUFTI. Como chamara? Como chamara?

TURKS. Giourdina, Giourdina.

MUFTI. Giourdina.
    (Leaping and looking in one direction and another)
    Giourdina? Giourdina? Giourdina?

TURKS. Giourdina! Giourdina! Giourdina![14]

12 A Zwinglian?/ No./ A Copt?/ No./ A Hussite?—The meaning of
"Morista" (a Moor?) and "Fronista" is not clear.
13 No. No. No./ No. No. No./ Be he a pagan?/ No./ A Lutheran?/
No./ A Puritan?/ No./ A Brahmin? ("Moffina" and "Zurina" are not
clear.)
14 No. No. No./ No. No. No./ A Mohammedan? A Mohammedan?/
Yes, by Allah! Yes, by Allah!/ What is his name? What is his name?/
Jourdain, etc.

MUFTI.

> Mahameta per Giourdina
> Mi pregar ser e matina:
> Voler far un Paladina
> De Giourdina, de Giourdina.
> Dar turbanta, e dar scarcina
> Con galera e brigantina
> Per deffender Palestina.
> Mahameta per Giourdina
> Mi pregar ser e matina.[15]
>
> Star bon Turca Giourdina?
> Star bon Turca Giourdina?

TURKS.

> Hey valla. Hey valla.
> Hey valla. Hey valla.[16]

MUFTI *(dancing and singing).* Hu la ba ba la chou ba la ba ba la da. *(Exit* MUFTI.*)*

TURKS *(dancing and singing).* Hu la ba ba la chou ba la ba ba la da.

Reenter the MUFTI *wearing an enormous ceremonial turban set with four or five rows of lighted candles. With him are two* DERVISHES, *wearing pointed hats also adorned with lighted candles, and bearing the Koran. The other two* DERVISHES *bring in* MONSIEUR JOURDAIN, *who is terrified by the ceremony, make him kneel down with his back to the* MUFTI *and rest his hands on the floor, and set the Koran on his back for the* MUFTI *to read. The* MUFTI *gives a burlesque invocation, frowning and opening his mouth without saying a word, then speaking vehemently, now softly, now as if possessed, slapping his sides as if to drive the words out, striking the Koran, turning its leaves very fast. Finally he raises his hands and cries out loudly: "Hou!"*

During the invocation the TURKS *sing "Hou, hou, hou!" alternately bowing and straightening up.*

[15] To Mahomet for Jourdain/ Me pray evening and morning./ Want to make a paladin/ Of Jourdain, of Jourdain./Give a turban and a scimitar/ With a galley and brigantine/ To defend Palestine./ To Mahomet for Jourdain/ Me pray evening and morning.

[16] Jourdain be good Turk?/ Jourdain be good Turk?/ Yes, by Allah! etc.

After the invocation the DERVISHES *take the Koran off* MONSIEUR JOURDAIN's *back; he exclaims "Ouf!" in relief from this tiring posture; and they lift him to his feet.*

MUFTI *(to* MONSIEUR JOURDAIN*)*. Ti non star furba?

TURKS. No, no, no.

MUFTI. Non star forfanta?

TURKS. No, no, no.

MUFTI. Donar turbanta. Donar turbanta.[17]   *(Exit the* MUFTI.*)*
     (The TURKS *repeat his words, singing and dancing, and present the turban to* MONSIEUR JOURDAIN. *Reenter the* MUFTI *with a scimitar.)*

MUFTI *(presenting the scimitar to* MONSIEUR JOURDAIN*)*.

Ti star nobile, e non star fabola.
Pigliar schiabola.[18]

(Exit the MUFTI.*)*
     (The TURKS *draw their scimitars and repeat his words. Six of them dance around* MONSIEUR JOURDAIN *and pretend to strike him with their scimitars. Reenter the* MUFTI, *who orders the* TURKS *to beat* MONSIEUR JOURDAIN.*)*

MUFTI. Dara, dara, bastonara, bastonara, bastonara.[19]

(Exit the MUFTI.*)*
     (The TURKS *repeat his words, dancing and beating* MONSIEUR JOURDAIN *with sticks in cadence. Reenter the* MUFTI.*)*

MUFTI.   Non tener honta:
Questa star l'ultima affronta.[20]
     (The TURKS *repeat his words. To the music of the whole orchestra the* MUFTI, *leaning on the* DERVISHES, *who support him with respect, makes a final invocation. The* TURKS, *dancing, lead off the* MUFTI *and* MONSIEUR JOURDAIN *in triumph, thus ending the* FOURTH INTERLUDE.*)*

---

17 You no be knave?/ No, no, no./ No be rascal?/ No, no, no./ Give turban, give turban.
18 You be noble, that be no fable./ Take scimitar.
19 Give, give, beat, beat, beat.
20 No feel shame:/ This be the final affront.

ACT V

Scene 1. MADAME JOURDAIN, MONSIEUR JOURDAIN

MADAME JOURDAIN. Oh! Lord have mercy! What in the world is all this? What a sight! Are you getting ready for a mummer's play, and is it a time for a masquerade? Speak up; what is all this? Who rigged you out like this?

MONSIEUR JOURDAIN. Look at your impertinence, to talk that way to a *Mamamouchi!*

MADAME JOURDAIN. How's that?

MONSIEUR JOURDAIN. Yes, you've got to show me some respect now; and I've just been made a *Mamamouchi.*

MADAME JOURDAIN. What do you mean with your *Mamamouchi?*

MONSIEUR JOURDAIN. *Mamamouchi,* I tell you. I'm a *Mamamouchi.*

MADAME JOURDAIN. What kind of animal is that?

MONSIEUR JOURDAIN. *Mamamouchi,* that is to say, in our language, Paladin.

MADAME JOURDAIN. A balladin'! Are you at an age for going around a-ballading?

MONSIEUR JOURDAIN. What an ignoramus! I said a Paladin. That's a dignity that's just been conferred on me with proper ceremony.

MADAME JOURDAIN. What kind of a ceremony?

MONSIEUR JOURDAIN. *Mahameta per Giourdina.*

MADAME JOURDAIN. What does that mean?

MONSIEUR JOURDAIN. *Giourdina,* that is to say Jourdain.

MADAME JOURDAIN. Well then, Jourdain? What about it?

MONSIEUR JOURDAIN. *Voler far un Paladina de Giourdina.*

MADAME JOURDAIN. What?

MONSIEUR JOURDAIN. *Dar turbanta con galera.*

MADAME JOURDAIN. What does that mean?

MONSIEUR JOURDAIN. *Per deffender Palestina.*

MADAME JOURDAIN. What is it you mean by that?

MONSIEUR JOURDAIN. *Dara dara bastonara.*

MADAME JOURDAIN. Just what is this jargon?

MONSIEUR JOURDAIN. *Non tener honta: questa star l'ultima affronta.*

MADAME JOURDAIN. Just what is all this?

MONSIEUR JOURDAIN *(dancing and singing).* Hou la ba ba la chou ba la ba ba la da.

MADAME JOURDAIN. Alas! Good Lord! My husband's gone crazy.

MONSIEUR JOURDAIN *(on his way out).* Peace, insolent woman! Show respect to Monsieur le *Mamamouchi.*

MADAME JOURDAIN. Why, where can he have lost his wits? Let's run and keep him from leaving. *(Sees* DORANTE *and* DORIMÈNE *entering.)* Aha! Sure enough, this is all we needed. I see nothing but trouble on every side.   *(Exit)*

Scene 2.   DORANTE, DORIMÈNE

DORANTE. Yes, Madame, you'll see the most amusing thing you ever could see; and I don't think it's possible still to find in all the world a man as crazy as that one. And then, Madame, we must try to serve Cléonte's love, and support his whole masquerade; he's a very decent chap who deserves our taking an interest on his behalf.

DORIMÈNE. I think a lot of him, and he deserves to have good fortune.

DORANTE. Besides that, Madame, we have a ballet coming to us here, which we shouldn't allow to be wasted; and I really must see whether my idea can work out.

DORIMÈNE. I saw some magnificent preparations there; and these are things, Dorante, that I can no longer put up with. Yes, I want to put a stop to your extravagance at last; and to cut short all the expenditures I see you making for me, I have resolved to marry you promptly. That's the real solution; all these things end with marriage.

DORANTE. Ah, Madame! Is it possible that you could have made such a sweet resolve on my behalf?

DORIMÈNE. It's only to keep you from ruining yourself; and without this I can easily see that in a short time you wouldn't have a penny.

DORANTE. How obliged I am, Madame, to your concern for preserving my property. It is entirely yours, as well as my heart, and you will use it in any way you please.

DORIMÈNE. I shall have good use for them both. But here's your man; he's a wonderful sight.

Scene 3.   MONSIEUR JOURDAIN, DORANTE, DORIMÈNE

DORANTE. Sir, Madame and I come to pay homage to your new dignity, and to rejoice with you at your daughter's coming marriage to the son of the Grand Turk.

MONSIEUR JOURDAIN (*after making his bows in Turkish fashion*). Sir, I wish you the strength of serpents and the prudence of lions.

DORIMÈNE. I was very glad to be one of the first, sir, to come and congratulate you on the high degree of glory you have risen to.

MONSIEUR JOURDAIN. Madame, I hope your rosebush may be in flower all year long. I am infinitely obliged to you for taking part in the honors that are coming to me, and I take great joy in seeing you here again so I can offer you my very humble apologies for my wife's outlandish behavior.

DORIMÈNE. That's nothing; I can excuse such an impulse in her. Your heart must be precious to her, and it's not strange that the possession of a man like you can give her some alarms.

MONSIEUR JOURDAIN. The possession of my heart is a thing that is entirely yours.

DORANTE. You see, Madame, that Monsieur Jourdain is not one of those people who are blinded by prosperity, and that in all his glory he still knows how to recognize his friends.

DORIMÈNE. That's the mark of a wholly noble soul.

DORANTE. Now where is his Turkish Highness? As friends of yours, we would like to pay him our respects.

MONSIEUR JOURDAIN. Here he comes, and I've sent for my daughter to give him her hand.

Scene 4. CLÉONTE, COVIELLE, MONSIEUR JOURDAIN, DORANTE, DORIMÈNE

DORANTE *(to* CLÉONTE*)*. Sir, as friends of your honorable father-in-law, we come to make obeisance to Your Highness and respectfully assure Your Highness of our very humble services.

MONSIEUR JOURDAIN. Where is the interpreter, to tell him who you are and make him understand what you're saying? You'll see that he'll answer you, and he speaks Turkish wonderfully. Hello! Where the deuce has he gone? *(To* CLÉONTE*)* *Strouf, strif, strof, straf.* This gentleman is a *grande Segnore, grande Segnore, grande Segnore;* and Madame is a *granda Dama, granda Dama, granda Dama.* *(Seeing that he is not understood)* Oh dear! Him, sir, him French *Mamamouchi,* and Madame French *Mamamouchie;* I can't say it more clearly. Good, here's the interpreter. Where are you going, anyway? We can't say a thing without you. Just tell him that the gentleman and the lady are persons of high rank, who have come to pay their respects to him, as my friends, and assure him of their services. *(To* DORANTE *and* DORIMÈNE*)* You'll see how he'll answer.

COVIELLE. *Alabala crociam acci boram alabamen.*

CLÉONTE. *Catalequi tubal ourin soter amalouchan.*

MONSIEUR JOURDAIN. You see?

COVIELLE. He says: "May the rain of prosperities forever water the garden of your family!"

MONSIEUR JOURDAIN. I told you, he speaks Turkish.

DORANTE. That's wonderful.

Scene. 5.   LUCILE, MONSIEUR JOURDAIN, DORANTE, DORIMÈNE, CLÉONTE, COVIELLE

MONSIEUR JOURDAIN. Come here, daughter; closer. Come and give your hand to this gentleman, who is doing you the honor of asking to marry you.

LUCILE. What's this, father? What a get-up! Are you acting in a play?

MONSIEUR JOURDAIN. No, no, it's no play, it's a very serious matter, and the most honorable for you that could be wished for. Here's the husband I am giving you.

LUCILE. Me, father?

MONSIEUR JOURDAIN. Yes, you. Come on, give him your hand, and thank Heaven for your good fortune.

LUCILE. I don't want to get married.

MONSIEUR JOURDAIN. I want you to, and I'm your father.

LUCILE. I'll do nothing of the kind.

MONSIEUR JOURDAIN. Oh! What a lot of fuss! Come on, I tell you. Here, your hand.

LUCILE. No, father, I've told you, there is no power that can oblige me to take any other husband than Cléonte; and I'll go to any extremes rather than . . . *(Recognizing* CLÉONTE*)* It is true that you are my father, I owe you entire obedience, and it is for you to dispose of me according to your will.

MONSIEUR JOURDAIN. Ah! I'm delighted to see you return to your duty so promptly, and I'm really pleased to have an obedient daughter.

Scene. 6. MADAME JOURDAIN, MONSIEUR JOURDAIN, LUCILE, CLÉONTE, COVIELLE, DORANTE, DORIMÈNE

MADAME JOURDAIN. How's this? What in the world is going on? They say you want to give your daughter in marriage to a Mardi Gras reveler.

MONSIEUR JOURDAIN. Will you be quiet, you impertinent woman? You're always coming thrusting your silly notions into everything, and there's no way of teaching you to be reasonable.

MADAME JOURDAIN. You're the one there's no way of getting any sense into, and you go from folly to folly. What is your intention, and what do you mean to do with this motley crew?

MONSIEUR JOURDAIN. I mean to marry our daughter to the son of the Grand Turk.

MADAME JOURDAIN. To the son of the Grand Turk!

MONSIEUR JOURDAIN. Yes, have the interpreter here pay him your compliments.

MADAME JOURDAIN. I have no use for the interpreter, and I'll tell him perfectly well myself to his face that he shan't have my daughter.

MONSIEUR JOURDAIN. Once more, will you be quiet?

DORANTE. What, Madame Jourdain, you oppose such good fortune as this? You refuse his Turkish Highness as a son-in-law?

MADAME JOURDAIN. Good Lord, sir, mind your own business.

DORIMÈNE. It's a great honor, which is not one to reject.

MADAME JOURDAIN. Madame, I beg you too not to bother yourself with what doesn't concern you.

DORANTE. It's our friendly feeling for you that makes us take an interest in whatever is to your advantage.

MADAME JOURDAIN. I'll get along fine without your friendly feeling.

DORANTE. Your daughter here consents to her father's will.

MADAME JOURDAIN. My daughter consents to marry a Turk!

DORANTE. Yes indeed.

MADAME JOURDAIN. She can forget Cléonte!

DORANTE. What won't a person do to be a great lady?

MADAME JOURDAIN. I'd strangle her with my own hands if she'd done a thing like that.

MONSIEUR JOURDAIN. That's a lot of cackle. I tell you this marriage shall take place.

MADAME JOURDAIN. And *I* tell *you* that it shall not.

MONSIEUR JOURDAIN. Oh, what a lot of fuss!

LUCILE. Mother.

MADAME JOURDAIN. Go on with you, you're a bad girl.

MONSIEUR JOURDAIN. What? You're scolding her because she obeys me?

MADAME JOURDAIN. Yes: she belongs to me as well as to you.

COVIELLE *(to* MADAME JOURDAIN*)*. Madame.

MADAME JOURDAIN. You, what are you trying to tell me?

COVIELLE. One word!

MADAME JOURDAIN. I don't want any part of your "word."

COVIELLE *(to* MONSIEUR JOURDAIN*)*. Sir, if she will listen to a word in private, I promise you to get her to consent to what you want.

MADAME JOURDAIN. I won't consent to it one bit.

COVIELLE. Just listen to me.

MADAME JOURDAIN. No.

MONSIEUR JOURDAIN. Listen to him.

MADAME JOURDAIN. No, I won't listen.

MONSIEUR JOURDAIN. He'll tell you . . .

MADAME JOURDAIN. I don't want him to tell me anything.

MONSIEUR JOURDAIN. There's an obstinate woman for you! Will it hurt you to hear him?

COVIELLE. Just listen to me; afterward you'll do as you please.

MADAME JOURDAIN. Well! What?

COVIELLE *(aside to* MADAME JOURDAIN*)*. Madame, we've been trying to make signs to you for an hour. Don't you see that all this is being done just to fall in with your husband's visions, that we're fooling him in this disguise, and that it's Cléonte himself who's the son of the Grand Turk?

MADAME JOURDAIN *(aside to* COVIELLE*)*. Aha!

COVIELLE *(aside to* MADAME JOURDAIN*)*. And I, Covielle, am the interpreter?

MADAME JOURDAIN *(aside to* COVIELLE*)*. Ah! In that case, I give in.

COVIELLE *(aside to* MADAME JOURDAIN*).* Don't let on to a thing!

MADAME JOURDAIN *(to* MONSIEUR JOURDAIN*).* Yes, that's settled, I consent to the marriage.

MONSIEUR JOURDAIN. Ah! Now everybody's reasonable. You wouldn't listen to him. I knew perfectly well that he'd explain what it is to be the son of the Grand Turk.

MADAME JOURDAIN. He explained it to me very well, and I'm satisfied. Let's send for a notary.

DORANTE. That's very well said. And, Madame Jourdain, so that your mind may be completely at ease, and that you may lose today any jealousy you might have conceived about your honorable husband, let me say that this lady and I will use the same notary to be married.

MADAME JOURDAIN. I consent to that too.

MONSIEUR JOURDAIN *(aside to* DORANTE*).* That's to pull the wool over her eyes.

DORANTE *(aside to* MONSIEUR JOURDAIN*).* We simply have to delude her with this pretense.

MONSIEUR JOURDAIN. *(Aside)* Fine, fine. *(Aloud)* Have the notary sent for, quick.

DORANTE. While he's coming and drawing up the contracts, let's see our ballet and offer it as an entertainment to his Turkish Highness.

MONSIEUR JOURDAIN. That's a very good idea. Let's go take our seats.

MADAME JOURDAIN. What about Nicole?

MONSIEUR JOURDAIN. I give her to the interpreter; and my wife to anyone that wants her.

COVIELLE. Sir, I thank you. *(Aside)* If you can find anyone crazier, I'll go publish it in Rome.

The play concludes with the short Ballet of the Nations, which has nothing to do with the rest of the play and is omitted from this version.

The Mischievous
Machinations
of Scapin

THE MISCHIEVOUS MACHINATIONS
OF SCAPIN

A prose comedy in three acts, first performed on May 24, 1671, at the Théâtre du Palais-Royal in Paris by Molière's Troupe du Roi. Molière played Scapin; La Thorillière, Silvestre; Mlle. Beauval, Zerbinette; the distribution of the other roles is not known. The play was warmly received and has always remained popular.

Molière's use of his sources is, as usual, considerable and free. The plot mainly follows that of Terence's *Phormio;* minor borrowings are from Plautus, Cyrano de Bergerac, Rotrou, and (for the business of the sack) Tabarin or some other contemporary or earlier farce writer. Boileau, a good friend and admirer of Molière, disapproved of the business of the sack, failing, as he said, to recognize in it the author of *The Misanthrope;* and many critics since his time have echoed his feelings. Recently, however, as farce has had a better press, the play has been hailed by many as a masterpiece of "pure theater."

Certainly the concern is all for theatrical fantasy and legerdemain, not for realism. The plot as such (the loves of Octave and Léandre for Hyacinte and Zerbinette, crossed by the plans of their stingy old fathers) is little more than a pretext for comic scenes and stories; the true plot, the action that intrigues us, is in effect created by Scapin as he goes along. He is the master manipulator; all the other characters dance when he whistles. His character, the only one that is more than sketched, is that of a virtuoso in love with his virtuosity; and in this it reflects that of Molière as craftsman.

In this play Molière shows no more concern with ideas or with serious involvement of the spectator than he does with realism or character. The comedy is a romp in the land of inventive make-believe. Scapin not only plays a variety of parts (Argante to Octave, a Basque, a Swiss and other soldiers, and so on) but also directs others (Octave, Silvestre), tells of other parts he has played (the werewolf), and stage-manages the whole action. When no one is acting a part, someone is likely to be telling a story; and the story-telling is also dramatic, since its comedy lies not in the story itself but in the story's relation to the teller and the listener. Zerbinette's account to Géronte of how Géronte was bilked would be dull repetition —except that the giddy Zerbinette tells the story to its victim; and the effect is similar in the final scene when Scapin, even in asking pardon of Géronte for the beating he gave him, mentions it repeatedly with obvious relish to the obvious discomfiture of Géronte.

In short, the play is an exercise in sheer virtuosity; and as anyone knows who has seen it performed, it works.

THE MISCHIEVOUS MACHINATIONS
OF SCAPIN

CHARACTERS

ARGANTE, *father of Octave and Zerbinette*
GÉRONTE, *father of Léandre and Hyacinte*
OCTAVE, *son of Argante, in love with Hyacinte*
LÉANDRE, *son of Géronte, in love with Zerbinette*
ZERBINETTE, *thought to be a Gypsy, recognized as the daughter of Argante; in love with Léandre*
HYACINTE, *daughter of Géronte, in love with Octave*
SCAPIN, *valet of Léandre, a trickster*
SILVESTRE, *valet of Octave*
NÉRINE, *nurse of Hyacinte*
CARLE, *a trickster*
Two PORTERS

The scene is Naples.

ACT I

Scene 1. OCTAVE, SILVESTRE

OCTAVE. Ah! Distressing news for a lover's heart! Harsh extremities that I am reduced to! Silvestre, you've just learned at the port that my father is coming back?

SILVESTRE. Yes.

OCTAVE. That he's arriving this very morning?

SILVESTRE. This very morning.

OCTAVE. And that he's coming back resolved to have me married?

SILVESTRE. Yes.

OCTAVE. To a daughter of Seigneur Géronte?

SILVESTRE. Of Seigneur Géronte.

OCTAVE. And that this girl is being sent for from Taranto for that?

SILVESTRE. Yes.

OCTAVE. And you have this news from my uncle?

SILVESTRE. From your uncle.

OCTAVE. To whom my father sent it in a letter?

SILVESTRE. In a letter.

OCTAVE. And this uncle, you say, knows all our affairs?

SILVESTRE. All our affairs.

OCTAVE. Oh! Speak up, will you, and don't make me drag the words out of your mouth this way.

SILVESTRE. Why should I say more? You're not forgetting a single circumstance, and you're telling things just exactly as they are.

OCTAVE. At least advise me, and tell me what I am to do in this cruel situation.

SILVESTRE. Faith! I'm as stumped about this as you are, and I could well use some advice myself.

OCTAVE. This cursed return of his slays me.

SILVESTRE. And me no less.

OCTAVE. When my father learns how things stand, I shall see a sudden storm of vehement reprimands burst over me.

SILVESTRE. Reprimands are nothing; would to Heaven I could get off at that price! But for my part I look like someone who will pay more dearly for your follies, and I can see forming, from afar, a storm of cudgel-blows that will break on my shoulders.

OCTAVE. O Heaven! How can I get out of the scrape I'm in?

SILVESTRE. That's what you should have thought about before you got in it.

OCTAVE. Oh, you kill me with your untimely lessons.

SILVESTRE. You kill me even more with your scatterbrained actions.

OCTAVE. What am I to do? What resolution shall I make? What remedy can I turn to?

Scene 2.   SCAPIN, OCTAVE, SILVESTRE

SCAPIN. What is it, Seigneur Octave? What's wrong with you? What's the matter? What is this disorder? I find you all upset.

OCTAVE. Ah, my poor dear Scapin, I'm lost, I'm desperate, I'm the most unfortunate of all men.

SCAPIN. How so?

OCTAVE. Haven't you heard anything about my situation?

SCAPIN. No.

OCTAVE. My father is arriving with Seigneur Géronte, and they want to get me married.

SCAPIN. Well! What's so disastrous about that?

OCTAVE. Alas! You don't know the cause of my anxiety.

SCAPIN. No; but it's up to you whether I'm to know it soon; and I'm a consolatory man, a man to take an interest in young people's affairs.

OCTAVE. Ah, Scapin! If you could find some device, forge some stratagem, to deliver me from the distress I'm in, I would think I owed you more than life itself.

SCAPIN. To tell you the truth, there are few things impossible
for me when I decide to get involved in them. Beyond a doubt,
I've received from Heaven a pretty fine genius for the fabri-
cation of all those nice turns of wit, all those ingenious intrigues, to which the ignorant vulgar give the name of mischievous machinations; and I may say without vanity that
hardly a man has ever been seen who was an abler artisan of
schemes and intrigues, who has acquired more glory than I in
that noble profession. But faith! Merit is too ill-treated today,
and I've given up everything since the chagrin of a certain
affair that happened to me.

OCTAVE. How's that? What affair, Scapin?

SCAPIN. An adventure in which I got into trouble with the law.

OCTAVE. The law!

SCAPIN. Yes, we had a bit of a tangle.

SILVESTRE. You and the law!

SCAPIN. Yes. It treated me very badly, and I got so angry at the
ingratitude of the times that I resolved not to do anything
more. Enough of that. Go ahead and tell me your story.

OCTAVE. You know, Scapin, that two months ago Seigneur
Géronte and my father embarked together on a voyage that
concerns a certain bit of business in which their interests are
involved together.

SCAPIN. I know that.

OCTAVE. And that Léandre and I were left by our fathers, I under
the guidance of Silvestre, and Léandre under your direction.

SCAPIN. Yes; I've acquitted myself of my commission very well.

OCTAVE. Some time after, Léandre met a young Gypsy girl and
fell in love with her.

SCAPIN. I know that too.

OCTAVE. Since we are great friends, he immediately took me into
his confidence about his love, and took me to see this girl,
whom I found to be beautiful indeed, but not as much as he
wanted me to think her. He talked to me of nothing but her
every day; at every moment exaggerated to me her beauty and

her grace; praised her wit, and spoke to me with ecstasy of the charms of her conversation, reporting it to me even to the slightest words, which he always strove to make me find the wittiest in the world. He would sometimes scold me for not being sensitive enough to the things he came to tell me, and would constantly blame me for the indifference I showed toward the flames of love.

SCAPIN. I don't yet see what all this is leading up to.

OCTAVE. One day when I was going with him to visit the people who watch over the object of his love, we heard, in a little house on an out-of-the-way street, some laments mingled with many sobs. We ask what the trouble is. A woman tells us, sighing, that we could see something pitiable there in the persons of some foreigners, and that unless we were insensible we would be touched.

SCAPIN. Where does that take us?

OCTAVE. Curiosity made me urge Léandre to see what it was. We go into a room where we see a dying old woman, attended by a maidservant uttering laments and a girl all melting in tears, the loveliest and most touching girl that anyone ever could see.

SCAPIN. Aha!

OCTAVE. Anyone else would have looked frightful in the state she was in; for she was wearing nothing but a wretched little petticoat with a night bodice of plain fustian; and on her head she had a yellow night cap, turned down at the top, which let her hair fall in disorder over her shoulders; and yet, dressed like that, she shone with a thousand attractions, and there were nothing but beauties and charms in her whole person.

SCAPIN. I can tell what's coming.

OCTAVE. If you'd seen her, Scapin, in the state I'm speaking of, you'd have thought she was wonderful.

SCAPIN. Oh! I've no doubt of it; and without having seen her, I see perfectly well that she was utterly charming.

OCTAVE. Her tears were none of those disagreeable tears that disfigure a face; there was a touching grace in her weeping, and her grief was the most beautiful in the world.

SCAPIN. I see all that.

OCTAVE. She made everyone dissolve in tears as she cast herself lovingly on the body of this dying woman, whom she called her dear mother; and there was no one whose soul would not have been pierced to see such natural goodness.

SCAPIN. Indeed, that is touching; and I can clearly see that this natural goodness made you love her.

OCTAVE. Ah, Scapin, even a barbarian would have loved her.

SCAPIN. Of course; how could anyone help it?

OCTAVE. After a few words with which I tried to assuage the grief of the charming sufferer, we left there; and when I asked Léandre what he thought of this person, he answered me coldly that he found her rather pretty. I was piqued at the coldness with which he spoke of her, and I decided not to reveal to him the effect that her beauties had had on my soul.

SILVSTRE. (To OCTAVE) If you don't abridge this story, we're in for it until tomorrow. Let me finish it in a few words. (To SCAPIN) His heart takes fire from that moment. He can't live any longer unless he goes to console his lovely sufferer. His frequent visits are rejected by the maidservant, who had become governess on the mother's decrease. Behold, my man in despair. He urges, supplicates, beseeches: nothing doing. He is told that the girl, although without means or support, is of a decent family; and that unless he is to marry her, his advances cannot be tolerated. Now his love is increased by difficulties. He mulls it over in his head, debates, reasons, hesitates, makes his resolve: now he's been married to her for three days.

SCAPIN. I understand.

SILVESTRE. Now add to that the unforeseen return of the father, who wasn't expected for two months; the disclosure by the uncle of the secret of this marriage of ours, and the other marriage they are planning between him and the daughter that Seigneur Géronte had by a second wife whom they say he married at Taranto.

OCTAVE. And also add, on top of all that, the poverty in which this lovely person finds herself, and my powerlessness to get the wherewithal to help her.

SCAPIN. Is that all? You're both mighty hung up over a trifle. That's a fine reason for such alarm! *(To* SILVESTRE*)* You, aren't you ashamed to fall short in such a small matter? What the devil! Here you are, tall and husky as your father and mother, and you can't find in your head or contrive in your mind some gallant ruse, some nice little stratagem, to set your affairs straight? Fie! Plague take the blockhead! I wish I'd been given these old men of ours to make dupes of long ago; I'd have led them both around by the nose; and I was no bigger than this *(holding his hand near the floor)* when I was already distinguishing myself by a hundred pretty tricks.

SILVESTRE. I admit that Heaven did not give me your talents, and that I haven't the wit, as you do, to get myself embroiled with the law.

OCTAVE. Here is my lovely Hyacinte.

Scene 3.   HYACINTE, OCTAVE, SCAPIN, SILVESTRE

HYACINTE. Ah! Octave, is it true, what Silvestre has just told Nérine, that your father is back and intends to have you married?

OCTAVE. Yes, lovely Hyacinte, and this news has been a cruel blow to me. But what do I see? You're weeping? Why these tears? Tell me, do you suspect me of some infidelity, and aren't you certain of the love I feel for you?

HYACINTE. Yes, Octave, I'm sure that you love me; but I'm not sure that you always will.

OCTAVE. Oh! Can anyone love you and not love you all his life?

HYACINTE. I've heard, Octave, that your sex loves less long than ours, and that the ardors men display to us are flames that burn out as easily as they are kindled.

OCTAVE. Ah! My dear Hyacinte, then my heart is not made like those of other men, and for my part I clearly feel that I will love you till the grave.

HYACINTE. I want to believe that you feel what you say, and I have no doubt that your words are sincere; but I fear a power that will combat in your heart the tender feelings you may have for me. You are dependent on a father who wants to have you married to another; and I'm sure I will die if this misfortune happens to me.

OCTAVE. No, lovely Hyacinte, no father can force me to break my word to you, and I shall be ready to leave my country, and life itself if necessary, rather than leave you. Without having seen her, I've already formed a frightful aversion for the woman who is destined for me; and without being cruel, I wish the sea would keep her from here forever. So don't weep, please, my dear Hyacinte, for your tears kill me, and I cannot see them without feeling my heart pierced.

HYACINTE. Since you will have it so, I'll dry my tears, and I'll await with a steady eye whatever Heaven is pleased to decree for me.

OCTAVE. Heaven will be favorable to us.

HYACINTE. It could not be contrary to me if you are faithful to me.

OCTAVE. That I shall certainly be.

HYACINTE. Then I shall be happy.

SCAPIN (aside). She's not such a fool, my word! and I think she's rather passable.

OCTAVE (pointing to SCAPIN) Here's a man who, if he would, could be a marvelous help to us in all our necessities.

SCAPIN. I have sworn great oaths to have nothing more to do with the world; but if you both ask me very persuasively, maybe . . .

OCTAVE. Ah! If all that's needed to get your help is to ask you very persuasively, I beseech you with all my heart to take on the direction of our little boat.

SCAPIN *(to* HYACINTE*)*. And you, have you nothing to say to me?

HYACINTE. I beseech you, just as he does, by all that is dearest to you in the world, to be willing to serve our love.

SCAPIN. We have to let ourselves be overcome, and have a little humanity. Go on, I'm willing to take a hand for you.

OCTAVE. Rest assured that . . .

SCAPIN. *(To* OCTAVE*)* Hush! *(To* HYACINTE*)* You go away, and rest easy.   *(Exit* HYACINTE.*)*
(To OCTAVE*)* And you, prepare to stand up firmly to meeting your father.

OCTAVE. I admit that that meeting makes me tremble in advance; and I have a natural timidity that I cannot conquer.

SCAPIN. However, you have to appear firm at the first clash, for fear that he may take advantage of your weakness to lead you about like a child. There, try to pull yourself together. A little boldness, and think how to give a resolute answer to anything he can say to you.

OCTAVE. I'll do the best I can.

SCAPIN. Here, let's practice a bit, to get you used to it. Let's rehearse your part a bit and see if you will play it well. Come on. Resolute face, head high, assured look.

OCTAVE. Like that?

SCAPIN. A little more still.

OCTAVE. So?

SCAPIN. Good. Imagine that I'm your father arriving, and answer me firmly as if you were answering himself. "What, blackguard, good-for-nothing, wretch, son unworthy of a man like me, do you really dare appear before my eyes after your fine behavior, after the cowardly trick you played on me during my absence? Is that the fruit of my cares, you scoundrel, is that the fruit of my cares, the respect you owe me, the respect you retain for me?" Come on now. "You have the insolence, you rascal, to get engaged without your father's consent, to contract a clandestine marriage? Answer me, rogue, answer me. Let's just see your fine reasons." Oh! What the devil! You stand there stupefied.

OCTAVE. The fact is I imagine it's my father I'm hearing.

SCAPIN. Why, yes. That's the reason why you mustn't act like an idiot.

OCTAVE. I'm going to be more resolute, and I'll reply firmly.

SCAPIN. Sure?

OCTAVE. Sure.

SILVESTRE. Here comes your father.

OCTAVE. O Heavens! I'm done for.   *(Runs off.)*

SCAPIN. Stop! Octave, stay here! Octave! There, he's fled. What a poor specimen of a man! Let's wait for the old man anyway.

SILVESTRE. What shall I say to him?

SCAPIN. Let *me* do the talking, and just follow my lead.

Scene 4.   ARGANTE, SCAPIN, SILVESTRE

ARGANTE *(for his first ten speeches, thinking himself alone).* Did anyone ever hear of such a thing?

SCAPIN *(to* SILVESTRE*).* He's already learned about the affair, and has it so much on his mind that even alone he's talking about it out loud.

ARGANTE. The nerve of them!

SCAPIN *(to* SILVESTRE*).* Let's listen to him a bit.

ARGANTE. I'd really like to know what they can tell me about this fine marriage.

SCAPIN *(aside).* We've thought about it.

ARGANTE. Will they try to deny the thing?

SCAPIN *(aside).* No, we're not thinking of that.

ARGANTE. Or suppose they undertake to excuse it?

SCAPIN *(aside)*. That just might be done.

ARGANTE. Will they hope to put me off with wild stories?

SCAPIN *(aside)*. Maybe.

ARGANTE. All their speeches will be no use.

SCAPIN *(aside)*. We shall see.

ARGANTE. They won't put anything over on me.

SCAPIN *(aside)*. Let's not swear to anything.

ARGANTE. I'll find a way to have my blackguard of a son put away in a safe place.

SCAPIN *(aside)*. We'll take care of that.

ARGANTE. And as for that rogue Silvestre, I'll tan his hide.

SILVESTRE *(to* SCAPIN*)*. I would have been mighty astonished if he'd forgotten me.

ARGANTE *(noticing* SILVESTRE*)*. Aha! So there you are, wise governor of a family, fine director of young people!

SCAPIN. Sir, I'm delighted to see you back.

ARGANTE. Hello, Scapin. *(To* SILVESTRE*)* You certainly followed my orders in a fine way, and my son behaved very wisely indeed in my absence.

SCAPIN. You're well, as far as I can see?

ARGANTE. Pretty well. *(To* SILVESTRE*)* You're not saying a word, you scoundrel, you're not saying a word.

SCAPIN. Did you have a good trip?

ARGANTE. Oh Lord! Very good. Let me do a little scolding in peace.

SCAPIN. You want to scold?

ARGANTE. Yes, I want to scold.

SCAPIN. Whom, sir?

ARGANTE *(pointing to* SILVESTRE*)*. That rogue there.

SCAPIN. Why?

ARGANTE. Didn't you hear what happened in my absence?

SCAPIN. I did hear of some small matter or other.

ARGANTE. What? Some small matter? A thing like that?

SCAPIN. You're somewhat right.

ARGANTE. A piece of effrontery like that?

SCAPIN. That's true.

ARGANTE. A son who gets married without his father's consent?

SCAPIN. Yes, there's something to be said about that. But I would think you shouldn't make a fuss about it.

ARGANTE. I wouldn't think so, for my part, and I want to make my bellyful of fuss. What? You don't think I have every reason in the world to be angry?

SCAPIN. Yes I do. I myself was angry at first when I learned about the thing, and I got involved on your behalf to the point of scolding your son. Just ask him what fine reprimands I made to him, and how I dressed him down on the scant respect he retained for a father whose footsteps he should kiss. No one could give him a better talking to, even if it were yourself. But what then? I gave way to reason, and came to the conclusion that at bottom he's not so much in the wrong as one might think.

ARGANTE. What kind of a story is this you're telling me? He's not so much in the wrong to go out on the spur of the moment and marry a stranger?

SCAPIN. What can you expect? He was driven to it by his destiny.

ARGANTE. Aha! That's one of the finest reasons in the world. All you have to do nowadays is commit every imaginable crime, cheat, steal, murder, and say for your excuse that you were driven to it by your destiny.

SCAPIN. Good Lord! You take my words too much like a philosopher. I mean he found himself fatally involved in this affair.

ARGANTE. And why did he get involved?

SCAPIN. Do you expect him to be as wise as you? Young folks

are young, and don't have all the prudence they would need to do nothing but what's reasonable; witness our Léandre, who, in spite of all my lessons, in spite of all my remonstrances, for his part has gone and done something even worse than your son. I'd really like to know whether you yourself weren't young once, and, in your day, didn't sow your wild oats like the rest. I myself have heard that once upon a time you were a gay blade with the women, that you had your fun with the liveliest of them at that time, and that you didn't approach any of them without going all the way.

ARGANTE. That's true, I agree; but I always confined myself to gallantry, and I never went as far as to do what he's done.

SCAPIN. What would you have him do? He sees a young girl who wishes him well (for he takes after you in being loved by all women). He finds her charming. He pays her visits, tells her sweet nothings, sighs gallantly, acts passionate. She surrenders to his pursuit. He presses his good fortune. There he is surprised with her by her relatives, who, by main force, oblige him to marry her.

SILVESTRE *(aside)*. What a clever trickster he is!

SCAPIN. Would you have wanted him to let himself be killed? At least it's better to be married than to be dead.

ARGANTE. They didn't tell me that was the way things happened.

SCAPIN *(pointing to* SILVESTRE*)*. Ask him then. He won't tell you the contrary.

ARGANTE *(to* SILVESTRE*)*. It was by force that he was married?

SILVESTRE. Yes, sir.

SCAPIN. Would I lie to you?

ARGANTE. Then he should have gone immediately and protested against the violence to a notary.

SCAPIN. That's what he wouldn't do.

ARGANTE. That would have made it easier for me to break up this marriage.

SCAPIN. Break up this marriage!

ARGANTE. Yes.

SCAPIN. You'll never break it up.

ARGANTE. I'll never break it up?

SCAPIN. No.

ARGANTE. What? I shan't have a father's rights on my side, and satisfaction for the violence they did to my son?

SCAPIN. That's something he won't agree to.

ARGANTE. He won't agree to it!

SCAPIN. No.

ARGANTE. My son?

SCAPIN. Your son. Do you want him to confess that he was capable of fear, and that it was by force he was made to do things? He's not likely to go and admit that. That would be doing himself a wrong, and showing himself unworthy of a father like you.

ARGANTE. I don't care a rap about that.

SCAPIN. He must, for his honor and yours, say wherever he goes that it was of his own free will that he married her.

ARGANTE. And *I*, for my honor and his, want him to say the opposite.

SCAPIN. No, I'm sure he won't do it.

ARGANTE. I'll surely force him to.

SCAPIN. He won't do it, I tell you.

ARGANTE. He'll do it, or I'll disinherit him.

SCAPIN. You?

ARGANTE. I.

SCAPIN. That's a good one.

ARGANTE. What do you mean, a good one?

SCAPIN. You won't disinherit him.

ARGANTE. I won't disinherit him?

SCAPIN. No.

ARGANTE. No?

SCAPIN. No.

ARGANTE. Ha! That's pretty funny. I won't disinherit my son.

SCAPIN. No, I tell you.

ARGANTE. Who'll stop me?

SCAPIN. Yourself.

ARGANTE. Me?

SCAPIN. Yes. You won't have the heart to.

ARGANTE. I will.

SCAPIN. You're joking.

ARGANTE. I am not joking.

SCAPIN. Paternal tenderness will play its part.

ARGANTE. It won't do a thing.

SCAPIN. Yes, yes.

ARGANTE. I tell you this shall be done.

SCAPIN. Nonsense.

ARGANTE. You mustn't say "nonsense."

SCAPIN. Good Lord! I know you, you're naturally good.

ARGANTE. I am not good, and I'm bad when I want to be. Let's end this talk; it's getting my bile up. *(To* SILVESTRE*)* Get along with you, you blackguard, get along with you and fetch me my rascal of a son, while I go join Seigneur Géronte and tell him my misfortune.

SCAPIN. Sir, if I can be useful to you in any way, you have only to command me.

ARGANTE. I thank you. *(Aside)* Ah! Why does he have to be my only son? And why do I not have now the daughter whom Heaven took from me, so I could make her my heiress?

Scene 5.   SCAPIN, SILVESTRE

SILVESTRE. I admit that you're a great man, and matters are going well; but on the other hand, we're pressed for money to live on, and we have people on all sides barking at our heels.

SCAPIN. Leave it to me, the plot's hatched. I'm just casting about in my mind for a man we can trust, to play a part I need. Wait. Hold still a minute. Pull your cap down like a tough guy. Take a stand on one leg. Put your hand to your side. Get some fury in your eyes. Strut about a bit like the king in a tragedy. That's fine. Follow me. I know secret ways to disguise your face and your voice.

SILVESTRE. I conjure you at least not to go and get me embroiled with the law.

SCAPIN. Go on, go on with you: we'll share the risks like brothers; and three years more or less in the galleys are not a thing to check a noble heart.

ACT II

Scene 1. GÉRONTE, ARGANTE

GÉRONTE. Yes, beyond a doubt, with this weather we'll have our people here today; and a sailor who has come from Taranto has assured me that he'd seen my man ready to embark. But my daughter's arrival will find things ill disposed for what we had in mind; and what you've just told me about your son utterly breaks up the arrangements we had made together.

ARGANTE. Don't worry about that; I guarantee to overcome that whole obstacle, and I'm going to work on it right away.

GÉRONTE. Faith, Seigneur Argante, shall I tell you what I think? The education of children is something that demands the hardest application.

ARGANTE. No doubt. What's this all about?

GÉRONTE. About the fact that the bad behavior of young folks most often comes from the bad education that their fathers give them.

ARGANTE. That sometimes happens. But what do you mean by that?

GÉRONTE. What do I mean by that?

ARGANTE. Yes.

GÉRONTE. That if, like a good father, you had brought your son into line properly, he wouldn't have played you the trick he has.

ARGANTE. Very good. So you brought yours into line much better?

GÉRONTE. Yes indeed, and I'd be very sorry if he'd done anything like that to me.

315

ARGANTE. And what if this son whom, like a good father, you have brought into line so properly, had done even worse than mine? Eh?

GÉRONTE. How's that?

ARGANTE. How's that?

GÉRONTE. What does that mean?

ARGANTE. That means, Seigneur Géronte, that you mustn't be so quick to condemn other people's conduct; and that those who want to criticize should take a good look to see if there isn't something wrong with them.

GÉRONTE. I don't understand this enigma.

ARGANTE. It'll be explained to you.

GÉRONTE. Could you have heard something about my son?

ARGANTE. That may be.

GÉRONTE. What, then?

ARGANTE. Your Scapin, while I was angry, told me the thing only in general; and from him, or from someone else, you can be informed about the details. As for me, I'm going quickly to consult a lawyer, and consider what course I am to take. Good-by.

Scene 2.   LÉANDRE, GÉRONTE

GÉRONTE *(alone).* What can this business be? Even worse than his? As for me, I don't see what anyone can do worse; and I think that marrying without your father's consent is an action that goes beyond anything that anyone can imagine. . . . Ah, there you are!

LÉANDRE *(running to him to embrace him).* Ah! Father, how happy I am to see you back!

GÉRONTE *(refusing to embrace him).* Easy now. Let's talk business a bit.

LÉANDRE. Allow me to embrace you, and to . . .

GÉRONTE *(still repulsing him)*. Easy now, I tell you.

LÉANDRE. What, father? You refuse to let me express my joy by my embraces?

GÉRONTE. Yes! We have something to straighten out together.

LÉANDRE. And what's that?

GÉRONTE. Hold still, let me look you in the face.

LÉANDRE. What?

GÉRONTE. Look me in the eyes.

LÉANDRE. Well?

GÉRONTE. Now, what's gone on here?

LÉANDRE. What's gone on?

GÉRONTE. Yes. What have you done in my absence?

LÉANDRE. Father, what do you expect I've done?

GÉRONTE. I'm not expecting you to have done, but I'm asking you what it is you've done.

LÉANDRE. I've done nothing that you have reason to complain of.

GÉRONTE. Nothing?

LÉANDRE. No.

GÉRONTE. You're quite certain.

LÉANDRE. That's because I'm sure of my innocence.

GÉRONTE. Yet Scapin has told things about you.

LÉANDRE. Scapin?

GÉRONTE. Aha! That name makes you blush.

LÉANDRE. He told you something about me?

GÉRONTE. This place isn't a very good one to settle this affair, and we'll go into it somewhere else. Go on home. I'll be back there shortly. Ah! Traitor, if you dishonor me, I renounce you as my son, and you can just make up your mind to flee my presence forever.

Scene 3.   OCTAVE, SCAPIN, LÉANDRE

LÉANDRE *(alone)*. To betray me in this way! A scoundrel who, for a hundred reasons, should be the first to conceal the things I confide in him, is the first to go and reveal them to my father! Ah! I swear to Heaven, this treachery shall not remain unpunished.

OCTAVE. My dear Scapin, what don't I owe to your efforts! What an admirable man you are! And how favorable Heaven is to me, to send you to my rescue!

LÉANDRE. Aha! There you are. I'm delighted to find you, Mr. Scoundrel.

SCAPIN. Sir, your servant. You do me too much honor.

LÉANDRE *(drawing his sword)*. You're a bad comic. Ah! I'll teach you . . .

SCAPIN *(falling on his knees)*. Sir!

OCTAVE *(stepping between them to keep LÉANDRE from striking)*. Ah! Léandre!

LÉANDRE. No, Octave, don't hold me back, please.

SCAPIN. Ah! Sir!

OCTAVE *(holding LÉANDRE back)*. Please!

LÉANDRE *(trying to strike SCAPIN)*. Let me satisfy my resentment.

OCTAVE. In the name of friendship, Léandre, don't mistreat him.

SCAPIN. Sir, what have I done to you?

LÉANDRE *(trying to strike him)*. What you've done to me, traitor?

OCTAVE *(holding LÉANDRE back)*. There! Gently.

LÉANDRE. No, Octave, I want him to confess to me himself,

right now, the perfidy he's committed against me. Yes, you scoundrel, I know the trick you've played on me, I've just learned of it; and perhaps you didn't think they would reveal this secret to me; but I want to have your confession of it from your own mouth, or I'm going to run this sword through your body.

SCAPIN. Ah, sir! Would you really have the heart to do that?

LÉANDRE. Then talk.

SCAPIN. Did I do something to you, sir?

LÉANDRE. Yes, you scoundrel, and your conscience tells you only too well what it is.

SCAPIN. I assure you, I don't know what it is.

LÉANDRE (advancing to strike him). You don't know!

OCTAVE (holding him back). Léandre!

SCAPIN. Well, sir, since you will have it, I confess that my friends and I drank up that quarter-cask of Spanish wine you were given a few days ago; and it was I who made a crack in the cask, and poured water all around to make you think the wine had run out.

LÉANDRE. It was you, you blackguard, who drank my Spanish wine, and were the reason why I scolded my serving-maid so, thinking that she was the one who had played me that trick?

SCAPIN. Yes, sir; I ask your pardon for it.

LÉANDRE. I'm very glad to learn that; but that's not the question now.

SCAPIN. It's not that, sir?

LÉANDRE. No, it's another matter that concerns me much more, and I want you to tell me about it.

SCAPIN. Sir, I don't remember doing anything else.

LÉANDRE (trying to hit him). You won't talk?

SCAPIN. Oh!

OCTAVE (holding back LÉANDRE). Gently!

SCAPIN. Yes, sir, it's true that three weeks ago when you sent me one evening to take a little watch to the young Gypsy girl whom you love, I came back with my clothes all covered with mud, and my face all bloody, and told you I'd run into some thieves who'd given me a good beating and robbed me of the watch. It was I, sir; I'd kept it.

LÉANDRE. It was you? You kept my watch?

SCAPIN. Yes, sir, so as to see what time it is.

LÉANDRE. Aha! I'm learning some pretty things here, and I certainly have a mighty faithful servant. But that still isn't what I'm asking.

SCAPIN. It's not that?

LÉANDRE. No, you wretch, it's something else again that I want you to confess to me.

SCAPIN. Confound it!

LÉANDRE. Speak up quick, I'm in a hurry.

SCAPIN. Sir, that's all I've done.

LÉANDRE (trying to strike SCAPIN). That's all?

OCTAVE (stepping in front of LÉANDRE). Hey!

SCAPIN. Oh well! Yes, sir. You remember that werewolf six months ago who gave you such a beating with a stick one night and nearly made you break your neck when you fell into a cellar as you ran away.

LÉANDRE. Well?

SCAPIN. It was I, sir, who played the werewolf.

LÉANDRE. It was you, traitor, who played the werewolf?

SCAPIN. Yes, sir, just to frighten you, and to make you stop wanting to make us chase around every night as you used to.

LÉANDRE. I'll remember all I've just learned at the proper time and place. But I want to come to the point, and for you to confess to me what you told my father.

SCAPIN. Your father?

LÉANDRE. Yes, you rogue, my father.

SCAPIN. I haven't even seen him since he got back.

LÉANDRE. You haven't seen him?

SCAPIN. No, sir.

LÉANDRE. Are you sure?

SCAPIN. I'm sure. That's something I'll get him to tell you himself.

LÉANDRE. Yet I have this from his own mouth.

SCAPIN. By your leave, he didn't tell you the truth.

Scene 4.   CARLE, SCAPIN, LÉANDRE, OCTAVE

CARLE. Sir, I bring you bad news for your love.

LÉANDRE. How's that?

CARLE. Your Gypsies are on the point of carrying off Zerbinette, and she herself, with tears in her eyes, charged me to come quickly and tell you that if, in two hours, you aren't minded to bring them the money they've asked of you for her, you're going to lose her forever.

LÉANDRE. In two hours?

CARLE. In two hours.

LÉANDRE. Oh! My dear Scapin, I implore you for your help!

SCAPIN (*walking in front of him with a haughty air*). "Oh! My dear Scapin." I'm "my dear Scapin" now that I'm needed.

LÉANDRE. Go on, I forgive you for everything you've told me, and for even worse, if you've done it.

SCAPIN. No, no, don't forgive me for anything. Run your sword through my body. I'd be delighted if you'd kill me.

LÉANDRE. No. Rather I conjure you to save my life by serving my love.

SCAPIN. Not at all, not at all; you'd do better to kill me.

LÉANDRE. You're too precious to me; and I beg you to be willing to use for me that admirable genius that can get around anything.

SCAPIN. No, kill me, I tell you.

LÉANDRE. Ah! For Heaven's sake, don't give any more thought to all that, and put your mind to giving me the help I'm asking of you!

OCTAVE. Scapin, you've got to do something for him.

SCAPIN. How can I, after an affront like that?

LÉANDRE. I beseech you to forget my temper and lend me your ingenuity.

OCTAVE. I join my prayers to his.

SCAPIN. I've taken that insult to heart.

OCTAVE. You must give up your resentment.

LÉANDRE. Would you abandon me, Scapin, to the cruel extremity in which my love is placed?

SCAPIN. To come and pay me, out of the blue, an affront like that!

LÉANDRE. I'm in the wrong, I confess.

SCAPIN. To call me a scoundrel, a rogue, a blackguard, a wretch!

LÉANDRE. I'm just as sorry as I can be.

SCAPIN. To want to run his sword through my body!

LÉANDRE. I ask your pardon for that with all my heart; and if all that's needed is for me to throw myself at your knees, here I am, Scapin, to beseech you once more not to abandon me.

OCTAVE. Ah! Faith, Scapin, you must give in to that!

SCAPIN. Rise. Another time, don't be so hasty.

LÉANDRE. Do you promise to work for me?

SCAPIN. I'll think about it.

LÉANDRE. But you know that time is pressing.

SCAPIN. Don't worry about it. How much do you need?

LÉANDRE. Five hundred crowns.

SCAPIN. And you?

OCTAVE. Two hundred pistoles.

SCAPIN. I mean to get the money out of your fathers. *(To* OCTAVE*)* As for yours, the scheme is all found already; *(to* LÉANDRE*)* and as for yours, although he's a miser to the last degree, he'll need less doing yet, for you know that as to wit, thank God, he has no great provision of it, and I set him down as a kind of man whom you can always lead to believe whatever you like. No offense to you: there's no suspicion of a resemblance between him and you; and you know well enough what everybody's opinion is, that he's your father only for form's sake.

LÉANDRE. Easy now, Scapin.

SCAPIN. All right, all right, so that bothers people a lot: are you serious? . . . But I see Octave's father coming. Let's begin with him, since here he is. Go away, both of you. *(To* OCTAVE*)* And you, notify your Silvestre to come quick and play his part.

Scene 5. ARGANTE, SCAPIN

SCAPIN *(aside)*. Here he is ruminating.

ARGANTE *(thinking himself alone)*. To have so little sense of behavior and consideration! To go and throw himself into an engagement like that! Ah! Ah! The witlessness of youth!

SCAPIN. Sir, your servant.

ARGANTE. Hello, Scapin.

SCAPIN. You're brooding about your son's affair.

ARGANTE. I admit I'm frightfully upset about it.

SCAPIN. Sir, life is mixed up with disappointments. It's a good thing to keep constantly prepared for them; and a long time ago I heard a remark of one of the ancients[1] that I've always remembered.

ARGANTE. What?

SCAPIN. That no matter how short a time the father of a family has been away from home, he should run his mind over all the distressing accidents he may encounter on his return: should imagine his house burned, his money stolen, his wife dead, his son crippled, his daughter seduced; and whatever he finds has not happened to him, impute it to good fortune. As for me, I've always practiced this lesson in my little philosophy; and I've never returned home without holding myself ready for the anger of my masters, for reprimands, insults, kicks in the ass, beatings with the stick and the strap; and whatever failed to happen to me, I thanked my lucky star for it.

ARGANTE. That's all very well. But this foolish marriage, which interferes with the one we want to bring about, is a thing I can't endure, and I've just consulted some lawyers to have it broken off.

SCAPIN. Faith, sir! If you'll take my word for it, you'll try to settle the affair in some other way. You know what lawsuits are in this country, and you're going to plunge yourself into some pretty thorny business.

ARGANTE. You're right, I see that well enough. But what other way?

SCAPIN. I think I've found one. I couldn't help feeling sorry for you just now, and that made me cast about in my mind for some way to get you out of trouble; for I can't see decent fathers upset by their children without being moved; and I've always felt a particular inclination for your person.

ARGANTE. I'm obliged to you.

SCAPIN. So I went to see the brother of this girl your son has married. He's one of those professional bravos, those people

[1] Terrence, *Phormio*, Act II, scene 1, ll. 231–246.

who are all sword thrusts, who talk of nothing but breaking someone's back, and have no more scruples about killing a man than about swallowing a glass of wine. I got him going on this marriage, pointed out to him how easy it would be to have it broken off by reason of violence, the prerogatives of your title of father, and the support you would get before the law by your right, your money, and your friends. In short, I twisted him about so in all directions that he lent an ear to the propositions I made him to settle the matter for a certain sum; and he'll give his consent to break off the marriage, provided you give him some money.

ARGANTE. And what did he ask?

SCAPIN. Oh! At first, the sky and all.

ARGANTE. Well, what?

SCAPIN. Wild things.

ARGANTE. But what?

SCAPIN. He was talking of nothing less than five or six hundred pistoles.

ARGANTE. Five or six hundred quartan fevers seize him! Is he trying to be funny?

SCAPIN. That's what I said to him. I utterly rejected any such propositions, and I clearly gave him to understand that you were no dupe, for him to ask you for five or six hundred pistoles. Finally, after a lot of talk, here's what the result of our discussion came down to. "We're at the time," he said to me, "when I must leave for the army. I'm busy getting equipped, and the fact that I need some money makes me consent, in spite of myself, to what is proposed. I need a regular horse, and I couldn't get one that's at all tolerable for less than sixty pistoles."

ARGANTE. Oh well! As for sixty pistoles, I'll give them.

SCAPIN. "I'll need the harness and the pistols; and that will come to a good twenty pistoles more."

ARGANTE. Twenty pistoles and sixty, that would be eighty.

SCAPIN. Exactly.

ARGANTE. That's a lot; but so be it, I consent to that.

SCAPIN. "I also need a horse for my valet to ride, which will cost fully thirty pistoles."

ARGANTE. What the devil! Let him walk! He shan't have a thing.

SCAPIN. Sir.

ARGANTE. No, he's out of line.

SCAPIN. Do you want his valet to go on foot?

ARGANTE. Let him go as he pleases, and the master too.

SCAPIN. Good Lord, sir! Don't stick at a little thing like that. Don't go to court, I beg you; give it all to keep out of the hands of the law.

ARGANTE. Oh well! All right, I'll agree to give him those thirty pistoles too.

SCAPIN. "I also need," he said, "a mule to carry . . ."

ARGANTE. Oh, let him go to the devil with his mule! That's too much, and we'll go before the judges.

SCAPIN. Please, sir . . .

ARGANTE. No, I'll do nothing of the sort.

SCAPIN. Sir, just a little mule.

ARGANTE. I wouldn't even give him a donkey.

SCAPIN. Consider . . .

ARGANTE. No! I'd rather go to law.

SCAPIN. Oh, sir! What are you talking about, what are you deciding? Cast your eyes over the devious course of the law: see how many appeals and degrees of jurisdiction, how many perplexing procedures, how many rapacious animals through whose claws you'll have to pass—sergeants, attorneys, counsels, clerks, substitutes, reporters, judges, and their clerks. There's not a one of all those people but is capable, for the merest trifle, of giving the best case in the world a slap in the face. A sergeant will serve false writs, on which you'll be condemned without knowing it. Your attorney will come to terms with your adversary and sell you out for hard cash.

Your counsel, won over in the same way, won't be there when they plead your case, or will give arguments that only beat about the bush and won't come to the point. The registrar will deliver sentences and decisions against you by default. The reporter's clerk will purloin documents, or the reporter himself won't say what he's seen. And when, by the greatest precautions in the world, you've parried all this, you'll be astonished that your judges will have been solicited against you, either by pious folk or by women they love. Oh, sir! If you can, save yourself from that hell. To be at law is to be damned already in this world; and the mere thought of a lawsuit would be enough to make me flee to the Indies.

ARGANTE. How much does he reckon for the mule?

SCAPIN. Sir, for the mule, his horse, his man's horse, the harness and the pistols, and to pay a little matter he owes his landlady, he asks in all for two hundred pistoles.

ARGANTE. Two hundred pistoles?

SCAPIN. Yes.

ARGANTE (*walking across the stage in anger*). Let's go, let's go, we'll go to court.

SCAPIN. Give it some thought . . .

ARGANTE. I'll go to court.

SCAPIN. Don't go cast yourself . . .

ARGANTE. I want to go to court.

SCAPIN. But to go to court, you'll need money. You'll need it for the summons, you'll need it for the registration, you'll need it for assigning the attorney, for appearance, counsel, evidence, and days spent by the attorney; you'll need it for the consultations and pleas of the lawyers, for the right to withdraw the briefs and for engrossing the documents; you'll need it for substitutes' reports; for the concluding presents to the judge; for registration by the clerk, provisional decree, sentences and arrests, rolls, signatures, and errands by their clerks, not to mention all the presents you'll have to make. Give this money to this man, and you're quit of the whole business.

ARGANTE. What, two hundred pistoles?

SCAPIN. Yes, you'll gain by it. I've made a little calculation in my head of all the costs of justice; and I've found that by giving two hundred pistoles to your man you'll have at least a hundred and fifty left over, without counting the worries, the steps, and the troubles you'll spare yourself. Even if all you had to put up with was the wise remarks made in front of everybody by lawyers who are nasty jokers, I would rather give three hundred pistoles than go to court.

ARGANTE. I don't care a rap about that, and I defy the lawyers to say anything about me.

SCAPIN. You'll do what you please; but if I were you, I'd avoid lawsuits.

ARGANTE. I won't give any two hundred pistoles.

SCAPIN. Here's the man we were talking about.

Scene 6.   SILVESTRE *(disguised as a bully)*, ARGANTE, SCAPIN

SILVESTRE. Scapin, just show me that man Argante, Octave's father.

SCAPIN. Why, sir?

SILVESTRE. I've just learned that he wants to bring suit against me and have my sister's marriage broken off by the law.

SCAPIN. I don't know if he has that in mind; but he won't consent to the two hundred pistoles you want, and he says it's too much.

SILVESTRE. 'Sdeath! By his head and guts! If I find him, I mean to break his back, even if I have to be broken alive on the wheel for it.

(ARGANTE *stands trembling behind* SCAPIN, *so as not to be seen.*)

SCAPIN. Sir, this father of Octave is a man of spirit, and perhaps he won't be at all afraid of you.

SILVESTRE. Him? Him? By his blood and head! If he were here, I'd run my sword through his stomach right now. *(Seeing* ARGANTE*)* Who's this man?

SCAPIN. He's not the one, sir, he's not the one.

SILVESTRE. Isn't he a friend of his?

SCAPIN. No, sir. On the contrary, he's his mortal enemy.

SILVESTRE. His mortal enemy?

SCAPIN. Yes.

SILVESTRE. Ah, gad! I'm delighted. You, sir, are the enemy of that scoundrel Argante, eh?

SCAPIN. Yes, yes, I'll answer to that.

SILVESTRE *(shaking his hand roughly).* Shake on it, shake. I give you my word, and swear to you on my honor, by the sword I wear, by all the oaths I could take, that before the end of the day I'll rid you of that arrant rogue, that scoundrel Argante. Rely on me.

SCAPIN. Sir, in this country violent acts are hardly tolerated.

SILVESTRE. I don't care about anything, and I've nothing to lose.

SCAPIN. He'll certainly be on his guard; and he has relatives, friends, and domestics whom he will use for help against your resentment.

SILVESTRE. That's what I want, 'sdeath! That's what I want! *(He draws his sword and thrusts in all directions, as if there were many people in front of him.)* Blood and guts! Why don't I find him here now with all his help? Why doesn't he appear before my eyes with thirty people around him? Why don't they swoop down upon me arms in hand? What, you scoundrels, you have the temerity to attack me? Come on, 'sdeath, kill! No quarter! Up and at 'em! Stand firm! Strike! Sure foot, sure eye. Ah! Scoundrels! Ah! Rabble, you're asking for it; I'll give you your bellyful. Stand firm, you rogues, stand firm. Let's go. Have at you here! Have at you there! Here! There! What, you're drawing back? Stand firm, 'sdeath! Stand firm.

SCAPIN. There, there, there, sir! We're not in this.

SILVESTRE. That'll teach you to dare to play tricks on me. *(Exit)*

SCAPIN. Well, you see how many people can be killed for two hundred pistoles. Oh, come on! I wish you good luck.

ARGANTE *(all trembling)*. Scapin.

SCAPIN. If you please?

ARGANTE. I've decided to give the two hundred pistoles.

SCAPIN. I'm delighted for your sake.

ARGANTE. Let's go find him, I have them on me.

SCAPIN. You've only to give them to me. For the sake of your honor, you mustn't appear here, after having passed here for someone other than you are; and furthermore, I'd be afraid that if you made yourself known he might go and take it into his head to ask for more.

ARGANTE. Yes; but I'd have been very glad to see how I give away my money.

SCAPIN. Do you mistrust me?

ARGANTE. No, but . . .

SCAPIN. By gad, sir, either I'm a rogue or I'm an honest man; it's one or the other. Would I want to deceive you, and in all this matter have I any other interest than yours, and that of my master, whom you want to be allied with? If I'm suspect to you, I'll have no more to do with the whole thing, and you can go right now and look for someone to fix up your affairs.

ARGANTE. Take it then.

SCAPIN. No, sir, don't trust me with your money. I'll be perfectly glad for you to make use of someone else.

ARGANTE. Good Lord! Take it!

SCAPIN. No, I tell you, don't trust me. Who knows whether I'm not trying to steal your money?

ARGANTE. Take it, I tell you, don't make me argue any more. But take care to get good security in dealing with him.

SCAPIN. Leave it to me, he's not dealing with a fool.

ARGANTE. I'll wait for you at my house.

SCAPIN. I won't fail to go there.   *(Exit* ARGANTE.*)*
And that's one! All I have to do is find the other. Ah! My word! Here he is. It seems as though Heaven brings them into my nets one after the other.

Scene 7.   GÉRONTE,   SCAPIN

SCAPIN. *(pretending not to see* GÉRONTE*).* O Heavens! O unforeseen disaster! O wretched father! Poor Géronte, what will you do?

GÉRONTE. What's that he's saying about me, with that unhappy face?

SCAPIN. Isn't there anyone who can tell me where Seigneur Géronte is?

GÉRONTE. What's wrong, Scapin?

SCAPIN. Where can I find him to tell him of this misfortune?

GÉRONTE. What is it then?

SCAPIN. In vain I'm running around in all directions to try to find him.

GÉRONTE. Here I am.

SCAPIN. He must be hidden in some place that no one can guess.

GÉRONTE. Stop it! Are you blind, that you don't see me?

SCAPIN. Ah, sir! There's just no way to find you.

GÉRONTE. I've been right in front of you for an hour. What in the world is the matter?

SCAPIN. Sir . . .

GÉRONTE. What?

SCAPIN. Sir, your son . . .

GÉRONTE. Well? My son . . . ?

SCAPIN. Has fallen into the strangest misfortune in the world.

GÉRONTE. And what's that?

SCAPIN. I found him just now quite sad about something or other you said to him, in which you brought me in where I didn't belong; and, trying to divert this sadness, we went for a walk in the port. There, among many other things, our eyes were caught by a rather well equipped Turkish galley. A nice-looking young Turk invited us to come aboard, and gave us his hand. We went aboard; he offered us a thousand civilities, gave us a collation in which we had the most excellent fruits to eat that you ever could see, and wine to drink that we considered the best in the world.

GÉRONTE. What's so terrible about all that?

SCAPIN. Wait, sir, we're getting there now. While we were eating, he had the galley put out to sea, and, when he saw he was well away from port, he had me put into a skiff, and then sends me to tell you that if you don't send five hundred crowns by me right away, he's going to take your son to Algiers.

GÉRONTE. What the devil! Five hundred crowns?

SCAPIN. Yes, sir; and furthermore, he gave me only two hours for it.

GÉRONTE. Ah! That villain of a Turk, to murder me in this way!

SCAPIN. It's up to you, sir, to be thinking promptly about ways of saving from slavery a son whom you love with such tenderness.

GÉRONTE. What the devil did he go into that galley for?

SCAPIN. He had no thought of what would happen.

GÉRONTE. Go along, Scapin, go along quick and tell that Turk that I'm going to send the police after him.

SCAPIN. The police in the open sea? Are you trying to be funny?

GÉRONTE. What the devil did he go into that galley for?

SCAPIN. Sometimes people are led by an evil destiny.

GÉRONTE. Scapin, in this you must play the part of a faithful servant; you must.

SCAPIN. What's that, sir?

GÉRONTE. You must go and tell this Turk to send me back my son, and that you'll take his place until I've raised the sum he's asking.

SCAPIN. Oh, sir! Are you aware of what you're saying? And do you suppose this Turk has so little sense as to go and accept a wretch like me in place of your son?

GÉRONTE. What the devil did he go into that galley for?

SCAPIN. He didn't anticipate this mishap. Keep in mind, sir, that he's given me only two hours.

GÉRONTE. You say he's asking . . .

SCAPIN. Five hundred crowns.

GÉRONTE. Five hundred crowns! Has he no conscience?

SCAPIN. Yes, indeed, a Turk's conscience.

GÉRONTE. Does he really know what five hundred crowns is?

SCAPIN. Yes, sir, he knows that it's a thousand five hundred francs.

GÉRONTE. Does the traitor think you can pick a thousand five hundred francs off a tree?

SCAPIN. These are people who don't understand reason.

GÉRONTE. But what the devil did he go into that galley for?

SCAPIN. That's true; but what can you expect? Nobody could foresee these things. Please, sir, hurry.

GÉRONTE. Here, this is the key to my cupboard.

SCAPIN. Good.

GÉRONTE. You'll open it.

SCAPIN. Very well.

GÉRONTE. You'll find a big key on the left-hand side, which is to my garret.

SCAPIN. Yes.

GÉRONTE. You'll go and get all the old clothes that are in that big hamper, and you'll sell them to the secondhand dealers to go and redeem my son.

SCAPIN *(returning the key to him)*. Oh, sir! Are you dreaming? I wouldn't get a hundred francs for all you're talking about; and besides, you know how little time they gave me.

GÉRONTE. But what the devil did he go into that galley for?

SCAPIN. Oh, what a lot of wasted words! Forget that galley, and bear in mind that time is pressing, and that you're running the risk of losing your son. Alas! My poor master, perhaps I'll never see you again in my life, and at the moment I'm speaking they're carrying you off to Algiers as a slave. But Heaven will be witness that I've done all I could for you, and that if you fail to be ransomed, the only thing to blame is the insufficient affection of a father.

GÉRONTE. Wait, Scapin, I'll go get that sum.

SCAPIN. Then hurry quick, sir, I tremble that the hour may strike.

GÉRONTE. Wasn't it four hundred crowns you said?

SCAPIN. No, five hundred crowns.

GÉRONTE. Five hundred crowns?

SCAPIN. Yes.

GÉRONTE. What the devil did he go into that galley for?

SCAPIN. You're right, but hurry up.

GÉRONTE. Wasn't there any other walk to take?

SCAPIN. That's true. But act promptly.

GÉRONTE. Oh, that cursed galley!

SCAPIN *(aside)*. He's got that galley on the brain.

GÉRONTE. Here, Scapin, I was forgetting that I just received that sum in gold, and I didn't think it would be snatched away from me so soon. *(He offers him his purse, but doesn't let go of it.)* Here. Go along and ransom my son.

SCAPIN *(holding out his hand, as he will do each time he speaks in the ensuing dialogue)*. Yes, sir.

GÉRONTE *(holding out the purse to* SCAPIN, *then pulling it back, as he will do each time he speaks in the ensuing dialogue)*. But tell that Turk that he's a villain.

SCAPIN. Yes.

GÉRONTE. A wretch.

SCAPIN. Yes.

GÉRONTE. A man of no faith, a robber.

SCAPIN. Leave it to me.

GÉRONTE. That he's extorting five hundred crowns from me contrary to all right and justice.

SCAPIN. Yes.

GÉRONTE. That I'm not giving them to him either till death or for life.

SCAPIN. Very well.

GÉRONTE. And that if I ever catch him, I'll have my revenge on him.

SCAPIN. Yes.

GÉRONTE *(putting the purse back in his pocket and moving off)*. Go on, go quick and bring back my son.

SCAPIN *(going after him)*. Stop, sir!

GÉRONTE. What?

SCAPIN. Then where's that money?

GÉRONTE. Didn't I give it to you?

SCAPIN. No, really, you put it back in your pocket.

GÉRONTE. Ah! It's grief that's confusing my mind.

SCAPIN. So I see.

GÉRONTE. What the devil did he go into that galley for? Ah!
Cursed galley! May all the devils in hell take that traitor of
a Turk!

SCAPIN *(alone)*. He can't stomach the five hundred crowns
that I'm tearing from him; but he's not quits with me yet,
and I mean to have him pay me in another coin for the lie he
told his son about me.

Scene 8.   OCTAVE, LÉANDRE, SCAPIN

OCTAVE. Well, Scapin! Did you succeed in what you undertook
for me?

LÉANDRE. Did you do anything to deliver my love from its
misery?

SCAPIN *(to OCTAVE)*. Here are two hundred pistoles that I got
out of your father.

OCTAVE. Ah! How happy you make me!

SCAPIN *(to LÉANDRE)*. For you I haven't been able to do anything.

LÉANDRE *(starting to go)*. Then I must go off and die; I have
no use for life if Zerbinette is taken from me.

SCAPIN. Hold on, hold on! Gently! How devilish quick you go
about things!

LÉANDRE *(turning back)*. What do you expect me to do?

SCAPIN. Come on, I have what you need here.

LÉANDRE *(coming back)*. Ah! You bring me back to life.

SCAPIN. But on condition that you allow *me* a little revenge
on your father for the trick he played on me.

LÉANDRE. Whatever you want.

SCAPIN. You promise me this before a witness?

LÉANDRE. Yes.

SCAPIN. Here you are, here are five hundred crowns.

LÉANDRE. Let's take it and promptly go purchase the girl I adore.

ACT III

Scene 1. ZERBINETTE, HYACINTE, SCAPIN, SILVESTRE

SILVESTRE. Yes, your suitors have decided between them that you should be together, and we are carrying out the orders they gave us.

HYACINTE *(to* ZERBINETTE*).* There's nothing about such an order but that is very agreeable to me. I accept such a companion with joy; and it won't be my fault if the friendship that exists between the persons we love does not spread out between the two of us.

ZERBINETTE. I accept the proposition, and I'm not a person to draw back when I'm approached with true friendship.

SCAPIN. And when it's with love that you're approached?

ZERBINETTE. As for love, that's another matter; in that you run a little more risk, and I'm not so bold.

SCAPIN. I think you are now, against my master; and what he's just done for you should give you heart to respond to his passion as you should.

ZERBINETTE. Thus far I trust in that only in a proper way; and what he's just done is not enough to give me complete assurance. I'm naturally gay, and I'm always laughing; but for all I may laugh, I'm serious about certain matters; and your master will be mistaken if he thinks it's enough for him to have purchased me in order to have me entirely his own. That must cost him something more than money; and to respond to his love in the way he wishes, I need to have him plight me his troth and season it with certain ceremonies that are considered necessary.

SCAPIN. That's how he looks at it too. His intentions toward you are strictly fair and honorable; and I wouldn't have been the man to be involved in this affair if he'd had any other ideas.

ZERBINETTE. That's what I want to believe, since you tell me so; but on the father's side I foresee some obstacles.

SCAPIN. We'll find ways to arrange things.

HYACINTE (to ZERBINETTE). The resemblance between our destinies should also contribute to bring about our friendship; and we both find ourselves exposed to the same alarms and the same misfortune.

ZERBINETTE. At least you have this advantage, that you know of whom you were born, and that the support of your parents, whom you can make known, can arrange everything, assure your happiness, and provide consent for a marriage already held. But as for me, I find no help in what I may be, and I'm in a state that won't soften the will of a father who considers only money.

HYACINTE. But also you have this advantage, that the man you love is not being tempted by another match.

ZERBINETTE. The change in a lover's heart is not the thing most to be feared. One may naturally think one has enough merit to keep one's conquest; and what I find most fearful in this sort of affair is the power of the father, to whom no merit is of any value.

HYACINTE. Alas! Why must just inclinations be crossed? What a sweet thing it is to love when you find no obstacle to those lovely chains with which two hearts bind themselves together!

SCAPIN. You're joking. Tranquillity in love is a disagreeable calm; a uniform happiness becomes boring to us; we need ups and downs in life; and the difficulties that intermingle in our affairs awaken ardors and augment pleasures.

ZERBINETTE. My goodness, Scapin, tell us this story which I've been told is so amusing, of the stratagem you thought of to extract money from your miserly old man. You know no one wastes his time telling me a story, and that I pay pretty well for it by the joy I take in it.

SCAPIN. Here's Silvestre, who will handle it as well as I would. I have a certain little revenge in mind, and I'm going to taste the pleasure of it.

SILVESTRE. Why do you go out of your way to try to bring troubles on your head?

SCAPIN. I like to attempt hazardous undertakings.

SILVESTRE. I've already told you, you'd give up your present plan if you'd take my word for it.

SCAPIN. Yes, but it's my word I'll take.

SILVESTRE. What the devil are you going to play around at?

SCAPIN. What the devil are you worrying about?

SILVESTRE. About seeing that, without any need, you're going to run the risk of bringing a shower of blows upon yourself.

SCAPIN. Well, it's at the expense of my back, not of yours.

SILVESTRE. It's true that you're master of your own shoulders, and you'll dispose of them as you please.

SCAPIN. This sort of risk has never stopped me, and I hate these pusillanimous hearts that see the consequences of things so well that they don't dare undertake anything.

ZERBINETTE (to SCAPIN). We'll need your help.

SCAPIN. Go along. I'll come and join you soon. It shall not be said that with impunity I was placed in a position to betray myself and to reveal secrets that were better not known.

Scene 2.   GÉRONTE, SCAPIN

GÉRONTE. Well, Scapin, how goes my son's affair?

SCAPIN. Your son, sir, is in a safe place; but now you yourself are running the greatest risk in the world, and I'd give a good deal for you to be at home.

GÉRONTE. Why, how's that?

SCAPIN. At the very moment I'm speaking, they're looking for you all over to kill you.

GÉRONTE. Me?

SCAPIN. Yes.

GÉRONTE. And who is it?

SCAPIN. The brother of this person that Octave has married. He thinks your plan to put your daughter in his sister's place is what is doing the most to break up their marriage; and with that notion in mind he has openly resolved to take out his despair on you and take away your life to avenge his honor. All his friends, swordsmen like himself, are looking all over for you and asking for news of you. I even saw here and there some soldiers of his company questioning the people they meet, and occupying in squads all the approaches to your house. So you can't go home, you can't take a step right or left, without falling into their hands.

GÉRONTE. What shall I do, my dear Scapin?

SCAPIN. I don't know, sir, and this is a bad business. I tremble for you from head to foot, and . . . Wait. (He turns around and pretends to go and look offstage to see if there is anyone there.)

GÉRONTE (trembling). Eh?

SCAPIN (coming back). No, no, no, it's nothing.

GÉRONTE. Couldn't you find some way to get me out of trouble?

SCAPIN. I can imagine one all right; but I'd run the risk of getting myself well beaten.

GÉRONTE. Oh, Scapin! Show yourself to be a zealous servant: don't desert me, I beg you!

SCAPIN. I'm willing to help. I'm too fond of you to leave you without help.

GÉRONTE. You'll have your reward for it, I assure you; and I promise you this suit, when I've gotten it a bit worn out.

SCAPIN. Wait. Here's something I've thought of that's just right to save you. You must get into this sack and . . .

GÉRONTE (*thinking he sees someone*). Oh!

SCAPIN. No, no, no, no, it's no one. You must get into it, I say, and keep from moving in any way. I'll load you on my back like a bundle of something or other, and that way I'll carry you through your enemies right into your house; and when we're once there, we can barricade ourselves and send for assistance against violence.

GÉRONTE. That's real ingenuity.

SCAPIN. The best in the world. You'll see. (*Aside*) You'll pay me for the trick.

GÉRONTE. Eh?

SCAPIN. I say that your enemies will be properly caught. Get right down to the bottom, and above all take care not to show yourself and not to move, whatever may happen.

GÉRONTE. Leave it to me. I'll manage to keep still.

SCAPIN. Hide. Here's a cutthroat looking for you. (*Disguising his voice as a Gascon*) "What? I won't have the advantage of to kill this Géronte, and someone out of charity won't tell me where he is?" (*To* GÉRONTE, *in his ordinary voice*) Don't budge. (*Resuming his disguised voice*) " 'Sdeath, I'll vind him, if he hid himself in the center of the earth." (*To* GÉRONTE, *in his natural voice*) Don't show yourself. (*From now on the Gascon talk, in quotation marks, is disguised, the rest is his own.*) "Oh, the man with the sack!" — Sir. — "I gib you one louis, and teach me where could be Géronte." — You're looking for Seigneur Géronte? — "Yes, 'sdeath, I be looking for him." — And on what business, sir? — "On vat business?" — Yes. — "I vant, zounds, to make him die of blows with a stick." — Oh, sir, blows with a stick are not given to people like him, and he's not a man to be treated in that way. — "Who, that fool Géronte, that rascal, that vum?" — Seigneur Géronte is neither a fool, nor a rascal, nor a bum, and, if you please, you should change your language. — "What, *you* treat *me* with that lovtiness" — I'm defending, as I must, a man of honor who is being insulted. — "Are you a vriend of this Géronte?" — Yes, sir, I am. — "Ah, zounds, you're a vriend of his, vell and good." *(He beats the sack with a stick repeatedly.)* "Here, this is what I gib you vor him." — Oh, oh, oh, oh! Sir! Oh, oh, sir! Gently! Oh, gently, oh, oh, oh! —"Go. Take him this vrom me. Varewell to you!" — Ah! The devil take that Gascon! Oh! *(He complains and wriggles his back as if he had received the beating.)*

GÉRONTE *(putting his head out of the sack).* Ah! Scapin! I can't go on.

SCAPIN. Ah! Sir! I'm beaten black and blue, and my shoulders hurt frightfully.

GÉRONTE. How so? It was mine he beat.

SCAPIN. No, sir, it was my back he was beating.

GÉRONTE. What do you mean? I certainly felt the blows, and I certainly feel them still.

SCAPIN. No, I tell you, it was only the end of the stick that reached your shoulders.

GÉRONTE. Then you ought to have moved away a bit to spare me.

SCAPIN *(putting* GÉRONTE's *head back in the sack).* Watch out! Here's another one that looks like a foreigner. *(Disguising his voice as a Swiss)* "By Gar! Me run around like a Basque, ant me no be able to fint all tay dat tefil Gironte." — Keep well hidden. — "Tell me a bit, you, mister man, if you please, you not know where is this Gironte that me looking for?" — No, sir, I don't know where Géronte is. — "You tell it to me frankly, me haf not much business with him. Just only to gif him a little treat of a dozen blows on the back mit der stick, and tree or four little swort trusts true his chest." — I assure you, sir, I don't know where he is. — "It seems to me I see something mofe in dis sack." — Pardon me, sir. — "Dere is assuretly some funny business in dere." — Not at all, sir. — "Me feel like giffing one swort trust in dat sack." — Ah, sir! Don't do anything of the sort. — "You just show me a bit what dat be dere." — Easy, sir! — "How's dat? Easy?" — You have no business wanting to see what I'm carrying. — "But me, I to want to see." — You shan't see. — "Aha! What a lot of trifling!" — These are old clothes that

belong to me. — "You show me, I tell you." — I'll do nothing
of the sort. — "You to nothing?" — No. — "Me gif this stick
on the shoulders of you." — I don't care a rap. — "Ah! You
be joker." — Ouch, ouch, ouch! Oh, sir, oh, oh, oh, oh! —
"Goot-by; that be one little lesson to teach to you to speak
insolentily!" — Oh! Plague take the jabbering fool! Oh!

GÉRONTE *(putting his head out of the sack)*. Ah! I'm beaten to
death!

SCAPIN. Ah! I'm dead!

GÉRONTE. Why the deuce must they strike on *my* back?

SCAPIN *(putting GÉRONTE's head back in the sack)*. Watch out,
here are half a dozen soldiers all together. *(He imitates several people together.)* "Come on, let's try to find that Géronte,
let's look everywhere. Let's not spare our steps. Let's run
through the whole town. Let's not forget any place. Let's
search everything. Let's ferret all over. Where shall we go?
Let's turn that way. No, this way. To the left. To the right.
No. Yes." — Keep well hidden. — "Ah, comrades, here's his
valet. Come on, you rogue, you've got to tell us where your
master is." — Oh, gentlemen! Don't maltreat me. — "Come on,
tell us where he is. Speak. Hurry up. Let's get a move on.
Make haste quick. Promptly." — Oh, gentlemen! Gently.
*(GÉRONTE puts his head gently out of the sack and perceives
SCAPIN's trick.)* — "If you don't help us find your master right
away, we'll rain a wave of cudgel-blows upon you." — I'd
rather endure anything than reveal my master to you. —
"We'll beat your brains out." — Do whatever you please. —
"You really want to be beaten." — I won't betray my master.
—"Oh! You want a taste. There . . . !" — Oh! *(As he is
ready to strike, GÉRONTE gets out of the sack, and SCAPIN runs
away.)*

GÉRONTE. Ah, you wretch! Ah, you traitor! Ah, you villain!
That's how you assassinate me!

Scene 3.   ZERBINETTE, GÉRONTE

ZERBINETTE *(laughing, not seeing* GÉRONTE*)*. Ha, ha! I guess I'll get a breath of air.

GÉRONTE *(aside, not seeing* ZERBINETTE*)*. You'll pay for this, I swear.

ZERBINETTE *(not seeing* GÉRONTE*)*. Ha, ha, ha, ha! What a funny story! And what a fine dupe of an old man!

GÉRONTE. There's nothing funny about this, and you have no business laughing about it.

ZERBINETTE. What? What do you mean, sir?

GÉRONTE. I mean that you mustn't make fun of me.

ZERBINETTE. Of you?

GÉRONTE. Yes.

ZERBINETTE. What? Who's thinking of making fun of you?

GÉRONTE. Why do you come here and laugh in my face?

ZERBINETTE. This has nothing to do with you, and I'm laughing to myself at a story I've just been told, the funniest you ever heard. I don't know whether it's because I'm involved in the thing; but I've never come across anything as funny as a trick that has just been played by a son on his father to get some money out of him.

GÉRONTE. By a son on his father, to get some money out of him?

ZERBINETTE. Yes. With the least bit of urging, you'll find me willing enough to tell you all about it, and I've a natural itch to communicate the stories I know.

GÉRONTE. Pray tell me this story.

ZERBINETTE. I'm willing. I won't risk very much by telling it to you, and it's an adventure that's not likely to be secret long. Destiny willed that I find myself among a band of these

people who are called Gypsies and who, roaming from province to province, involve themselves in telling fortunes, and
sometimes in many other things. When we arrived in this
town, a young man saw me and fell in love with me. From
that moment on he has followed me around, and at first he
was like all these young fellows, who think all they have to do
is to speak and that at the slightest word they say to us their
business is done; but he found a pride that made him correct
his original ideas a little. He made his passion known to the
people whose hands I was in, and he found them disposed
to give me up to him in consideration for a certain sum. But
the trouble with the business was that my suitor found himself
in the state in which we very often see most young men of
good condition, that is to say that he was a bit bare of money;
and he has a father who, though rich, is an arrant skinflint,
the meanest man in the world. Wait! Can't I even remember
his name? Hey! Help me a little. Can't you tell me the name
of someone in this town who is known for being a miser to
the highest degree?

GÉRONTE. No.

ZERBINETTE. There's a *ron* in his name, *ronte. Or . . . Oronte.*
No. *Gé . . . Géronte;* yes, Géronte, that's just it; that's my
miser, I've got it, that's the skinflint I'm talking about. To
come to our story, today our people wanted to leave this town;
and my sweetheart was going to lose me for want of money, if,
in order to get some out of his father, he hadn't found help
in the ingenuity of a servant he has. As for the servant's name,
I know it perfectly; his name is Scapin; he's an incomparable
man, and he deserves all the praise that can be given.

GÉRONTE (*aside*). Ah! You scoundrel!

ZERBINETTE. Here's the stratagem he used to catch his dupe.
Ha, ha, ha, ha! I can't think back on it without laughing with
all my heart. Ha, ha, ha! He went and found this dog of a
miser, ha, ha, ha! and told him that as he was walking in the
port with his son, hee, hee! they had seen a Turkish galley,
and been invited to go aboard; that a young Turk had given
them a collation, ha! that while they were eating, the galley
had put out to sea; and that the Turk had sent him back to
land, alone, in a skiff, with orders to tell his master's father

that he was taking his son to Algiers unless he sent him five hundred crowns right away. Ha, ha, ha! There is my skinflint, my miser in frenzied anguish; and the tenderness he has for his son puts on a weird combat with his avarice. Five hundred crowns that they demand of him are precisely five hundred dagger thrusts. Ha, ha, ha! He can't bring himself to tear this sum from his entrails; and the pain he suffers makes him find a hundred ridiculous ways of getting his son back. Ha, ha, ha! He wants to send the police to sea after the Turk's galley. Ha, ha, ha! He solicits his valet to go and offer himself in his son's place until he has raised the money that he doesn't want to give. Ha, ha, ha! To make up the five hundred crowns, he gives up four or five old suits that aren't worth thirty. Ha, ha, ha! The valet makes him understand, at every turn, the pointlessness of his propositions, and each reflection is lugubriously accompanied by a "But what the devil did he go into that galley for? Ah! Cursed galley! Traitor of a Turk!" Finally, after many evasions, after long having groaned and sighed . . . But it seems to me that you're not laughing at my story? What do you think of it?

GÉRONTE. I say that the young man is an insolent gallowsbird who shall be punished by his father for the trick he played on him; that the Gypsy girl is an impertinent scatterbrain to insult a man of honor who will teach her to come here and debauch sons of good families; and that the valet is a villain, who will be sent to the gallows by Géronte before tomorrow morning.

Scene 4.   SILVESTRE, ZERBINETTE

SILVESTRE. What are you up to? Do you realize that you've just been talking to your sweetheart's father?

ZERBINETTE. I've just suspected so; and I spoke to him without thinking of that, and told him his own story.

SILVESTRE. How's that, his own story?

ZERBINETTE. Yes, I was full of the story and burning to repeat it. But what does it matter? So much the worse for him. I don't see how things can be either worse or better thereby for us.

SILVESTRE. You had a great itch to babble; and a person has a loose tongue who can't keep quiet about his own affairs.

ZERBINETTE. Wouldn't he have learned it from someone else?

Scene 5.   ARGANTE, SILVESTRE

ARGANTE. Hold on, Silvestre!

SILVESTRE *(to* ZERBINETTE*)*. Go back in the house. There's my master calling me.

ARGANTE. So you were in it together, you scoundrel? You were in it together, Scapin, you, and my son, to cheat me; and you think I'll put up with it?

SILVESTRE. Faith, sir! If Scapin is cheating you, I wash my hands of it, and I assure you that I'm not involved in it in any way.

ARGANTE. We'll see about this business, you gallowsbird, we'll see about this business, and I don't intend to be hoodwinked.

Scene 6.   GÉRONTE, ARGANTE, SILVESTRE

GÉRONTE. Ah, Seigneur Argante! You find me overwhelmed by misfortune.

ARGANTE. You find me too in frightful despondency.

GÉRONTE. That blackguard Scapin, by one of his machinations, has gotten five hundred crowns out of me.

ARGANTE. That same blackguard Scapin, also by one of his machinations, has gotten two hundred pistoles out of me.

GÉRONTE. He didn't content himself with getting five hundred crowns out of me; he treated me in a way I'm ashamed to tell. But he'll pay for it.

ARGANTE. I want him to give me satisfaction for the trick he played on me.

GÉRONTE. And I mean to take exemplary vengeance on him.

SILVESTRE (aside). Please Heaven that I don't have my part in all this!

GÉRONTE. But that's not yet all, Seigneur Argante; and one misfortune always leads to another. I was rejoicing today in the hope of having my daughter back, in whom I placed all my consolation; and I've just learned from my man that she left Taranto a long time ago, and that they think she has perished in the ship she embarked in.

ARGANTE. But why, pray, did you keep her at Taranto, and not give yourself the joy of having her with you?

GÉRONTE. I had my reasons for that; and family interests obliged me up to now to keep this second marriage very secret. But what's this I see?

Scene 7.   NÉRINE, ARGANTE, GÉRONTE, SILVESTRE

GÉRONTE. Ah! It's you, nurse.

NÉRINE (casting herself at his knees). Ah! Seigneur Pandolphe, let me . . .

GÉRONTE. Call me Géronte, and don't use that name any more. The reasons have ceased which obliged me to assume it among you at Taranto.

NÉRINE. Alas! How many troubles and worries that change of name has caused us in our efforts to come and look for you here!

GÉRONTE. Where's my daughter, and her mother?

NÉRINE. Your daughter, sir, is not far from here. But before I let you see her, I must ask your pardon for having gotten her married, in the abandonment I found myself in with her for want of meeting with you.

GÉRONTE. My daughter married?

NÉRINE. Yes, sir.

GÉRONTE. And to whom?

NÉRINE. To a young man named Octave, son of a certain Seigneur Argante.

GÉRONTE. Heavens!

ARGANTE. What a coincidence!

GÉRONTE. Take us to where she is, take us promptly.

NÉRINE. You have only to enter this house.

GÉRONTE. Go ahead. Follow me, follow me, Seigneur Argante.

SILVESTRE (alone). That's a really amazing adventure.

Scene 8.   SCAPIN, SILVESTRE

SCAPIN. Well, Silvestre! What are our people doing?

SILVESTRE. I have two pieces of information to give you. First, that Octave's affair is settled. Our Hyacinte has turned out to be Seigneur Géronte's daughter; and chance accomplished what the prudence of the two fathers had planned. The other thing is that the two old men are making frightful threats against you, and especially Seigneur Géronte.

SCAPIN. That's nothing. Threats have never done me any harm; they are clouds that pass far above our heads.

SILVESTRE. Watch out for yourself. The sons might very well make it up with the fathers, and you'd be left in the trap.

SCAPIN. Leave it to me; I'll find a way to appease their wrath, and . . .

SILVESTRE. Get out of here, they're coming out now.

Scene 9. GÉRONTE, ARGANTE, SILVESTRE, NÉRINE, HYACINTE

GÉRONTE. Come on, my daughter, come to my house. My joy would have been perfect if I could have seen your mother there with you.

ARGANTE. Here's Octave, just at the right moment.

Scene 10. OCTAVE, ARGANTE, GÉRONTE, HYACINTE, NÉRINE,
ZERBINETTE, SILVESTRE

ARGANTE. Come, my son, come and rejoice with us at the happy adventure of your marriage. Heaven . . .

OCTAVE *(not seeing* HYACINTE*)*. No, father, all your plans for marriage will be in vain. I must take off the mask with you, and you've been told of my commitment.

ARGANTE. Yes; but you don't know . . .

OCTAVE. I know all I have to know.

ARGANTE. I want to tell you that Seigneur Géronte's daughter . . .

OCTAVE. Seigneur Géronte's daughter will never be anything to me.

GÉRONTE. She's the one . . .

OCTAVE. No, sir! I ask your pardon; my resolution is fixed.

SILVESTRE. Listen . . .

OCTAVE. No, be quiet, I won't listen to a thing.

ARGANTE. Your wife . . .

OCTAVE. No, I tell you, father, I'll die rather than leave my lovely Hyacinte. *(Crosses stage and stands beside her.)* Yes, no matter what you do, here is the one to whom my faith is plighted; I'll love her all my life and I won't have any other wife.

ARGANTE. Well! She's the one I'm giving you. What a darned scatterbrain, always sticking to your point!

HYACINTE. Yes, Octave, this is my father that I've found, and our troubles are over.

GÉRONTE. Let's go to my house; we'll have a better place to talk than here.

HYACINTE. Ah, father! I beg you as a favor not to have me separated from the charming person whom you see; she has a merit that, when you know it, will give you esteem for her.

GÉRONTE. You want me to keep in my house a person whom your brother is in love with, and who just now told me, to my face, a thousand stupid things about me?

ZERBINETTE. Sir, I beg you to excuse me. I wouldn't have spoken in that way if I'd known it was you; I knew you only by reputation.

GÉRONTE. How's that, only by reputation?

HYACINTE. Father, my brother's passion for her has nothing criminal about it, and I'll answer for her virtue.

GÉRONTE. That's certainly very fine. Wouldn't they have me get my son married to her? An unknown girl who's a street-walker by profession!

Scene 11. LÉANDRE, OCTAVE, HYACINTE, ZERBINETTE, ARGANTE,
GÉRONTE, SILVESTRE, NÉRINE

LÉANDRE. Father, don't complain that I love an unknown girl
without birth or property. The people from whom I purchased
her have just revealed to me that she is from this city, and
of an honorable family; that it was they who stole her at the
age of four; and here is a bracelet they gave me, which may
help us find her parents.

ARGANTE. Alas! To see this bracelet, she's my daughter, whom I
lost at the age you say.

GÉRONTE. Your daughter?

ARGANTE. Yes, she is, and I see all the features that can make
me assured of it.

HYACINTE. O Heavens! What a lot of extraordinary coincidences!

Scene 12. CARLE, LÉANDRE, OCTAVE, GÉRONTE, ARGANTE,
HYACINTE, ZERBINETTE, SILVESTRE, NÉRINE

CARLE. Ah! Gentlemen, a strange accident has just happened.

GÉRONTE. What?

CARLE. Poor Scapin . . .

GÉRONTE. He's a scoundrel whom I want to have hanged.

CARLE. Alas, sir! You won't need to take the trouble for that.
As he passed next to a building, a stonecutter's hammer fell
on his head, broke the bone, and laid his whole brains open.
He's dying; and he asked to be brought here to be able to
talk to you before he died.

ARGANTE. Where is he?

CARLE. Here he is.

Scene 13.   SCAPIN, CARLE, GÉRONTE, ARGANTE, LÉANDRE,
OCTAVE, HYACINTE, ZERBINETTE, SILVESTRE, NÉRINE,
PORTERS

SCAPIN *(carried on by two men, his head swathed in bandages,
as if he had been seriously wounded)*. Oh, oh! Gentlemen,
you see me . . . Oh! You see me in a sad state. I didn't want
to die without coming to ask for pardon from all the persons
I may have offended. Oh! Yes, gentlemen, before I utter my
last sigh, I conjure you all, with all my heart, to be willing to
forgive me for what I may have done to you, especially
Seigneur Argante and Seigneur Géronte. Oh!

ARGANTE. As for me, I forgive you; go, die in peace.

SCAPIN *(to* GÉRONTE*)*. It's you, sir, whom I offended most, by
the beating that . . .

GÉRONTE. Say no more, I forgive you too.

SCAPIN. It was a very great temerity on my part, the cudgel-blows
that I . . .

GÉRONTE. Let's let it go.

SCAPIN. I have inconceivable sorrow, in dying, for the cudgel-
blows that . . .

GÉRONTE. Good Lord! Be quiet.

SCAPIN. The unfortunate cudgel-blows that I . . .

GÉRONTE. Be quiet, I tell you, I'm forgetting everything.

SCAPIN. Alas! What goodness! But is it wholeheartedly, sir, that
you pardon me the cudgel-blows that . . . ?

GÉRONTE. Oh, yes! Let's say no more about anything; I forgive
you for everything, and that's that.

SCAPIN. Ah! Sir, I feel all relieved since those words.

GÉRONTE. Yes; but I forgive you on condition that you die.

SCAPIN. How's that, sir?

GÉRONTE. I take back my word if you get well.

SCAPIN. Oh, oh! There goes my faintness seizing me again.

ARGANTE. Seigneur Géronte, for the sake of our joy, you must forgive him unconditionally.

GÉRONTE. So be it.

ARGANTE. Let's go and have supper together, the better to relish our pleasure.

SCAPIN (*jumping to his feet, taking off his bandages, and being carried off by the* PORTERS). And as for me, have them carry me to the end of the table, while they wait for me to die.

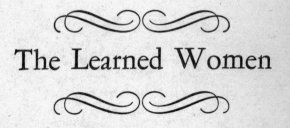

The Learned Women

THE LEARNED WOMEN

A verse comedy in five acts, first performed on March 11, 1672 at the Théâtre du Palais-Royal in Paris by Molière's Troupe du Roi. Molière played Chrysale; Baron, Ariste; La Grange, Clitandre; La Thorillière, Trissotin; Du Croisy, Vadius; Hubert, Philaminte; Mlle. Villeaubrun, Bélise; Mlle. de Brie, Armande; Mlle. Molière, Henriette; and Martine was probably played by Mlle. Beauval.[1] The play was well received.

Molière seems to have had this play in mind for over three years, ever since he was criticized for presenting five acts of prose in *The Miser*. In many ways it recalls his first great success, *The Ridiculous Précieuses;* for it is another lampoon of their kind. What is surprising here is the sharpness and personality of Molière's attack, not so much on the learned women themselves as on the pedantic would-be poets Vadius and especially Trissotin. Vadius clearly represents the Hellenist Gilles Ménage, and Trissotin—whom Molière had apparently once thought of naming *Tricotin*—the Abbé Cotin; the quarrel between the two is attested in anecdotal history. In making Trissotin not only ridiculous but rather despicable, Molière has carried reprisals far. Some have considered this a blot on his name; but since Cotin had been pretty venomous himself, I find this less distressing than a certain heavy-handedness that occasionally detracts from the comedy.

However, this is a natural risk of another of Molière's ventures into the "serious" comedy of values. The learned women are not merely silly, like the *précieuses;* the power they wield is an actual danger. Besides dominating the pusillanimous Chrysale

[1] One report states that Martine was played by a servant of Molière who bore that name; but this seems unlikely.

and thereby ruling his family, they plan a woman's academy that shall be an absolute arbiter of taste. Their values are false in that they take words for things and—as happens so often in Molière—seek to "escape from the man" by rejecting all the physical side of human nature. Or perhaps they do not seek so much as claim this; for Armande still wishes to be courted by Clitandre, and Bélise enjoys the delightful fancy that every man is secretly and submissively in love with her. In this and other ways the learned women often fail to practice what they preach. They regularly deceive themselves, constructing a verbal world and taking it to be real, so that the ultimate sin comes to be that of Martine against grammar. Their delusion extends to their motives, mistaking arrogant one-sidedness for sublimity, and lust for power for idealism. Hence the confrontation of them with the others, and with it the overall tone of the play, remains comic.

Another difference from the *Précieuses* is that *The Learned Women* is mainly a comedy of character: the conceit of Trissotin, and to a lesser extent of Vadius; the happy delusions of Bélise; the dilemma of Armande, who spurns marriage but craves dangling suitors; the adroit arrogance of Philaminte; and the brave posture of the henpecked Chrysale—as long as Philaminte is not there. The best comic scenes are those confronting the learned women with the sturdily ungrammatical Martine and with the ineffable inanity of Trissotin's poetry.

The conclusion resolves the plot happily. The learned women are not converted; Molière's comic characters never are. Philaminte's recognition is not of Trissotin's inanity, merely of his mercenary motives. However, even this may open the door to a healthy breeze of self-doubt; and she does promptly accept Clitandre as son-in-law even though this means coming over to her husband's side. A full conversion would have fitted a melodrama or a moral tract; and Molière, happily for us, was writing a comedy.

THE LEARNED WOMEN

CHARACTERS

CHRYSALE, *a member of a good bourgeois family*
PHILAMINTE, *wife of Chrysale*
ARMANDE } *daughters of Chrysale and*
HENRIETTE } *Philaminte*
ARISTE, *brother of Chrysale*
BÉLISE, *sister of Chrysale*
CLITANDRE, *sweetheart of Henriette*
TRISSOTIN, *a wit*
VADIUS, *a learned man*
MARTINE, *a kitchen servant*
L'ÉPINE, *a lackey*
JULIEN, *valet of Vadius*
The NOTARY

The scene is Paris, in Chrysale's house.

ACT I

Scene 1. ARMANDE, HENRIETTE

ARMANDE. What, sister, is your eagerness so great
   To quit the sweetness of your maiden state?
   And dare you be so pleased at being wed?
   Can such a vulgar plan enter your head?

HENRIETTE. Yes, sister.

ARMANDE.   How can one endure that "yes"?
How can one stomach it without distress?

HENRIETTE. Why should the thought afflict you in this way,
Sister . . . ?

ARMANDE.   Oh, fie!

HENRIETTE.   How's that?

ARMANDE.   Oh, fie, I say!
Why, don't you understand how such a word
10   Can be offensive any time it's heard?
It brings a squalid picture to the mind;
The thoughts it prompts are of the ugliest kind.
Doesn't it make you quake to recognize
The consequences that this word implies?

HENRIETTE. The consequences it suggests to me
Are husband, children, home, a family;
And on reflection, I see nothing there
That makes me tremble or that I can't bear.

ARMANDE. Do such relationships appeal to you?

20   HENRIETTE. At my age, are there better things to do
Than find a man with whom to spend your life
As his dearly beloved and loving wife,
And from this union, formed in tenderness,
Fashion a life of blameless happiness?
Hasn't a well-matched marriage some appeal?

ARMANDE. Lord, what a sordid mind your words reveal!
Believe me, it's a sorry role you'll play,
Cooped up with household chores day after day,
And nothing to induce a lofty mood
30   But a hero husband and a squalling brood!
Leave such affairs and their ignoble sport
To common people of the cruder sort;
Set up higher objectives for your leisures,
Try to acquire a taste for nobler pleasures,
And, treating sense and matter with disdain,
Devote yourself to mind with might and main.

Your mother's an example and a guide
Honored for scholarship on every side;
Try to be her true daughter, just like me,
Fit member of a brilliant family,   *40*
And welcome in your spirit and your heart
The joys that love of study can impart;
Rather than be a slave to any man,
Marry philosophy, while still you can,
Which raises us above all humankind
And gives the sovereign power to the mind,
Bringing our animal part under control,
Which makes us like a beast without a soul.
This is the love, this is the dedication
Which should fill our existence with elation;   *50*
The cares some women cherish, I confess,
Seem to my eyes horrible pettiness.

HENRIETTE. Almighty Heaven, which orders all on earth,
Shapes us for different functions from our birth;
Not every mind can muster, I'm afraid,
The stuff of which philosophers are made.
If yours is born to live upon the heights
Ascended by the learned in their flights,
Mine, sister, is at home upon the ground;
In petty cares its frailty is found.   *60*
Rather than trouble Heaven's just regulations,
Let each of us follow her inclinations.
Your great and noble genius makes you free
To tread the summits of philosophy,
While my poor spirit, in this lower sphere,
Delights in marriage and its earthly cheer.
Thus, while our lives differ from one another,
We each of us will emulate our mother:
You by the soul, with all its noble treasures;
I by the senses and their cruder pleasures;   *70*
You by the fruits of light and of the mind;
I by those of a more material kind.

ARMANDE. When there is someone we would emulate,
It is her good points we should imitate;
We don't model ourselves on her one bit
By being like her when we cough or spit.

HENRIETTE. But you would not be here with all your pride
If Mother had not had another side;
And, sister, it is well for you that she
Had other interests than philosophy.
Allow me certain base reactions, pray,
Thanks to which you now see the light of day;
And don't suppress, by giving me your scorn,
Some tiny scholar waiting to be born.

ARMANDE. I see your mind is in a hopeless state
From your insane resolve to get a mate;
But who's the man for whom your heart's inclined?
I trust it's not Clitandre you have in mind.

HENRIETTE. And can you tell me why he shouldn't be?
Or don't you think he's good enough for me?

ARMANDE. No; but it's a dishonorable plan
To try to steal another woman's man;
And surely no one fails to realize
That I have been the object of his sighs.

HENRIETTE. Yes; but these sighs, for you, are all in vain,
And you're above our basely human plane;
You have renounced marriage for evermore,
And it's philosophy that you adore.
Since you don't want Clitandre in any case,
Why do you care if someone takes your place?

ARMANDE. Reason may hold the senses in control,
And yet attentions gratify the soul;
A worthy man may seek our hand in vain
And yet be welcome as a faithful swain.

HENRIETTE. I've never held him back, by word or sign,
From any adoration at your shrine;
And when your firm refusal set him free,
I simply let him pay his court to me.

ARMANDE. When a rejected suitor turns to you,
Can you be satisfied his vows are true?
Do you think you're the one he yearns to wed,
And that his love for me is wholly dead?

HENRIETTE. He says so. What he tells me I believe.

ARMANDE. Sister, don't be so easy to deceive;
For when he claims he loves *you* now, you'll find
He's self-deluded, not in his right mind.

HENRIETTE. I do not know; however, if you please,
Let's find this out and set our minds at ease.
I see him coming; and while he is here,
I'm sure that he can make this matter clear.   *120*

Scene 2.   CLITANDRE, ARMANDE, HENRIETTE

HENRIETTE. Some things my sister says leave me in doubt;
So please, between the two of us, speak out.
Clitandre, please tell us without circumspection
Which of us has a claim to your affection.

ARMANDE. No, no; it might afford you too much pain
If both of us required you to explain;
It is embarrassing and out of place
To have to make such statements face to face.

CLITANDRE. No, Madame, my heart shuns dissimulation,
And will not grudge you a free explanation;   *130*
I'm not embarrassed by it, for my part,
And I shall tell you frankly, from the heart,
That those sweet bonds with which my soul is tied,
My love, my wishes, all *(pointing to* HENRIETTE*)* are on
    this side.
Don't be dismayed at hearing this from me:
This is the way you wanted things to be.
Your charms had won me, and my tender sighs
Proved what desire there shone out of my eyes;
My heart had vowed to love you evermore;
But by your conquest you set little store.   *140*
Your eyes reduced me to a sorry role
And proudly lorded it over my soul.
And so I sought, weary of all these pains,
A kinder mistress and less cruel chains.

(Pointing to HENRIETTE*)* All this I found, Madame,
    within these eyes,
Whose gracious radiance I shall always prize;
They dried my tears with just one pitying glance;
Your rebuff did not make them look askance.
Such rare kindness has won my heart forever;
150   My present bonds nothing can make me sever;
And now I dare, Madame, to conjure you
Not to attempt, by anything you do,
To summon back the heart you owned before,
For it has found its love for evermore.

ARMANDE. What makes you think, sir, that I have this aim,
    And that I'd like to fan your former flame?
There is a funny side to your assumption,
And telling me about it is presumption.

HENRIETTE. Come, sister, gently. Where's that self-control
160   That curbs the animal portion of the soul,
And leads the force of anger to submit?

ARMANDE. But you who talk so, do you practice it,
    By holding yourself ready to receive
This show of love without your parents' leave?
Duty affords them the decisive voice;
We are not free to love save by their choice;
Over our hearts they have the final say,
And it's a crime to want to have our way.

HENRIETTE. I thank you for the goodness you reveal
170   In telling me my duty with such zeal;
My heart welcomes the lessons that you teach,
And, so you'll see I practice what you preach,
Clitandre, if you would have me for your wife,
Gain the consent of those who gave me life;
Legitimize your power over my flame,
And give me leave to love you without shame.

CLITANDRE. To reach that goal shall be my firm intent,
    And I was waiting for your sweet consent.

ARMANDE. Sister, what a triumphant mood you're in
180   To think that all this fills me with chagrin!

HENRIETTE. I, sister? Not at all. Within your soul
   Reason, I know, holds sense in strict control;
   And in you wisdom's lessons so prevail
   That you'd not stoop to anything so frail.
   Far from supposing you in misery,
   I think you'll deign to do your best for me,
   Back his petition, and help consummate
   The marriage that we eagerly await.
   I pray you'll do so; and, to work your best . . .

ARMANDE. I see your petty mind is moved to jest,   *190*
   And that you're proud of a heart that's tossed to you.

HENRIETTE. Tossed though it be, you seem to like it too;
   And if your eyes could capture back your swain,
   You'd cast them down on him without much pain.

ARMANDE. To that I will not deign to say one word;
   And such remarks are better left unheard.

HENRIETTE. That is well done for you; your moderation
   Elicits my unbounded admiration.

Scene 3. CLITANDRE, HENRIETTE

HENRIETTE. Your frank avowal took her by surprise.

CLITANDRE. She will not let me have it otherwise,   *200*
   And it's her foolish pride she has to thank
   For forcing me to be completely frank.
   But since I may, it's time I had begun;
   I'll see your father . . .

HENRIETTE.   Mother is the one.
   Father is readier to give consent,
   But then his resolution is soon bent;
   Heaven gave to him a kindliness of heart
   That makes him yield to Mother from the start.
   Her rule is absolute; all her decrees

210 Soon become law, and with the greatest ease.
 With her and with my aunt, I'd like to see
 Your soul a bit more ready to agree;
 If you could look more kindly on their views,
 You would have much to gain, little to lose.

CLITANDRE. They've ways of which I never have been fond,
 Not even in the person of Armande,
 And women scholars simply aren't my kind.
 Of course, a woman ought to have a mind,
 But I'd forbid her that outrageous yearning
220 To learn a lot just for the sake of learning;
 I'd have her know, for questions people pose,
 How not to know some of the things she knows;
 I'd have her study be for her alone;
 Let her have knowledge; but not make it known,
 Drop authors' names, emit pompous quotations,
 Or witticize her simplest observations.
 I do respect her mother Philaminte;
 But countenance her wholly, that I can't,
 Nor echo all she says, I must admit,
230 Nor idolize her paragon of wit.
 Her Monsieur Trissotin's a crashing bore;
 I cannot see what she esteems him for,
 Or how she sets in such a lofty sphere
 A fool whose every work provokes a jeer,
 Whose pedant pen supplies, with doubtful grace,
 The wrapping paper for the market place.

HENRIETTE. His speech, his writings cast a deadly pall;
 Indeed I share your feelings one and all;
 But since he holds my mother in his spell,
240 You ought to do your best to treat him well.
 A lover must not rest till he has won
 The unreserved support of everyone;
 And so that he may have no enemies,
 Even the family dog he tries to please.

CLITANDRE. You're right, of course; of that I'm well aware;
 But Monsieur Trissotin I cannot bear.
 And even to gain favor in his sight,
 I cannot stoop to praise what he can write.

You see, I'd read his works, to my regret,
And knew the man before we ever met.   *250*
His jumbled writings brought into full view
The man himself, a pedant through and through:
His lofty arrogance, so freely flaunted,
The self-esteem that never can be daunted,
The happy and luxuriant conceit
That makes his self-assurance so complete,
Renders his worth one of his chief delights,
And gives him joy in everything he writes,
So that he would not change his place and name
For that of a general with all his fame.   *260*

HENRIETTE. To see all that you need to have good eyes.

CLITANDRE. Even his face, too, I could visualize,
And from his wretched verses I could see
What kind of man the poet had to be;
I'd guessed his looks so well in every way
That when I saw a man the other day
Among the shops, I bet he was the one—
Our Trissotin. You know, I would have won.

HENRIETTE. No!

CLITANDRE.   That's the way it was. But here's Bélise.
I trust you will allow me, if you please,   *270*
To be quite frank, and try to win your aunt
To help us with your mother Philaminte.

Scene 4. CLITANDRE, BÉLISE

CLITANDRE. Ah, pray, Madame, allow a happy swain
Not to let such a moment pass in vain,
For I'm in love, and simply must reveal . . .

BÉLISE. Gently, sir; pray don't tell me all you feel.
If I've become the object of your sighs,
Your only spokesman, sir, must be your eyes;

Theirs is the only language to convey
280   Desires that would offend another way.
Yes, love me, sigh, burn: that I will permit;
But pray allow me not to know of it;
I need not bridle at your secret suit
As long as your interpreters are mute;
But if your lips should ever speak your plight,
I'd have to banish you out of my sight.

CLITANDRE. My plans, Madame, give you no cause for fear:
Henriette is the one I hold so dear;
And I implore you to be on my side
290   And try to help me win her for my bride.

BÉLISE. Oh! that's a neat evasion, I must say,
Which earns the highest praise in every way;
In all the novels I have read, I've never
Encountered anything that was so clever.

CLITANDRE. Madame, let me say one thing from the start:
It's no evasion, but what's in my heart.
With Henriette I'm ardently in love
By a decree that comes from Heaven above;
Henriette is the one for whom I pine,
300   I dream that Henriette one day be mine.
You can help greatly, and my one request
Is that on my behalf you do your best.

BÉLISE. Ingenious as you are, I realize
What you are getting at under this guise;
The trick is clever, and I'll play my part
By not revealing what is in my heart;
But Henriette views marriage with disdain,
And if you love her, you will love in vain.

CLITANDRE. Oh come, Madame, why make so much ado,
310   And cling to notions that are just not true?

BÉLISE. Heavens! Let's stop this fencing. Why deny
What I have seen your glances signify?
Enough for you to know that I'm content
With what your love was able to invent,
And, knowing your respect for good repute,
I can be willing to permit your suit,

Provided that your transports you refine
And offer a pure worship at my shrine.

CLITANDRE. But . . .

BÉLISE.   No, that is enough for now. Good day.
I've told you more than I had meant to say.   *320*

CLITANDRE. But your mistake . . .

BÉLISE.   Stop! Not so fast; don't rush:
Offended modesty has made me blush.

CLITANDRE. Hanged if it's you I love! That's too absurd!

BÉLISE. No, no, I will not hear another word.   *(Exit)*

CLITANDRE. The deuce with her and her mad prepossessions!
Who ever saw the like of these obsessions?
I'll pass on this commission if I can,
And try to get help from some wiser man.

ACT II

Scene 1. ARISTE

ARISTE *(to* CLITANDRE *offstage).* Yes, I'll bring back your
    answer at top speed;
330 I'll back you, urge him—everything you need.
    How a lover will talk! He never tires.
    How eagerly he wants what he desires!
    Never . . .

Scene 2. CHRYSALE, ARISTE

ARISTE.   God save you, brother.

CHRYSALE.   And you too,
  Brother.

ARISTE.   D'you know what brings me here to you?

CHRYSALE. No, but I hope you'll tell me anyhow.

ARISTE. You've known Clitandre, I think, for some time
    now?

CHRYSALE. Indeed; he's always with us, it would seem.

ARISTE. And, brother, do you hold him in esteem?

CHRYSALE. A man of honor, conduct, heart, and mind;
340 And I see too few people of his kind.

ARISTE. It is at his request that I've come by,
    And I'm delighted that you rate him high.

CHRYSALE. I knew his late father in Rome.

ARISTE.   That's good.

CHRYSALE. A fine gentleman.

ARISTE.   So I understood.

CHRYSALE. We both were only twenty-eight, and gad!
    Each of us was a mighty lusty lad.

ARISTE. I'm sure.

CHRYSALE.   Those Roman belles, matrons, and maids!
    The whole town talked about our escapades.
    We made men jealous.

ARISTE.   Yes, I have no doubt.
    But let's come to the point. Please hear me out.   *350*

Scene 3.   BÉLISE, CHRYSALE, ARISTE

ARISTE. I've come to see you at his son's demand.
    Clitandre loves Henriette, and seeks her hand.

CHRYSALE. My daughter?

ARISTE.   Yes, Clitandre's enamored of her;
    I never saw so passionate a lover.

BÉLISE. No; you don't know his complicated scheme;
    In this affair things are not what they seem.

ARISTE. How's that, sister?

BÉLISE.   Don't be mistaken, brother;
    Clitandre is really smitten with another.

ARISTE. What, not with Henriette? How do you know?

BÉLISE. I'm sure of it.

ARISTE.   He himself told me so.   *360*

BÉLISE. Oh, yes!

ARISTE.   Sister, he sent me here today
    To ask her hand for him. Explain that, pray.

BÉLISE. That's fine.

ARISTE.   He even asked me if I would
    Hasten the marriage any way I could.

BÉLISE. Oh, better yet. His gallantry's a joy.
    Between us, Henriette is a decoy,
    A pretext, brother, an astute disguise
    To hide another love from people's eyes;
    And I would like to undeceive you two.

370 ARISTE. But, sister, knowing all the things you do,
    Tell us who his real love is, if you please.

BÉLISE. You want to know?

ARISTE.   Yes.

BÉLISE.   I.

ARISTE.   You?

BÉLISE.   I, Bélise.

ARISTE. Oh, sister!

BÉLISE.   Now that "oh" was most ill-bred.
    What's so surprising about what I said?
    I do not think I am so destitute
    Of charms, as to have just one single suit.
    And Lycidas, Dorante, Damis, Cléonte
    Are there to prove this is no idle vaunt.

ARISTE. These people love you?

BÉLISE.   Yes, desperately.

ARISTE. They've told you so?

380 BÉLISE.   Not one has been so free;
    They have revered me so up to this day
    That not a one of them has said his say;
    But to offer their service and their heart,
    Their silent spokesmen all have done their part.

ARISTE. I haven't seen Damis here for some time.

BÉLISE. No, his submissiveness is quite sublime.

ARISTE. All Dorante says of you is bitter quips.

BÉLISE. It's jealous rage that brings them to his lips.

ARISTE. Cléonte and Lycidas each have a wife.

BÉLISE. Yes, crossed in love, despairing of their life.   *390*

ARISTE. Sister, these are sheer visions, I should say.

CHRYSALE. Yes, they are fancies you must put away.

BÉLISE. Oh, fancies! These are fancies, you maintain!
Me, fancies! Oh yes, fancies, that's quite plain!
Fancies indeed, brothers! How nice for me!
I never knew my fancies were so free.

Scene 4.   CHRYSALE, ARISTE

CHRYSALE. Our sister's mad.

ARISTE.   Yes, not much hope for her.
But let's get back, once more, to where we were.
Clitandre requests the hand of Henriette:
Have you decided on your answer yet?   *400*

CHRYSALE. How can you ask? I consent heartily.
It's a great honor for our family.

ARISTE. You know he does not have money to burn,
And . . .

CHRYSALE. That's an accident of no concern.
His virtue's wealth enough for anyone,
And then his father and I were once as one.

ARISTE. Let's see your wife, and get her to agree . . .

CHRYSALE. Enough: he is the son-in-law for me.

ARISTE. But even though you're clear in your intent,

410   It would be well to gain your wife's consent.
      Let's go . . .
      CHRYSALE.   You're joking; there's no need for that.
      I'll vouch for her, and handle this; that's flat.

ARISTE. But . . .

      CHRYSALE.   Leave it to me, I say, and have no care;
      I'll soon win her assent to this affair.

ARISTE. I'll speak to Henriette, then, and return
      To see . . .

      CHRYSALE.   It's done. Enough of your concern.
      I'll tell my wife without further ado.

Scene 5.   MARTINE, CHRYSALE

MARTINE. That's just my luck! My lack! The saying's true:
      If you want to drown your dog, declare him mad.
420   And servants are not heirs, which is too bad.

CHRYSALE. What's wrong, Martine?

MARTINE.   What's wrong? If you
      insist . . .

CHRYSALE. I do.

MARTINE.   What's wrong is that I've been dismissed,
      Today, sir.

CHRYSALE.   You, dismissed?

MARTINE.   Yes, by Madame.

CHRYSALE. I still don't understand.

MARTINE.   Threatened I am,
      With cudgeling, unless I go away.

CHRYSALE. No, I am pleased with you; no, you shall stay.
      My wife is often overly severe,
      And *I* won't have . . .

Scene 6.   PHILAMINTE, BÉLISE, CHRYSALE, MARTINE

PHILAMINTE.   What, hussy, you're still here?
  Quick, wench, get out; come on, out of this place,
  I want never again to see your face.   *430*

CHRYSALE. Gently.

PHILAMINTE.   No, no, that's that.

CHRYSALE.   Oh!

PHILAMINTE.   She must go.

CHRYSALE. But what's she done, for you to treat her so?

PHILAMINTE. What? You're supporting her, then?

CHRYSALE.   Not one
      jot.

PHILAMINTE. You'd take her side against me?

CHRYSALE.   Indeed not.
  I only ask how she's infringed the laws.

PHILAMINTE. You think I'd banish her without due cause?

CHRYSALE. I don't say that; but still we must allow . . .

PHILAMINTE. No, I say, she must leave this house, and now.

CHRYSALE. All right, does anybody say you nay?

PHILAMINTE. In all these matters I must have my way.   *440*

CHRYSALE. Granted.

PHILAMINTE.   And you, in view of our relation,
  Should take my side, and share my indignation.

CHRYSALE. And so I do. *(To* MARTINE*)* Your crime was a
      disgrace;
  My wife is right to send you from this place.

MARTINE. What have I done, then?

CHRYSALE.   My word, I don't know.

PHILAMINTE. She's just the type to think I'd let it go.

CHRYSALE. What has she done to earn your bitter hate?
Broken some looking glass or precious plate?

PHILAMINTE. Would I dismiss the girl, do you suppose,
450   For accidents as trivial as those?

CHRYSALE. What does that mean? A serious affair?

PHILAMINTE. Of course. If not, why do you think I'd care

CHRYSALE. Did she allow, through careless unconcern,
Someone to steal a silver jug or urn?

PHILAMINTE. That would be nothing.

CHRYSALE.   A plague upon the
beauty!
Have you found her delinquent in her duty?

PHILAMINTE. It's worse than that.

CHRYSALE.   Worse than that?

PHILAMINTE.   Quite a
bit.

CHRYSALE. What the devil! That wench! Did she commit . . . ?

PHILAMINTE. Yes, she, with unexampled insolence,
460   For all her lessons, shocked my ear and sense
With an improper word, both crude and coarse,
Which Vaugelas[2] condemns without recourse.

CHRYSALE. Is that . . . ?

PHILAMINTE.   Should she, in spite of all we said
Attack all learning at its fountainhead,
Grammar, which even mighty kings obey,
And which subjects them to its awful sway?

CHRYSALE. I thought you had some heinous crime in mind.

---

[2] Claude Favre de Vaugelas (1585–1650), a grammarian who, in
his *Remarks on the French Language* (1643), had sought to improve
French usage. In his Preface he had noted that even kings must obey
the rules of grammar.

PHILAMINTE. What? You'd condone an outrage of this kind?

CHRYSALE. Oh, no.

PHILAMINTE.   I'd like to see you make excuses.

CHRYSALE. Not I.

BÉLISE.   It's true that hers are sad abuses: *470*
   She just demolishes every construction,
   Despite repeated, competent instruction.

MARTINE. I'm sure all this you preach is mighty cute,
   But I can't talk your jargon worth a hoot.

PHILAMINTE. To call this jargon is linguistic treason,
   For it is based on usage and on reason.

MARTINE. We talk all right when we are understood,
   And all your precious rules don't do no good.

PHILAMINTE. Listen to that! See, there she goes again!
   Don't do no good!

BÉLISE.   Oh, what a stubborn brain!   *480*
   It seems that you are one whom none can teach;
   For all our work, we cannot mend your speech.
   Your ignorance of grammar rules is sad,
   And double negatives are just too bad.

MARTINE. Lordy! I never studied none, like you;
   I talks straight out like all my home folks do.

PHILAMINTE. Unbearable!

BÉLISE.   That solecism drear!

PHILAMINTE. Mortal affront to any delicate ear!

BÉLISE. Your mind, I fear, in matter is interred.
   Listen: *I* is first person, *talks* is third.   *490*
   Against good grammar must you always sin?

MARTINE. Gran'ma or gran'pa—where do they come in?

PHILAMINTE. Heavens!

BÉLISE.   I said *grammar*, not your family tree.
   I've told you where the word comes from.

MARTINE.   Could be.
　Chaillot, Auteuil, Pontoise—you call the roll,
　I don't care where it's from.

BÉLISE.   O peasant soul!
　The laws of adjective and substantive,
　Of verbal usage and of nominative:
　These grammar teaches us.

MARTINE.   Madame, I say
　That I don't know them folks.

500 PHILAMINTE.   Oh! lackaday!

BÉLISE. Those are the names of words, and one must see
　In what respects one must make them agree.

MARTINE. Let them agree, or fight. What do I care?

PHILAMINTE (to her sister). Finish this talk; it's more than
　I can bear.
　(To her husband) Well, won't you pack her off, and have
　some peace?

CHRYSALE. All right. (Aside) I must consent to her caprice.
　(To MARTINE) Come on, Martine, don't vex her; off you
　go.

PHILAMINTE. Why do you fear to offend the hussy so?
　The tone you use to her is soft and mild.

510 CHRYSALE. I? Not at all. (To MARTINE, roughly) Get out.
　(Gently) Go on, poor child.

Scene 7. PHILAMINTE, CHRYSALE, BÉLISE

CHRYSALE. All right, she's gone, I hope you're satisfied;
　But I don't think that this was justified;
　She works well and she knows what she's about;
　Yours was a poor reason to kick her out.

PHILAMINTE. You mean you'd want me still to keep her here
  For the everlasting torment of my ear?
  To flout the laws of reason and of use
  With barbarisms quite beyond excuse?
  With fractured phrases, patched up here and there
  With proverbs dragged up from the market square?   *520*

BÉLISE. True, one can't bear the things she finds to say;
  She butchers Vaugelas ten times a day;
  Cacophony and pleonasm are
  The mildest sins that she commits by far.

CHRYSALE. What if she fails to know Vaugelas' book.
  Provided she's no failure as a cook?
  I'd rather have her, as she cleans her herbs,
  Use nouns in disagreement with her verbs,
  And utter language low and indiscreet,
  Than put on too much salt, or burn my meat.   *530*
  I need good soup, not all this balderdash.
  Vaugelas's not much help for making hash;
  And Balzac and Malherbe,[3] with all their rules,
  In any kitchen might have been plain fools.

PHILAMINTE. These crude remarks are a distressing blow!
  How can a human being sink so low,
  And, always busy with material things,
  Never try out his spiritual wings?
  Is our body so precious that we ought
  To give to such a rag a single thought?   *540*
  Shouldn't we leave that far behind indeed?

CHRYSALE. My body is myself, and worth my heed.
  A rag if you will—to me *my* rag is dear.

BÉLISE. Body and mind together must appear;
  But if you heed what all the learned say,
  The soul must lead, the body must obey;
  And our main care, our primary concern,
  Must be to feed the soul what it can learn.

---

[3] Jean-Louis Guez de Balzac (1597–1654; no relation to the novelist) and François de Malherbe (1555–1628) were classical reformers of great authority in prose and poetry respectively.

CHRYSALE. My word! If it's your wish to feed the mind,
550   Such food is not the most nutritious kind;
       And you have no concern, no just unease,
       For . . .

PHILAMINTE. Oh, *unease* offends my hearing. Please!
       Really, it stinks; it's terribly outdated.

BÉLISE. Indeed, that word is superannuated.

CHRYSALE. Listen to me. I've got to make a scene,
       Take off the mask at last, and vent my spleen.
       Folks treat you both as mad, and if I knew . . .

PHILAMINTE. How's that?

CHRYSALE.   I'm speaking now, sister, to you.
       You wince at slips and solecisms in speech,
560   But your conduct displays plenty of each.
       Your everlasting books, they please me not,
       And you should burn the entire useless lot
       —Except that Plutarch, where I keep my bands—
       And leave your learning in the scholars' hands;
       Should take out of the attic and my sight
       That telescope that gives people a fright,
       And all those knickknacks that would shame a loon;
       Care not for what goes on up in the moon,
       But what goes on here, in your residence,
570   Where nothing I can see makes any sense.
       A woman should be willing to forego
       The love of study and the lust to know.
       To train her children's minds to be well-bred,
       Manage the household, see that all are fed,
       Control the servants, use economy:
       This is her study, her philosophy.
       In this respect our fathers were discerning
       To say a woman has enough of learning
       When her intellect, at its farthest reaches,
580   Can tell a doublet from a pair of breeches.
       Their wives read nothing, but they lived full well;
       Their households were the lore they had to tell,
       Their books a thimble, needles, and some thread,

With which they made their daughters' clothes instead.
For today's women that is far too trite:
They want to become authors, they must write.
For them no science can be too profound;
And less so here than anywhere around;
For this is where the deepest thoughts are thought;
Here they know everything but what they ought.   *590*
They know the motion of the moon and stars
—A lot I care—of Venus, Saturn, Mars;
And with this vain, farfetched learning of theirs,
My pot goes unobserved and no one cares.
My help aspires to learning, to please you,
And leaves undone just what it ought to do;
My household reasons busily all day,
And reasoning drives reason far away:
One lets my roast burn while he reads some tale;
One dreams up verses when I call for ale;   *600*
In short, your fine example is observed,
And I have servants, and I am not served.
At least one serving-woman still was there
Not yet infected by this noxious air,
And so you kick her out with much *éclat*
Because she fails to speak good Vaugelas.
I tell you, I take all these things amiss
(It's to you, sister, I'm addressing this);
I don't like all your Latinizers here,
Especially Trissotin, whom you revere;   *610*
He it was ridiculed you both in verse;
All that he says is balderdash or worse;
After he speaks, you wonder what he said,
And I don't think he's quite right in the head.

PHILAMINTE. O Heavens, what crudity of speech and soul!

BÉLISE. Can tiny atoms[4] form a heavier whole?
  Can a mind be formed of seeds so middle-class?
  And can it be I'm of his blood, alas?
  I'm mortified that I am of your race,
  And in confusion I shall leave this place.   *620*

4 The "atoms" or "seeds" of Epicurean philosophy.

Scene 8. PHILAMINTE, CHRYSALE

PHILAMINTE. Well, is there more, or have you had your fun?

CHRYSALE. I? No. Don't speak of quarrels; that's all done.
Now, then. Marriage, if I perceive aright,
Lacks glamour in your elder daughter's sight;
She's a philosopher by predilection.
She's well brought up, so I have no objection.
But Henriette is different. As for me,
I think we should provide for her, and see
About a husband . . .

630 PHILAMINTE.   I am so inclined,
And let me tell you what I have in mind.
That Monsieur Trissotin whom you despise,
Who finds only disfavor in your eyes,
He is the man I choose to be her mate,
And I know better than you his true estate.
My mind's made up, on full deliberation,
And there's no point in any protestation.
No word of this to her, I conjure you;
I want to talk to her before you do;
I have strong reasons for her, well rehearsed,
640 And I shall know it if you've seen her first.

Scene 9. ARISTE, CHRYSALE

ARISTE. Well then? There goes your wife, and I infer
That you've just had yourself a talk with her.

CHRYSALE. Yes.

ARISTE.   Well, what luck? Do we get Henriette?
Has she consented? Is it settled yet?

CHRYSALE. Not quite.

ARISTE.   Does she refuse?

CHRYSALE   No, that not it.

ARISTE. Then is she hesitating?

CHRYSALE.   Not a bit.

ARISTE. Then?

CHRYSALE.   She has another son-in-law in view.

ARISTE. Another son-in-law?

CHRYSALE.   Another.

ARISTE.   Who?

CHRYSALE. Trissotin.

ARISTE.   Trissotin? You mean the one . . . ?

CHRYSALE. Whose Latin and whose verse are never done.   650

ARISTE. And you accepted him?

CHRYSALE.   I? God forbid.

ARISTE. So you said . . . ?

CHRYSALE.   Nothing, and I'm glad I did.
  By saying nothing, I gave no consent.

ARISTE. Well, I suppose that's an accomplishment.
  Did you at least bring up Clitandre's name?

CHRYSALE. No; seeing that our choice was not the same,
  I thought that this was not the time to speak.

ARISTE. Your prudence, honestly, is quite unique!
  Aren't you a bit ashamed to be so placid?
  And can a man be quite so weak and flaccid   660
  As to bow to his wife in word and deed
  And never dare attack what she's decreed?

CHRYSALE. Lord! It's not hard for you to talk about;
  You don't know how her racket puts me out.
  I'm fond of gentleness, repose, and peace,
  And my wife's temper gives me no surcease.

She claims philosophy as her demesne,
But does not let that mitigate her spleen;
And her ideals, which frown on wealth as vile,
670   Do nothing to reduce her flow of bile.
If I oppose her, if I dare to speak,
I get a frightful tempest for a week.
She's like a dragon when she takes that tone;
I tremble, and just want to be alone;
And yet, for all the grief she puts me through,
I have to call her "sweetheart," and I do.

ARISTE. Come, face the facts. Your cowardice, I say,
Is all that gives your wife this sovereign sway.
Your weakness is her source of power, you know,
680   And if she's masterful, you've made her so;
You feed her despotism, at the least;
She leads you by the nose like some poor beast.
Since others know this, don't you think you can
Resolve once and for all to be a man,
Oblige a headstrong woman to be still,
And have the heart to say: "This is my will"?
You'll see your daughter sacrificed, it seems,
Without shame, to your family's crazy dreams,
And pass your whole estate on to a fool
690   For some six Latin words he learned in school,
A pedant whom your doting wife sees fit
To praise as a philosopher and wit,
Writer of gallant verse with brilliant ease—
And who, we know, is not a one of these.
Once more, this whole thing is a sorry jest;
Your cowardice deserves a laugh, at best.

CHRYSALE. Yes, you're quite right, and I can see I'm wrong.
All right, I'll make an effort to be strong,
Brother.

ARISTE.   Well said.

CHRYSALE.   It is a coward's role
700   To be so subject to a wife's control.

ARISTE. Quite right.

CHRYSALE.   She's profited by my docility.

ARISTE. That's true.

CHRYSALE.   And made the most of my facility.

ARISTE. No doubt.

CHRYSALE.   And I shall let her know today
My daughter is mine too, and *I* shall say
Who my choice for her husband is to be.

ARISTE. That's sensible, and what I like to see.

CHRYSALE. You know where Clitandre lives, and he's your
          man:
Have him see me as quickly as he can.

ARISTE. I go in haste.

CHRYSALE.   My sufferance is done;
710   I'll be a man in spite of everyone.

ACT III

Scene 1. PHILAMINTE, ARMANDE, BÉLISE, TRISSOTIN, L'ÉPINE

PHILAMINTE. Ah! let's be comfortable, that we may hear
  This verse, which warrants an attentive ear.

ARMANDE. I simply burn to see it.

BÉLISE.   So do we.

PHILAMINTE. Whatever *you* write casts a spell on me.

ARMANDE. Just listening is incomparably sweet.

BÉLISE. My ear could not enjoy a greater treat.

PHILAMINTE. Don't make us pine; have pity on our plight.

ARMANDE. Hurry.

BÉLISE.   Be quick, and hasten our delight.

PHILAMINTE. We cannot wait to hear your epigram.

720 TRISSOTIN. Alas! It is a newborn child, Madame.
  You should have pity on its fate, I vow,
  For in your court I brought it forth just now.

PHILAMINTE. Its father guarantees it my affection.

TRISSOTIN. Your favor gives it motherly protection.

BÉLISE. Ah, what a wit!

Scene. 2.   HENRIETTE, PHILAMINTE, ARMANDE, BÉLISE,
TRISSOTIN, L'ÉPINE

PHILAMINTE *(to* HENRIETTE, *who starts to come in, then
turns to leave).*   Here now! Why do you flee?

HENRIETTE. Lest I disturb so sweet a *causerie.*

PHILAMINTE. Then come on in and lend an eager ear
To all the wondrous things that you shall hear.

HENRIETTE. I am no judge of writing, I admit,
Nor quite at home in the domain of wit.   730

PHILAMINTE. No matter; there is something else as well;
A secret for you that I have to tell.

TRISSOTIN. Learning has nothing to inflame your heart,
And to be charming is your chosen art.

HENRIETTE. No, neither one, and I am scarcely wild
To . . .

BÉLISE   Pray, let's think about the newborn child.

PHILAMINTE *(to* L'ÉPINE). Come, hurry, bring a chair, you
little clown.
     (The LACKEY *falls as he brings the chair.)*
The saucy knave! Should anyone fall down
Who's studied equilibrium and all?

BÉLISE. Oaf, don't you see the causes of your fall,   740
And that you had your body so inclined
Your center of gravity was left behind?

L'ÉPINE. Madame, I learned that on the floor, alas!

PHILAMINTE. The clod!

TRISSOTIN.   He's lucky he's not made of glass.

ARMANDE. Such wit!

BÉLISE.   It never fails him in the least.

PHILAMINTE. Come, quick now, serve us your delightful
feast.

TRISSOTIN. For such a hunger as I find in you
An eight-line dish, I fear, will never do;
The epigram or madrigal's too short,
750 And I propose to add, in its support,
The tidbit of a sonnet, which was made
The subject of a princess' accolade.
Its every line with Attic salt is laced,
And I believe you'll find it in good taste.

ARMANDE. Oh! I've no doubt of it.

PHILAMINTE.   Let's hear it, now.

BÉLISE *(interrupting each time he tries to read)*. My heart
trembles with eagerness, I vow.
I love poetry with a burning passion,
Especially when it's turned in gallant fashion.

PHILAMINTE. If we keep talking, he can't say a word.

TRISSOTIN. "Son—."

760 BÉLISE *(to* HENRIETTE). Silence, my niece!

TRISSOTIN. "Sonnet to Princess Uranie upon Her Fever"[5]

> *Your prudence must have gone astray*
> *To treat with such magnificence*
> *And harbor in such opulence*
> *Your worst foe as a stowaway.*

BÉLISE. Oh, what a pretty start!

ARMANDE.   My, he has flair!

---

5 The sonnet, composed in 1659, is from the *Oeuvres galantes*
(*Gallant Works*) of Abbé Cotin, where it was addressed to Mademoiselle de Longueville, duchess of Nemours, upon her quartan
fever. The princess referred to above (line 752) is the King's cousin,
Mlle. de Montpensier. The use of culinary terms (lines 747–754) is
probably a reference to Cotin's *Festin poétique* (*Poetic Feast*).

PHILAMINTE. His verse alone has such a gallant air!

ARMANDE. *Prudence astray!* Why, I throw down my arms.

BÉLISE. And *harbor your worst foe* is full of charms.

PHILAMINTE. I like *opulence* and *magnificence,*
   Two nouns equally rich in sound and sense.   770

BÉLISE. Let's hear the rest.

TRISSOTIN.   *Your prudence must have gone astray*
          To treat with such magnificence
          And harbor in such opulence
          Your worst foe as a stowaway.

ARMANDE. *Prudence astray!*

BÉLISE. *Harbor your foe!*

PHILAMINTE. *Opulence* and *magnificence!*

TRISSOTIN. *Make her go out, whate'er they say,*
          From your delightful residence,
          Where, with ungrateful insolence,
          She seeks to steal your life away.

BÉLISE. Gently! Leave me a chance for respiration.

ARMANDE. I pray you, give me time for admiration.

PHILAMINTE. Those verses thrill one to one's inmost soul
   And bring one to a swoon beyond control.

ARMANDE. *Make her go out, what'ever they say.*
        From your delightful residence.
   Delightful residence—a charming phrase!   780
   What witty things the metaphor conveys!

PHILAMINTE. *Make her go out, whate'er they say.*
   Whate'er they say: what admirable taste!
   My debt for that can never be erased.

ARMANDE. *Whate'er they say:* that is the clause for me.

BÉLISE. *Whate'er they say!* Lovely, I quite agree.

ARMANDE. I wish I'd said it.

BÉLISE.   Better than a play.

PHILAMINTE. D'you see the subtle things the words convey?

ARMANDE and BÉLISE. Oh, oh!

PHILAMINTE. *Make her go out, whate'er*
   they say:
There are those who espouse the fever's part,
So don't take anything they say to heart.
      Make her go out, whate'er they say.
      Whate'er they say, whate'er they say.
790 *Whate'er they say* speaks more than some could see.
I don't know whether everyone's like me,
But those words tell me more than volumes could.

BÉLISE. Short as they are, they leave much understood.

PHILAMINTE *(to* TRISSOTIN*)*.
But when you wrote that sweet *whate'er they say,*
Did you know all the power those words display?
Were you aware of all we find in it,
And did you think to put in so much wit?

TRISSOTIN. Heh, heh!

ARMANDE.   I have *ungrateful* on my mind:
Ungrateful fever, yes, unjust, unkind,
800 Who mistreats those who have her as their guest.

PHILAMINTE. In short, the quatrains both are of the best.
So let's turn promptly to the tercets, pray.

ARMANDE. Oh, please! Just one more time, *whate'er they say.*

TRISSOTIN. *Make her go out, whate'er they say,*

PHILAMINTE, ARMANDE and BÉLISE. *Whate'er they say!*

TRISSOTIN. *From your delightful residence,*

PHILAMINTE, ARMANDE, and BÉLISE. *Delightful residence!*

TRISSOTIN. *Where with ungrateful insolence,*

PHILAMINTE, ARMANDE, and BÉLISE. *Ungrateful fever!*

TRISSOTIN. *She seeks to steal your life away.*

PHILAMINTE. *Your life away!*

BÉLISE. Ah!

TRISSOTIN. *Without respect for rank and birth,*
She robs your blood of all its worth,

PHILAMINTE, ARMANDE, and BÉLISE. Ah!

TRISSOTIN. *And does you harm the clock around!*

If she goes with you to the baths,
Give up your temporizing paths,
Use your own hands and see her drowned.

PHILAMINTE. One can't go on.

BÉLISE.   One swoons.

ARMANDE.   One dies of bliss.   810

PHILAMINTE. A thousand shivers seize one, hearing this.

ARMANDE. *If she goes with you to the baths,*

BÉLISE. *Give up your temporizing paths,*

PHILAMINTE. *Use your own hands and see her drowned:*
With your own hands, in the baths, see her drowned.

ARMANDE. Each step brings joy in everything you write.

BÉLISE. Where'er we walk, we meet some fresh delight.

PHILAMINTE. On nothing but the loveliest things we tread.

ARMANDE. They're little roads bedecked with roses red.

TRISSOTIN. You find the sonnet . . .

PHILAMINTE.   Admirable, new;
No one has ever done as well as you.

BÉLISE. What? No emotion while you heard this piece?
You cut a sorry figure there, my niece!   820

HENRIETTE. Why try to cut a figure that we can't?
Not everyone can be a wit, my aunt.

TRISSOTIN. Perhaps my verses do not please Madame.

HENRIETTE. I'm just no listener.

PHILAMINTE.   Come! The epigram.

TRISSOTIN. "On a Marigold-Colored Carriage, Given to a Lady Who is a Friend of His"[6]

PHILAMINTE. These titles are unique, no doubt of it.

ARMANDE. Their novelty prepares us for his wit.

TRISSOTIN. *Love sold his bondage to me at a price,*

BÉLISE, ARMANDE, and PHILAMINTE. Ah!

TRISSOTIN. *That costs me half my wealth, to be precise;*
    Seeing this carriage (and its cost),
830   *With gold so lavishly embossed*
    That it astounds the countryside
    And sounds my Laïs' triumph far and wide,

PHILAMINTE. Aha! *My Laïs!* That's a learned note.

BÉLISE. Yes, it's an admirable protective coat.

TRISSOTIN. *Seeing this carriage (and its cost),*
    With gold so lavishly embossed
    That it astounds the countryside
    And sounds my Laïs' triumph far and wide,
    No longer say it's marigold,
    But rather say it's made of gold.

ARMANDE. Oh, oh! That is a marvelous surprise!

PHILAMINTE. Nobody else can write verse in this wise.

BÉLISE. *No longer say it's marigold,*
    But rather say it's made of gold.
  You can almost decline it: *gold, of gold, i' gold.*

PHILAMINTE. I may be too impressed; I cannot say;
840   But since I knew you first, in every way
  I have admired your prose and verse, you know.

TRISSOTIN. If there were something you would care to show,
  Our admiration too could be in season.

PHILAMINTE. I've nothing new in verse, but I have reason

6 Again, taken from Cotin's *Gallant Works*, where the title was "On an Amaranth-Colored Carriage Bought for a Lady: A Madrigal." This translator could not render the pun without changing the color and the flower.

To hope to show you, confidentially,
Eight chapters on our planned Academy.
In his *Republic* Plato outlined one,
But did not finish what he had begun.
A complete treatment is what I propose,
And now I have most of it down in prose.   *850*
For I confess it vexes me to find
That men won't give us credit for a mind,
And I mean to avenge us if I can
For the low rank accorded us by man,
Who limits us to mere futilities
And bars the door to eternal verities.

ARMANDE. To our whole sex it is a great offense
For us to limit our intelligence
To judging how a skirt or cloak is made,
The beauties of some lace or some brocade.   *860*

BÉLISE. This gross unbalance must be overthrown;
Our minds need freedom to be on their own.

TRISSOTIN. The merits of the sex I recognize,
And if I vaunt the beauty of their eyes,
I honor too the brilliance of their wit.

PHILAMINTE. And we reciprocate, no doubt of it;
But there are some to whom we'd make it plain
(Whose haughty learning treats us with disdain)
That women are equipped with knowledge too.
We can have learned meetings, as they do,   *870*
In many aspects better regulated,
Uniting what is elsewhere separated,
Mingling beautiful words with lofty lore,[7]
Revealing secrets undisclosed before,
And, on the questions set by anyone,
Inviting in each sect, espousing none.

TRISSOTIN. For order, Aristotle is my meat.

PHILAMINTE. But for abstractions, Plato's hard to beat.

ARMANDE. Epicurus is strong, and meets my needs.

---

[7] The French Academy of Sciences had recently (1666) been instituted, distinct from the French Academy (founded in 1635).

880 BÉLISE. I like his doctrine of the *little seeds*,
    But I do find his *void* hard to digest,
    And to me, *subtle matter* is the best.[8]

TRISSOTIN. On the magnet, Descartes and I agree.

ARMANDE. I like his *vortex*.

PHILAMINTE.   *Falling worlds* for me!

ARMANDE. I yearn to start this congress of the mind
    And signalize ourselves by some rare find.

TRISSOTIN. Your keenness offers grounds for hope, it's true,
    And nature can keep little hid from you.

PHILAMINTE. I've one discovery to publish soon,
890   For I have clearly seen men in the moon.[9]

BÉLISE. I've not seen men, I think not, anyway,
    But I've seen steeples just as clear as day.

ARMANDE. We shall explore, besides the universe,
    History, grammar, morals, law, and verse.

PHILAMINTE. Moral questions arouse my interest,
    And once the greatest thinkers loved them best;
    But there the Stoics are the ones for me,
    And their sage is as fine as fine can be.

ARMANDE. For language, we shall soon reveal our rules,
900   And we expect to overturn the schools.
    Justly or naturally, we abhor
    And each harbor a deadly hatred for
    Certain locutions, whether verbs or nouns,
    Which we abandon to each other's frowns.
    We're planning bans to punish their transgressions,
    And we should open up our learned sessions
    By placing a proscription or a curse
    On words we want to purge from prose and verse.

---

[8] For Epicurus the world is composed of atoms, or little seeds of things, and the void through which they fall. For Descartes, subtle matter fills the space between bodies; the magnet is a fifth element; matter is moved in vortices or whirlwinds; and comets fall from whirlwind to whirlwind.

[9] Their existence was a very live question in seventeenth-century France.

PHILAMINTE. But the best plan of our Academy,
  Whose execution I can't wait to see,   *910*
  A glorious scheme, which will elicit praise
  From all the finest minds in future days,
  Is the excision of those dirty parts
  Which, in the fairest words, offend pure hearts,
  Those playthings of the fools of every age,
  Which nasty jokers have made all the rage,
  Sources of puns unworthy of the name,
  With which men wound a woman's sense of shame.

TRISSOTIN. Most admirable plans, beyond a doubt!

BÉLISE. You'll see our statutes when we've worked them out. *920*

TRISSOTIN. They'll be both fair and wise, assuredly.

ARMANDE. We'll judge all works, for so our laws decree;
  Our laws place prose and verse beneath our rule;
  None shall have wit except us and our school;
  We'll find flaws everywhere, to our delight,
  And see that no one else knows how to write.

Scene 3.   L'ÉPINE, TRISSOTIN, PHILAMINTE, BÉLISE,
ARMANDE, HENRIETTE, VADIUS

L'ÉPINE. Sir, there's a man to speak to you out there.
  He's dressed in black, and has a quiet air.

TRISSOTIN. That learned man who made such an ado
  To have the honor soon of meeting you.   *930*

PHILAMINTE. You've every right to introduce the man.
              (TRISSOTIN *goes to do so.*)
  Well, let us show our wit as best we can.
  (*To* HENRIETTE) You there! I told you clearly, didn't I,
  That I have need of you?

HENRIETTE.   May I ask why?

PHILAMINTE. Come; soon your wish to know shall be contented.

TRISSOTIN. Here is a man dying to be presented.
I could not be accused except in vain
Of bringing to you one of the profane:
Among the keenest wits he holds his own.

940   PHILAMINTE. Your sponsoring hand's enough to make that known.

TRISSOTIN. He knows the ancients better than any man;
No one in France can read Greek as he can.

PHILAMINTE. Good Heavens, Greek! Greek! Sister, he knows Greek!

BÉLISE. My niece, Greek!

ARMANDE.   Greek! How lovely! How unique!

PHILAMINTE. The gentleman knows Greek? Let each of us,
Sir, for the love of Greek, embrace you—thus.
(Kisses him. He kisses all the women except HENRIETTE, *who refuses.)*

HENRIETTE. Excuse me, sir, but Greek I do not speak.

PHILAMINTE. I've marvelous respect for books in Greek.

VADIUS. I fear to bother you, but burn to pay,
950   Madame, sincere homage to you today.
I trust I've not disturbed some learned chat.

PHILAMINTE. With Greek? There's nothing you could spoil with that.

TRISSOTIN. His verses are as brilliant as his prose,
And if urged, he could show you some of those.

VADIUS. Authors are prone, with everything they write,
To fall on conversation like a blight;
At table, alcove, or the Cours-la-Reine,[10]
They read their verse while others yawn in vain.
Nothing, it seems to me, betrays less sense
960   Than for an author to cadge compliments,

[10] A favorite place to walk in Molière's time.

And, to a bystander's reluctant ear,
Deliver what he cannot choose but hear.
A captive audience I do not seek;
I share the feeling of a certain Greek[11]
Who once forbade his sage—in black and white—
To gratify this itching to recite.
Now: for the young in love this verse is meant;
I should be glad to hear your sentiment.

TRISSOTIN. Yours is the only poetry that soars.

VADIUS. Love and the Graces rule in all of yours.   970

TRISSOTIN. Your style is free, your words afford delight.

VADIUS. *Ithos* and *pathos*[12] shine in all you write.

TRISSOTIN. We have seen eclogues issued from your pen
Beyond Theocritus' and Virgil's ken.

VADIUS. Your odes have something gallant and refined
That leaves your old friend Horace far behind.

TRISSOTIN. Your chansonnettes have such a loving fall!

VADIUS. Nothing can match your sonnets, nothing at all.

TRISSOTIN. Your rondeaus! Is there anything more charming?

VADIUS. Your madrigals! So witty, so disarming!   980

TRISSOTIN. Your *ballades* I wholeheartedly admire.

VADIUS. And of your crambo-verse[13] I never tire.

TRISSOTIN. If only France could recognize your worth, . . .

VADIUS. If brilliance were acknowledged here on earth, . . .

TRISSOTIN. A gilded coach would take you everywhere.

VADIUS. Your statue'd be in every public square.

---

11 This Greek sounds rather like the Roman Horace.
12 *Ethos* (characters) and *pathos* (passions), according to ancient
rhetoricians, are important oratorical effects. Modern Greek pronounces the former word "ithos."
13 The French is *bouts-rimés:* verses composed on given verse-
endings.

Ahem! It's a *ballade;* your judgment on it
Is what I . . .

TRISSOTIN.   Did you hear a little sonnet
On the fever of Princess Uranie?

990 VADIUS. Oh yes, I heard it read in company.

TRISSOTIN. You know who wrote it?

VADIUS.   No, but I know this:
It's nothing anyone would ever miss.

TRISSOTIN. Yet many folk think it deserves great fame.

VADIUS. It's a very bad sonnet all the same;
And if you've seen it, you will side with me.

TRISSOTIN. Not at all, I completely disagree;
Few people could have written such a sonnet.

VADIUS. Well, Heaven preserve me from having done it!

TRISSOTIN. I maintain it's incomparably fine;
1000   And my main reason is: the poem is mine.

VADIUS. Yours!

TRISSOTIN.   Mine.

VADIUS.   I can't see how that came to pass.

TRISSOTIN. My sonnet failed to please your ear, alas!

VADIUS. I must have had something else in my head,
Or else the poem must have been badly read.
But here is my *ballade,* if you're inclined.

TRISSOTIN. The *ballade* is a dull form, to my mind,
Old-fashioned and completely out of date.

VADIUS. It has its charms for some, at any rate.

TRISSOTIN. To me it's still a sorry form of verse.

1010 VADIUS. Your feeling does not make it any worse.

TRISSOTIN. Well, pedants love it dearly, that is clear.

VADIUS. And yet we see it does not please your ear.

TRISSOTIN. You see yourself in others, stupidly.

VADIUS. You have the nerve to pin your traits on me.

TRISSOTIN. You scribbling hack, go, get along with you.

VADIUS. You dime a dozen laureate, you too.

TRISSOTIN. You impudent, text-snatching plagiarist!

VADIUS. You pedant . . .

PHILAMINTE.   Gentlemen, I must insist!

TRISSOTIN. You owe the Latins and the Greeks your soul.
Come on, give them back all you basely stole.   *1020*

VADIUS. You took Horace and cut him at both ends.
Go to Parnassus then, and make amends.

TRISSOTIN. Your book came out unnoticed, don't forget.

VADIUS. Nor you, your publisher immersed in debt.

TRISSOTIN. In vain you try to smirch my fame, you know.

VADIUS. Oh, yes, your fame! Yes, tell it to Boileau![14]

TRISSOTIN. Tell him your own.

VADIUS.   Of this I'm satisfied:
He treats me better; that can't be denied.
He strikes me just the tiniest of blows,
Among the authors everybody knows;   *1030*
But in his verse you're never left in peace:
His arrows rain on you and never cease.

TRISSOTIN. And that's what shows that he thinks more
   of me.
He lumps you with the men of low degree.
He thinks one blow enough to set you back,
And you're not honored with renewed attack;
But he assails me as an adversary
Who makes his fullest effort necessary;
And each new blow reveals to everyone
That victory for him is never won.   *1040*

---

14 The French reads: "the author of the *Satires*." In these Boileau
criticizes Ménage once, Cotin often.

VADIUS. My pen will give a sample of my strength.

TRISSOTIN. And mine will show my mastery at length.

VADIUS. Verse, prose, Greek, Latin, I defy you then.   *(Exit)*

TRISSOTIN. I'll meet you at the bookstore,[15] pen to pen.

Scene 4.   TRISSOTIN, PHILAMINTE, ARMANDE,
BÉLISE, HENRIETTE

TRISSOTIN. Don't wonder I'm as angry as I am:
    The fact is, he impugned your taste, Madame,
    By daring to attack my sonnet's merits.

PHILAMINTE. I'll try to bring you back to better spirits.
    Let's change the subject. Come here, Henriette.
1050 For quite some time my soul has been upset
    To find you lacking any trace of wit;
    But I've a way to have you get a bit.

HENRIETTE. That would be an unnecessary care:
    Learned discussions are not my affair;
    I like my ease, and it is not my way
    To strive for wit in everything I say.
    That, Mother, is no part of my ambition;
    I'm happy to be dull, with your permission;
    I'd rather be content with common speech
1060 Than strain for wit that lies beyond my reach.

PHILAMINTE. Yes, but it hurts me too, and drives me wild
    To find myself disgraced by my own child.
    The beauty of the face can never last,
    It's like a flower, whose bloom is quickly past,
    And it resides no deeper than the skin;
    That of the mind is firmly lodged within.
    So I've long sought some means to have you gain
    This beauty that the years attack in vain,

15 The French reads *"chez Barbin,"* a bookseller who published
Molière and Boileau, among others.

To fill you with a salutary yearning
To savor the delicious fruits of learning;   1070
And I have found the way to manage it:
By marrying you to a man of wit,
(Pointing to TRISSOTIN*)* This gentleman, in whom you are
    to see
The husband picked for you by my decree.

HENRIETTE. Me, mother?

PHILAMINTE.   You. Go on, act innocent.

BÉLISE *(to* TRISSOTIN*)*. I understand: your eyes ask my
    consent
To reassign a heart that I possess.
All right, I give you up; the answer's yes.
Yours will be an auspicious wedding day.

TRISSOTIN. In my delight I don't know what to say,   1080
Madame, I'm honored so that Henriette
Will . . .

HENRIETTE. Gently, sir, it's not concluded yet.
Don't hurry so.

PHILAMINTE *(to* HENRIETTE*)*. For that, you make a scene?
D'you know that if . . . Well, you know what I mean.
(To TRISSOTIN*)* Leave her alone, there's nothing else
    to do.

Scene 5. HENRIETTE, ARMANDE

ARMANDE. You see the trouble Mother takes for you.
I can't believe a more illustrious match . . .

HENRIETTE. Why don't you take him, if he's such a catch?

ARMANDE. He's for you, not for me; that is the plan.

HENRIETTE. You are my elder; welcome to the man.   1090

ARMANDE. If marriage found such favor in my sight,
   I would accept your offer with delight.

HENRIETTE. If, like you, I had pedants on the brain,
   I might accept his hand and not complain.

ARMANDE. Although our tastes are different, I'm afraid,
   Our parents' will, sister, must be obeyed.
   A mother's power over us is entire,
   And in vain by resisting you aspire . . .

Scene 6.   CHRYSALE, ARISTE, CLITANDRE, HENRIETTE, ARMANDE

CHRYSALE *(presenting* CLITANDRE *to* HENRIETTE*)*. Come,
   daughter, you must do as I have planned:
1100   Remove your glove, and take this gentleman's hand,
   And from now on put this into your head:
   This is the man I mean to have you wed.

ARMANDE. Sister, you hardly seem to be dismayed.

HENRIETTE. Sister, our parents' will must be obeyed.
   A father's power over us is entire.

ARMANDE. A mother needs obedience like a sire.

CHRYSALE. What does that mean?

ARMANDE.   It means it seems to me
   That on this Mother and you do not agree;
   And she has someone else . . .

CHRYSALE.   Prattler, be still!
1110   Go philosophize with her all you will,
   And just leave me and my affairs alone.
   Tell her my plan. I want it clearly known
   That she's not to come storming at my ears.
   Quick, on your way.

ARISTE.   That's wonderful: three cheers!

CLITANDRE. What joy! What ecstasy! We shall be wed!

CHRYSALE. All right then, take her hand, and go ahead,
    Escort her to her room. What a sweet caress!
    My heart is stirred by all this tenderness,
    Old age's apathy is left behind,
    And all my youthful loves come back to mind.   1120

ACT IV

Scene 1. ARMANDE, PHILAMINTE

ARMANDE. Yes, without even a show of reticence
    She made a virtue of obedience.
    Her heart, eager to give itself away,
    Could scarcely wait to hear what he would say,
    And in her action it appeared she rather
    Defied a mother than obeyed a father.

PHILAMINTE. I'll show her clearly which one of us two
    Reason selects to tell her what to do,
    And whether he or I should have control,
1130   Matter or form, the body or the soul.

ARMANDE. That little man might have displayed more tact.
    Instead he chose a funny way to act,
    To be your son-in-law against your will.

PHILAMINTE. Oh, well, he has some distance to go still.
    I liked his looks, and seconded your love;
    But there are things he has no notion of.
    He knows that writing's a pursuit of mine,
    And never has he asked to hear a line.

Scene 2. CLITANDRE *(at first unobserved)*, ARMANDE, PHILAMINTE

ARMANDE. If I were in your place, I'd never let
1140   Clitandre be the groom of Henriette.
    No one who knows me would make the mistake

Of thinking I had anything at stake,
And that the way he's played his coward's part
Has left some deep resentment in my heart.
Philosophy, against blows of this sort,
Provides the soul with resolute support,
And with its aid we rise high above all.
But his treatment has pushed you to the wall:
Honor demands that you oppose his will,
And that young man must surely make you ill.   1150
In all our talk he's never shown for you
The genuine esteem that is your due.

PHILAMINTE. The little fool!

ARMANDE.   Despite your well-earned fame,
His praise has always seemed frigid and lame.

PHILAMINTE. The clod!

ARMANDE.   Often, to put him to the test,
I've read your verse, and he was not impressed.

PHILAMINTE. What insolence!

ARMANDE.   And then, when I demurred,
You won't believe how utterly absurd . . .

CLITANDRE (to ARMANDE). Oh! Gently, pray! I beg of you,
    be kind,
Madame, or at least keep an open mind.   1160
What harm have I done you? What's my offense
That arms against me all your eloquence?
Why seek to lay me low, and give such heed
To make me odious to those I need?
Speak, tell me, what has caused this frightful grudge?
Madame will be our equitable judge.

ARMANDE. If I did bear a grudge, as you insist,
There would be ample reasons I could list:
You would deserve it; and our earliest flames
Establish on our souls such sacred claims   1170
That we should cast fortune and life away
Rather than ever let our ardor stray;
To change our vows is a repugnant crime,
And every faithless heart is smirched with grime.

CLITANDRE. Madame, d'you call it infidelity
　　To do what your soul's pride commanded me?
　　I merely am obedient to its laws;
　　If I offend you, it's the only cause.
　　At first your charms possessed my heart entire;
1180　It burned two years with an unceasing fire;
　　Care, respect, service—nothing would suffice;
　　It paid you every lover's sacrifice.
　　My ardor and my care have no fruition;
　　My fondest hopes are met with opposition.
　　I offer someone else what you decline—
　　Come now, Madame, is the fault yours or mine?
　　Am I, or you, causing this turnabout?
　　Did I leave you, or did you drive me out?

ARMANDE. Do I oppose the wishes of your heart
1190　When I seek to root out their vulgar part,
　　And ask a purity in your desires
　　Consistent with what perfect love requires?
　　You couldn't school your thoughts to abstinence,
　　For me, from the degrading claims of sense?
　　And you've no taste for the serene delight
　　Felt when two disembodied hearts unite?
　　You can live only in this brutish wise?
　　Only with all the train of fleshly ties?
　　And to nourish the fires produced in you
1200　You must have marriage, and what follows too?
　　Oh, what a strange love! Hear me, if you please:
　　Noble souls burn with no such flames as these!
　　In all their glow the senses have no part,
　　And all they seek to marry is the heart;
　　With scorn they leave aside other desires.
　　Their flames are pure, like the celestial fires.
　　Their love gives vent only to virtuous sighs,
　　And crass desires they utterly despise.
　　Nothing impure contaminates their goals;
1210　They love for love alone, a love of souls;
　　Their transports are directed to the mind;
　　The body is ignored and left behind.

CLITANDRE. Alas, Madame, with no offense to you,
　　I have a soul, but I've a body too;

It sticks too closely to be set apart;
Of such dismemberings I lack the art.
Heaven has denied me that philosophy,
And soul and body walk abreast with me.
Nothing could be more beautiful, I own,
Than purified desire for mind alone,   *1220*
Unions of hearts, the tender innocence
Of thoughts completely undefiled by sense.
And yet such loves for me are too refined;
I am a trifle earthily inclined;
When I'm in love, it's with a love entire
For the whole person to whom I aspire.
That's not a matter for great punishments,
And—no offense to your fine sentiments—
The world acknowledges my kind of passion,
And marriage is sufficiently in fashion,   *1230*
Is thought a sweet, good enough way of life
To have made me want to have you as my wife
Without the liberty of such a notion
Giving offense or causing such commotion.

ARMANDE. Well then, sir! Well then! Since you give no heed
To any voice but that of brutish greed;
Since I can make of you a faithful swain
Only by fleshly bonds, a bodily chain,
If Mother wills it, I make up my mind,
For your sake, to a union of that kind.   *1240*

CLITANDRE. Too late, Madame; another has your place;
And I could not return without bad grace,
Mistreating my asylum, giving pain
To her who rescued me from your disdain.

PHILAMINTE. But, sir, are you expecting my consent
For this new marriage on which you're intent?
And in your visions, have you reckoned yet
That I've another man for Henriette?

CLITANDRE. Madame, pray think about this choice you
    make:
Expose me to less shame, for pity's sake,   *1250*
And spare me the ridiculous position
Of having Trissotin for competition.

The love of wits, which makes you scorn me so,
Could not provide me a less noble foe.
The bad taste of the times, and the inflation
Of wit, have given some a reputation;
But Trissotin could make a dupe of none;
His is a well-deserved oblivion.
He's valued at his worth, outside of here;
1260   And twenty times I have been stunned to hear
How you can raise up nonsense to the skies,
Which, had you written it, you would despise.

PHILAMINTE. If you judge him otherwise than we do,
We look at him with other eyes than you.

Scene 3.   TRISSOTIN, ARMANDE, PHILAMINTE, CLITANDRE

TRISSOTIN. I come with news that is extremely grave.
Last night, Madame, we had a narrow shave:
Another world passed near us at full length,
Falling across our vortex in its strength;
And a collision, had it come to pass,
1270   Would have shattered our earth like so much glass.

PHILAMINTE. Let's put this talk off for another season:
This man would find in it no rhyme nor reason;
The love of ignorance is his profession,
And hating wit and learning, an obsession.

CLITANDRE. Let me tone down that truth and set it straight.
The only wit and learning that I hate
Are those that spoil a person unaware.
These are things in themselves both good and fair;
But ignorant indeed I'd rather be
1280   Than learned as are certain folk I see.

TRISSOTIN. For my part I don't hold, whate'er befall,
That learning can spoil anything at all.

CLITANDRE. And I believe that people often make

Great dunces of themselves for learning's sake.

TRISSOTIN. That's quite a paradox.

CLITANDRE.   Though I'm no wit,
I think I could make easy proof of it:
If reasons failed, I'm sure in any case
That famed examples would be commonplace.

TRISSOTIN. Some you might choose to cite would be in vain.

CLITANDRE. I'd not look far to make the matter plain.   *1290*

TRISSOTIN. These famed examples all escape my mind.

CLITANDRE. To me they are so clear they strike me blind.

TRISSOTIN. Till now I've always thought it was the rule
That ignorance, not learning, made the fool.

CLITANDRE. You have thought wrong. Ask me, ask anyone:
A learned fool's worse than a simpleton.

TRISSOTIN. Your views fly in the face of common sense,
Since fool and dullard are equivalents.

CLITANDRE. If usage is what you'll be guided by,
Pedant and fool have yet a closer tie.   *1300*

TRISSOTIN. Stupidity shines pure in an ignorant face.

CLITANDRE. Study aids nature in the other case.

TRISSOTIN. But learning in itself deserves respect.

CLITANDRE. But learning in a dunce is a defect.

TRISSOTIN. For you ignorance must have potent charms,
Since its defense prompts you to take up arms.

CLITANDRE. If ignorance has potent charms for me,
It's since I've seen some learned men I see.

TRISSOTIN. Just get to know those learned men; they may
Be well worth others who are on display.   *1310*

CLITANDRE. Yes, if you go by just those learned men;
Other men's views are something else again.

PHILAMINTE. It seems to me, sir . . .

CLITANDRE.   Madame, not you too.
He's surely self-sufficient without you;
My hands are full with such a doughty foe,
And I give ground before his every blow.

ARMANDE. But the offensive rancor of your wit
Is . . .

CLITANDRE. What? Another second? Then I quit.

PHILAMINTE. This kind of combat can be fought with tact,
1320   Provided that the person's not attacked.

CLITANDRE. There's nothing here to make him look askance;
He'll take a joke with any man in France;
He's felt the sting of sharper darts by half
And greeted them with a complacent laugh.

TRISSOTIN. In this sharp skirmish, it is no surprise
To see this gentleman quick to criticize.
He's rooted in the court, you see, that's it;
The court, we all know, has no use for wit;
Ignorance readily wins its support,
1330   And his defense of it smacks of the court.

CLITANDRE. Your spite against the court is great, I fear,
And its misfortune is each day to hear
You wits belabor it with might and main,
Hold it responsible for every pain,
Incriminate it for its tastelessness,
And blame on it alone your ill success.
Allow me, Monsieur Trissotin, I pray,
With all respect for your good name, to say
You and your colleagues would do well to speak
1340   About the court with just a bit less pique;
It's not so foolish, take it as it goes,
As all you learned gentlemen suppose;
It judges by the light of common sense;
It can teach men good taste without pretense;
Indeed, its worldly wit is worth far more
Than all of pedantry's recondite lore.

TRISSOTIN. We see, sir, the effects of its good taste.

CLITANDRE. And where, sir, do you find it so debased?

TRISSOTIN. I see this, sir, that by their erudition,
 Rasius and Baldus[16] win us recognition,   *1350*
 And that their merit brings them no support
 Because they lack the favor of the court.

CLITANDRE. I see you're vexed, and that your modesty
 Is all that keeps you from their company.
 And so, leaving you out of the debate,
 How do your able heroes help the State?
 What service, rendered by their writings rare,
 Leads them to claim the court is so unfair,
 And everywhere moan that their names are missed
 When courtiers select a pension list?   *1360*
 France could not get along without their learning,
 And for their every book the court is yearning.
 These wretches, whose presumption makes me laugh,
 Think that to be in print and bound in calf
 Makes them in all the State important men;
 That they make or break kingdoms with their pen;
 That the least word of what they're putting out
 Should bring the pensions flying round about;
 That all the world has eyes for them alone;
 That everywhere their glory is well known;   *1370*
 That they are famous prodigies of lore
 For knowing what others have said before,
 For thirty years of using ears and sight,
 For some ten thousand times spending the night
 Daubing themselves with Latin and with Greek,
 Loading their minds with everything antique,
 And combing dusty books for worthless junk:
 People whose learning merely makes them drunk,
 Their merit, that they're rich in tedious chatter,
 Empty of sense, inept in every matter,   *1380*
 Full of enough impertinence, I swear,
 To decry wit and learning everywhere.

PHILAMINTE. Your warmth, I do declare, is very great,
 And this attack proclaims your natural hate.
 The prospect of this rivalry shows how . . .

16 Names of imaginary pedants.

Scene 4.   JULIEN, TRISSOTIN, PHILAMINTE, CLITANDRE,
ARMANDE

JULIEN. The learned man who came to call just now,
        And whose most humble servitor I am,
        Exhorts you to peruse this note, Madame.

PHILAMINTE. However much this letter may portend,
1390   Learn that it is stupidity, my friend,
        To come and break into a conversation;
        The servants should receive your application
        And let you in as a well-trained valet.

JULIEN. Madame, I'm noting everything you say.

PHILAMINTE (reads). *Trissotin has boasted, Madame, that
        he would marry your daughter. I give you notice that his
        philosophy has eyes only for your riches, and that you will
        do well not to conclude this marriage until you have seen
        the poem I am composing against him. While you are
        waiting for this painting, in which I intend to portray him
        to you in all his colors, I send you Horace, Virgil, Terence,
        and Catullus, where you will see noted in the margin all
        the places he has pillaged.*

PHILAMINTE (goes on). This man, to whom my daughter
            goes as bride,
        Is pressed by enemies on every side;
        And these attacks prompt me to expedite
        The thing that's surest to confound their spite,
        And let them know the efforts that they make
1400   Will bring about the tie they seek to break.
        Report that to your master, when you go,
        And tell him that—so as to let him know
        How much I take his counsel in good part
        And how his words are printed on my heart—
        I'll have the two married this very night.
        (To CLITANDRE) Sir, as a family friend, it's only right

That you should see this contract duly signed,
And I invite you with an open mind.
Armande, be sure the Notary is there,
And notify your sister of the affair.   *1410*

ARMANDE. For me to notify her there's no need;
This gentleman has graciously agreed
To run and bear this news without delay,
And make her heart rebel at what you say.

PHILAMINTE. We'll see who will prevail with Henriette,
And whether I can bring her to reason yet.   *(Exit)*

ARMANDE. I'm sorry, sir, to see things go amiss
And stand in opposition to your bliss.

CLITANDRE. And I shall do my utmost, for my part,
Madame, to take this sorrow from your heart.   *1420*

ARMANDE. I fear that all your effort still may fail.

CLITANDRE. Perhaps you'll find your fear of no avail.

ARMANDE. I hope you may be right.

CLITANDRE.   I'm sure you do,
And that for help I can rely on you.

ARMANDE. Yes, I will serve your cause as best I can.

CLITANDRE. Do so, and I shall be a grateful man.

Scene 5.   CHRYSALE, ARISTE, HENRIETTE, CLITANDRE

CLITANDRE. Without your help, sir, I am destitute:
Your wife, refusing to allow my suit,
Wants Henriette and Trissotin to wed.

CHRYSALE. What crazy notion has she in her head?   *1430*
Why she wants Monsieur Trissotin, Heaven knows!

ARISTE. He almost rhymes with *Latin;* I suppose
That's why he's found such favor in her sight.

CLITANDRE. She means to marry them this very night.

CHRYSALE. Tonight?

CLITANDRE.   Tonight.

CHRYSALE.   Tonight what I shall do
Is go and marry off the two of you.

CLITANDRE. She's called the Notary to write the deed.

CHRYSALE. I'll send for him to draw the one we need.

CLITANDRE. Her sister is to make Madame aware
1440 Of the marriage for which they want her to prepare.

CHRYSALE. And *I* give her an absolute command
That she be ready to give *you* her hand.
Let them just find out, if they want to try,
If there's another master here than I.
(To HENRIETTE*)* Please wait for us; we'll be back pres-
ently.
(To ARISTE *and* CLITANDRE*)* Come, brother, son-in-law,
pray follow me.   *(Exit)*

HENRIETTE. Oh! keep him always in this humor, pray.

ARISTE. I'll strive to serve your love in every way.

CLITANDRE. Though I were promised more help than I am,
1450 My strongest hope is in your heart, Madame.

HENRIETTE. As for my heart, its stanch support is sure.

CLITANDRE. Then I am happy, knowing that's secure.

HENRIETTE. You see the loathsome bonds that they design.

CLITANDRE. I'll have no fear as long as your heart is mine.

HENRIETTE. I'll try my best to make our wish come true,
And if I can't be yours whatever I do,
I'll take the vows, do anything I can
Not to belong to any other man.

CLITANDRE. Just Heaven! May I never be witness of
1460 Any such baneful token of your love!

ACT V

Scene 1.   HENRIETTE, TRISSOTIN

HENRIETTE. About this marriage which my mother has set,
   I've wanted, sir, to have a tête-à-tête;
   And with the family all confused, I thought
   You might listen to reason as you ought.
   I know you think that I can bring to you,
   Besides my hand, a good-sized dowry too;
   But money, by which many set such store,
   To a true sage is not worth striving for.
   The scorn for wordly greatness that you've shown
   Should not be manifest in words alone.   1470

TRISSOTIN. And that is not what I so dearly prize.
   Your brilliant charms, your sweet but piercing eyes,
   Your grace—these were the riches, from the start,
   That won you my affection and my heart.
   These treasures are my one and only aim.

HENRIETTE. I'm grateful for your honorable flame.
   It fills me with confusion, and I find
   I'm sorry, sir, I can't respond in kind.
   Esteem for you, that I have plenty of,
   But there's an obstacle to any love: 1480
   A heart, you know, cannot belong to two;
   Mine's for Clitandre; it cannot be for you.
   I grant the merit on your side is great,
   That I'm not good at picking out a mate,
   That all the handsome talents you reveal
   Should win my love; but that's not what I feel;
   And all that reasoning can do, I find,
   Is make me feel ashamed to be so blind.

TRISSOTIN. Just give your hand, and that will be the start

1490   That will enable me to win your heart;
          And from countless attentions you will learn
          —So I presume—to love me in return.

HENRIETTE. No, sir, my first allegiance is intact,
          And nothing you can do will change that fact.
          I'm speaking frankly and without ado,
          And what I say should be no shock to you.
          The tenderness that sets a heart aglow
          Does not arise from merit, as you know;
          Caprice too plays a part; hard as we try,

1500   When we're in love, often we can't say why.
          If wisdom, sir, determined love's selection,
          You would have all my heart, all my affection;
          But it is otherwise with love, we see.
          Blind as I am, I beg you, let me be,
          And don't let them resort to violence
          To wring from me a forced obedience.
          No good man wants to owe a woman's hand
          Just to her parents' power to command,
          Nor wants his love to play a victim's part,

1510   Nor any but a freely given heart.
          My mother's wish, you know, is not my own;
          Don't seek to win me by her choice alone;
          No, take your love away; at other doors
          Offer a heart as highly prized as yours.

TRISSOTIN. How can this heart bring such a thing about?
          Give it commands that it can carry out.
          How, Madame, can it move in that direction,
          Unless you stop arousing man's affection
          By all the heavenly charms that you display?

1520 HENRIETTE. Come now, Monsieur! I hope you've had your
          say.
          What! All the Irises that fill your verse,
          The Phyllises whose beauties you rehearse,
          And from whose side you vow never to part . . . ?

TRISSOTIN. To those my mind is speaking, not my heart.
          For them only a poet's love I feel;
          For the fair Henriette my love is real.

HENRIETTE. Oh, sir, I beg of you . . .

TRISSOTIN. If I offend,
I fear that my offense may never end.
This flame, which you've not noticed hitherto,
Fixes its hopes eternally on you; 1530
Nothing can keep its loving transports down;
And though you greet my efforts with a frown,
A mother's help I cannot turn aside,
Who'd crown my flame by making you my bride;
Provided I enjoy this ecstasy,
The way it happens matters not to me.

HENRIETTE. But do you know you play a risky part
In using force upon a woman's heart?
It's not the safest thing, you must confess,
When a girl marries you under duress; 1540
And such constraint may put it in her head
To take reprisals that a man must dread.

TRISSOTIN. Such talk does not make me at all alarmed.
Against all accidents the sage is armed;
Thanks to the help reason alone can bring,
He rises far above that sort of thing,
And feels no bitterness within his soul
At anything outside of his control.

HENRIETTE. Honestly, sir, I'm overjoyed with you;
And I'd not thought philosophy could do 1550
All that I see it can, thus to prepare
Men for the accidents they have to bear.
This strength of soul, in you so manifest,
Deserves to undergo a glorious test,
And find a mate who'll labor every day,
With loving care, to put it on display;
And since, to tell the truth, I'm not the one
To give it the place it merits in the sun,
I leave it to another, and now state
That I give up all claims to be your mate. 1560

TRISSOTIN. We'll soon see the result of the affair,
And now I think the Notary is there.

Scene 2.   CHRYSALE, CLITANDRE, MARTINE, HENRIETTE

CHRYSALE. Ah, daughter! I'm so glad to see you here.
    Come on and do your duty; it is clear;
    Your father's will must be a law to you.
    I mean to teach your mother a thing or two,
    And the better to defy her, here's Martine,
    Whom herewith I bring back upon the scene.

HENRIETTE. Your resolutions I can only praise.
1570   Be sure, father, you do not change your ways.
    Be firm in willing what you once decide,
    And don't let kindness throw you off your stride;
    Do not let down, but see that you so act
    That Mother will not win the day in fact.

CHRYSALE. What's this? You think I am a willing tool?

HENRIETTE. Heaven forbid!

CHRYSALE.   Perhaps an utter fool?

HENRIETTE. I don't say that.

CHRYSALE.   Then you don't think I can
    Act like a firm and reasonable man?

HENRIETTE. Of course, father.

CHRYSALE.   Then do I lack the skill
1580   To make my family respect my will?

HENRIETTE. No, no.

CHRYSALE.   Then I'm so feeble, I suppose,
    As to let my wife lead me by the nose?

HENRIETTE. Oh no, father.

CHRYSALE.   Then what's this all about?
    You have a funny way of speaking out.

HENRIETTE. If I offended you, I didn't mean it.

CHRYSALE. I rule this house and everything that's in it.

HENRIETTE. Quite so, father.

CHRYSALE.   And no one here but me
   Can give the orders.

HENRIETTE.   Yes, I quite agree.

CHRYSALE. Mine is the headship here, the sole command.

HENRIETTE. Indeed.

CHRYSALE.   I must dispense my daughter's hand.   *1590*

HENRIETTE. Oh, yes!

CHRYSALE.   Heaven gives me power over your fate.

HENRIETTE. Who would deny it?

CHRYSALE.   When you take a mate,
   Although your mother tries to have her way,
   It is your father that you must obey.

HENRIETTE. To see you have your will is all I ask.
   I only hope you're equal to the task.

CHRYSALE. I'll give my wife the orders, and see how . . .

CLITANDRE. She and the Notary are coming now.

CHRYSALE. All of you lend a hand.

MARTINE.   Leave it to me.
   I'll help you out, if help there needs to be.   *1600*

Scene 3. PHILAMINTE, BÉLISE, ARMANDE, TRISSOTIN,
the NOTARY, CHRYSALE, CLITANDRE, HENRIETTE, MARTINE

PHILAMINTE. You cannot change the uncouth style you use,
   And write the contract nicely if you choose?

NOTARY. Our style is good, and I would be absurd,
   Madame, to try to change a single word.

BÉLISE. Ah! What barbarity in France today!
    But at least honor learning in one way:
    In minas and in talents pray set down
    The dowry; not a word of franc or crown;
    In ides and calends have the dates expressed.

1610 NOTARY. I, Madame? If I did what you request,
    My colleagues all would hoot with might and main.

PHILAMINTE. We grieve at this barbarity in vain.
    Come, sir, sit at the table now and write.
    (Seeing MARTINE*)* Aha! This wench still dares affront my
      sight?
    In my house? Who allowed her to return?

CHRYSALE. Presently, at our leisure, you shall learn.
    But now we've other matters to decide.

NOTARY. Now, to the contract. Where's the future bride?

PHILAMINTE. I'm marrying off the younger.

NOTARY.   I'll just set
    That down.

1620 CHRYSALE.   She's here; her name is Henriette.

NOTARY. All right. The groom?

PHILAMINTE.   I give her as her mate
    (Pointing to TRISSOTIN*)* This gentleman.

CHRYSALE.   And I am here
    to state
    (Pointing to CLITANDRE*)* This is the gentleman for her,
    I vow.

NOTARY. Two grooms! That's one too many.

PHILAMINTE.   Don't stop
    now!
    Put down Trissotin for my daughter's hand.

CHRYSALE. Put down Clitandre as groom; that's a command.

NOTARY. You'd better talk this over, and agree
    Which of the two your son-in-law shall be.

PHILAMINTE. Be guided, sir, be guided by my choice.

CHRYSALE. Just hearken, sir, just hearken to my voice.   *1630*

NOTARY. Tell me, which of you two shall I obey?

PHILAMINTE. What? Do you go against the things I say?

CHRYSALE. A man should seek my daughter for his bride
   Just for our money? That I can't abide.

PHILAMINTE. A lot he cares about your precious money!
   Such a thought for a sage? Why, don't be funny!

CHRYSALE. My choice is made; Clitandre's the man for her.

PHILAMINTE. And for her mate this person I prefer;
   On this point I've made up my mind alone.

CHRYSALE. Well! That's a pretty high and mighty tone!   *1640*

MARTINE. Women should not give orders, and I ben
   For always yielding the upper hand to men.

CHRYSALE. Well said.

MARTINE.   I may get sacked, but still I know
   The hen must wait and let the rooster crow.

CHRYSALE. No doubt.

MARTINE.   People look at a man askance
   When it's his wife at home who wears the pants.

CHRYSALE. That's true.

MARTINE.   I tell you, if I had a spouse,
   I'd want him to be master of the house;
   I wouldn't love one who'd let *me* boss *him;*
   And if I argued too much, by some whim,   *1650*
   Or talked too loud, I'd think it would be fine
   If with a slap he brought me back in line.

CHRYSALE. Well spoken.

MARTINE.   Master's doing as he oughter
   To want a proper husband for his daughter.

CHRYSALE. Yes.

MARTINE.   Why not leave her have her way. Lord knows
          Clitandre is young and handsome. Why impose
          This scholar and his endless monologue?
          She wants a husband, not a pedagogue.
          Latin and Greek are not her cup of tea,
1660   Nor Monsieur Trissotin, if you ask me.

CHRYSALE. That's good.

PHILAMINTE.   We have to listen to her speech.

MARTINE. Pedants are good for nothing but to preach;
          And for my husband, once more I submit,
          I'd never want to take a man of wit.
          Wit will not help a couple in rough weather,
          And books and marriage do not go together.
          If I marry, I want my husband's needs
          To make of me the only book he reads;
          By your leave, Ma'am, he shan't know A from B,
1670   And he shall be a doctor just for me.

PHILAMINTE. Is it done? Is your worthy spokesman through?
          I've held my temper.

CHRYSALE.   What she said is true.

PHILAMINTE. And I, to bring this squabble to an end,
          Must carry out my will in this, my friend.
          This man shall marry Henriette today.
          I want it. There is nothing more to say.
          If you have pledged him Henriette to wed,
          Then offer him the elder's hand instead.

CHRYSALE. *There's* a suggestion for a settlement.
1680   What do you say, you two? Do you consent?

HENRIETTE. Oh, father!

CLITANDRE.   Oh, sir!

BÉLISE   I can well believe
          There are offers he rather would receive;
          But we're establishing a kind of love
          As pure as is the morning star above:
          The thinking substance has a place in it,
          But the extensive substance, not a bit.

Scene 4. ARISTE, CHRYSALE, PHILAMINTE, BÉLISE,
HENRIETTE, ARMANDE, TRISSOTIN, *the* NOTARY,
CLITANDRE, MARTINE

ARISTE. I hate to vex this joyful gathering
  By the bad tidings that I have to bring.
  These letters both bear news that I deplore,
  Because I feel the grief you have in store.   1690
  (To PHILAMINTE*)* For you, from your attorney, I bring
    this.
  (To CHRYSALE*)* This is for you from Lyon.

PHILAMINTE.   What's amiss,
  I wonder, that deserves such great concern?

ARISTE. If you will read this letter, you will learn.

PHILAMINTE *(reads). Madame, I have requested your
  brother to give you this letter, which will tell you what I
  did not dare come to tell you. Your great negligence for
  your affairs was the reason why the clerk of your judge of
  first instance did not notify me, and you have irrevocably
  lost your suit, which you should have won.*

CHRYSALE. Your suit is lost!

PHILAMINTE.   Why trouble yourself so?
  My heart is quite unshaken by this blow.
  Pray, pray, show a less ordinary soul,
  And accept fortune's shafts with self-control.

PHILAMINTE *(reads). The scant care that you take is costing
  you forty thousand crowns, and it is to pay this sum,
  together with the costs, that you are condemned by the
  decision of the court.*

PHILAMINTE *(speaks). Condemned!* That shocking word
    does not belong
  Except to criminals.

ARISTE.   Indeed he's wrong,   1700

And your complaint was just and for the best.
He should have said that there was a request—
And from the court—to pay up for your suit
The forty thousand crowns, and costs to boot.

PHILAMINTE. Let's see the other.

CHRYSALE *(reads). Sir, the friendship that binds me to your
brother makes me take an interest in all that concerns you.
I know that you have put your property in the hands of
Argante and Damon, and I inform you that on the same
day they both went bankrupt.*

CHRYSALE *(speaks).* Heavens! All at once to lose my whole
estate!

PHILAMINTE. Oh, what a shameful outburst! That's just fate.
A truly wise man never suffers pains,
And if he loses all, himself remains.
Let's wind up our affair, and stop your fuss:
1710   His wealth will be enough for him and us.

TRISSOTIN. No, Madame, your persistence is in vain.
You're all against this marriage, that is plain,
And I will not impose myself by force.

PHILAMINTE. This is a very sudden change of course!
It follows close on our reduced condition.

TRISSOTIN. I'm tired at last of so much opposition.
All this to-do impels me to resign,
And I don't want a heart that won't be mine.

PHILAMINTE. I see, I see, with disenchanted eyes,
1720   What up to now I would not recognize.

TRISSOTIN. You may see anything you want to see,
And how you take it matters not to me.
I'm not the man to suffer the disgrace
Of the rebuffs that here I have to face.
I deserve more esteem than I receive.
You don't want me? I kiss your hands and leave. *(Exit)*

PHILAMINTE. How he has bared his mercenary soul
And fallen short of a philosopher's role!

CLITANDRE. I'm no philosopher, but none the less,
 I wish to share your lot in your distress.   *1730*
 And I make bold to offer, with my hand,
 Whatever wealth I have at my command.

PHILAMINTE. Such generous conduct, sir, I do admire,
 And I am glad to crown your heart's desire.
 Your eager ardor wins you Henriette . . .

HENRIETTE. I've changed my mind, Mother, and I regret
 That I must go against your will in this.

CLITANDRE. What? Will you then oppose my hopes for bliss?
 And when my love wins over each and all . . .

HENRIETTE. Clitandre, I know that your estate is small,   *1740*
 And when I thought it good for your affairs,
 I hoped to satisfy my fondest prayers,
 And always wished to have you for my mate;
 But now that we are set apart by fate,
 I love you enough, in this extremity,
 Not to load you with our adversity.

CLITANDRE. But with you any fate would be most fair;
 Without you there's no fate that I could bear.

HENRIETTE. Love always talks this way, but then forgets;
 Let us avoid a later day's regrets.   *1750*
 Nothing so surely frays the marriage-knot
 As lack of simple things that we have not;
 And often even commonplace vexations
 Lead to regrettable recriminations.

ARISTE. Is that the only reason, may I know,
 Why you now plan to let Clitandre go?

HENRIETTE. Yes, but for that his hand I'd gladly take,
 And I have turned him down just for love's sake.

ARISTE. Accept this bond then without more ado.
 The news that I just gave you is untrue.   *1760*
 It was a trick that I made trial of,
 Hoping to be of service to your love,
 Open my sister's eyes, and manifest
 How her philosopher would meet the test.

CHRYSALE. Heaven be praised!

PHILAMINTE.					This thought makes me re-
joice:
That base deserter will regret his choice.
His sordid avarice will be chastised,
Seeing this marriage grandly solemnized.

CHRYSALE (to CLITANDRE). You'll marry her all right. I
always knew it.

1770 ARMANDE (to PHILAMINTE). You sacrifice me then. How can
you do it?

PHILAMINTE. No, I will not be sacrificing you,
And you've philosophy to help you through
To see their ardor crowned without dismay.

BÉLISE. Let him take note, I'm in his heart to stay.
When despair leads a man to take a wife,
He may repent at leisure all his life.

CHRYSALE (to the NOTARY). Come, sir, follow the order I've
decreed,
And as I've said, draw up the marriage-deed.

The Imaginary Invalid

THE IMAGINARY INVALID

A comedy in three acts in prose, mingled with music and dance, first performed on February 10, 1673 at the Théâtre du Palais-Royal in Paris by Molière's Troupe du Roi. Molière played Argan; Mlle. Molière, Angélique; La Grange, Cléante; Beauval, Thomas Diafoirus; Mlle. Beauval, Toinette; Louise Beauval, Louison. The play was a success; but at the fourth performance, on February 17, Molière was seized with a coughing spell, coughed up blood, finished his part, but died later in the day.

His last year had been a hard one. Death had taken Madeleine Béjart one year to the day before it took him, and in the fall his infant son Pierre. The musician Lulli, ever popular with the King, had become a greedier rival than ever, monopolizing all musical spectacles at court and securing sole rights to all the entertainments in which—often with Molière—he had collaborated. Molière had hoped to present *The Imaginary Invalid* before the King, but no invitation was forthcoming. An earlier slap of a different kind, to which *The Imaginary Invalid* is an extraordinary answer, was the publication in 1670 of a rather venomous skit at his expense, whose title speaks for itself, Le Boulanger de Chalussay's *Élomire hypocondre*.[1]

The coincidences and ironies surrounding the play are extraordinary and macabre, making the humor often seem black. An author-actor who is desperately ill and knows it writes a play about a completely imaginary invalid such as some had accused him of being; plays that role himself; in the role invites (or at least says that if he were a doctor he would invite) Molière to "Croak, croak" for his blasphemous impertinence in making fun of medicine; and in his fourth performance of the role is seized

[1] *Élomire the Hypochondriac.* Élomire is of course an anagram of Molière.

431

with a fatal attack of his illness, thus almost literally dying in the part.

There are other serious overtones. Many critics have noted that the doctors in this play offer many analogies with theologians. They speak with the same formidable authority, anathematize with the same deadly enthusiasm, and welcome candidates with somewhat similar rites. I doubt that this is deliberate on Molière's part; but it is hard to imagine that he was wholly unaware of it, and he may not have minded much. He had had a hard time with theologians; he valued human nature and never liked tyrants, especially when they happened to be pedants as well.

Yet the play sparkles with humor, from the great opening scene in which Argan tots up his medical bills, argues with his apothecary *in absentia*, and methodically cuts them all down, through the elaborate addresses of the robot Thomas Diafoirus, the mock solemnity of Dr. Purgon's curse, and Toinette's inspired play as a doctor-to-end-all-doctors, to the pig Latin ceremony that swiftly makes Argan a doctor himself. The demonstration that disease is a career to Argan; the constant clash between his choleric health and his role as invalid; the perpetual interplay of illusion and reality; the deft teasing of Toinette—all these contribute richly to the fun.

Just as in *The Learned Women,* the trick that reveals to Argan the true feelings of those around him brings about the happy ending but does not cure him; for the play is a comedy, and Molière's heroes are not to be cured. From first to last *The Imaginary Invalid* is a triumph of comic make-believe over grim reality.

THE IMAGINARY INVALID

CHARACTERS

ARGAN, *an imaginary invalid*
BÉLINE, *Argan's second wife*
ANGÉLIQUE, *daughter of Argan by his first marriage, in love with Cléante*
LOUISON, *young daughter of Argan by his first marriage, sister of Angélique*
BÉRALDE, *Argan's brother*
CLÉANTE, *in love with Angélique*
MONSIEUR DIAFOIRUS,[2] *a doctor*
THOMAS DIAFOIRUS, *his son, suitor of Angélique*
MONSIEUR PURGON, *Argan's doctor*
MONSIEUR FLEURANT, *an apothecary*
MONSIEUR BONNEFOY, *notary*
TOINETTE, *maidservant*

The scene is Argan's bedroom in his house in Paris.

PROLOGUE

(At the first performance, on February 10, 1673, the play opened with a pastoral ballet honoring the recent military victories of Louis XIV in Holland. This was superseded in 1674 by a shorter one announcing the play but having no other relation to the action. Neither prologue is given here.)

2 Many of Molière's characters' names in this play are suggestive. Diafoirus would be rather like Diarrheus or Diaturdus in English; Fleurant, like Sniffer or Smeller; Bonnefoy means Good Faith; Purgon speaks for itself.

ACT I

Scene 1. ARGAN

ARGAN *(sitting alone at a table in his bedroom, adding up his apothecary's bills with counters, and talking to himself as he does).* Three and two makes five, and five makes ten, and ten makes twenty. Three and two makes five. "Plus, on the twenty-fourth, a little enema, insinuative, preparatory, and emollient, to soften up, moisten, and refresh the gentleman's bowels." What I like about Monsieur Fleurant, my apothecary, is that his bills are always very civil: "the gentleman's bowels, thirty sous." Yes, but, Monsieur Fleurant, being civil isn't everything, you've got to be reasonable too, and not fleece your patients. Thirty sous for an enema! I'm your very humble servant, and I've told you so already. You put them down in my other bills at only twenty sous, and twenty sous in apothecary's language means ten sous. Here they are, ten sous *(dropping some counters into a slot).* "Plus, on the said day, a good detergent enema composed of double catholicon,[3] rhubarb, rose honey, etc., according to the prescription, to flush, clean, and scour the gentleman's lower intestine, thirty sous." With your permission, ten sous. "Plus, on the said day, in the evening, a hepatic, soporific, and somniferous julep compounded to put the gentleman to sleep, thirty-five sous." I've no complaint about that one, for it made me sleep well. Ten, fifteen, sixteen, and seventeen sous, six deniers.[4] "Plus, on the twenty-fifth, a good purgative and tonic concoction of fresh cassia with Levantine senna, etc.,

---

[3] Rhubarb and senna.
[4] Twelve deniers make one sou, twenty sous make one franc. In all these calculations Argan plans—as was customary enough in his time—to pay exactly half of the apothecary's adjusted bill.

according to Monsieur Purgon's prescription, to expel and
evacuate the gentleman's bile, four francs." Ah, Monsieur
Fleurant, you're joking; you have to live with your patients.
Monsieur Purgon didn't prescribe for you to put down four
francs. Put down . . . put down three francs, if you please.
Twenty . . . thirty sous. "Plus, on the said day, an anodine
and astringent potion, to make the gentleman rest, thirty
sous." All right, ten . . . fifteen sous. "Plus, on the twenty-
sixth, a carminative enema, to drive out the gentleman's
wind, thirty sous." Ten sous, Monsieur Fleurant. "Plus, the
gentleman's enema repeated in the evening, as above, thirty
sous." Monsieur Fleurant, ten sous. "Plus, on the twenty-
seventh, a good medicine compounded to speed along and
drive out the gentleman's noxious humors, three francs." All
right, twenty . . . thirty sous; I'm very glad you're being
reasonable. "Plus, on the twenty-eighth, a dose of whey,
clarified and edulcorated, to dulcify, lenify, temper, and refresh the gentleman's blood, twenty sous." All right, ten
sous. "Plus a cordial and preservative potion, compounded
with twelve grains of bezoar, lemon and pomegranate syrups,
etc., according to the prescription, five francs." Ah! Monsieur
Fleurant, gently, if you please; if you treat people like that,
they won't want to be sick any more; content yourself with
four francs. Twenty . . . and forty sous. Three and two makes
five, and five makes ten, and ten makes twenty. Sixty-three
francs four sous six deniers. So this month I've taken one,
two, three, four, five, six, seven, eight doses of medicine and
one, two, three, four, five, six, seven, eight, nine, ten, eleven,
twelve enemas; and last month there were twelve doses of
medicine and twenty enemas. I don't wonder that I'm not
as well this month as last. I'll tell Monsieur Purgon this, so
that he'll set this right. Come on, have all this taken
away! . . . There's nobody here. No matter what I say, they
always leave me alone; there's no way to keep them here.
(He rings a bell to summon his servants.) They don't hear
a thing, and my bell doesn't make enough noise. *(Ringing
and calling out at the same time, more and more loudly and
angrily)* Ting-a-ling, ting-a-ling, ting-a-ling: nothing doing.
Ting-a-ling a-ling a-ling: they're deaf. Toinette! Ting-a-ling
a-ling a-ling: just as if I wasn't ringing. You slut, you hussy!
Ting-a-ling a-ling a-ling: I'm getting mad. *(Throws away the*

bell and simply shouts.) Ting-a-ling a-ling a-ling: you jade, go to the devil! Is it possible that they should leave a poor invalid all alone like this? Ting-a-ling a-ling a-ling: that's really pitiful! Ting-a-ling a-ling a-ling: oh, good Lord! They're going to leave me here to die. Ting-a-ling a-ling a-ling!

Scene 2. TOINETTE, ARGAN

TOINETTE *(coming into the room)*. Here we are.

ARGAN. Oh, you slut! Oh, you hussy . . . !

TOINETTE *(pretending to have bumped her head)*. Confound your impatience! You hurry people so that I got a big bang on the head on the corner of the shutter.

ARGAN *(angrily)*. Ah, you traitress . . . !

TOINETTE *(interrupting him and trying to keep him from shouting by always wailing)*. Oh!

ARGAN. It's been . . .

TOINETTE. Oh!

ARGAN. It's been an hour . . .

TOINETTE. Oh!

ARGAN. Since you left me . . .

TOINETTE. Oh!

ARGAN. Will you shut up, you hussy, and let me scold you?

TOINETTE. Indeedy! My word! That's nice, after what I've done to myself.

ARGAN. You made me shout myself hoarse, you slut.

TOINETTE. And you, you made me bang my head; that's just as bad; we'll call it quits, if you like.

ARGAN. What, you hussy . . . ?

TOINETTE. If you scold me, I'll cry.

ARGAN. You'd leave me, you traitress . . .

TOINETTE *(still interrupting him).* Oh!

ARGAN. You wench, you want . . .

TOINETTE. Oh!

ARGAN. What! I won't even have the pleasure of scolding her?

TOINETTE. Scold me, have your fill of it, I'm willing.

ARGAN. You stop me, you wench, by interrupting me at every turn.

TOINETTE. If you have the pleasure of scolding me, for my part, I must have the pleasure of crying. To each his own, that's only fair. Oh!

ARGAN. All right, I've got to put up with it. Take this away, you hussy, take this away. *(Gets up from his chair.)* Did my enema today work well?

TOINETTE. Your enema?

ARGAN. Yes. Did I produce plenty of bile?

TOINETTE. Faith! I don't get mixed up in those affairs. It's up to Monsieur Fleurant to poke his nose into it, since he makes his profit from it.

ARGAN. See that they have some hot water ready, for the other that I'm to take in a while.

TOINETTE. That Monsieur Fleurant and that Monsieur Purgon are having a gay old time over your body; they have a good milch cow in you; and I'd really like to ask them what ails you, for them to give you so many remedies.

ARGAN. Be quiet, you ignoramus, it's not up to you to question the doctor's orders. Have my daughter Angélique sent in, I have something to say to her.

TOINETTE. Here she comes of her own accord; she must have guessed what was on your mind.

Scene 3. ANGÉLIQUE, TOINETTE, ARGAN

ARGAN. Come here, Angélique; you've come at a good time; I wanted to talk to you.

ANGÉLIQUE. Here I am ready to hear you.

ARGAN (running over to the basin). Wait. Give me my stick. I'll be right back.

TOINETTE (teasing him). Go quick, sir, go. Monsieur Fleurant gives us plenty of business to do.

Scene 4. ANGÉLIQUE, TOINETTE

ANGÉLIQUE (confidentially, with a languishing look). Toinette.

TOINETTE. What?

ANGÉLIQUE. Look at me a minute.

TOINETTE. Well! I'm looking at you.

ANGÉLIQUE. Toinette.

TOINETTE. Well, what, "Toinette"?

ANGÉLIQUE. Don't you guess what I want to talk about?

TOINETTE. I have a pretty good suspicion: about our young suitor; for it's about him that all our conversations have been for six days; and you're not well if you're not talking about him every moment.

ANGÉLIQUE. Since you know that, then why aren't you the first to talk to me about him, and why don't you spare me the pains of getting you started on the subject?

TOINETTE. You don't give me time to, and you're so eager about it that it's hard to get ahead of you.

ANGÉLIQUE. I confess to you that I couldn't possibly tire of talking about him, and that my heart warmly takes advantage of every chance to open itself to you. But tell me, Toinette, do you condemn the feelings I have for him?

TOINETTE. I wouldn't dream of it.

ANGÉLIQUE. Am I wrong to abandon myself to these sweet impressions?

TOINETTE. I don't say that.

ANGÉLIQUE. And would you have me be insensible to the tender protestations of the ardent passion he manifests for me?

TOINETTE. God forbid!

ANGÉLIQUE. Just tell me, don't you agree with me in seeing something providential, some act of destiny, in the unforeseen way we became acquainted?

TOINETTE. Yes.

ANGÉLIQUE. Don't you think that the act of coming to my defense without knowing me is the mark of a really gallant gentleman?

TOINETTE. Yes.

ANGÉLIQUE. That it's impossible to act more nobly?

TOINETTE. Agreed.

ANGÉLIQUE. And that he did all that with the best grace in the world?

TOINETTE. Oh, yes!

ANGÉLIQUE. Toinette, don't you think he's good looking?

TOINETTE. Assuredly.

ANGÉLIQUE. That he has the nicest manners in the world?

TOINETTE. Beyond a doubt.

ANGÉLIQUE. That there's something noble about his words as well as his actions?

TOINETTE. That's sure.

ANGÉLIQUE. That you could never hear anything more passionate than everything he says to me?

TOINETTE. That's true.

ANGÉLIQUE. And that there's nothing more irritating than the constraint I'm kept in, which blocks all communication of the sweet transports of that mutual ardor that Heaven inspires in us?

TOINETTE. You're right.

ANGÉLIQUE. But, my dear Toinette, do you think he loves me as much as he tells me he does?

TOINETTE. Mm hmm! Those things are sometimes subject to caution. Love's grimaces are a lot like the real thing; and I've seen some great actors in that field.

ANGÉLIQUE. Oh, Toinette! What are you saying? Alas! With the way he talks, would it really be possible that he wasn't telling me the truth?

TOINETTE. In any case, you'll soon be enlightened about that; and his resolution, that he wrote you about yesterday, to ask for your hand in marriage, is a quick way to let you know whether he's telling you the truth or not. That will be the real proof of it.

ANGÉLIQUE. Ah, Toinette! If that man deceives me, I'll never believe any man as long as I live.

TOINETTE. Here's your father coming back.

Scene 5. ARGAN, ANGÉLIQUE, TOINETTE

ARGAN (*sitting down in his chair*). Well now, daughter, I'm going to tell you a bit of news that you may not be expecting. Your hand is being requested in marriage. What's that? You're laughing. That word *marriage* is amusing, yes; there's nothing more laughable for girls. Ah! Nature, nature! From what I can see, daughter, I have no need to ask you if you are willing to get married.

ANGÉLIQUE. Father, I must do whatever you are pleased to order me to.

ARGAN. I'm very glad to have such an obedient daughter. So the matter is settled, and I have promised your hand.

ANGÉLIQUE. It is for me, father, to follow all your wishes blindly.

ARGAN. My wife, your stepmother, wanted me to make you a nun, and your little sister Louison as well; she's been set on that all along.

TOINETTE (*aside*). That innocent creature has her reasons.

ARGAN. She wouldn't consent to this marriage, but I won out, and my word is given.

ANGÉLIQUE. Ah, father! How grateful I am to you for all your goodness!

TOINETTE. In truth, I am grateful to you for that, and that's the most sensible thing you've done in your life.

ARGAN. I haven't yet seen the person; but I've been told that I'd be pleased with him, and you too.

ANGÉLIQUE. Certainly, father.

ARGAN. What, have you seen him?

ANGÉLIQUE. Since your consent authorizes me to be able to open my heart to you, I shall not hesitate to tell you that chance made us acquainted six days ago, and that the request made of you is an effect of the inclination that we formed for each other at first sight.

ARGAN. They didn't tell me that; but I'm very glad of it, and so much the better that things are that way. They say he's a tall, nice looking young man.

ANGÉLIQUE. Yes, father.

ARGAN. Well built.

ANGÉLIQUE. Undoubtedly.

ARGAN. Personally attractive.

ANGÉLIQUE. Yes indeed.

ARGAN. Good looking.

ANGÉLIQUE. Very good looking.

ARGAN. Sensible, and well born.

ANGÉLIQUE. Absolutely.

ARGAN. A very fine chap.

ANGÉLIQUE. As fine as can be.

ARGAN. And speaking good Latin and Greek.

ANGÉLIQUE. That I don't know.

ARGAN. And he'll be accepted as a doctor in three days.

ANGÉLIQUE. He, father?

ARGAN. Yes. Didn't he tell you so?

ANGÉLIQUE. No, really. Who told *you*?

ARGAN. Monsieur Purgon.

ANGÉLIQUE. Does Monsieur Purgon know him?

ARGAN. A fine question! Indeed he must know him, since he's his nephew.

ANGÉLIQUE. Cléante, Monsieur Purgon's nephew?

ARGAN. What Cléante? We're talking about the man for whom your hand has been asked in marriage.

ANGÉLIQUE. Indeed yes!

ARGAN. Well, he's Monsieur Purgon's nephew, son of his brother-in-law the doctor, Monsieur Diafoirus; and this son's name is Thomas Diafoirus, not Cléante; and we arranged that marriage this morning, Monsieur Purgon, Monsieur Fleurant, and I; and tomorrow this prospective son-in-law is to be brought to see me by his father. What's the matter? You look all flabbergasted!

ANGÉLIQUE. That, father, is because I now know that you were talking about one person, and I understood you to mean another.

TOINETTE. What, sir? You could have made such a ludicrous plan? And with all the money you have you'd like to marry your daughter to a doctor?

ARGAN. Yes. What business is it of yours, you impudent hussy?

TOINETTE. Good Lord! Easy now. You start right in with invectives. Can't we reason together without getting into a temper? There now, let's talk calmly. What is your reason, if you please, for such a marriage?

ARGAN. My reason is that, seeing myself sick and infirm as I am, I want to have doctors for a son-in-law and relatives, so as to assure myself of good assistance against my illness, to have in my family the sources of the remedies I need, and to be within reach of consultations and prescriptions.

TOINETTE. Well, that's telling me a reason, and it's a pleasure to be answering one another gently. But, sir, put your hand on your conscience: are you sick?

ARGAN. What, you wench, am I sick? Am I sick, you hussy?

TOINETTE. Well then, yes, sir, you're sick, let's have no quarrel about that; yes, you're very sick, I grant you that, and sicker than you think: that's settled. But your daughter should marry a husband for herself; and since she's not sick, it's not necessary to give her a doctor.

ARGAN. It's for me that I'm giving her this doctor; and a daughter with the right nature should be delighted to marry whatever is useful to her father's health.

TOINETTE. Faith, sir! Do you want me to give you a piece of advice, as a friend?

ARGAN. What is this advice?

TOINETTE. Not to think of this marriage.

ARGAN. And the reason?

TOINETTE. The reason? That your daughter won't consent to it.

ARGAN. She won't consent to it?

TOINETTE. No.

ARGAN. My daughter?

TOINETTE. Your daughter. She'll tell you that she wants no part of Monsieur Diafoirus, nor of his son Thomas Diafoirus, nor of all the Diafoiruses in the world.

ARGAN. Well, I want them. Besides, the match is more advantageous than you think. Monsieur Diafoirus has only that son for his sole heir, and what's more, Monsieur Purgon, who has neither wife nor children, will leave him his entire estate in view of this marriage; and Monsieur Purgon is a man who has a good eight thousand francs a year of income.

TOINETTE. He must have killed a lot of people to get so rich.

ARGAN. Eight thousand francs a year is something, without counting the father's money.

TOINETTE. Sir, all that is very well and good; but I still come back to my point. I advise you, between ourselves, to choose her another husband, and she's not cut out to be Madame Diafoirus.

ARGAN. And *I* want that to be.

TOINETTE. Oh, fie! Don't say that.

ARGAN. What do you mean, I shouldn't say that?

TOINETTE. Why, no.

ARGAN. And why shan't I say it?

TOINETTE. People will say you don't know what you're saying.

ARGAN. They'll say what they like; but I tell you, I want her to carry out the promise I've given.

TOINETTE. No: I'm sure she won't do it.

ARGAN. I'll darned well make her.

TOINETTE. She won't do it, I tell you.

ARGAN. She'll do it, or I'll put her in a convent.

TOINETTE. You?

ARGAN. I.

TOINETTE. Fine.

ARGAN. What do you mean, "fine"?

TOINETTE. You won't put her in a convent.

ARGAN. I won't put her in a convent?

TOINETTE. No.

ARGAN. No?

TOINETTE. No.

ARGAN. Well now! That's a good one! I won't put my daughter in a convent if I want to?

TOINETTE. No, I tell you.

ARGAN. Who'll stop me?

TOINETTE. You yourself.

ARGAN. I?

TOINETTE. Yes, you won't have the heart to do it.

ARGAN. I will.

TOINETTE. You're joking.

ARGAN. I'm not joking one bit.

TOINETTE. Fatherly affection will get the better of you.

ARGAN. It won't get the better of me.

TOINETTE. A little tear or two, two arms around your neck,

a tenderly uttered "my dear little papa," will be enough to touch you.

ARGAN. All that won't do a thing.

TOINETTE. Yes, yes.

ARGAN. I tell you I won't back down.

TOINETTE. Fiddlesticks.

ARGAN. You mustn't say "fiddlesticks."

TOINETTE. Good Lord! I know you; you're naturally good.

ARGAN *(angrily)*. I am not good, I'm bad when I want to be.

TOINETTE. Gently, sir; you're forgetting that you're sick.

ARGAN. I absolutely command her to prepare to take the husband I say.

TOINETTE. And *I* absolutely forbid her to do anything of the sort.

ARGAN. What are we coming to? And what kind of effrontery is that, for a slut of a maidservant to talk that way in front of her master?

TOINETTE. When a master doesn't think what he's doing, a sensible servant has the right to correct him.

ARGAN *(running after Toinette)*. Oh! You insolent hussy, I'll brain you!

TOINETTE *(running away from him)*. It's my duty to oppose anything that may dishonor you.

ARGAN *(in a fury, chasing her around his chair, stick in hand)*. Come here, come here, I'll teach you how to talk.

TOINETTE *(running around the chair ahead of Argan)*. I'm concerned, as I should be, with not letting you do anything foolish.

ARGAN. Slut!

TOINETTE. No, I'll never consent to this marriage.

ARGAN. Gallows bait!

TOINETTE. I don't want her to marry your Thomas Diafoirus.

ARGAN. Jade!

TOINETTE. And she'll obey me rather than you.

ARGAN. Angélique, won't you stop this hussy?

ANGÉLIQUE. Oh, father! Don't make yourself sick.

ARGAN. If you don't stop her for me, I'll put my curse on you.

TOINETTE. And *I'll* disinherit her if she obeys you.

ARGAN (*weary of running after her, throwing himself into his chair*). Oh! Oh! I'm done for. It's enough to kill me.

Scene 6.   BÉLINE, ANGÉLIQUE, TOINETTE, ARGAN

ARGAN. Ah! My wife, come here.

BÉLINE. What's wrong, my poor husband?

ARGAN. Come over here and help me.

BÉLINE. What in the world is it, my sweet boy?

ARGAN. My darling!

BÉLINE. My dearest!

ARGAN. They've just made me angry!

BÉLINE. Alas! Poor little hubby! How did it happen, my dear?

ARGAN. That scoundrelly Toinette of yours got more insolent than ever.

BÉLINE. Then don't get excited.

ARGAN. She put me in a rage, darling.

BÉLINE. Easy, sweet boy.

ARGAN. For one whole hour she opposed the things I want to do.

BÉLINE. There, there, gently.

ARGAN. And had the effrontery to tell me I'm not sick.

BÉLINE. She's an impertinent hussy.

ARGAN. You know, sweetheart, how it really is.

BÉLINE. Yes, sweetheart, she's wrong.

ARGAN. My love, that slut will be the death of me.

BÉLINE. There now, there now!

ARGAN. She's the cause of all the bile I'm producing.

BÉLINE. Don't get so upset.

ARGAN. And I've been telling you for I don't know how long to dismiss her.

BÉLINE. Good Lord, dear boy! There are no servants, men or women, who don't have their faults. Sometimes one is forced to put up with their bad qualities on account of the good ones. This one is adroit, careful, diligent, and above all faithful; and you know that nowadays you need great precautions about the people you take on. Here now! Toinette!

TOINETTE. Madame?

BÉLINE. Why in the world do you make my husband angry?

TOINETTE (sweetly). I, Madame? Alas! I don't know what you mean, and all I think of is pleasing the master in all things.

ARGAN. Oh, the traitress!

TOINETTE. He told us he wanted to give his daughter in marriage to the son of Monsieur Diafoirus; I answered that I thought it was an advantageous match for her, but that I thought he'd do better to put her in a convent.

BÉLINE. There's no great harm in that, and I think she's right.

ARGAN. Ah, my love! You believe her! She's a scoundrel: she said all kinds of insolent things to me.

BÉLINE. Well, I believe you, my dear. There, pull yourself together. Listen, Toinette, if you ever make my husband angry, I'll put you out. Here, give me his fur-lined cloak and some pillows, so I can get him comfortable in his chair. You're all every which way. Pull your night cap well down over your ears; there's nothing like getting air in your ears for catching cold.

ARGAN. Oh, my darling! I'm so grateful to you for all the care you take of me!

BÉLINE *(putting the pillows around Argan and arranging them).* Get up, let me put this under you. Let's put this one here for you to lean on, and that one on the other side. Let's put this one behind your back, and that other one there to prop up your head.

TOINETTE *(putting a pillow roughly over his head and running off).* And this one to protect you from the evening dew.

ARGAN *(getting up in anger and throwing all the pillows at Toinette).* Ah, you scoundrel, you're trying to smother me!

BÉLINE. There now, there now! Why, what's the matter?

ARGAN *(out of breath, throwing himself into his chair).* Oh, oh, oh! I'm all in!

BÉLINE. Why do you get so angry? She meant well.

ARGAN. My love, you don't know the malice of that she-devil. Ah! She's got me beside myself; and I'll need more than eight doses of medicine and a dozen enemas to make up for all this.

BÉLINE. There, there, my little sweet, calm down a bit.

ARGAN. Honey, you're my only consolation.

BÉLINE. Poor dear boy.

ARGAN. To try to show my gratitude for the love you bear me, sweetheart, I want, as I told you, to make my will.

BÉLINE. Ah, my darling! Let's not talk about that, I beg you. I can't abide the thought of it, and the very word *will* makes me shudder with pain.

ARGAN. I had told you to speak to your notary about that.

BÉLINE. There he is in there; I brought him with me.

ARGAN. Then have him come in, my love.

BÉLINE. Alas, my dear! When someone really loves her husband, she's hardly in any condition to think about all that.

Scene 7. *The* NOTARY, BÉLINE, ARGAN

ARGAN. Come here, Monsieur de Bonnefoy, come here. Have a
seat, please. My wife has told me, sir, that you're a very reliable man and quite a good friend of hers; and I've asked
her to speak to you about a will I want to make.

BÉLINE. Alas! I just can't talk about those things.

NOTARY. She explained your intentions to me, sir, and the plan
you have for her; and on that score I have this to tell you,
that you can't give anything to your wife by your will.

ARGAN. But why not?

NOTARY. Common law opposes it. If you were in a region of
statute law, that could be done; but in Paris and the regions
of common law, at least most of them, that can't be done, and
that disposition would be null and void. The only provision
that man and woman conjoined in marriage can make for
each other is a mutual gift *inter vivos;* even then there must
be no children, whether of the two conjoined, or of either
one of them, at the time of the decease of the first to die.

ARGAN. That's a mighty impertinent common law, that a man
can't leave anything to a wife who loves him tenderly and
takes such care of him. I'd like to consult my lawyer to see
how I might do something.

NOTARY. It's not lawyers you should go to, for ordinarily they're
strict about those things and imagine it's a great crime to
deal with the law by fraud. They're people who make difficulties and are ignorant of the detours of conscience. There are
other people to consult who are much more accommodating,
who have expedients for quietly getting around the law and
making something just that isn't permitted; who know how
to smooth out the difficulties of an affair and find ways
to elude the common law by some indirect advantage. Without that, where would we be every day? There has to be

some facility in things; otherwise we wouldn't get anything done, and I wouldn't give you a sou for our business.

ARGAN. Indeed, my wife had told me that you were very able, and a very reliable man. How can I go about it, if you please, to give her my estate and keep it from my children?

NOTARY. How can you go about it? You can quietly pick out some intimate friend of your wife, to whom in your will you'll give in due form all that you can; and then this friend will give everything back to her. Or again, you can contract a large number of obligations, all above board, toward various creditors, who will lend their names to your wife, and will put into her hands a declaration that what they've done was only to serve her. You can also, while you are alive, put ready cash in her hands, or notes that you may have, made payable to the bearer.

BÉLINE. Good Lord! You mustn't worry yourself about all that. If ever I don't have you, my sweet boy, I don't want to stay in this world.

ARGAN. My darling!

BÉLINE. Yes, my darling, if I'm unhappy enough to lose you . . .

ARGAN. My dear wife!

BÉLINE. Life won't mean a thing to me anymore.

ARGAN. My love!

BÉLINE. And I'll follow in your footsteps, to let you know the affection I have for you.

ARGAN. My darling, you're breaking my heart. Console yourself, please.

NOTARY. These tears are out of season, and things haven't come to that yet.

BÉLINE. Ah, sir! You don't know what it is to have a husband you love tenderly.

ARGAN. The only regret I'll have if I die, my darling, is not to have a child by you. Monsieur Purgon told me he'd have me have one.

NOTARY. That may still come.

ARGAN. I'll have to make my will, my love, in the way the
gentleman says; but as a precaution, I want to put into your
hands twenty thousand francs in gold, which I have in the
panel of my alcove, and two notes payable to the bearer
that are due me, one from Monsieur Damon, and the other
from Monsieur Gérante.

BÉLINE. No, no, I don't want any of that at all . . . Ah! How
much did you say there was in your alcove?

ARGAN. Twenty thousand francs, my love.

BÉLINE. Don't talk to me about money, I beg you . . . Ah!
How much are the two notes?

ARGAN. My darling, one is for four thousand francs, and the
other for six.

BÉLINE. All the money in the world, my darling, is nothing to
me compared with you.

NOTARY. Shall we proceed to the will?

ARGAN. Yes, sir; but we'll be better in my little study. *(Gets
up, then remembers his illness.)* My love, take me in, please.

BÉLINE. Come on, my poor sweet little boy.

Scene 8. ANGÉLIQUE, TOINETTE

TOINETTE. There they are with a notary, and I heard them
talking about a will. Your stepmother isn't falling asleep,
and no doubt it's some conspiracy against your interests
that she's pushing your father into.

ANGÉLIQUE. Let him dispose of his money as he likes, provided
he doesn't dispose of my heart. You see, Toinette, the plans
they're making to do violence to it. Don't abandon me, I
beg you, in the extremity I'm in.

TOINETTE. I, abandon you? I'd rather die. Your stepmother can make me her confidante and try to get me to work for her all she likes, but I've never been able to have any inclination for her, and I've always been on your side. Leave it to me: I'll do everything to serve you; but to serve you more effectively I want to change my line of attack, cover up the zeal I have for you, and pretend to fall in with the feelings of your father and your stepmother.

ANGÉLIQUE. Try, I beseech you, to let Cléante know about the marriage they've arranged.

TOINETTE. I have no one to use for that purpose but my sweetheart Punchinello, the old usurer, and it will cost me a few sweet nothings that I'm willing to spend for you. For today it's too late; but tomorrow bright and early I'll send for him, and he'll be delighted to . . .

BÉLINE (offstage). Toinette!

TOINETTE. They're calling me. Good night. Rely on me.

FIRST INTERLUDE

(Punchinello, coming to serenade his mistress, is interrupted by the violinists, then by the watch, whom he has to pay off to avoid being beaten. Since this interlude has nothing to do with the rest of the play, it is omitted here.)

ACT II

Scene 1. TOINETTE, CLÉANTE *(disguised)*

TOINETTE *(not recognizing* CLÉANTE*).* What do you want, sir?

CLÉANTE. What do I want?

TOINETTE *(recognizing him).* Aha! It's you? What a surprise! What have you come here for?

CLÉANTE. To learn my destiny, speak to the lovely Angélique, inquire about the feelings of her heart, and ask her what she has resolved about this fatal marriage I've been informed about.

TOINETTE. Yes, but you don't talk point-blank like that to Angélique. There have to be mysteries, and you've been told of the tight guard she's kept under, how they don't let her go out, or talk to anyone, and that it was only the curiosity of an elderly aunt of hers that got us permission to go to that play that was the scene of the birth of your passion; and we have taken good care not to speak of that adventure.

CLÉANTE. So I'm not coming here as Cléante and in the role of her sweetheart, but as a friend of her music teacher, who has authorized me to say that he's sending me in his place.

TOINETTE. Here's her father. Go out for a bit, and let me tell him that you're here.

Scene 2. ARGAN, TOINETTE, CLÉANTE

ARGAN. Monsieur Purgon told me to take a walk in my room in the morning, twelve times up and back; but I forgot to ask him whether he meant lengthwise or crosswise.

TOINETTE. Sir, here is a . . .

ARGAN. Speak softly, you slut; you're shaking up my whole brain, and you forget that you mustn't speak so loud to the sick.

TOINETTE. I wanted to tell you, sir . . .

ARGAN. Speak low, I tell you.

TOINETTE. Sir . . . *(Pretending to speak.)*

ARGAN. Eh?

TOINETTE. I tell you that . . . *(Pretending to speak.)*

ARGAN. What's that you say?

TOINETTE *(shouting).* I tell you that there's a man who wants to speak to you.

ARGAN. Have him come in. *(TOINETTE beckons to CLÉANTE to come forward.)*

CLÉANTE. Sir . . .

TOINETTE *(teasing).* Don't speak so loud, for fear of shaking up the master's brain.

CLÉANTE. Sir, I'm delighted to find you up and around and to see that you're better.

TOINETTE *(pretending to be angry).* What do you mean, he's better? That's not true. The master is always ill.

CLÉANTE. I heard that the gentleman was better, and I think he looks well.

TOINETTE. What do you mean, he looks well? The master looks

very badly, and the people who told you he was better don't know what they're talking about. He's never been so ill.

ARGAN. She's right.

TOINETTE. He walks, sleeps, eats, and drinks just like anyone else; but that doesn't keep him from being very sick.

ARGAN. That's true.

CLÉANTE. Sir, I'm terribly sorry. I've come on behalf of your daughter's singing teacher. He had to go to the country for a few days; and he sends me, as his intimate friend, in his place, to continue her lessons for him, for fear that by interrupting them she might come to forget what she already knows.

ARGAN. Very well. Call Angélique.

TOINETTE. I think, sir, it will be better for me to take the gentleman to her room.

ARGAN. No; have her come.

TOINETTE. He won't be able to give her a lesson properly unless they are alone.

ARGAN. Yes he will, yes he will.

TOINETTE. Sir, it will only deafen you, and it doesn't take anything to upset you in the state you're in, and shake up your brain.

ARGAN. Not at all, not at all; I like music, and I'll be very glad to. . . . Ah! Here she is! You, go see if my wife is dressed.

Scene 3.   ARGAN, ANGÉLIQUE, CLÉANTE

ARGAN. Come here, daughter; your music teacher has gone to the country, and here's someone he's sending in his place to teach you.

ANGÉLIQUE (*recognizing* CLÉANTE *as he turns to face her*). Ah, Heavens!

ARGAN. What is it? Why this surprise?

ANGÉLIQUE. It's . . .

ARGAN. What? What moves you so?

ANGÉLIQUE. Father, it's a surprising coincidence I find here.

ARGAN. How's that?

ANGÉLIQUE. I dreamed last night that I was in the worst predicament in the world, and that someone who looked just like this gentleman presented himself, I asked him for help, and he came and got me out of the trouble I was in; and my surprise was great to see unexpectedly, on arriving here, what I had in mind all night.

CLÉANTE. That's no unhappy lot, to occupy your mind whether you're asleep or awake, and my happiness would unquestionably be great if you were in some trouble that you thought me worthy to get you out of; and there's nothing I wouldn't do to . . .

Scene 4.   TOINETTE, CLÉANTE, ANGÉLIQUE, ARGAN

TOINETTE *(in derision)*. Faith, sir, I'm for you now, and I take back all I was saying yesterday. Here are Monsieur Diafoirus the father and Monsieur Diafoirus the son, come to pay you a visit. How well son-in-lawed[5] you will be! You're going to see the handsomest young fellow in the world, and the wittiest. He said just two words, which delighted me, and your daughter's going to be charmed with him.

ARGAN *(to* CLÉANTE, *who pretends he wants to go)*. Don't go away, sir. You see, I'm marrying off my daughter; and now they're bringing her her prospective husband, whom she hasn't yet seen.

CLÉANTE. That's doing me a great honor, to want me to be witness to such a charming interview.

5 The French (*engendré*) also, and normally, means "engendered."

ARGAN. He's the son of an able doctor, and the marriage will take place in four days.

CLÉANTE. Very good.

ARGAN. Just tell her music teacher about it, so he'll be at the wedding.

CLÉANTE. I won't fail to.

ARGAN. I'm inviting you too.

CLÉANTE. You do me much honor.

TOINETTE. Come, make room, here they are.

Scene 5.   MONSIEUR DIAFOIRUS, THOMAS DIAFOIRUS, ARGAN,
ANGÉLIQUE, CLÉANTE, TOINETTE

ARGAN (putting his hand to his hat without taking it off). Sir, Monsieur Purgon has forbidden me to uncover my head. You're in the business, you know the consequences.

MONSIEUR DIAFOIRUS. In all our visits we are there to bring help to the sick, and not to bring them any discomfort.

ARGAN. Sir, I receive . . .

(They both speak at the same time, interrupting each other.)

MONSIEUR DIAFOIRUS. We come here, sir . . .

ARGAN. With great joy . . .

MONSIEUR DIAFOIRUS. My son Thomas and I . . .

ARGAN. The honor you do me . . .

MONSIEUR DIAFOIRUS. To let you know, sir . . .

ARGAN. And I would have wished . . .

MONSIEUR DIAFOIRUS. The delight that is ours . . .

ARGAN. To be able to go to your house . . .

MONSIEUR DIAFOIRUS. For the kindness you do us . . .

ARGAN. To assure you . . .

MONSIEUR DIAFOIRUS. In being willing to receive us . . .

ARGAN. But you know, sir . . .

MONSIEUR DIAFOIRUS. Into the honor, sir . . .

ARGAN. What a poor invalid is . . .

MONSIEUR DIAFOIRUS. Of an alliance with you . . .

ARGAN. Who can do nothing else . . .

MONSIEUR DIAFOIRUS. And to assure you . . .

ARGAN. Than to tell you now . . .

MONSIEUR DIAFOIRUS. That in all matters that depend on my profession . . .

ARGAN. That he will seek every occasion . . .

MONSIEUR DIAFOIRUS. As well as in all others . . .

ARGAN. To let you know, sir . . .

MONSIEUR DIAFOIRUS. We shall always be ready, sir . . .

ARGAN. That he is entirely at your service.

MONSIEUR DIAFOIRUS. To demonstrate our zeal to you. *(Turning back to his son)* Come on, Thomas, step forward. Pay your compliments.

THOMAS DIAFOIRUS *(a great simpleton, recently issued from the schools, who does everything clumsily and at the wrong time).* Isn't it the father I'm supposed to begin with?

MONSIEUR DIAFOIRUS. Yes.

THOMAS DIAFOIRUS. Sir, I come to salute, recognize, cherish, and revere in you a second father; but a second father to whom I take the liberty of saying that I am more indebted than to the first. The first engendered me, but you have chosen me. He received me through necessity, but you have accepted me through kindness. What I have from him is a work of his body; but what I have from you is a work of your will; and the more the spiritual faculties are above the corporeal, the more I owe you, and the more I hold precious this future filiation, for which I come today to pay in advance my most humble and most respectful homage.

TOINETTE. Hurrah for the schools, which produce such able men!

THOMAS DIAFOIRUS. Was that all right, father?

MONSIEUR DIAFOIRUS. *Optime.*

ARGAN *(to* ANGÉLIQUE*).* Come on, greet the gentleman. *(*ANGÉLIQUE *curtseys.)*

THOMAS DIAFOIRUS. Do I kiss?

MONSIEUR DIAFOIRUS. Yes, yes.

THOMAS DIAFOIRUS *(to* ANGÉLIQUE*).* Madame, it is with justice that Heaven has granted you the fair name of mother-in-law,[6] since we . . .

ARGAN. It's not my wife, it's my daughter you're speaking to.

THOMAS DIAFOIRUS. Then where is she?

ARGAN. She's coming.

THOMAS DIAFOIRUS. Do I wait, father, till she comes?

MONSIEUR DIAFOIRUS. Go ahead and pay your compliment to Mademoiselle.

THOMAS DIAFOIRUS. Mademoiselle, no more nor less than the statue of Memnon gave forth a harmonious sound when it came to be lit by the sun's rays, even so I feel myself animated by a sweet transport at the apparition of the sun of your beauties. And as the naturalists note that the flower named heliotrope turns incessantly toward that day star, so my heart shall henceforth always turn toward the resplendent stars of your adorable eyes, as toward its only pole. So permit me, Mademoiselle, to append to the altar of your charms the offering of this heart, which breathes and aspires to no other glory than to be all its life, Mademoiselle, your most humble, most obedient, and most faithful servant and husband.

TOINETTE *(mocking him).* That's what it is to study, you learn to say beautiful things.

---

[6] The French is *belle-mère,* literally "beautiful-mother." It also means "stepmother," and might mean that here; but I think not.

ARGAN *(to* CLÉANTE*)*. Well! What do you say to that?

CLÉANTE. That the gentleman does wonders, and that if he's as good a doctor as he is an orator, it will be a pleasure to be a patient of his.

TOINETTE. Yes indeed. It will be something wonderful if he cures as well as he makes speeches.

ARGAN. Come, quick, my chair, and seats for everybody. You sit there, daughter. You see, sir, that everyone admires your son, and I think you're very fortunate to have a boy like that.

MONSIEUR DIAFOIRUS. Sir, it's not because I'm his father, but I may say that I have reason to be pleased with him, and that everyone who sees him speaks of him as a boy who has no wickedness in him. He has never had a very lively imagination, nor that sparkling wit that you notice in some; but it's by this that I have always augured well of his judgment, a quality required for the exercise of our art. When he was small, he never was what you'd call mischievous or lively. He was always mild, peaceful, and taciturn, never saying a word, and never playing all those little games that we call childish. We had all the trouble in the world in teaching him to read, and he was nine years old before he ever knew his letters. "All right," I used to say to myself, "the late-growing trees are the ones that bear the best fruit; you have much more trouble engraving on marble than on sand; but things are preserved there much longer, and this slowness of understanding, this heaviness of imagination, is the sign of a good judgment to come." When I sent him to school, he had trouble; but he stood firm against the difficulties, and his teachers always praised him to me for his assiduity and his hard work. Finally, by keeping hard at it, he succeeded in earning his *licence* gloriously; and I may say without vanity that in the two years he's been on the benches there is no candidate that has made more noise than he in all the disputations in our school. He's made himself redoubtable at this, and no act is ever passed without his arguing to the last ditch for the opposite proposition. He is firm in dispute, strong as a Turk on his principles, he never gives up his opinion, and he follows a line of reasoning down to the last recesses of logic. But what I like about him above all else, and in which he follows my example, is that he attaches himself blindly to the opinions of our ancients, and he has never been willing to understand or listen to the reasons and experiments of the so-called discoveries of our century, about the circulation of the blood, and other opinions of the same ilk.

THOMAS DIAFOIRUS (*drawing a great rolled thesis from his pocket and presenting it to* ANGÉLIQUE). I have maintained a thesis against the circulators, which, with the gentleman's permission, I make bold to present to Mademoiselle, as a homage I owe her of the first fruits of my mind.

ANGÉLIQUE. Sir, that's a useless article for me, and I'm no expert in those matters.

TOINETTE. Give it here, give it here; it's always worth taking for the picture; it will serve to decorate our bedroom.

THOMAS DIAFOIRUS. Also with the gentleman's permission, I invite you to come one of these days, for your entertainment, to see the dissection of a woman, on which I am to make a dissertation.

TOINETTE. That will be a delightful entertainment. There are some who put on a play for their sweethearts; but to put on a dissection is a much more gallant thing.

MONSIEUR DIAFOIRUS (*confidentially, to* ARGAN). For the rest, as regards the qualities requisite for marriage and propagation, I assure you that, according to the rules of our doctors, he is just as one could wish; he possesses the prolific virtue to a laudable degree, and he is of the proper temperament to engender and procreate well-conditioned children.

ARGAN. Isn't it your intention, sir, to push him at court and get him a position as a doctor there?

MONSIEUR DIAFOIRUS. To be frank with you, our profession among the great has never seemed agreeable to me, and I have always found it better for us to stick to the general public. The public is easy to deal with. You don't have to answer to anyone for your actions; and provided you follow the current of the rules of our art, you don't have to worry about anything that can happen. But what is annoying with the great is that when they fall ill they absolutely insist that their doctors cure them.

TOINETTE. That's a funny one, and they are mighty presumptuous to insist that you gentlemen cure them; you're not there for that; you're there only to receive your fees and prescribe remedies for them; it's up to them to be cured if they can.

MONSIEUR DIAFOIRUS. That's true. We're obliged only to treat people according to the proper forms.

ARGAN (to CLÉANTE). Sir, have my daughter sing a bit for the company.

CLÉANTE. I was awaiting your orders, sir, and it occurred to me, to entertain the company, to sing with Mademoiselle a scene from a little opera that was composed recently. (To ANGÉLIQUE) Here, this is your part. (Gives her a piece of paper.)

ANGÉLIQUE. Me? (Gets up and takes the paper.)

CLÉANTE (to ANGÉLIQUE). Don't refuse, please, and let me make you understand what the scene is that we are to sing. (To all) I have no singing voice, but it's enough here for me to make myself heard, and you will be good enough to excuse me because of the necessity I'm in to have Mademoiselle sing.

ARGAN. Are the verses nice?

CLÉANTE. This is really a little impromptu opera, and all you'll hear sung is rhythmic prose, or a kind of free verse, such as passion and necessity can inspire in two persons who say what they say by themselves, and speak extemporaneously.

ARGAN. Very well. Let's listen.

CLÉANTE. Here is the subject of the scene. A shepherd was attentive to the beauties of a performance, which had just begun, when his attention was distracted by a noise he heard nearby. He turns around and sees a brutish fellow mistreating a shepherdess with insolent words. Immediately he espouses the interests of a sex to which all men owe homage; and after giving the brute the punishment due to his insolence, he comes to the shepherdess and sees a young person who, from the two most beautiful eyes he had ever seen, was shedding tears, which he thought the most beautiful in the world. "Alas!" he says to himself, "is it possible for anyone to outrage so lovely a person? And what inhuman barbarian would not be touched by such tears?" He takes pains to stop them, these tears that he finds so beautiful; and the lovely shepherdess takes pains at the same time to thank him for this slight service of his, but in a manner so charming, so tender, and so passionate, that the shepherd cannot resist it; and each word, each glance is a flaming dart which he feels penetrating his heart. "Is there anything," he says, "that can deserve the lovely expression of such thanks? And what would a man not do, what service and what danger would he not hasten in delight to undergo, to win a single moment of the touching tenderness of so grateful a soul?"

The whole performance takes place without his paying any attention to it; but he complains that it is too short, because the end separates him from his adorable shepherdess; and from that first sight, from that first moment, he takes home with him all the greatest violence of several years of love. Now immediately he feels all the pangs of absence, and he is tormented at seeing no more what he has seen so little. He does all he can to see once again this vision, of which he retains night and day so dear an image; but the great constraint in which his shepherdess is kept deprives him of any means of doing so. The violence of his passion makes him resolve to ask to marry the adorable beauty without whom he can no longer live, and he obtains her permission to do so by a note which adroitly he succeeds in putting into her hands. But at the same time he is informed that the father of this beauty has arranged her marriage to another, and that all is being prepared to celebrate the ceremony.

Think what a cruel blow this is to the heart of this sad shepherd. Behold him stricken with a mortal sorrow. He cannot bear the frightful idea of seeing the one he loves in another's arms; and his love, in despair, makes him find a way to enter the house of his shepherdess, to learn her feelings and find out from her the destiny he must accept. There he finds the preparations for all he fears; there he sees the unworthy rival come whom a father's caprice opposes to the tenderness of his love. He sees this ridiculous rival, triumphant, with the lovely shepherdess, as with a conquest of which he is assured;

and this sight fills him with an anger which he finds hard to master. He casts pained glances at the one he adores; and his respect, and the presence of her father, keep him from saying anything except with his eyes. But finally he overcomes all constraint, and the transport of his love obliges him to speak to her thus:

> (Sings) *Fair Phyllis, too much pain have I;*
> *Break this harsh silence, tell me how you feel.*
> *My destiny you must reveal:*
> *Am I to live or shall I die?*

ANGÉLIQUE (*singing in response*)
> *You see me, Tircis, sad and melancholy,*
> *Confronted by this marriage that you dread;*
> *I raise my eyes to Heaven, I look at you, I sigh,*
> *And that is enough said.*

ARGAN. Well, well! I didn't think my daughter was good enough to sing at sight like that without hesitation.

CLÉANTE.
> *Alas! O lovely Phyllis,*
> *Can it be true that ever-loving Tircis*
> *Has such rapture for his part*
> *As to hold some small place within your heart?*

ANGÉLIQUE. *I've no defense in my extreme distress:*
> *Tircis, I love you, yes.*

CLÉANTE.
> *O words full of delight!*
> *Alas! Can I have heard aright?*
> *Say them again, Phyllis, and put my doubts to flight.*

ANGÉLIQUE.   *Yes, Tircis, I love you.*

CLÉANTE.   *Pray, Phyllis, one more time.*

ANGÉLIQUE   *I love you.*

CLÉANTE. *Begin again a hundred times, and never tire.*

ANGÉLIQUE.
> *I love you, I love you,*
> *Yes, Tircis, I love you.*

CLÉANTE. *O Gods, O kings, who see the world beneath your feet,*
> *Can you compare your happiness with mine?*
> *But, Phyllis, there's one thought*

> *That comes to mar my bliss:*
> *A rival, a rival . . .*

ANGÉLIQUE.   *Ah! I hate him more than death.*
And his presence is to me,
A torment, as it is to you.

CLÉANTE. *But your father's will can set your hopes awry.*

ANGÉLIQUE.   *I'd rather, rather die*
Than ever to comply,
Rather, rather die, rather die.

ARGAN. And what does the father say to all that?

CLÉANTE *(back to earth, after a pause).* He doesn't say a thing.

ARGAN. That's a stupid father, that father, to put up with all that nonsense without saying a thing.

CLÉANTE *(sings).*   *Ah! My love . . .*

ARGAN. No, no, that's enough of that. That play sets a very bad example. The shepherd Tircis is an impertinent fellow, and the shepherdess Phyllis an impudent girl, to talk that way in front of her father. Show me that paper. *(*ANGÉLIQUE *hands it over reluctantly.)* Aha! Why, where are the words you spoke? There's nothing written here but music.

CLÉANTE. Don't you know, sir, that they've recently invented a way to write the words with the notes themselves?

ARGAN. Very well. I'm your servant, sir; good-by. We could have gotten along very nicely without your silly opera.

CLÉANTE. I thought it would entertain you.

ARGAN. Stupid things aren't entertaining. Ah! Here's my wife.

Scene 6. BÉLINE, ARGAN, TOINETTE, ANGÉLIQUE, MONSIEUR DIAFOIRUS, THOMAS DIAFOIRUS

ARGAN. My love, here is the son of Monsieur Diafoirus.

THOMAS DIAFOIRUS *(beginning a memorized compliment, but unable to continue when his memory fails him).* Madame, it is with justice that Heaven has granted you the fair name of mother-in-law, since we see on your face . . .

BÉLINE. Sir, I am delighted to have come here at the right time to have the honor of seeing you.

THOMAS DIAFOIRUS. Since we see on your face . . . since we see on your face . . . Madame, you interrupted me in the middle of my sentence, and that has troubled my memory.

MONSIEUR DIAFOIRUS. Thomas, save that for another time.

ARGAN. Honey, I wish you'd been here just now.

TOINETTE. Ah, Madame! You missed a lot by not being here for the second father, the statue of Memnon, and the flower called heliotrope.

ARGAN. Come, daughter, take the gentleman's hand, and plight him your troth as your husband.

ANGÉLIQUE. Father.

ARGAN. Well then! "Father?" What does that mean?

ANGÉLIQUE. I beseech you, don't hurry things. At least give us the time to come to know each other, and to see within us the birth of that inclination for one another that is so necessary to make up a perfect union.

THOMAS DIAFOIRUS. As for me, Mademoiselle, it is already full born in me, and I have no need to wait any longer.

ANGÉLIQUE. If you are so prompt, sir, it is not the same with me, and I admit to you that your merit has not yet made enough impression on my soul.

ARGAN. Oh, well, well! There'll be plenty of time for that to develop when you're married to each other.

ANGÉLIQUE. Ah, father! Give me time, I beg you. Marriage is a bond that should never be imposed on a heart by force; and if the gentleman is an honorable man, he must not want to accept a person who would belong to him by constraint.

THOMAS DIAFOIRUS. *Nego consequentiam,*[7] Mademoiselle, and I can be an honorable man and still be willing to accept you from the hands of your father.

ANGÉLIQUE. That's a bad way to make someone love you, to do her violence.

THOMAS DIAFOIRUS. We read of the ancients, Mademoiselle, that it was their custom to carry off by force from the fathers' house the daughters they were taking to marry, so that it should not seem that it was by their own consent that they flew off in a man's arms.

ANGÉLIQUE. The ancients, sir, are the ancients, and we are the people of today. Pretences are not necessary in our time; and when we are pleased with a marriage, we are perfectly capable of going to it without being dragged. Have patience: if you love me, sir, you should want everything I want.

THOMAS DIAFOIRUS. Yes, Mademoiselle, up to but not including the interests of my love.

ANGÉLIQUE. But the great mark of love is to submit to the will of the one you love.

THOMAS DIAFOIRUS. *Distinguo,* Mademoiselle. In what does not concern the possession of her, *concedo*; but in what concerns it, *nego.*[8]

TOINETTE *(to* ANGÉLIQUE*)*. There's no use your arguing. The gentleman is fresh out of school, and he'll always have the upper hand. Why do you resist so, and refuse the glory of being attached to the staff of the Faculty?

BÉLINE. Perhaps she has some other inclination in her head.

7 "I deny the consequence," a phrase used in scholastic debate.
8 *Distinguo,* "I make a distinction." *Concedo,* "I concede the point." *Nego,* "I deny it."

ANGÉLIQUE. If I had, Madame, it would be such a one as reason and decency would permit.

ARGAN. Well! I'm playing a funny part here.

BÉLINE. If I were you, dear boy, I wouldn't force her to get married, and I know very well what I'd do.

ANGÉLIQUE. I know what you mean, Madame, and the kindness you have for me; but perhaps your advice won't have the good fortune to be carried out.

BÉLINE. That's because decent well-behaved daughters like you laugh at being obedient and submissive to their fathers' will. It was better in the old days.

ANGÉLIQUE. A daughter's duty has limits, Madame, and reason and the laws do not extend it to every kind of matter.

BÉLINE. That is to say that your thoughts are all for marriage, but you want to choose a husband to suit your fancy.

ANGÉLIQUE. If my father won't give me a husband I like, I shall at least conjure him not to force me to marry one I cannot love.

ARGAN. Gentlemen, I beg your pardon for all this.

ANGÉLIQUE. Everyone has his own aim in getting married. As for me, since I want a husband only to love him truly, and since I mean to attach myself entirely to him for life, I admit I want some precautions. There are some women who take a husband only to extricate themselves from the constraint of their parents and get in a position to do whatever they want. There are others, Madame, who make of marriage a matter of pure self-interest, who marry only to get inheritances, only to get rich by the death of the men they marry, and run without scruple from husband to husband to appropriate their spoils. Those persons, in truth, are not so particular, and care little who the person may be.

BÉLINE. You're quite a reasoner today, and I'd very much like to know what you mean by that.

ANGÉLIQUE. I, Madame? What should I mean except what I say?

BÉLINE. You're so stupid, my dear, you're really unbearable.

ANGÉLIQUE. Madame, you'd like to provoke me into some impertinent reply; but I warn you that you shall not have that advantage.

BÉLINE. I've never seen the like of your insolence.

ANGÉLIQUE. No, Madame, it's no use your talking.

BÉLINE. And you have a ridiculous pride, an impertinent presumption, that makes people shrug their shoulders.

ANGÉLIQUE. All that, Madame, will be no use. I'll be well-behaved in spite of you; and to deprive you of any hope of being able to succeed in what you want, I'm going to remove myself from your sight.

ARGAN. Listen, there's no middle ground in this. Make up your mind to marry, within four days, either this gentleman, or a convent.   *(Exit* ANGÉLIQUE.*)*
Don't worry. I'll bring her around.

BÉLINE. I'm sorry to leave you, sweet boy, but I have business in town that I must attend to. I'll be back soon.

ARGAN. Go ahead, my love, and stop at your notary's, so that he'll expedite you know what.

BÉLINE. Good-by, my little darling.

ARGAN. Good-by, my dear.   *(Exit* BÉLINE.*)*
There's a woman who loves me so. . . . It's incredible.

MONSIEUR DIAFOIRUS. Sir, we're going to take leave of you.

ARGAN. I beg you, sir, just to tell me how I am.

MONSIEUR DIAFOIRUS *(taking his pulse).* Come on, Thomas, take the gentleman's other arm, to see if you can make a good judgment about his pulse. *Quid dicis?*

THOMAS DIAFOIRUS. *Dico* that the gentleman's pulse is the pulse of a man who is not well.

MONSIEUR DIAFOIRUS. Good.

THOMAS DIAFOIRUS. That it is a wee bit hardish, not to say hard.

MONSIEUR DIAFOIRUS. Very good.

THOMAS DIAFOIRUS. Beating strongly.

MONSIEUR DIAFOIRUS. *Bene.*

THOMAS DIAFOIRUS. And even a little capricious.

MONSIEUR DIAFOIRUS. *Optime.*

THOMAS DIAFOIRUS. Which indicates an intemperance in the splenic parenchyma, that is to say the spleen.

MONSIEUR DIAFOIRUS. Very good.

ARGAN. No. Monsieur Purgon says it's my liver that's sick.

MONSIEUR DIAFOIRUS. Oh, yes! If anyone says *parenchyma,* he says both, because of the close sympathy they have with each other, by means of the *vas breve* of the *pylorus,* and often of the *choledochal meatuses.* No doubt he orders you to eat a lot of roast meat?

ARGAN. No, nothing but boiled.

MONSIEUR DIAFOIRUS. Oh, yes! Roast, boiled, all the same thing. He prescribes for you very prudently, and you couldn't be in better hands.

ARGAN. Sir, how many grains of salt should one put on an egg?

MONSIEUR DIAFOIRUS. Six, eight, or ten, in even numbers; just as with medicines, in odd numbers.

ARGAN. Good-by, sir.

Scene 7.   BÉLINE, ARGAN

BÉLINE. Before I go out, dear boy, I've come to inform you about something you must watch out for. As I passed in front of Angélique's room, I saw a young man with her, who ran away as soon as he saw me.

ARGAN. A young man with my daughter?

BÉLINE. Yes. Your little daughter Louison was with them, and can tell you some things about it.

ARGAN. Send her here, my love, send her here. Ah, the brazen girl! No wonder she resisted so.

Scene 8.   LOUISON, ARGAN

LOUISON. What do you want, papa? My stepmother said you're asking for me.

ARGAN. Yes, come here. Come nearer. There. Turn around, raise your eyes, look at me. Well?

LOUISON. What, papa?

ARGAN. Here now.

LOUISON. What?

ARGAN. Haven't you anything to tell me?

LOUISON. If you want, I'll tell you, to divert you, the story of the Ass's Skin or the fable of the Fox and the Crow, which was taught me recently.

ARGAN. That's not what I'm asking.

LOUISON. What, then?

ARGAN. Ah, you sly girl! You know very well what I mean.

LOUISON. I beg your pardon, papa.

ARGAN. Is this how you obey me?

LOUISON. What?

ARGAN. Didn't I ask you to come and tell me right away anything you see?

LOUISON. Yes, papa.

ARGAN. Have you done that?

LOUISON. Yes, papa. I came and told you everything I've seen.

ARGAN. And haven't you seen anything today?

LOUISON. No, papa.

ARGAN. No?

LOUISON. No, papa.

ARGAN. Are you sure?

LOUISON. I'm sure.

ARGAN. Oh, now really! *I'm* going to make you see something. *(He goes and picks up a switch.)*

LOUISON. Oh, papa!

ARGAN. Aha! You little minx, you didn't tell me that you saw a man in your sister's room.

LOUISON. Papa!

ARGAN. Here's something that'll teach you to lie.

LOUISON *(falling on her knees)*. Oh, papa, I ask your pardon. You see, sister had told me not to tell you; but I'm going to tell you everything.

ARGAN. First you've got to have a whipping for lying. Then afterward we'll see about the rest.

LOUISON. Forgive me, papa!

ARGAN. No, no.

LOUISON. Dear papa, don't give me a whipping!

ARGAN. You shall have it.

LOUISON. In Heaven's name, papa, don't whip me!

ARGAN *(taking hold of her to whip her)*. Come on, come on.

LOUISON. Oh, papa, you've hurt me! Stop, I'm dead. *(She plays dead.)*

ARGAN. Hey! What's this? Louison! Louison! Oh, good Lord! Louison! Oh, my daughter! Oh, unhappy me, my poor daughter is dead! What have I done, wretch that I am? Oh, blast this switch! Plague take all switches! Oh, my poor daughter, my poor little Louison!

LOUISON. There, there, papa, don't cry so hard, I'm not dead—quite.

ARGAN. Will you look at that little trickster? Oh, all right! I forgive you this time, provided you really tell me everything.

LOUISON. Oh, yes, papa!

ARGAN. Anyway, be good and sure you do, for here's my little finger that knows everything and will tell me if you lie.

LOUISON. But, papa, don't tell my sister I told you.

ARGAN. No, no.

LOUISON. The fact is, papa, a man did come into sister's room while I was there.

ARGAN. Well?

LOUISON. I asked him what he wanted, and he told me he was her singing teacher.

ARGAN. Oho! So that's the game. Well?

LOUISON. Then sister came.

ARGAN. Well?

LOUISON. She said to him: "Go, go, go! Good Lord, go! You're driving me to despair."

ARGAN. Well?

LOUISON. Well, *he* didn't want to go.

ARGAN. What did he say to her?

LOUISON. He said I don't know how many things.

ARGAN. And then what?

LOUISON. He told her all this and all that, that he loved her dearly, and that she was the most beautiful girl in the world.

ARGAN. And after that?

LOUISON. And after that, he got on his knees before her.

ARGAN. And after that?

LOUISON. And after that, he kissed her hands.

ARGAN. And after that?

LOUISON. And after that, my stepmama came to the door, and he ran away.

ARGAN. There's nothing else?

LOUISON. No, papa.

ARGAN. But here's my little finger mumbling something. *(Putting his finger to his ear)* Wait! Eh? Aha! Yes? Oho! Here's my little finger telling me there's something you saw and that you haven't told me.

LOUISON. Oh, papa! Your little finger's a liar.

ARGAN. Take care!

LOUISON. No, papa, don't believe it, it's lying, I assure you.

ARGAN. Oh, all right, all right! We'll see about that. Run along, and keep an eye out for everything. Go on.

(Exit LOUISON.*)*

Ah! There are no children any more. Oh! What a lot of troubles! I don't even have time to think about my illness. Really, I'm done for. *(Sits down in his chair again.)*

Scene 9.   BÉRALDE, ARGAN

BÉRALDE. Well, brother, what's up? How are you?

ARGAN. Ah, brother! Very bad.

BÉRALDE. How do you mean, very bad?

ARGAN. Yes, I'm so weak you wouldn't believe it.

BÉRALDE. That's too bad.

ARGAN. I haven't even the strength to be able to speak.

BÉRALDE. I've come here, brother, to propose to you a match for my niece Angélique.

ARGAN (*speaking furiously, and rising from his chair*). Brother, don't talk to me about that wicked girl! She's an impertinent, brazen hussy, and I'll put her into a convent before two days are up.

BÉRALDE. Oh! That's fine. I'm very glad that your strength is coming back a bit, and that my visit is doing you good. Oh, well, we'll talk about business later. I'm bringing you an entertainment I came across that will banish your melancholy and make your soul better disposed for the things we have to talk about. They are Gypsies dressed as Moors, who put on dances mingled with songs. I'm sure you'll enjoy them, and they'll do you as much good as one of Monsieur Purgon's prescriptions. Come on.

SECOND INTERLUDE

(*A troop of Gypsies dance and sing songs in praise of love, and their pet monkeys join in one of the dances. Since the songs have nothing to do with the rest of the play, they are omitted here.*)

ACT III

Scene 1. BÉRALDE, ARGAN, TOINETTE

BÉRALDE. Well, brother, what do you say to that? Isn't that as good as a dose of senna?

TOINETTE. Hm! Good senna is good.

BÉRALDE. Well, now! Would you like to have a little talk together?

ARGAN. Be patient a bit, brother, I'll be back.

TOINETTE. Wait, sir, you're forgetting that you can't walk without a stick.

ARGAN. You're right.

Scene 2. BÉRALDE, TOINETTE

TOINETTE. Please don't abandon your niece's interests.

BÉRALDE. I'll do everything I can to get her what she wants.

TOINETTE. It's absolutely necessary to prevent this crazy marriage that he's taken into his head, and I had thought to myself that it would have been a good idea to be able to bring in here a doctor of our own choosing, to give him a distaste for his Monsieur Purgon and disparage his methods. But since we have no one in hand for that, I've resolved to play a trick out of my head.

BÉRALDE. How's that?

TOINETTE. It's a wild idea. Maybe it will be more lucky than it is sensible. Leave it to me; for your part, do what you can. Here's our man.

Scene 3. ARGAN, BÉRALDE

BÉRALDE. Allow me, brother, to ask you above all not to get excited during our conversation.

ARGAN. That's settled.

BÉRALDE. To answer any things I may say to you without bitterness.

ARGAN. Yes.

BÉRALDE. And to reason together on the things we have to talk about with a mind detached from any passion.

ARGAN. Good Lord, yes! That's a lot of preamble.

BÉRALDE. How does it happen, brother, that with the money you have, and no children but one daughter, for I'm not counting the little one, how does it happen, I say, that you're talking about putting her into a convent?

ARGAN. How does it happen, brother, that I am master in my family to do what seems good to me?

BÉRALDE. Your wife doesn't fail to advise you to get rid of both your daughters thus, and I have no doubt that, out of a spirit of charity, she would be delighted to see both of them be good nuns.

ARGAN. Aha! Here we go. You've got my poor wife into it right away: she's the one who does all the harm, and everyone has it in for her.

BÉRALDE. No, brother; let's let her be; she's a woman who has the best intentions in the world for your family, free of any sort of self-interest, who has a marvelous tenderness for you, and displays for your children an affection and a kindness which are inconceivable; that's certain. Let's not talk about her, and let's come back to your daughter. What's your idea, brother, in wanting to give her in marriage to a doctor's son?

ARGAN. My idea, brother, is to give myself the kind of son-in-law I need.

BÉRALDE. That, brother, isn't the thing for your daughter, and there's a match available that's more suitable for her.

ARGAN. Yes, brother, but this one is more suitable for me.

BÉRALDE. But, brother, should the husband she is to take be for her or for you?

ARGAN. He should be, brother, both for her and for me, and I want to bring into my family the people I need.

BÉRALDE. On that reasoning, if your little one was grown up, you'd give her in marriage to an apothecary?

ARGAN. Why not?

BÉRALDE. Is it possible that you will always be infatuated with your apothecaries and your doctors, and that you intend to be sick in spite of everyone and of nature herself?

ARGAN. How do you mean that, brother?

BÉRALDE. I mean, brother, that I don't see one single man who is less sick than you, and that I wouldn't ask for a better constitution than yours. One great sign that you are healthy and that you have a perfectly well set up body is that with all the cares you have taken you haven't yet succeeded in ruining the soundness of your system, and that you haven't burst with all the medicines they've had you take.

ARGAN. But do you realize, brother, that that's what's keeping me alive, and that Monsieur Purgon says I would succumb if he went even three days without taking care of me?

BÉRALDE. If you're not careful, he'll take such care of you that he'll send you into the other world.

ARGAN. But let's discuss this a little, brother. So you don't believe in medicine?

BÉRALDE. No, brother, and I don't believe it's necessary, for our salvation, to believe in it.

ARGAN. What? You don't believe in the truth of a thing established by everyone, and which every age has revered?

BÉRALDE. Very far from believing in its truth, I consider it, between us, one of the greatest follies there is among men; and looking at things as a philosopher, I can see no more comical piece of mummery, I can see nothing more ridiculous, than one man wanting to undertake to cure another.

ARGAN. Brother, why won't you allow that one man can cure another?

BÉRALDE. For this reason, brother: that the functioning of our machine is a mystery in which up to now men can't see a thing, and nature has put before our eyes veils too thick to allow us to know anything about it.

ARGAN. So the doctors don't know anything, by your account?

BÉRALDE. Oh yes, they do, brother. Most of them know a lot in the humanities, know how to talk in fine Latin, know how to name all the diseases in Greek, define them, and classify them; but as for curing them, that's what they don't know how to do at all.

ARGAN. But still you must agree that on this matter the doctors know more than others.

BÉRALDE. Brother, they know what I've told you, which doesn't cure anyone of very much; and the whole excellence of their art consists of a pompous mumbo-jumbo, a specious chatter, which gives you words for reasons, and promises for results.

ARGAN. But after all, brother, there are people as wise and as clever as you; and we see that in time of sickness, everyone has recourse to the doctors.

BÉRALDE. That's a sign of human weakness, and not of the truth of their art.

ARGAN. But the doctors must certainly believe their art is true, since they use it for themselves.

BÉRALDE. That's because there are some among them who themselves share the popular delusion, by which they profit, and others who profit by it without sharing it. Your Monsieur

Purgon, for example, doesn't try to fool anybody: he's a man who's all doctor, from head to foot, a man who believes in his rules more than in all the demonstrations of mathematics, and who would think it a crime to want to examine them; who sees in medicine nothing obscure, nothing doubtful, nothing difficult, and who, with impetuous prejudice, rigid self-confidence, brutish common sense and reason, gives purgations and bleedings right and left and never ponders a thing. You mustn't bear him ill will for anything he may do to you; it's in the best faith in the world that he'll expedite you; and in killing you he will do only what he's done to his wife and children, and what, if the need arose, he would do to himself.

ARGAN. The fact is, brother, you've always had it in for him. But anyway, let's come to the point. Then what should you do when you're sick?

BÉRALDE. Nothing, brother.

ARGAN. Nothing?

BÉRALDE. Nothing. All you have to do is rest. Nature, by herself, when we let her be, gently makes her way out of the disorder into which she has fallen. It's our anxiety, our impatience that spoils everything, and almost all men die of their remedies, and not of their diseases.

ARGAN. But you must agree, brother, that we can assist nature in certain ways.

BÉRALDE. Good Lord, brother, those are pure notions that we like to feed on; and in every age there have been pretty fancies that have insinuated themselves among men, which we come to believe because they flatter us and because it would be most desirable that they should be true. When a doctor talks to you about aiding, helping, relieving nature, taking away from it what harms it and giving it what it lacks, setting it right again and restoring it to a full state of ease in its functions; when he talks to you about rectifying the blood, tempering the bowels and the brain, deflating the spleen, redressing the lungs, repairing the liver, fortifying the heart, re-establishing and conserving the natural heat, and having secrets to extend your life for many long years, he is telling you precisely the fairy tale of medicine. But when you come down to truth and experience, you find nothing of all that, and it's like those beautiful dreams that leave you, when you wake, nothing but chagrin at having believed them.

ARGAN. That is to say that all the knowledge in the world is enclosed in your head, and you claim to know more about it than all the great doctors of our time.

BÉRALDE. Your great doctors are two different kinds of people in words and in deeds. Hear them talk: the ablest men in the world. See them at work: the most ignorant of all men.

ARGAN. Well! You're a great doctor, I can see that; and I wish there was one of those gentlemen here to refute your arguments and humble your chatter.

BÉRALDE. Brother, I don't take it upon myself to combat medicine; and everyone, at his own risk and peril, may believe all he likes. What I'm saying about it is just between us, and I would have liked to be able to bring you a little way out of the error you're in, and, to amuse you, take you to see one of Molière's comedies on the subject.

ARGAN. He's a really impertinent fellow, your Molière, with his comedies, and it's very amusing of him to go and make fun of worthy men like the doctors.

BÉRALDE. It's not the doctors he makes fun of, but the absurdities of medicine.

ARGAN. I suppose it's his business to undertake to criticize medicine. He's a fine kind of impertinent fool to ridicule consultations and prescriptions, to attack the medical profession, and to put on his stage venerable people like those gentlemen!

BÉRALDE. What would you have him put on his stage but the various professions of men? Every day they put on princes and kings, who are of just as good birth as the doctors.

ARGAN. By all that's holy—or unholy! If I were a doctor, I'd take revenge on his impertinence; and when he's sick, I'd let him die without any help. He could say or do what he likes, I wouldn't prescribe the slightest little bleeding, the least little enema; and I'd say to him: "Croak! Croak! That'll teach you another time to make fun of the Faculty of Medicine!"

BÉRALDE. You really are angry at him!

ARGAN. Yes, he's a stupid joker, and if the doctors are smart they'll do what I'm saying.

BÉRALDE. He'll be even smarter than your doctors, for he won't ask them for any help.

ARGAN. So much the worse for him, if he doesn't have recourse to any remedies.

BÉRALDE. He has his reasons for not wanting any, and he maintains that they are permissible only for vigorous, robust people who have strength to spare to bear the remedies as well as the disease; but that for his part he has only just strength enough to bear his illness.

ARGAN. What stupid arguments those are! Look, brother, let's not talk about that man any more, for it rouses my bile, and it would bring on my illness.

BÉRALDE. I'm perfectly willing, brother; and to change the subject, I will tell you that just because your daughter shows some slight opposition, you shouldn't make the violent resolve to put her into a convent; that in choosing a son-in-law, you shouldn't blindly follow the passion that carries you away; and that in this matter one should make some accommodation to a daughter's inclinations, since it's for her whole life, and since on that depends the whole happiness of a marriage.

Scene 4. MONSIEUR FLEURANT (syringe in hand),
ARGAN, BÉRALDE

ARGAN. Ah, brother, with your permission . . .

BÉRALDE. How's that? What do you want to do?

ARGAN. Take this little enema; I'll be done soon.

BÉRALDE. You must be joking. Can't you go one moment without an enema or a dose of medicine? Put it off for another time, and take a little rest.

ARGAN. Monsieur Fleurant, I'll see you this evening, or tomorrow morning.

MONSIEUR FLEURANT (to BÉRALDE). What business is it of yours to oppose the prescriptions of medicine, and to keep the gentleman from taking my enema? Your audacity is mighty comical!

BÉRALDE. Come, sir, it's easy to see that you're not accustomed to talking to people's faces.

MONSIEUR FLEURANT. A person has no business making fun of remedies and making me waste my time. I came here only on a proper prescription, and I'm going to tell Monsieur Purgon how I've been kept from executing his orders and performing my function. You'll see, you'll see . . .   (Exit)

ARGAN. Brother, you're going to be the cause of some misfortune here.

BÉRALDE. A great misfortune, not to take an enema that Monsieur Purgon prescribed! Once again, brother, is it possible that there's no way to cure you of the malady of doctors, and that you want to be buried in their remedies all your life?

ARGAN. Good Lord, brother! You're talking about this as a well man; but if you were in my place, you'd really change your tune. It's easy to talk against medicine when you're in perfect health.

BÉRALDE. But what illness *do* you have?

ARGAN. You're enough to drive me crazy. I wish *you* had my illness, to see if you'd prattle so much. Oh! Here's Monsieur Purgon.

Scene 5.   MONSIEUR PURGON, ARGAN, BÉRALDE, TOINETTE

MONSIEUR PURGON. I've just learned, here at the door, a pretty piece of news: that people have made light of my prescriptions, and have refused to take the remedy I had prescribed.

ARGAN. Sir, it wasn't . . .

MONSIEUR PURGON. That's a great piece of audacity, an extraordinary rebellion by a patient against his doctor!

TOINETTE. That is frightful.

MONSIEUR PURGON. An enema that I had taken pleasure in concocting myself!

ARGAN. It wasn't I . . .

MONSIEUR PURGON. Invented and fashioned according to all the rules of the art!

TOINETTE. He was wrong.

MONSIEUR PURGON. And that was destined to have a marvelous effect on the bowels.

ARGAN. Brother?

MONSIEUR PURGON. To send it away with disdain!

ARGAN. He's the one . . .

MONSIEUR PURGON. It's an unconscionable act.

TOINETTE. That's true.

MONSIEUR PURGON. A shocking attack on medicine.

ARGAN. He's the cause . . .

MONSIEUR PURGON. A crime of *lèse-faculté*, which cannot be punished severely enough.

TOINETTE. You're right.

MONSIEUR PURGON. I declare to you that I am breaking off relations with you.

ARGAN. It was my brother . . .

MONSIEUR PURGON. That I want no more family alliance with you.

TOINETTE. You'll be doing the right thing.

MONSIEUR PURGON. And that to end all dealings with you, here is the donation I was making to my nephew in favor of the marriage. *(Tears it up.)*

ARGAN. It was my brother that did all the harm.

MONSIEUR PURGON. To disdain my enema!

ARGAN. Bring it here, I'll take it right away.

MONSIEUR PURGON. I would have got you out of this in next to no time.

TOINETTE. He doesn't deserve it.

MONSIEUR PURGON. I was going to clean out your body and completely evacuate the evil humors.

ARGAN. Ah, brother!

MONSIEUR PURGON. And all I wanted was another dozen doses of medicine to empty the bottom of the sack.

TOINETTE. He is unworthy of your care.

MONSIEUR PURGON. But since you wouldn't be cured at my hands . . .

ARGAN. It wasn't my fault.

MONSIEUR PURGON. Since you absconded from the obedience that a man owes to his doctor . . .

TOINETTE. That cries for vengeance.

MONSIEUR PURGON. Since you have declared yourself a rebel against the remedies I was prescribing for you . . .

ARGAN. Oh! Not at all!

MONSIEUR PURGON. I have this to tell you: that I abandon you to your bad constitution, to the intemperance of your bowels, to the corruption of your blood, to the bitterness of your bile, and to the turbidity of your humors.

TOINETTE. Well done!

ARGAN. Good Lord!

MONSIEUR PURGON. And I will that before four days are up you get into an incurable state.

ARGAN. Ah! Mercy!

MONSIEUR PURGON. That you fall into bradypepsia . . .[9]

---

[9] Bradypepsia: slow digestion. Dyspepsia: bad digestion. Apepsia: lack of digestion. Lientery: a form of diarrhea.

ARGAN. Monsieur Purgon!

MONSIEUR PURGON. From bradypepsia into dyspepsia . . .

ARGAN. Monsieur Purgon!

MONSIEUR PURGON. From dyspepsia into apepsia . . .

ARGAN. Monsieur Purgon!

MONSIEUR PURGON. From apepsia into lientery . . .

ARGAN. Monsieur Purgon!

MONSIEUR PURGON. From lientery into dysentery . . .

ARGAN. Monsieur Purgon!

MONSIEUR PURGON. From dysentery into dropsy . . .

ARGAN. Monsieur Purgon!

MONSIEUR PURGON. And from dropsy into loss of life, to which your folly will have led you.

Scene 6.   ARGAN, BÉRALDE

ARGAN. Oh, good Lord! I'm a dead man. Brother, you've ruined me.

BÉRALDE. What? What's the matter?

ARGAN. I'm done for. Already I feel medicine taking its revenge.

BÉRALDE. Faith, brother! You're crazy, and I wouldn't for anything want to have you be seen doing what you're doing. Examine yourself a bit, please, come back to yourself, and don't give so much play to your imagination.

ARGAN. Brother, you heard the awful diseases he threatened me with.

BÉRALDE. What a simpleton you are!

ARGAN. He says I'll become incurable in less than four days.

BÉRALDE. And what he says, what has that to do with the case? Was it an oracle that spoke? It seems, to hear you, that Monsieur Purgon holds the thread of your days in his hands, and that by supreme authority he lengthens it and shortens it for you as he pleases. Remember that the principles of your life are in yourself, and that the wrath of Monsieur Purgon is as little capable of making you die as are his remedies of making you live. Here is an adventure, if you will, to rid you of doctors; or, if you are born to be unable to do without them, it is easy to get another, with whom, brother, you might run a little less risk.

ARGAN. Ah, brother! He knows my whole constitution and the way I have to be treated.

BÉRALDE. I must confess to you that you're a man of great obstinacy, and that you see things through a strange pair of eyes.

Scene 7.   TOINETTE, ARGAN, BÉRALDE

TOINETTE. Sir, there's a doctor here asking to see you.

ARGAN. And what doctor?

TOINETTE. A doctor of doctoring.

ARGAN. I ask you who he is?

TOINETTE. I don't know him, but he and I look as much alike as two peas in a pod; and if I wasn't sure that my mother was an honest woman, I'd say that he's probably some little brother she'd given me since my father's death.

ARGAN. Show him in.   (*Exit* TOINETTE.)

BÉRALDE. You're served to your heart's content: one doctor leaves you, another presents himself.

ARGAN. I'm very much afraid that you'll be the cause of some misfortune.

BÉRALDE. Again? You're still coming back to that?

ARGAN. You see, I have all these illnesses I don't know anything about on my mind, these . . .

Scene 8.   TOINETTE *(disguised as a doctor)*, ARGAN,
BÉRALDE

TOINETTE. Sir, allow me to come and pay you a visit and offer you my modest services for any bleedings and purges you may need.

ARGAN. Sir, I am much obliged to you. *(To* BÉRALDE*)* My word, he looks just like Toinette herself!

TOINETTE. Sir, I beg you to excuse me; I forgot to give an order to my valet; I'll be right back.

ARGAN. Eh! Wouldn't you say it really is Toinette?

BÉRALDE. It's true that the resemblance is extremely great. But this is not the first time that this sort of thing has been observed, and the histories are only too full of these freaks of nature.

ARGAN. For my part, I'm surprised, and . . .

Scene 9.   TOINETTE, ARGAN, BÉRALDE

TOINETTE *(having shed her doctor's gown so fast that it's hard to believe that it was she who appeared as a doctor)*. What do you want, sir?

ARGAN. What?

TOINETTE. Didn't you call me?

ARGAN. I? No.

TOINETTE. My ears must have been burning.

ARGAN. Stay here a bit to see how much this doctor looks like you.

TOINETTE. Yes indeed! I've plenty to do downstairs, and I've seen him enough.   *(Exit)*

ARGAN. If I didn't see them both, I'd think there was only one of them.

BÉRALDE. I've read some surprising things about this kind of resemblance, and we've seen some in our time that fooled everybody.

ARGAN. As for me, I would have been fooled by this one, and I would have sworn it was the same person.

Scene 10.   TOINETTE *(as a doctor)*, ARGAN, BÉRALDE

TOINETTE. Sir, with all my heart I ask your pardon.

ARGAN. That's amazing!

TOINETTE. If you please, you won't take amiss the curiosity I've had to see an illustrious invalid like yourself; and your reputation, which has spread everywhere, may excuse the liberty I have taken.

ARGAN. Sir, I am your servant.

TOINETTE. I see, sir, that you're looking at me fixedly. How old do you really think I am?

ARGAN. I think you may be twenty-six or twenty-seven at the very most.

TOINETTE. Ha, ha, ha, ha, ha! I'm ninety.

ARGAN. Ninety?

TOINETTE. Yes. You see one effect of the secrets of my art, to keep myself fresh and vigorous in this way.

ARGAN. Faith! Here's a handsome young old man for ninety!

TOINETTE. I'm a traveling doctor, who go from town to town, from province to province, from kingdom to kingdom, seeking illustrious subjects for my capacity, trying to find patients worthy of my attention, capable of exercising the fine great secrets I have discovered in medicine. I disdain to waste my time on that petty jumble of ordinary illnesses, on those trifles rheumatism and catarrhs, on those pathetic little fevers, those vapors, and those migraines. I want important illnesses: good continuous fevers with spells of delirium, good scarlet fevers, good plagues, good well-formed dropsies, good pleurisies with inflammation of the lungs: that's what I enjoy, that's where I triumph. And I wish, sir, that you had all the illnesses I've just mentioned, that you were abandoned by all the doctors, desperate, in agony, to show you the excellence of my remedies and my keen desire to do you service.

ARGAN. I am obliged to you, sir, for all your kindness to me.

TOINETTE. Give me your pulse. Come on now, beat properly. Aha! I'll make you work as you should all right. Hey, this pulse is trying to be impertinent: I see very well that you don't know me yet. Who is your doctor?

ARGAN. Monsieur Purgon.

TOINETTE. That man is not inscribed on my list among the great doctors. What does he say you're sick with?

ARGAN. He says it's the liver, and others say it's the spleen.

TOINETTE. They're all ignoramuses: it's in the lungs that you're sick.

ARGAN. The lungs?

TOINETTE. Yes. What do you feel?

ARGAN. From time to time I have headaches.

TOINETTE. Precisely, the lungs.

ARGAN. It seems to me sometimes that I have a veil before my eyes.

TOINETTE. The lungs.

ARGAN. I sometimes have pains in my heart.

TOINETTE. The lungs.

ARGAN. Now and then I feel a weariness in every limb.

TOINETTE. The lungs.

ARGAN. And sometimes I have pains in my stomach, as if it were colic.

TOINETTE. The lungs. You have an appetite for what you eat?

ARGAN. Yes, sir.

TOINETTE. The lungs. You like to drink a little wine?

ARGAN. Yes, sir.

TOINETTE. The lungs. You get a little sleepy after a meal, and feel glad of a nap?

ARGAN. Yes, sir.

TOINETTE. The lungs, the lungs, I tell you. What does your doctor prescribe for your diet?

ARGAN. He prescribes soup.

TOINETTE. Ignoramus.

ARGAN. Poultry.

TOINETTE. Ignoramus.

ARGAN. Veal.

TOINETTE. Ignoramus.

ARGAN. Broths.

TOINETTE. Ignoramus.

ARGAN. Fresh eggs.

TOINETTE. Ignoramus.

ARGAN. And some little prunes in the evening as a laxative.

TOINETTE. Ignoramus.

ARGAN. And above all to drink my wine mixed with a lot of water.

TOINETTE. *Ignorantus, ignoranta, ignorantum.* You must drink your wine straight; and to thicken your blood, which is too thin, you must eat good fat beef, good fat pork, good Holland cheese, gruel and rice, and chestnuts and wafers, to bind and conglutinate. Your doctor is an ass. I mean to send you one of my own choosing, and I'll come and see you from time to time while I'm in town.

ARGAN. I'm much obliged to you.

TOINETTE. What the devil do you do with that arm?

ARGAN. How's that?

TOINETTE. That's an arm I'd have cut off right away, if I were you.

ARGAN. And why?

TOINETTE. Don't you see that it's drawing all the nourishment to itself, and keeping that whole side from profiting?

ARGAN. Yes, but I need my arm.

TOINETTE. You also have a right eye there that I'd have put out, if I were in your place.

ARGAN. Put out an eye?

TOINETTE. Don't you see that it's disadvantaging the other one and stealing its nourishment? Believe me, have it put out as soon as possible, you'll see better out of the left eye.

ARGAN. There's no hurry.

TOINETTE. Good-by. I'm sorry to leave you so soon, but I've got to be at a big consultation to be held for a man who died yesterday.

ARGAN. For a man who died yesterday?

TOINETTE. Yes, to deliberate and see what should have been done to cure him. Good-by.

ARGAN. You know that patients don't show you out.

(Exit TOINETTE.*)*

BÉRALDE. There's a doctor who really seems very able.

ARGAN. Yes, but he goes about things pretty fast.

BÉRALDE. All great doctors are like that.

ARGAN. Cut off one of my arms, and put out one of my eyes, so that the other one will be healthier? I'd much rather it wasn't so healthy. A fine operation, to make me one-eyed and one-armed!

Scene 11.   TOINETTE, ARGAN, BÉRALDE

TOINETTE (calling offstage). Come, come, I'm your servant, I'm not in the mood for fun.

ARGAN. What is it?

TOINETTE. Faith, your doctor! He wanted to feel my pulse.

ARGAN. What do you know! At ninety!

BÉRALDE. Now then, brother, since your Monsieur Purgon is on bad terms with you, won't you let me talk to you about the suitor who's seeking my niece's hand?

ARGAN. No, brother; I want to put her in a convent, since she has opposed my wishes. I see very well that there's some little love affair at the bottom of this, and I've found out about a certain secret interview that they don't know I've found out about.

BÉRALDE. Well, brother, even if there were some slight inclination, would that be so criminal, and can anything offend you when it all leads only to honorable things like marriage?

ARGAN. Be that as it may, brother, she shall be a nun; that's settled.

BÉRALDE. You're trying to please someone.

ARGAN. I understand you: you always come back to that, and you have my wife on the brain.

BÉRALDE. Well, yes, brother, since I must speak open-heartedly, it is your wife that I mean; and no more than your infatuation with medicine can I bear the infatuation you have for her, or see you fall head down into all the traps she lays for you.

TOINETTE. Ah, sir, don't speak of Madame! She's a woman against whom there's nothing to be said, a woman without artifice, and who loves Monsieur, who loves him . . . you can't put it into words.

ARGAN *(to BÉRALDE)*. Just ask *her* how she caresses me.

TOINETTE. That's true.

ARGAN. How worried she is about my illness.

TOINETTE. Unquestionably.

ARGAN. And the care and trouble she takes for me.

TOINETTE. That's certain. *(To BÉRALDE)* Do you want me to convince you, and show you right now how Madame loves Monsieur? *(To ARGAN)* Sir, allow me to show him how childish he is, and undeceive him.

ARGAN. How?

TOINETTE. Madame is just coming back. Stretch out full length in this chair and pretend to be dead. You'll see what her grief is like when I tell her the news.

ARGAN. I'm willing.

TOINETTE. Yes, but don't leave her long in despair, for she might well die of it.

ARGAN. Leave it to me.

TOINETTE *(to BÉRALDE)*. You, hide yourself in that corner.

ARGAN. Isn't there some danger in pretending to be dead?

TOINETTE. No, no. What danger could there be? Just stretch out there. *(Whispering, to ARGAN)* It'll be a pleasure to confound your brother. Here's Madame. Keep good and still.

Scene 12. BÉLINE, TOINETTE, ARGAN, BÉRALDE

TOINETTE *(wailing loudly)*. Oh, good Lord! Oh, what a shame! What a terrible accident!

BÉLINE. What is it, Toinette?

TOINETTE. Oh, Madame!

BÉLINE. What's the matter?

TOINETTE. Your husband is dead.

BÉLINE. My husband is dead?

TOINETTE. Alas! Yes. The poor deceased has passed on.

BÉLINE. Are you quite sure?

TOINETTE. Quite sure. No one knows it's happened yet, and I was here all alone. He's just passed away in my arms. Look, there he is stretched out full length in this chair.

BÉLINE. Heaven be praised! I'm delivered from a heavy burden. How stupid you are, Toinette, to take on over his death.

TOINETTE. Madame, I thought I ought to cry.

BÉLINE. Come, come, it's not worth it. What are we losing in him? And what good on earth was he? A man who was a nuisance to everyone, dirty, disgusting, always with an enema or a dose of medicine in his stomach; always blowing his nose, coughing, and spitting; devoid of wit, boring, bad-humored, constantly wearying people, and scolding all the servants day and night.

TOINETTE. That's a nice funeral oration.

BÉLINE. Toinette, you must help me carry out my plan, and believe me, in serving me your reward is sure. Since by a stroke of good fortune no one is yet informed of the matter, let's carry him to his bed and keep this death quiet until I've done some business of mine. There are some papers, there's some money I want to get hold of, and it isn't fair that I should have spent the best years of my life with him without some reward. Come on, Toinette, first let's take all his keys.

ARGAN *(rising suddenly)*. Gently.

BÉLINE *(surprised and terrified)*. Oh!

ARGAN. Yes, my lady and wife, so that's how you love me?

TOINETTE. Ha, ha! The deceased isn't dead.

ARGAN *(to BÉLINE)*. I'm very glad to see how you love me and to have heard the fine panegyric you gave about me.

(Exit BÉLINE.)

There's a warning to the reader that will make me wiser in the future and keep me from doing a lot of things.

BÉRALDE *(coming out of his hiding-place)*. Well, brother, you see the way it is.

TOINETTE. Upon my word, I never would have believed it. But I hear your daughter; get back the way you were, and let's see how she receives your death. That's a thing that it's not bad to test out; and while you're at it, that way you'll learn the feelings your whole family has for you.

Scene 13.   ANGÉLIQUE, ARGAN, TOINETTE, BÉRALDE

TOINETTE *(wailing)*. O Heavens! Ah, what a sad thing! Unhappy day!

ANGÉLIQUE. What's the matter, Toinette, and what are you crying about?

TOINETTE. Alas! I have sad news to give you.

ANGÉLIQUE. Why, what?

TOINETTE. Your father is dead.

ANGÉLIQUE. My father is dead, Toinette?

TOINETTE. Yes. There you see him. He's just died, just now, of a spell of weakness that seized him.

ANGÉLIQUE. O Heaven! What a misfortune! What a cruel blow! Alas! Must I lose my father, the only thing left to me in the world? And moreover, to add to my despair, lose him at a time when he was irritated with me? What is to become of me, wretched girl that I am, and what consolation can I find after so great a loss?

Scene 14.   CLÉANTE, ANGÉLIQUE, ARGAN, TOINETTE, BÉRALDE

CLÉANTE. Why, what's wrong, lovely Angélique? And what misfortune is making you weep?

ANGÉLIQUE. Alas! I'm weeping for the dearest and most precious thing I could lose in life: I'm weeping for the death of my father.

CLÉANTE. O Heavens! What a calamity! What an unexpected blow! Alas! After I'd implored your uncle to ask your hand of him on my behalf, I was coming to present myself to him and try, by my respects and my prayers, to make his heart disposed to grant you to my wishes.

ANGÉLIQUE. Ah, Cléante, let's not talk any more about any of that. Let's leave behind all thoughts of marriage. After the loss of my father, I want no part of the world any more, and I give it up forever. Yes, father, if I resisted your wishes just now, I want to follow at least one of your intentions, and thereby make amends for the unhappiness I blame myself for having given you. Allow me, father, to give you my word for this here and now, and to kiss you to testify my feeling to you.

ARGAN (rising). Ah, my daughter!

ANGÉLIQUE (frightened). Oh!

ARGAN. Come. Don't be afraid, I'm not dead. Come, come, you

are my own flesh and blood, my true daughter; and I'm delighted to have seen how good your nature really is.

ANGÉLIQUE. Oh, what a delightful surprise, father! Since, by extreme good fortune, Heaven restores you to my love, allow me here and now to throw myself at your feet to beseech you for one thing. If you are not favorable to the inclination of my heart, if you refuse me Cléante for a husband, I conjure you at least not to force me to marry another. That's all the boon I ask of you.

CLÉANTE *(throwing himself on his knees)*. Ah, sir, let yourself be touched by her prayers and mine, and don't take a stand against the mutual ardor of such a fair inclination.

BÉRALDE. Brother, can you hold out against that?

TOINETTE. Sir, will you be insensible to so much love?

ARGAN. Let him become a doctor, and I'll consent to the marriage. Yes, become a doctor, and I'll give you my daughter.

CLÉANTE. Very gladly, sir; if that's all that's needed to be your son-in-law, I'll become a doctor, even an apothecary, if you want. That's no great matter, and I'd do far more than that to win the lovely Angélique.

BÉRALDE. But, brother, a thought occurs to me: become a doctor yourself. The convenience would be even greater, to have everything you need in yourself.

TOINETTE. That's true. That's the real way to get well soon; and there is no illness so daring as to trifle with the person of a doctor.

ARGAN. Brother, I think you're making fun of me. Am I of an age to be a student?

BÉRALDE. Be a student? That's a good one! You're learned enough; and there are many of them who are no smarter than you.

ARGAN. But you have to know how to speak Latin well, and know the illnesses and the remedies you need to use for them.

BÉRALDE. As you receive the doctor's cap and gown you'll learn all that, and afterward you'll be even smarter than you want.

ARGAN. What? A man knows how to discourse upon illnesses when he has that costume?

BÉRALDE. Yes. One has only to talk with a cap and gown on. Any gibberish becomes learned, and any nonsense becomes reason.

TOINETTE. Look here, sir, if all you had was your beard, that's already a lot, and a beard makes more than half a doctor.

CLÉANTE. In any case, I'm ready for anything.

BÉRALDE. Do you want to have the thing done right away?

ARGAN. What do you mean, right away?

BÉRALDE. Yes, and in your own house.

ARGAN. In my own house?

BÉRALDE. Yes. I have friends on the Faculty who will come right away and perform the ceremony here in your room. It won't cost you a thing.

ARGAN. But for my part, what I am to say, what am I to answer?

BÉRALDE. They'll give you instructions in a few words, and give you in writing what you have to say. Go along and put on proper clothes; I'm going to send for them.

ARGAN. All right, let's see about it. *(Exit)*

CLÉANTE. What do you mean, and what do you have in mind with these friends on the Faculty . . . ?

TOINETTE. What's your plan, anyway?

BÉRALDE. To have a little fun this evening. I have some actors who have composed a little act about accepting a man as a doctor, with music and dances. I want us to enjoy the entertainment together, and I want my brother to play the leading part.

ANGÉLIQUE. But, uncle, it seems to me that you're making a bit too much fun of my father.

BÉRALDE. But, niece, it's not so much making fun of him as accommodating ourselves to his fancies. All this is just between us. We can also each of us take a part, and thus put on a comedy for one another. Carnival time authorizes that. Let's go quickly and get everything prepared.

CLÉANTE *(to* ANGÉLIQUE*).* Do you consent?

ANGÉLIQUE. Yes, since my uncle is leading the way.

FINALE

A burlesque, with recitative, song, and dance, of the conferral of the degree of Doctor of Medicine on a candidate (a Bachelor) by the Faculty. It is in macaronic Latin—sprinkled with French and a little Italian in Molière's text, with English here—easily intelligible to Molière's audience.

Several attendants, to music, prepare the room and set out the benches. Then enter the whole assembly—eight syringe-bearers, six apothecaries, twenty-two doctors, the candidate (Bachelierus, in this case ARGAN*), eight surgeons dancing and two singing. All take their places according to their ranks. The Presiding Officer (Praeses) takes his place in a pulpit.*

PRAESES.

> Learnedissimi doctores,
> Medicinae professores,
> Qui hic assemblati estis,
> Et vos, altri Messiores,
> Sententiarum facultatis
> Fideles executores,
> Surgeoni, apothecari,
> Atque tota company,
> Salus, honor, et argentum,
> Atque bonum appetitum.
>
> Non possum, docti Confreri,
> In me satis admirari
> Qualis bona inventio
> Est medici professio,
> How fine a thinga est, et well trovata,
> Medicina illa benedicta,
> Quae suo nomine solo,
> Surprisingi miraculo,
> For such a longo tempore

i

Has made à gogo vivere
So many omni genere.

Per totam terram videmus
Grandam vogam ubi sumus,
Et quod omnes, great and small,
Sunt infatuated with us all.
Totus mundus, currens ad nostros remedios,
Nos regardat sicut Deos;
Et nostris ordonnanciis
Principes et reges submissive videtis.

Therefore 'tis nostrae sapientiae,
Boni sensus atque prudentiae,
Sturdily to laborare
A nos bene conservare
In tali credito, voga, et honore,
And take good care to non receivere
In nostro docto corpore
Quam personas capabiles,
Et totas dignas to fillire
Has plaças honorabiles.

This is why nunc convocati estis:
Et credo quod findabitis
Dignam materiam medici
In learned man whom here you see,
Whom, in thingsis omnibus,
Dono ad interrogandum,
Et in depth examinandum
Vostris capacitatibus.

PRIMUS DOCTOR.
Si mihi licentiam dat Dominus Praeses,
Et tanti docti Doctores,
Et assistantes illustres:
Very learned Bacheliero,
Quem estimo et honoro,
Demandabo causam et rationem quare
Opium facit dormire.

BACHELIERUS (ARGAN).

Mihi by docto Doctore
Demandatur causam et rationem quare
Opium facit dormire:
To which respondeo
Quia est in eo
Virtus dormitiva,
Cuius est natura
Sensus stupefire.

CHORUS.

Bene, bene, bene, bene respondere:
Dignus, dignus est entrare
In nostro docto corpore.

SECUNDUS DOCTOR.

Cum permissione Domini Praesidis,
Doctissimae Facultatis,
Et totius his nostris actis
Companiae assistantis,
Demandabo tibi, docte Bacheliere,
Quae sunt remedia
Quae in maladia
Known as hydropisia
Convenit facere.

BACHELIERUS (ARGAN).

Enema donare,
Postea bleedare,
After that purgare.[10]

CHORUS.

Bene, bene, bene, bene respondere:
Dignus, dignus est entrare
In nostro docto corpore.

TERTIUS DOCTOR.

Si bonum seems Domini Praesidi,
Doctissimae Facultati,
Et companiae praesenti,

---

[10] Morris Bishop has given an inspired free version of this refrain, which I feel sure Molière would have relished, in *The Would-Be Invalid* (Crofts Classics, Appleton-Century Crofts, New York, 1950, pp. 74–75).

> Demandabo tibi, docte Bacheliere,
>> Quae remedia eticis,
>> Pulmonicis, atque asmaticis,
>> You think it right to facere.

BACHELIERUS (ARGAN).
>> Enema donare,
>> Postea bleedare,
>> After that purgare.

CHORUS.
> Bene, bene, bene, bene respondere:
>> Dignus, dignus est entrare
>> In nostro docto corpore.

QUARTUS DOCTOR.
>> Super illas maladias
> Doctus Bachelierus dixit marvelias,
> But si non annoyo Dominum Praesidem,
>> Doctissimam Facultatem,
>> Et totam honorabilem
>> Companiam listenantem,
> Faciam illi unam quaestionem.
>> Yesterday maladus unus
>> Fellavit into meas manus;
> Habet grandam feveram cum redoublamentis,
>> Grandam dolorem capitis,
>> Et grandum malum in the side,
>> Cum granda difficultate
>> Et paina to respirare:
>> Be so kind as to tell mihi,
>> Docte Bacheliere,
>> Quid illi facere?

BACHELIERUS (ARGAN).
>> Enema donare,
>> Postea bleedare,
>> After that purgare.

QUINTUS DOCTOR.
>> But if maladia,
>> With obstinacia,
>> Non vult se curire,
>> Quid illi facere?

BACHELIERUS *(ARGAN)*.

> *Enema donare,*
> *Postea bleedare,*
> *After that purgare.*

CHORUS.

> *Bene, bene, bene, bene respondere:*
> *Dignus, dignus est entrare*
> *In nostro docto corpore.*

PRAESES.

> *Juras keepare statuta*
> *Per Facultatem praescripta*
> *Cum sensu et judgeamento?*

BACHELIERUS *(ARGAN)*.

> *Juro.*[11]

PRAESES.

> *Essere in omnibus*
> *Consultationibus*
> *True to opinion oldo,*
> > *Aut bono,*
> > *Aut baddo?*

BACHELIERUS *(ARGAN)*.

> *Juro.*

PRAESES.

> *Never to usire*
> *Any remediis*
> *But only those of doctae Facultatis,*
> > *Though maladus croakare,*
> > *Et mori de suo malo?*

BACHELIERUS *(ARGAN)*.

> *Juro.*

PRAESES.

> *Ego, cum isto boneto*
> *Venerabili et docto,*

11 It was here or hereabouts that at the fourth performance of the play (February 17, 1673) Molière suffered an attack of his lung trouble that made him cough up blood. He finished the performance but died that evening.

Dono tibi et concedo
Virtutem et poweriam
   Medicandi,
   Purgandi,
   Bleedandi,
   Pierceandi,
   Carvandi,
   Cutandi,
   Et killendi
Impune per totam terram.

(All the surgeons and apothecaries come and do reverence to
ARGAN, *to music.)*

BACHELIERUS (ARGAN).
   Grandes doctores doctrinae
   Of rhubarb and of senna,
'Twould be no doubt the action of a foola,
   Inepta et ridicula,
   If I went and m'engageare
   Praises unto you donare,
And undertook to add-on-are
   Any lightas to the sunno,
   And any staras to the skyo,
   Waveas to the oceano,
   And rosas to the springo.
   Pray allow that with one wordo,
   As grateful as you ever heardo,
I give thanks to corpori tam docto.
   Vobis, vobis debeo
Much more than to naturae and to patri meo:
   Natura et pater meus
   Hominem me habent factum;
   But vos me—a great big plus—
   Havetis factum medicum,
   Honor, favor, et gratia
   Qui, in hoc corde you have here,
   Imprimant ressentimenta
   Which will endure in saecula.

CHORUS.
   Vivat, vivat, vivat, vivat, a hundred times vivat

Novus Doctor, qui tam bene speakat!
Mille, mille annis et eatet et drinkat
Et bleedet et killat!

(All the surgeons and apothecaries dance to the sound of instruments and voices, hand-clapping, and apothecaries' mortars.)

CHIRURGUS.

May he see doctas
Suas ordonnancias
Omnium chirurgorum
Et apothecarum
Fill up the shoppas!

CHORUS:

Vivat, vivat, vivat, vivat, a hundred times vivat
Novus Doctor, qui tam bene speakat!
Mille, mille annis et eatet et drinkat,
Et bleedet et killat!

CHIRURGUS.

May all his anni
Be to him boni
And favorable,
And always be full
Of pestas, poxas,
Feveras, pleurisias,
Of bloody fluxions and dysenterias!

CHORUS.

Vivat, vivat, vivat, vivat, a hundred times vivat
Novus Doctor, qui tam bene speakat!
Mille, mille annis et eatet et drinkat
Et bleedet et killat!

Selected Bibliography

*Other Plays of Molière: French Titles and Dates of
First Performance*[1]

La Jalousie du barbouillé (c. 1650?)	*Mélicerte* (Dec. 1666)
Le Médecin volant (c. 1650?)	*Le Sicilien* (Feb. 1667)
L'Étourdi (1655?)	*Amphitryon* (Jan. 1668)
Le Dépit amoureux (Dec. 1656)	*George Dandin* (July 1668)
Sganarelle (May 1660)	*Monsieur de Pourceaugnac* (Sept. 1669)
Dom Garcie de Navarre (Feb. 1661)	*Les Amants magnifiques* (Feb. 1670)
Les Fâcheux (Aug. 1661)	*Psyché* (Jan. 1671)
Le Mariage forcé (Jan. 1664)	*La Comtesse d'Escarbagnas* (Dec. 1671)
La Princesse d'Élide (May 1664)	
L'Amour médecin (Sept. 1665)	

Works about Molière Available Only in French

Particularly useful to me have been three general treatments: Daniel Mornet's *Molière* (1943), terse, scrupulous, learned, and pertinent; Antoine Adam's enlightening pages in his *Histoire de la littérature française au XVIIᵉ siècle*, Vol. III (1952) ; and Jacques Guicharnaud's penetrating and illuminating study of *Tartuffe, Don Juan,* and *The Misanthrope* in *Molière: Une Aventure théâtrale* (1963); for Molière's biography, Gustave Michaut's three volumes (1922-25), which firmly distinguish fact from fiction and legend; and for the theatrical background, Jacques Schérer's rich *La Dramaturgie classique en France* (1950?).

Works about Molière Available in English

Bergson, Henri. *Laughter* (*Le Rire,* 1900), in George Meredith and Henri Bergson, *Comedy.* New York: Doubleday & Co., Inc., Anchor Books, 1956. (An outstanding theory of comedy—as mechanization —based largely on Molière.)

Chapman, Percy, A. *The Spirit of Molière.* Princeton, N.J.: Princeton University Press, 1940.

[1] These are available in the translations of Baker and Miller and of Van Laun (see our Introduction, above; *L'Amour médecin* and *Le Sicilien* are also in Wood.

Dussane, Béatrix. *An Actor Named Molière* (*Un Comédien nommé Molière*, 1936). New York: Charles Scribner's Sons, 1937. (Good fictionalized biography.)

Fernandez, Ramon: *Molière: The Man Seen through the Plays* (*La Vie de Molière*, 1929). New York: Hill and Wang, 1958. (Fascinating biography which welcomes probabilities where certainties are lacking.)

Gossman, Lionel. *Men and Masks: A Study of Molière*. Baltimore: The Johns Hopkins Press, 1963.

Hubert, J. D. *Molière: The Comedy of Intellect*. Berkeley: University of California Press, 1962.

Moore, W. G. *Molière: A New Criticism*. Revised ed. New York: Oxford University Press, 1953; New York: Doubleday & Co., Inc., Anchor Books, 1962. (A seminal work in modern Molière criticism.)

Palmer, John. *Molière*. New York: Brewer and Warren, 1930.

Turnell, Martin. *The Classical Moment: Studies of Corneille, Molière, Racine*. London: Hamish Hamilton, Ltd., 1947.